Language, Meaning, and Use in Indian Philosophy

ALSO AVAILABLE FROM BLOOMSBURY

An Introduction to Indian Philosophy, by Christopher Bartley
Philosophy of the Bhagavad Gita, by Keya Maitra
The Bloomsbury Research Handbook of Indian Aesthetics and the Philosophy of Art, edited by Arindam Chakrabarti
Understanding Asian Philosophy, by Alexus McLeod

Language, Meaning, and Use in Indian Philosophy

An Introduction to Mukula's "Fundamentals of the Communicative Function"

Malcolm Keating

BLOOMSBURY ACADEMIC
LONDON • NEW YORK • OXFORD • NEW DELHI • SYDNEY

BLOOMSBURY ACADEMIC
Bloomsbury Publishing Plc
50 Bedford Square, London, WC1B 3DP, UK
1385 Broadway, New York, NY 10018, USA

BLOOMSBURY, BLOOMSBURY ACADEMIC and the Diana logo are trademarks of Bloomsbury Publishing Plc

First published in Great Britain 2019

Cover design by Toby Way

A catalogue record for this book is available from the British Library.

A catalog record for this book is available from the Library of Congress.

ISBN: HB: 978-1-3500-6077-7
PB: 978-1-3500-3076-0
ePDF: 978-1-3500-6075-3
eBook: 978-1-3500-6073-9

Typeset by Deanta Global Publishing Services, Chennai, India

इदमन्धं तमः कृत्स्नं जायेत भुवनत्रयम् ।
यदि शब्दाह्वयं ज्योतिरासंसारं न दीप्यते ।।
दण्डस्य काव्यदर्शः

idam andhaṃ tamaḥ kṛtsnaṃ jāyeta bhuvanatrayam |
yadi śabdāhvayaṃ jyotirāsaṃsāraṃ na dīpyate ||
Kāvyadarśa of Daṇḍin

This whole universe would be blinded by darkness
If the luminous rays called "speech" did not shine.
Daṇḍin's *Mirror on Poetry*

Contents

List of Illustrations x
Foreword xii
Acknowledgments xv
Note on Text/Translation xvi
How to Use this Book xvii

Part I Introduction

Why did Mukula Bhaṭṭa Write the *Fundamentals*? 5
Indication and Resolving Incongruity: Mukula's Response 10
Understanding Mukula's Context 17
Further Reading by Topic 39

Part II English Translation of "The Fundamentals of the Communicative Function"

About this Translation 45
Introduction 46
Verses 1–15 47
Appendix 1: Outline of the Fundamentals of the Communicative Function 75

Appendix 2: Linguistic Examples used by Mukula 82

Part III Commentary on "The Fundamentals of the Communicative Function"

About this Commentary 87
Introduction 88
Verses 1–15 91

Part IV Sanskrit Text of the Abhidhāvṛttamātṛkā

Transliteration Conventions 197
Introduction 198
Verses 1–15 199

Part V Mukula and Contemporary Linguistic Philosophy

Mukula Bhaṭṭa on Sentence Meaning and the Semantics-Pragmatics Distinction 221
Mukula Bhaṭṭa on Primary and Secondary Meaning 223
A Contemporary Approach to What is Said: François Recanati 231

What is Said, What is Expressed 236
Lessons and Future Inquiry 242

Part VI Study Resources

Glossary 247
Sanskrit Pronunciation 253
Chronology of Important Figures and Dates 254
Indices 255

Notes 259
Bibliography 286
Index of Names, Works, and Terms 295

List of Illustrations

Figures

Figure 1 Mukula's analysis of the communicative function 94
Figure 2 Indication involving transfer 111
Figure 3 Ānandavardhana's primary function 120
Figure 4 Ānandavardhana's secondary function 120
Figure 5 Ānandavardhana's suggestive function 121
Figure 6 Mukula's indicatory function with semantic imbuing 123
Figure 7 Ānandavardhana, suggestion, and intention to express 175
Figure 8 Mukula Bhaṭṭa, suggestion, and intention to express 177
Figure 9 Mukula's varieties of relationship and intention to express 178
Figure 10 "The umbrella-holders go" 182
Figure 11 Mukula's analysis of the communicative function 190

Tables

Table 1 Ānandavardhana's theory of meaning 9
Table 2 Mukula's theory of meaning 13
Table 3 Analysis of primary meaning 95
Table 4 Mukula's first and second analysis, compared 104
Table 5 Mukula's complete analysis of indication 117
Table 6 Novel indication based on speaker, sentence, expressed meaning 138
Table 7 First and second sentence theories, compared 159
Table 8 Combined view of sentence meaning 162
Table 9 Relationships between primary and indicated meanings 167
Table 10 Five relationships in terms of expressed meaning 178

Foreword

While the late ninth-/early tenth-century Kashmiri critic and linguistic philosopher Mukula Bhaṭṭa has left us only one rather brief work, his influence on the development of Indian language theory and literary semantics has been immense, although modern scholarship has nevertheless long overlooked his pivotal work or failed to take proper account of its role in the larger stream of Indian thought on the modes of linguistic expression. The present study represents the most serious effort to date to remedy this deficiency and, one hopes, will mark a watershed in the study of this important but long-neglected work.

Mukula's *Fundamentals of the Communicative Function* offered the first comprehensive synthesis of what had by his time become standard thinking on the main varieties of linguistic expression, both literal and nonliteral. As such, it incorporates elements from multiple divergent traditions of Brahmanical linguistic thought, but does not uniformly affiliate itself with any one of these traditions. This places the work at the center of late first-millennium Indian linguistic theory while, at the same time, rendering it somewhat atypical within the traditional Sanskrit disciplinary order. Mukula draws heavily on several of the major traditions of classical Indian linguistic thought, especially grammar, and two main schools of scriptural hermeneutics (that of Kumārila Bhaṭṭa and his rival Prabhākara), in developing his typology of the modes of linguistic expression, but he does not mark himself as a follower of any one of these traditions, and his final synthesis is not entirely consistent with any of them. This, in an intellectual environment where practically all authors of philosophical or theoretical works explicitly present themselves as followers and often as commentators on some preexisting text tradition, makes his work something of an anomaly. Not belonging obviously to any preexisting camp or school of linguistic thought, Mukula's work lay outside the main doxographic pigeonholes that have often guided philosophical debate and scholarship both in traditional India and among modern scholars, and it is likely this that accounts for the undue neglect it has long suffered under. Nevertheless, as a perusal of the present work will show, Mukula proved to be a major force in the development of Indian semantic theory, and his analysis and typology of the modes of primary and secondary signification became standard for many later authors.

Mukula's most powerful influence was indirect, via the adoption and inclusion of his account of primary and secondary signification in the extremely popular *Kāvyaprakāśa* ("Light on Poetry") of the eleventh-century Kashmiri literary theorist Mammaṭa. Mammaṭa's discussion of these two modes of signification is very closely modeled on Mukula's. Mammaṭa, as a follower and systematizer of the *dhvani* theory of Ānandavardhana, makes room for a third mode of signification, the "suggestive," in addition to the primary and secondary signification treated by Mukula. This sets the two thinkers at odds since, as can clearly be seen from Keating's translation and commentary, and as I have sought to show in my own earlier work, Mukula's primary purpose in writing the *Fundamentals of the Communicative Function* was precisely to attack Ānandavardhana's theory, and to demonstrate that all supposed instances of suggestion can be incorporated within the already established rubric of secondary signification. Yet, despite Mammaṭa's split with Mukula over the existence of suggestion as a distinct mode of signification, Mammaṭa's account of the two universally recognized primary and secondary modes is wholly indebted to Mukula, replicating his typology precisely, incorporating most of his examples, and even copying his wording verbatim in many places. Through its incorporation in the almost universally known and profusely commented *Kāvyaprakāśa*, Mukula's theory gained extremely wide purchase, albeit without his name explicitly attached to it. The earlier commentators on Mammaṭa's *Kāvyaprakāśa* were clearly thoroughly familiar with Mukula's work, and knew well how deeply Mammaṭa was indebted to him, though they most often refer directly to him only on the comparatively rare occasions when Mammaṭa dissents from Mukula's account of primary or secondary signification. In time, however, direct references to Mukula and his *Fundamentals of the Communicative Function* become rarer, and it is less clear that later commentators and literary theorists are fully aware of the roots of Mammaṭa's semantics in Mukula's work. Apart from its obvious and central importance in later poetic theory, Mukula's treatment of the semantic modes exercised an important influence in other fields, wherever the topic of the modes of signification took on special importance, especially in the language theories of Vedānta and Nyāya. His account of secondary signification in particular provides the broadly accepted foundation for nearly all later thinking on the topic. While it was not universally accepted in all its details, and certain elements of its typology and its theory of the modes of signification remained controversial, Mukula's *Fundamentals of the*

Communicative Function constructed what in effect became the baseline, commonsense account of both everyday and literary semantics for nearly a millennium after his time.

Yet, despite the undeniably deep and wide influence of Mukula's theory in later Indian thinking on linguistic expression, modern Indological scholarship has largely ignored his work or overlooked its decisive impact on the development of traditional Indian semantic theory. Early scholarly interest in Mukula's work was almost entirely prosopographical in character, taking note of Mukula's quotation of rare or otherwise unknown works (such as the lost Mīmāmsā treatise of Bhartṛmitra), or of the chronological significance of his early references to the *dhvani* theory of Ānandavardhana, but almost no attention is given to his semantic theories, or to his vast influence on Mammaṭa and the later tradition. Even when his work did begin to draw more pointed attention from scholars, his theories and his historical role were often glaringly mischaracterized. K. Venugopalan, for example, in his annotations to the only existing English translation prior to the present one, claims that Mukula "accepts the *dhvani* view indirectly" (p. 262), when it is quite clear that the main purpose of his work is precisely to attack this theory; Edwin Gerow, who comments only briefly on Mukula in his *Indian Poetics* (p. 58), anachronistically suggests that Mukula's work preceded and was known to Ānandavardhana, when the reverse is quite obviously true. It is only in past few decades that Mukula's importance as the first major critic of Ānandavardhana's *dhvani* theory, and his as one of the most original and influential theorists of both literary and nonliterary signification, has finally come into focus.

Malcolm Keating's translation and study of Mukula Bhaṭṭa's *Fundamentals of the Communicative Function*, the first book-length study of this work, represents the culmination of this recent trend, standing as the most thorough and concerted analysis of Mukula's semantics and its intellectual context. Elevating Mukula to his proper place in the study of Indian philosophy and language theory renders an immensely important service to scholars within the field, as well as to interested observers outside it. One may reasonably hope that this work will play a substantial role not only in bringing broader appreciation of Mukula and his work, but in promoting a fuller understanding of the sophisticated problematics and the substantial achievements of the traditional Indian philosophy of language. In a time when the need for a non-Eurocentric "world philosophy" is increasingly being recognized, this must surely be seen as a welcome development.

Lawrence McCrea, Cornell University

Acknowledgments

This project began at the University of Texas at Austin, where I first read Mukula Bhaṭṭa's text with Stephen Phillips. It was he who encouraged me to take on this topic in the first place, and I will always be indebted to his guidance at Texas. I also benefited greatly from Larry McCrea's work in Alaṅkāraśāstra generally, Mukula more specifically, and his comments on this manuscript's draft form. I thank Ray Buchanan, Josh Dever, and Hans Kamp for pushing me to make Mukula's work accessible to an audience of philosophers unfamiliar with Sanskrit. Along the way, my thinking has been refined by conversations with many colleagues, but to name a few, I am grateful to David Buchta, Daniele Cuneo, Matthew Dasti, Elisa Freschi, Mrinal Kaul, and Andrew Ollett. At Yale-NUS College, I benefited from the entire philosophy faculty's support as well as funding from the College and the Singapore Ministry of Education for trips, research materials, and a manuscript workshop (grant numbers R-607-263-325-121, R-607-263-230-121, and BMW17-002). A number of colleagues helpfully read parts of the final translation: Andrew Bailey, Sandra Field, Neil Mehta, and Robin Zheng. I thank my 2016 Classical Indian Philosophy of Language class at Yale-NUS: Abel Ang En Pei, Shina Chua, Le Van Cahn, Lee Zheng Yang Vincent, Ng Sai Ying, Peter Ooi Teik Aun, Sherice Ngaserin Ng Jing Ya, and Yun Do Ung. They all read early drafts of the translation and commentary, suggesting revisions and asking insightful questions. Sherice Ngaserin shared with me her lively drawings of Mukula's examples for this volume. The faculty at Jawaharlal Nehru University gave feedback on a presentation of parts of my commentary, and the audiences at the India International Centre gave feedback on a version of the introduction as part of a workshop organized by Studio Abhyas Trust and Manipal University. Finally, I am immensely grateful to Harvard University for hosting a manuscript workshop and to the participants of that workshop—Parimal Patil, Larry McCrea, Anand Vaidya, and Brendan Gillon, along with Anand Venkatakrishnan, Tyler Richard, and Lee Ling Ting. The discussion at that workshop was invaluable for refining the final version of this book.

Note on Text/Translation

Unless indicated otherwise, the Sanskrit translations in this book are the work of the author.

How to Use this Book

If you are new to Indian philosophy, begin by reading the Introduction. There, you will learn who Mukula Bhaṭṭa is, what his aims are, and become acquainted with important background concepts to understand his text. You'll also find recommended readings, arranged by topic, which will help you go further into Indian linguistic philosophy. Before beginning to read the translation itself, you may wish to read Appendix 1, which outlines the text. When you read the translation, you may find it helpful to read it along with the immediately subsequent analytic commentary, organized by verse. This commentary explains Mukula's arguments by expanding on what is compressed, discussing the thinkers he quotes, and giving English analogs for the Sanskrit expressions he analyzes. It also includes several tables which clarify the structure of his argument. Finally, as you read, make use of the Glossary which includes important Sanskrit terms (highlighted in bold throughout the text) as well as select terms from contemporary philosophy and linguistics. A Sanskrit pronunciation guide is included as well.

If you are using this book in a class on Indian philosophy, I also suggest your students also begin with the Introduction. Students could either read Mukula's text in its entirety (which I recommend they do on their own before reading the commentary) or excerpts along with additional readings. For instance, they might read his discussion of word meanings along with the recommended readings in the Introduction. Instructors can use these recommended readings to develop a topical syllabus coordinated with selections. Encourage students to come up with their own cases for analysis using Mukula's categories. A list of Mukula's own examples is provided in Appendix 2 to facilitate this approach.

If you are already familiar with Mukula's work or with Indian philosophy generally, you may not need the Introduction, but might want to go straight to the translation. Sanskritists will probably want to read along with the Sanskrit, which you can do with the aid of square brackets which indicate the location in the included transliteration as well as Dvivedi (1973). Paragraph breaks between Sanskrit text and transliteration are coordinated so you can find your place easily. Finally, both specialists and newcomers can read Part V: Mukula and Contemporary Linguistics Philosophy at any time, as it is a chapter which brings together Mukula's work with modern philosophical thought. The chapter can serve as an introduction to themes in the text for readers familiar with modern philosophy, or it can serve as concluding reflections about where Mukula's work, and the Indian intellectual traditions of grammar, philosophy, and poetics can take us next.

Part I

Introduction

Why did Mukula Bhaṭṭa Write the *Fundamentals*?
Indication and Resolving Incongruity: Mukula's Response
Understanding Mukula's Context
Further Reading by Topic

Suppose your friend is telling you about a coworker who constantly talks over people at the office. Your friend complains, "Ajay is a bulldozer." Chances are, you immediately understand what your friend means—Ajay is like a bulldozer in pushing through people to get to his goal. Or, take the expression "Two heads are better than one." It doesn't refer to inert heads bereft of bodies, but to a pair of people who have heads and use them, together, for thinking. Likewise, we often talk about governments by using names of buildings: "The White House held a press conference," or "Downing Street called for a referendum," but no one thinks that these buildings are alive. This way of using language, going beyond the ordinary meaning of words to communicate something else, is pervasive, no matter which language people are speaking. Now consider poetry. When William Shakespeare writes in Sonnet 19 "Devouring Time, blunt thou the lion's paws and make the earth devour her own sweet brood" what does he mean?[1] This meaning is less easy to understand. There are study guides written on Shakespeare's poetry and literary critics have written (and continue to write) volumes analyzing it. Still, people do understand something from this and other poems like it.

We might wonder, though, is the way that we understand Shakespeare the same way that we understand the others, about Ajay and the White House? If it is the same process, then what explains why poetry seems different from everyday speech? And if it is a different process, what is it?

In the late ninth or early tenth century CE, Mukula Bhaṭṭa, a thinker writing in Sanskrit and located in Kashmir, wrote a treatise explaining how communication works, and answering these questions. Mukula's treatise, the *Fundamentals of the Communicative Function* (*Abhidhā-vṛtta-mātṛkā*), sets out a framework for how communication happens, from what words mean to how sentences are constructed to how people use language beyond its ordinary meanings. We know little about him except that his father is Bhaṭṭa Kallaṭa, the author of the *Commentary on the Verses on Vibration* (*Spanda-kārika-vṛtti*), and that he had two students, Pratīhāra Indurāja and Sahadeva. The *Fundamentals* is an important work for the study of poetry and aesthetics in India (known as *alaṅkāra-śāstra*, or henceforth, Alaṅkāra). The tremendously influential twelfth-century writer Mammaṭa adopts large sections of it verbatim, even while criticizing other aspects of Mukula's view. However, although Mukula's text can be understood as a positive theory of communication, he writes it with a polemical aim: to argue against a new theory of language put forward by Ānandavardhana, another Kashmiri thinker living a little earlier than Mukula, in the mid to late ninth century CE. Mukula's thesis, that understanding ordinary and poetic language involves the same fundamental processes, sets the stage for a debate which will continue for hundreds of years. Contemporary philosophers, though typically unaware of the Indian tradition (they usually draw on ancient Greek philosophy if appealing to historical sources), are still discussing the questions Mukula raises, a thousand years later.[2] For this reason, the book's cover includes the word for "speech" in multiple languages, to reflect the universality of the topic.

In what follows, I will explain the basics of Ānanda's new theory with the aim of showing how Mukula responds to him.[3] In the second half of the introduction, we will take a step back to understand the broader context for Mukula's reply. Around ninth century CE, Ānanda, who was a poet, Kashmiri literary theorist, and philosopher, writes a treatise in which he argues that there is a previously undiscovered process of understanding meanings, known as **suggestion (*dhvani*)**. This process accounts for poetry like Shakespeare's sonnets—although Ānanda of course focuses on the *Rāmāyaṇa*, *Mahābhārata*, and other poems written in Sanskrit and Prakrit.[4] Mukula responds by arguing that we can explain this putative process of "suggestion" through a fairly ordinary process which thinkers had already discussed, a process known as **indication (*lakṣaṇā*).** Indication accounts for our ability to understand the sentences about Ajay the bulldozer and Downing Street, thus making our understanding of poetic meaning simply an extension of our natural linguistic abilities, even if one that requires advanced skill and knowledge about the world. Further, Mukula thinks that part of what happens in indication is that hearers "solve" a linguistic puzzle or incongruity, and what is indicated is the solution to that puzzle. Poetry for Mukula is just like any other case of linguistic communication in the way we understand it. Essentially, if our theory cannot account for poetry as a human use of language, then something is wrong with it.

Why did Mukula Bhaṭṭa Write the *Fundamentals*?

Ānandavardhana's *A Light on Suggestion* (*Dhvanyâloka*) lays out a number of arguments for his claim that we need to postulate a new process of understanding, suggestion, to account for poetry.[1] In order to understand the main lines of reasoning, we need to understand how he thinks ordinary language works. First, it's important to recognize that while Ānanda is concerned with how people come to know what words and sentences mean, he does not focus on the distinction between what a person means and what someone mistakenly takes them to mean. In other words, he is working on the assumption that there is a certain **meaning (*artha*)** communicated by an expression (be it a word, a sentence, or an entire poem) and that the hearer can come to understand these meanings, which are the same as the meanings intended by the speaker. When he's focusing on the process of understanding, he's assuming this is correct understanding. Put more specifically, he's concerned with the **function of speech (*śabda-vyāpāra*)** which is to cause hearers to understand certain meanings. Thus a hearer's comprehension of linguistic meaning is also characterized in terms of a capacity of words. We are setting aside problems of misinterpretation, failed communication, and so on, and are only concerned with a competent hearer.

Second, Ānanda, along with many thinkers before him, distinguishes between two main functions of speech: the primary function and the secondary function. The Sanskrit terms for these functions vary, but the basic idea is the same. The primary function is what a word expresses directly, whereas the secondary function works indirectly, based on the first, primary meaning. Ānanda argues that we need a third function, suggestion, for two main reasons:

- **a** Suggested meanings vary in contexts, so they are not the result of the primary function, which results in the same meaning in each context.
- **b** Suggested meanings can occur without figures of speech, so they are not the result of secondary meaning.

Let's take a modern example to explain these ideas. Someone says

1 I had to go two streets over to find a parking meter.

The phrase "parking meter" communicates through its primary function the meaning *device that charges fees for parking cars nearby*. This is what someone would understand directly from "parking meter." It is consistent across contexts—if it were not, we wouldn't be able to understand new sentences. But assuming that words have primary meanings which remain fixed allows us to explain this ability. However, in this example, our speaker isn't just looking for a parking meter. She wants to find a place to park which has a meter. Thus from the primary meaning of "parking meter" we understand a further meaning.

2 I had to go two streets over to find a *spot next to a* parking meter.

This meaning, in italics, is understood through the secondary function of words. This function does not happen all of the time. The phrase "parking meter" doesn't always mean "spot next to a parking meter," but only in certain contexts. In fact, according to Indian thinkers, there are three necessary conditions which must be met for the secondary function to work:

a *Incongruity.* There must be an incongruity in the primary meaning.
b *Relationship.* There must be some relationship between the secondary and primary meanings.
c *Motive.* There must be some motive to understand the secondary meaning.

These conditions are present in our example case above. To take our speaker as looking for just a meter doesn't make sense with the facts we know—it is an incongruity. There is a relationship between a meter and a parking spot, that of spatial contiguity, since they are found next to each other all regularly. Finally, in this case, it's a matter of convention to refer to a parking spot with the term "meter," but sometimes there are unusual, unconventional motives. For instance, in our first example

3 Ajay is a bulldozer

the incongruity is that people are not bulldozers. However, there is a relationship of similarity between Ajay and bulldozers: both move through obstacles, both keep going regardless of what's in front of them, etc. And finally, regarding motive, our speaker might choose this term to dehumanize

Ajay, or perhaps for plausible deniability if someone overhears her (oh, I meant to say that he keeps going at all costs!).[2] Both of these examples, what are today typically called "metonymy" and "metaphor," respectively, are examples of the secondary function at work. Ānanda distinguishes the function of suggestion from both primary and secondary functions. Let's look at one of his examples:

> **4** While the heavenly visitor was speaking, Pārvatī,
> standing with lowered face beside her father,
> counted the petals of the lotus in her hand.[3]

In this example, taken from 6.84 of Kālidāsa's *The Origin of the Young God* (*Kumāra-saṃbhava*), Pārvatī is standing next to her father and a sage while the two discuss her betrothal to the god Śiva. From the primary function we understand the ordinary meaning of the sentence, just that Pārvatī is counting the petals of a lotus flower which she holds in her hand. There is no obstacle in understanding this, and so there is no figure of speech. But, still, Ānandavardhana argues that this verse suggests that Pārvatī is shy (and from this it suggests that she is in love). This is what the function of suggestion does—it conveys something beyond the primary meaning which does not require an incongruity.

Further, suggestion is the whole point of poetry. That Pārvatī is in love is the point of the poem. But no poet worth their salt conveys love by stating "Pārvatī is in love." Rather, they convey this fact implicitly, by their choice of words and by the figures of speech they use. Ānanda argues that, in good poetry, conveying suggested meanings is the purpose of every aspect of the poem. While poets can be clever—they can use double entendré, metaphors, alliteration, and so on—if these figures of speech are the focal point of a poem, it has failed. Poetry should suggest what Ānandavardhana and thinkers before him call ***rasa***, a word literally meaning "flavor" or "sap," and which, for Ānanda, leads to aesthetic beauty. However, we must pause here. Ānanda calls *rasa* a meaning, alongside of the meanings communicated by the primary and secondary functions. It is a meaning that is understood differently, yes, but he is not talking about emotions that hearers experience. It is found in the text, in the characters of a poem, for instance. For him, *rasa* is a meaning communicated by words, through what he calls "suggestion."

Finally, although the main point of poetry is to suggest *rasa*, suggestion can yield two other kinds of meanings. Suggestion can convey facts or narrative matter (*vastu*) and it can convey figures of speech. An example of a suggested fact is this verse:

5 Mother-in-law sleeps here, I there:
look traveler, while it is light.
For at night when you cannot see
you must not fall into my bed.[4]

As with the case of Pārvatī, Ānanda would say that there is no obstacle to taking this in its primary meaning. However, a reader familiar with the relevant poetic motifs would immediately know that the speaker (who is a married woman) is coyly inviting a (male) traveler into her bed. This invitation is suggested. It is not explicitly stated, nor is it a metaphor or double meaning. Rather, it is implicit in the woman's manner of speaking. Figures of speech can also be suggested, as in this verse which Ānandavardhana himself wrote:

6 Truly insensate is the ocean
that it is not now stirred by this your smiling face,
tremulous-eyed beauty,
which fills the horizon with the splendor of its loveliness.[5]

This verse suggests a metaphor: your face is the moon. The tides of the ocean are implicitly compared to how someone's heart is moved by a beautiful woman. Nowhere in the verse is this comparison stated, and even if there is some secondary meaning in the verse (for instance, an ocean cannot be "stirred" like a person's heart and so we might take that word differently), the central metaphor is suggested. We might think of Shakespeare again for an English example. The soliloquy in *As You Like It* which begins "All the world's a stage" could be taken to suggest a further metaphor: life is a play. For Ānanda, suggestion is responsible for figures of speech which emerge out of the individual parts of a poem. However, these suggested figures of speech and previously mentioned suggested facts, in excellent poetry, are subsidiary to the main goal, of suggesting *rasa*.

Before concluding and moving on to Mukula's response, let us summarize Ānanda's theory of meaning. Table 1 illustrates the three functions of speech, each with their respective meanings, and an example.

Table 1 Ānandavardhana's theory of meaning

Function	Meaning	Example
Primary	Ordinary word meanings	"parking meter" means *device that charges fees for parking cars nearby*
Secondary	Figures of speech	"parking meter" secondarily means *spot next to a* parking meter "bulldozer" secondarily means *running over obstacles*
Suggestion	Facts	"you must not fall into my bed" means *you are invited into my bed*
	Figures of speech	"Truly insensate is the ocean" means *your face is the moon*
	Rasa	"Pārvatī counted the petals" means that *Pārvatī is shy* and *Pārvatī is in love*

Indication and Resolving Incongruity: Mukula's Response

Mukula argues that Ānandavardhana has unnecessarily added a new function of speech, since the secondary function is able to communicate facts, figures of speech, and *rasa*. This requires that he explain cases like "Pārvatī . . . counted the petals" where there is not any obvious secondary meaning present. His strategy is to show that the three requirements for secondary meaning are present in these cases. These requirements are, again

- **a** *Incongruity.* There must be an incongruity in the primary meaning.
- **b** *Relationship.* There must be some relationship between the secondary and primary meanings.
- **c** *Motive.* There must be some motive to understand the secondary meaning.

Mukula's argument depends on the claim that what counts as an "incongruity" is broader than Ānanda thinks. He argues that there are a number of incongruities that might lead to secondary meaning. He calls secondary meaning "indicated meaning," as it arises from the **indicatory function** (***lākṣanika-vyāpāra***), also sometimes simply called indication (*lakṣaṇā*). He also explains how each of the three conditions can be brought about, often analyzing the same examples as Ānanda did, in order to show his analysis is equally powerful.

Earlier we illustrated the incongruity condition with "Ajay is a bulldozer" and the case of the parking meter. These sentences are examples where the incongruity is within the words of the sentence. They are sentence-internal problems. Unless we resolve the incongruity, we cannot understand the sentence as a syntactically unified sequence of words.[1] Mukula thinks that secondary meaning does include these cases, just like Ānanda does. However, Mukula argues that there are several other features of a speech situation that we should take into account: the speaker, the sentence, the expressed meaning, the place, the time, the circumstances, and individuality (of the thing being described). Like Ānanda, Mukula uses love poetry to illustrate his examples. The role of the speaker is clear in a case where a woman whom we know is unvirtuous tells her neighbor:

7 Hey there neighbor, will you watch our house for a bit, as well?
This child's father won't drink the tasteless well-water at all.
I go now, all alone, from here to the forest stream full of tamala trees.
Let the stiff, broken ends of the knotted reeds scratch my body.[2]

Mukula argues that since we know that the woman has a bad nature, her prediction about the scratches indicates, through the indicatory function, that she expects to have marks from an amorous (and adulterous) fling. There is nothing faulty about the sentence, unlike the case of bulldozer Ajay. However, if we know something about the speaker, her statement doesn't make sense unless we assume that she has a hidden meaning.[3] Here, the indicated meaning, which is that the woman is going to an adulterous rendezvous, is not a figure of speech. It is what Ānanda would call a "fact." So Mukula has argued that, like with the earlier disguised invitation into bed, speakers can indicate meanings which are the opposite of the primary meaning. What's necessary is some incongruity between a speaker and her statement. There is also a relationship between the primary meaning and the indicated meaning: opposition. This might be characterized as irony, then. Finally, the motivation for speaking in this manner is that the woman wishes to hide her true intentions. By saying something which is plausible in its ordinary meaning, but which can also be understood to convey a hidden meaning, she retains deniability. Perhaps her neighbor can be trusted with the truth, perhaps not—but she now has a cover story for her indiscretions.

Mukula also argues that figures of speech, not just facts, can be communicated through the indicatory function. He analyzes a poem that Ānanda also analyzed as a case of suggested metaphor.

"He has already taken Śrī, so why stir up pain by churning me?
I cannot believe one so active would want to sleep like before.
And why would he build a bridge again, when the lords of all the islands serve him?"
The ocean's trembling when your Majesty marches near is like it has these doubts. (81)

In this poem, the ocean is explicitly anthropomorphized: "It is as if" the ocean were thinking to itself as the king goes by, along with all of his army. The water's waves ripple at the impact of the horses' hooves pounding on the shore, and these ripples are compared to how a person shakes when they are in worried and doubting. The first three lines describe three heroic actions performed by the god Viṣṇu, who took his wife Śrī from the oceans, who sleeps upon the oceans in between the times of world-creation, and who built a bridge over the ocean to Laṅkā (in his incarnation as Rāma). However, the king in the poem is not Viṣṇu, so there is an obstacle in understanding what is expressed by the phrase "your Majesty." Why would the ocean think about the king in this way when the king did not do any of these things? Mukula argues that the solution is to take the poem as indicating that the king is Viṣṇu. This metaphor resolves the obstacle. As for what the relationship is between the primary and indicated meaning, the king and Viṣṇu are similar in their actions. Like Viṣṇu, the king is heroic and does great things. As a piece of praise poetry (a panegyric), this verse participates in a genre which lauds kings by comparison to well-known gods and heroes. This is the motive for speaking this way: to praise.

Finally, Mukula takes up another stanza, which he says indicates the *rasa* of love, in particular, love-in-separation.

> The flower-tipped arrows of the love-god are hard to avoid: spring blossoms everywhere.
> The bright moon's rays make my heart crazy and the cuckoos capture my mind.
> This young age, with these heavy breasts, is a hard burden to bear.
> These burdensome five fires—now, how can I endure them, my friend? (83)

In this verse, Mukula argues that there is an indicated meaning expressed by a metaphor: the five fires referred to by "these" are the five phenomena in the verses (arrows, blossoms, moon, cuckoos, youth). This process of indication requires some obstacle (e.g., that arrows are not fires), but it results in a perfectly acceptable explicitly communicated metaphorical meaning. There is also nothing we know about the speaker which leads us to think there is any other indicated meaning. But Mukula argues that it is by reflecting on the metaphor that another meaning is indicated, and in fact indicated as the predominant meaning: that there is love-in-separation. What he argues is that the expressed meaning of the verse is not justified unless we assume that there is a purpose for them. For we ask, why would the speaker say these things are hard to endure? All of the things they are describing, the love-god's arrows, the beauty of spring blossoms, and so on, do not seem like burdens. However, if we assume that the speaker is separated from their beloved, then the poem makes sense. They have written about how beautiful reminders of their beloved are causes of pain. This they are motivated by expressing love-in-separation, and we can understand this indicated meaning by reflecting on the cause-and-effect relationship between the primary meaning and the indicated meaning. This love-in-separation is the main thing we are to understand from the verse, and Mukula argues that we understand it through the same process we do all other indicated meanings: we recognize there is an obstacle, the speaker has a particular motive, and there is a relationship between the primary and secondary meaning. We can represent Mukula's understanding of primary and secondary meaning with Table 2.

In all of these examples, Mukula explains the process which leads us to the indicated meaning with the same pattern, involving two conditions.

Some meaning *q* is postulated from some expression "*p*" and *m* if and only if

1 *Knowledge condition.* "*p*" is a testimonial utterance and *m* is background knowledge
2 *Incongruity condition.* Only the postulation of *q* makes *p* congruous with *m*.

The background knowledge represented by *m* varies, and how we determine what resolves incongruity also varies depending on what relationships we rely on, and what motives we can ascertain. But in general, this is the approach he uses, and it is no accident. This process is identified with an epistemic instrument known as **postulation (*arthāpatti*)** in Indian philosophy, and it has a history of being used by some philosophers, known as Mīmāṃsakas, as part of linguistic interpretation. At one point in his treatise, Mukula explains a standard example of postulation as being an important kind of indication

Table 2 Mukula's theory of meaning

Function	Meaning	Example
Primary	Ordinary word meanings	"parking meter" means *device that charges fees for parking cars nearby*
Secondary	Figures of speech (within sentences)	"parking meter" secondarily means *spot next to a* parking meter "bulldozer" secondarily means *running over obstacles*
	Facts	"hey there neighbor" means *I go to a rendezvous*
	Figures of speech	"He has already taken Śrī" means *The king is Viṣṇu*
	Rasa	"The flower-tipped arrows" means that *the poet/speaker has the rasa love-in-separation*

known as **inclusion (*upādāna*)**. All of the above examples, in which Mukula argues that suggestion can be replaced with indication, are cases of inclusion. While he is not explicit that suggestion is explained by postulation, he leaves textual and conceptual hints throughout the treatise.[4]

With this in mind, let's go back to the example of Pārvatī, using Mukula's approach. We must identify an obstacle, a motive, and a relationship to explain how the meaning that Pārvatī is in love can be understood by indication from "Pārvatī . . . counted the petals on the lotus." As we saw before, there is nothing syntactically or semantically wrong with the sentence. And unlike some earlier cases, there is not even any figure of speech involved. However, Mukula has told us that we can appeal to any of the seven features to identify an incongruity: speaker, sentence, expressed meaning, place, time, circumstance, and individuality. Perhaps circumstance holds the key. Let's employ the model of postulation:

That Pārvatī is shy is postulated from some expression "Pārvatī counted the petals on her lotus" and *the fact that Pārvatī is being betrothed* if and only if

1 *Knowledge condition*: "Pārvatī counted the petals on her lotus" is a testimonial utterance and *the fact that Pārvatī is being betrothed* is background knowledge
2 *Incongruity condition.* Only the postulation *that Pārvatī is shy* makes "Pārvatī counted the petals on her lotus" congruous with *the fact that Pārvatī is being betrothed.*

Why do we need to make Pārvatī's counting the petals on her lotus congruous with the circumstances, that she is being bethrothed? We might think that what is appropriate in the case of bethrothal is to show interest in the future marriage. However, Pārvatī does the opposite: she does not show interest in the future marriage. This might lead us to think that Pārvatī is not in love. But what we understand is (1) that she is shy and, subsequently (2) that she is in love. So there are two steps involved. We postulate that she is shy, as this explains her looking at the petals instead of showing interest. Once we understand she is shy, we can understand shyness as an indicator of love. Maybe this is a matter of convention or maybe it's a matter of postulation. We are speculating on what Mukula would say. Whatever the details, we now have two of the three conditions in place:

a *Incongruity.* Looking at flower petals and showing disinterest is incongruous with the circumstances of being betrothed.
b *Relationship.* The primary meaning (looking at petals) is an effect of the secondary meaning (love and shyness).

The final condition is motive, and here we need to know something about the conventions of Sanskrit poetry and courtship, but even lacking this information, a reader could imagine that showing a woman as demure might be considered more appropriate and beautiful than to openly show her interest in marriage to an attractive god.[5]

c *Motive.* Portraying Pārvatī as shy conveys her love in a beautiful manner.

This is just one hypothetical account of how Mukula's analysis could be extended to refute to Ānandavardhana's explanation of supposed cases of suggestion. Mukula's work is short, terse, and lacking the details we need to further evaluate its success. If it is correct that he is drawing on the epistemic instrument of postulation in order to explain suggestion, then we might like to know how precise the deliverances of postulation are. In the case of poetry, it seems as if not only one single determinate meaning (or a conjunction of several) is meant, but rather a diffuse range of possibilities. But in Indian epistemology, the result of an epistemic instrument is a determinate cognition (*niścaya*). How can we square the open-ended sense of poetic meaning with the requirement that a certain thing (or things) be meant? Second, our confidence in these more diffuse poetic meanings is often lower than our confidence in the ordinary meaning. In contemporary terms, we think of these further meanings as defeasible, in that further evidence can overturn our interpretation. But postulation, at least on some understandings of its nature, results in a necessary conclusion based on a constrained set of alternatives.[6] We know, for a fact, that if Devadatta is fat and he does not eat during the day, he must eat at night, given the background knowledge that he does not drink during the day or night. Can we construct such an inference for the case of Pārvatī and her lotus?

The answers to these questions depend in part on how Mukula understands postulation (and to what extent it is implicated in his theory), as well as how Mukula understands poetic interpretation. To the extent that poetry is dependent on the ordinary meanings of words and their syntactic and semantic properties, its meaning(s) would seem to be constrained by these regularities. On the other hand, poetry is a place where words are used to communicate in novel ways, as Mukula emphasizes, conveying things for which we previously had no language. By bringing suggestion back into the range of indication and ordinary epistemic practices, Mukula emphasizes that poetry must be knowable. Of course, Ānanda, anticipating such an approach, responds to it with laughter, arguing that to treat poetry with the tools of logic is a category mistake.[7]

Mukula's account of communication goes beyond what we have sketched above. He explains how it is that the secondary meaning can be understood as predominant, what distinguishes between conventional and novel poetic language, and he explores the structure of indication in great detail. Whether his challenge is successful (and later Indian thinkers do give objections to his argument), Mukula's treatise challenges us to think clearly about the relationship between ordinary language and poetry, and how it is we understand their meanings. Further, if we can understand the relationship between words and their meanings, then his theory has implications for writers of poetry: they can predict what meanings their hearers will understand from the words we use. As a result, one's writing will be clear. As he says at the conclusion of his work:

> [The] communicative function is reflected in the sciences of words, sentences, and epistemic instruments. The one who employs it in composition has words which shine clearly (100).

After all, unless a poet can predict what meanings her words will communicate, all of the work she does in selecting the right words is for nothing. Mukula's treatise implicitly argues that this ability to pair word and meaning undermines the argument for suggestion, even when that relationship is highly context-dependent and subtly understood. For him, since we can reconstruct the relationship between these putatively suggested meanings and primary meaning in terms of secondary meaning, there is no need to adduce an additional linguistic capacity.

Understanding Mukula's Context

To understand Mukula's arguments within his context, this next section introduces the intellectual resources he is drawing on. In what follows, we will discuss the broad contours of linguistic theory in India before the tenth century. Since Mukula's arguments are innovative in large part through their deployment of previous concepts in a new context, in Section 1: Locating Linguistic Philosophy in Indian Thought we will introduce the major thinkers whose work he cites or alludes to, thinkers who are primarily from three textual traditions: Mīmāṃsā (Vedic hermeneutics), Sanskrit grammar, and Alaṅkāra (poetic and aesthetic theory). In Section 2: Theories of Word Meaning we will introduce several problems related to what words mean and how we know their meanings. Section 3: Theories of Sentence Meaning examines competing theories of how words combine into sentential unity. In Section 4: Poetics and Linguistics we will survey some of the important foundational concepts which inform Ānandavardhana and Mukula's debate. Finally, in Section 5: After Mukula we take a brief look at some of the thinkers after Mukula, for readers who may wish to follow this debate beyond this text. At the end of the introduction, there is a brief and lightly annotated list of resources as a guide for further exploration.

A brief note on method: In what follows, we will avoid drawing strong parallels with any particular modern thinkers, although readers may consult footnotes for some occasional pointers. This is for two reasons. First, the aim of this text is to introduce readers to Indian philosophy who may not already be well versed in contemporary linguistics or analytic philosophy of language. Thus drawing parallels might not serve an illuminating purpose, and in fact, could be obscuring. On the other hand, it isn't possible to entirely avoid frameworks which are outside of Mukula's original context. This is because explicating Mukula's ideas for a twenty-first-century English-reading audience necessarily requires some interpretation into familiar terms and ideas. So we will be introducing concepts like reference, epistemology, the type-token distinction, etc.

However, within the introduction and the rest of the book, hopefully it will become clear the manner in which these ideas are grounded in the texts themselves, and as these concepts are debated in contemporary thought, so, too in the premodern Indian context. Thus the second reason for avoiding strong parallel claims is that too-easy identification of, say, an "Indian Grice" or *lakṣaṇā* as a Sanskrit equivalent for Gricean implicature risks obscuring genuine differences between the traditions. While it is not surprising to find thinkers separated by time, language, and culture, converging on similar, or even the same positions, it would be surprising to find that all of their motivations and arguments converge. Leaving open the possibility of such a surprising result, in this book, readers will find aids for their own inquiry into how Indian thinkers understood communication, so that they may then consider their relationships with other thinkers around the world.

Locating linguistic philosophy in Indian thought

Mukula Bhaṭṭa's *Fundamentals of the Communicative Function* (*Abhidhā-vṛtta-mātṛkā*) is situated at the intersection of three major strands of textual reflection: philosophy, grammar, and poetic/aesthetic inquiry. These systematic textual disciplines, or sciences, are known as *śāstra*s, and each of them includes linguistic analysis in various ways.

The science often referred to today as "philosophy," sets out the viewpoints (*darśana*s) of Indian intellectual traditions. Each tradition typically identifies itself as such in relationship to a foundational or root text (*sūtra*), written in an aphoristic style, and ascribed to an authoritative teacher, often as the result of an oral tradition preceding the teacher (who may or may not be the historical author of the text). Philosophical development typically occurs by way of commentary on the foundational text—and subcommentaries on commentaries, and so on. These texts investigate metaphysical topics (Does the self exist or not? Are universals real?) as well as epistemological ones (In virtue of what do we have knowledge? What is the relationship between testimony and inference?). Illustrating the importance of the commentarial style for Indian thought, especially in the "classical" period (roughly 200 CE to 1300 CE) is the fact that Mukula's *Fundamentals,* although he is the sole author, is written in the style of a commentary, in which he writes commentary on his own verses. Among the philosophical *darśanas*, Mukula draws most heavily from the intellectual tradition known as Mīmāṃsā. The Mīmāṃsakas, as these thinkers are known, develop a system of hermeneutics for texts which prescribe rituals, and as they do, they investigate the conditions necessary to make a unit of speech a coherent whole, the relative strength of various interpretive principles, the relationship between different sentences in a discourse unit, and more. For its focus on the sentence as a unit of analysis, Mīmāṃsā is known as the "science of sentences," although they, like other thinkers, also considered questions of metaphysics, knowledge, and ethics, and more. Mukula quotes or alludes to a number of Mīmāṃsākas, whose views on language we will consider in more detail below.

Before we move on to reflections about language in the other sciences, let us pause to introduce an important concept from Mīmāṃsā which is not typically taken to be only about language. This is the **epistemic instrument (*pramāṇa*)** known as postulation (*arthāpatti*), which we were introduced to briefly above.[1] Epistemic instruments are the ways by which human beings come to know the world. For instance, perception and inference are two of the most paradigmatic, and many Indian thinkers (especially that loose collection known as *Pramāṇavādins*, or "members of the School of Epistemology") were concerned with understanding how epistemic instruments function, what cognitive states they result in, and what guarantees their authority in epistemic matters. Mukula Bhaṭṭa does not discuss inference or perception, but he does discuss postulation. Mīmāṃsā philosophers took postulation to explain cases when we come to know something on the basis of a doubt or a conflict that arises on the basis of two apparently incongruous pieces of knowledge. While the structure of postulation is a difficult question, subject to much philosophical debate, one way to characterize it is reasoning to the only possible explanation on the basis of a limited set of options. It has applications beyond linguistic cases, such as postulating that someone is outside and alive when we find them not in the house and have every reason to believe they are alive. However, its importance for Mīmāṃsakas lay primarily in its usefulness in completing incomplete (elliptical) utterances, where the utterance makes no sense unless we postulate another part of the expression.

For instance, postulation is involved in recovering the missing parts of elliptical expressions such as "the door," when what we want to say is "Close the door." What Mukula does which is interesting is to identify one of these stock examples of postulation as also being an example of secondary meaning (see below). While he is careful to remain neutral on the more technical matters that engaged various thinkers in debate, Mukula agrees with Mīmāṃsakas that postulation is a way to come to know linguistic meanings which are not explicitly uttered. Based on this claim, in tandem with his discussion of the structure of secondary meaning throughout the text, we can extrapolate that he believes postulation is responsible for at least some kinds of poetic meaning (as well as nonpoetic meaning). In fact, in the commentarial chapter, I argue that his case against Ānandavardhana depends on the fact that there is an epistemic instrument which enables us to understand implicit or indirect meanings. This makes Mukula the first thinker to appeal to an epistemic instrument as an alternative for suggestion, and in this he is followed by Mahima Bhaṭṭa, though he prefers inference as the alternative.

Returning to the three major sciences, the science of grammar (*vyākaraṇa*) includes what philosophers today would recognize as theories of reference, sentential unity, the role of context, and so on. One of the earliest and most important works of Sanskrit grammar we have is Pāṇini's *Eight Chapters* (*Aṣṭâdhyāyī*), circa second to fourth century BCE, which laid out the rules for what we now know as Classical Sanskrit. Just as with the philosophical *darśanas*, the textual tradition of grammar self-consciously traces itself back to this root text. In Mukula's treatise, he refers to Pāṇini's *Eight Chapters* to settle whether expressions are grammatical or not, and he also cites Pāṇini's important commentator, Patañjali, whose roughly second-century-BCE *Great Commentary on the Eight Chapters* (*Mahā-bhāṣya*) includes explicit philosophical reflection on the relationship between sound and meaning, theories of word reference, and so on. Grammar was a discipline essential for some very practical reasons, as well: since the orthoprax religious texts known as the Vedas are in Sanskrit, proper religious practice necessitated learning rules of pronunciation, along with Sanskrit grammar. The religious technocratic caste, the brahmins, learn from an early age how to chant and sing Sanskrit in a ritual context, where proper utterance guarantees sacrificial efficacy. However, despite the centrality of Vedic praxis to Sanskrit grammatical science, the latter goes beyond mere grammatical textbook to sophisticated discussion of competing theories of reference and meaning. In the circa sixth-century-CE *Treatise on Sentences and Words* (*Vākya-padīya*) of Bhartṛhari, another important interlocutor for Mukula, the grammarian explicitly brings together theorizing on ordinary human language with issues relevant for Vedic praxis, along the way investigating the metaphysical grounds for language use. We will see Mukula allude to Bhartṛhari's thought throughout his text, concluding with a lengthy reflection on the relationship between language and the world we see around us, a world which we think of as involving distinctions but which, on Bhartṛhari's view, ultimately lacks them.

The last science which we will take up as a locus of philosophical reflection on language lacks a foundational *sūtra* text. This textual tradition, though it can be traced back in some ways to a seminal work of dramaturgy, the *Treatise on Dramaturgy* (*Nāṭya-śāstra*) of Bharata Muṇi (with date estimates varying widely from second century BCE to third century CE), does not evolve primarily through commentaries on this text. Further, putting the tradition into English terms is challenging: it is known as *alaṅ-kāra-śāstra*, the science of figuration, or quite literally, "the science of making beautiful." On the one hand, we might call this "poetics," but we might also call it "aesthetics" as these thinkers also analyze cognitive processes relevant to appreciating poetry and drama. Hence, in this book we simply retain the term Alaṅkāra. The thinkers in this discipline (Ālaṅkārikas) consider the internal logic of poetry and especially of figurative language: What is the most foundational figure of speech? What faults prevent figurative language from being effective? They also take up issues involving the reader or hearer's experience of poetry, what emotional moods poetry cultivates, in what ways, and how these moods are related to the language—figurative and otherwise—of the poem. Mukula, of course, is responding to an important Ālaṅkārika we have already met, Ānandavardhana. However, he also draws on another Ālaṅkārika, Udbhaṭa, who lived around the late eighth to early ninth centuries CE, and whose work in many ways anticipates Ānandavardhana, in particular in his use of Mīmāṃsā philosophy to help him analyze poetic language. Mukula not only draws on theorists of poetry, but he quotes from well-known poetic compositions known as *kāvya*, a courtly poetry tradition. Some of these stanzas we can identify, such as an excerpt from Māgha's *The Killing of Śiśupāla* (*Śiśupāla-vadha*), whereas others may come from lost compositions or have been "stray verses," individual stanzas written as works in themselves.

Just this brief summary of three sciences and Mukula's use of them should give the sense that he is what today we might call an "interdisciplinary thinker." His *Fundamentals* is not a commentary on any of the foundational texts in these textual traditions, although he makes use of the work of thinkers within each. While, as we have already said, his treatise is designed to refute Ānandavardhana's revolutionary claims in the *Light on Suggestion*, he also presents his own views on word and sentence meaning, through creative repurposing of earlier theories.

Perhaps because of its ambiguous position in terms of textual traditions, Mukula's treatise, although one of the earliest substantial replies to the *Light*, has not been given much attention by modern scholarship until relatively recently, in the work of McCrea (2008). This is regrettable, since it was influential in Sanskrit poetic theory and is a notably interdisciplinary text. Mammaṭa (c. 1150 CE), a tremendous figure in Sanskrit poetic theory, borrowed parts of it verbatim for his twelfth-century *An Investigation into the Function of Speech* (*Śabda-vyāpāra-vicāra*). Mukula had at least two students, Pratīhāra Indurāja and Sahadeva (c. 1050 CE), who both note that Mukula has not only informed their understanding of aesthetics, but that he was responsible for rediscovering the work of Vāmana (c. 750 CE), an important earlier aesthetic theorist. Abhinavagupta's famous commentary (c. 1075 CE) on the *Light on Suggestion*, the *Eye* (*Locana*), may show his awareness of Mukula's work, as it deals with the objection that suggestion should be understood as indication.

In what follows, we will trace out some major conceptual themes which are found in all three of these sciences which set the stage for Mukula's work.

Theories of word meaning

Indian thinkers are concerned with a range of questions when it comes to word meaning. To understand their questions, we must first distinguish between a word as a **type,** or an abstraction from its many uses in different contexts, and a word as a **token**, or when it is used in a particular context. Grammarians like Pāṇini inquire into morphology, the principles which govern how word types and their smaller component parts change according to grammatical principles. However, since words are used by speakers for practical purposes, and in particular, since speech is a central part of religious practice—not just the Vedic scriptures, but also the words of the Buddha, the Jain scriptures—Indian thought focuses heavily on how language, through its word tokens, functions as an epistemic instrument. With language, human beings come to know things, whether ordinary or supraordinary facts, and so, for instance, Mīmāṃsā thinkers such as Śabara (fourth to fifth century CE) and Kumārila (seventh century CE) inquire into how such testimony works.

Taking a cue from the grammatical analysis of parts of speech, which distinguishes between an agent, an action, an instrument, and an object,

Indian thinkers understand the structure of an epistemic instrument in the following way: an epistemic instrument involves a knowing agent engaged in the action of knowing by means of the instrument of testimony, whose object is a mental event, known as a **cognition**. When someone utters a sentence, "The book is on the table," if this is a genuine case of testimony, the hearer will come to know something true about the world, namely, that the book is on the table. This knowledge, which is a mental event, is a result of, among other things, understanding the words spoken, and, most Indian thinkers argue, of understanding what those words refer to in the world. Inquiry into language, then, involves what contemporary disciplinary boundaries might consider philosophy of mind as well as epistemology and philosophy of language.[2]

Testimony involves sentences which are taken to be semantically meaningful wholes composed of smaller meaningful units: words. Thus sentence meaning is determined (at least in part) by word meaning. Not everyone accepts this approach (as we will see when we get to Bhartṛhari's "Burst" Theory), and there is a further question of how to individuate words. Is the Sanskrit sound /*akṣa*/, which can mean "gambling die" and "eye," a single polysemous word with two meanings, or a two homophonous words, with one meaning each? Typically, Indian thinkers prefer a one-to-one denotation relationship between words and their meanings, insofar as is possible, explaining further meanings as derivative, or indirect. We will discuss this in a moment, but first treat the topic of what Indian thinkers call "primary meaning" or *mukhya*, the meaning of words which contribute compositionally to sentence meaning and which is understood directly from an utterance. For most everyone, save some Buddhists, primary word meaning is about **reference**—Buddhists generally characterize word meaning as a concept entertained by the human mind, rather than a referent in the world.

On the view that words pick out, or designate, things in the world, Indian thinkers must explain how it is that people come to know this relationship between the word and its object, reference. Reference is understood to require epistemic access to the object as well as a process of pairing speech sounds with objects, so that when children hear "cow" they have an appropriate cognition. Instead of pointing to a cow and saying the single word, "cow," the process known as ostension, Indian thinkers tend to explain language-learning by the process of hearing commands in different contexts and extrapolating from complete sentences the meaning of the sub-sentential parts. When the request to bring a cow and not a horse has been successfully fulfilled, the language-learner comes to distinguish between "cow" and "horse." Mukula refers to this process throughout his treatise, and even though his concern eventually becomes the subtleties of poetic language, he begins with the starting premise that without a grip on reference, we have no way of employing language for any of its multiple purposes.

Early theories about word reference are found in grammatical as well as philosophical literature. These distinctions are important for Mukula's work for two reasons. First, he is writing a treatise which aims to convince as many interlocutors as possible of his view—and so he tries to be neutral with regard to these distinctions as is possible. Second, there are some places where neutrality is impossible, because one's theory of primary word meaning influences one's theory of secondary word meaning (which we will see in what follows), and he must take a position. As a broad characterization, we can say that Nyāya philosophers (Naiyāyikas) emphasize the importance of words playing different functions in context, and thus they refuse to identify a particular kind of entity or entities to which all words refer. Bhāṭṭa Mīmāṃsā philosophers, who follow Kumārila Bhaṭṭa, emphasize the repeatability of words across contexts, and thus argue that the universal is the primary referent for words, as it allows this pattern of use, especially when considering commands. Another group of Mīmāṃsā philosophers, those who follow Prabhākara (seventh century CE) and are thus called "Prābhākaras," disagree with both the Bhāṭṭa and Nyāya thinkers, arguing that words do not refer to any kind of entity, but to entities-in-relation together.[3] Finally, the early grammarian Patañjali identifies four kinds of referents—universals, individuals, actions, and qualities—to which words can refer.

This debate shows us that Indian thinkers are concerned with a number of things in their theorizing about word meanings. They are concerned with both *semantic* and *foundational theories* of word meaning. One way to get at this distinction is to say that while semantic theories of word meaning tell us what words are paired with in order to be meaningful, foundational theories tell us what makes this pairing possible. In the Indian context, semantic theorizing takes up the question of whether words refer to universals or particulars—adding into the mix qualities, actions, and some other categories. Foundational theorizing takes up the roles of cognition and causation. Most Indian theorists start with the view that word meanings depend upon a causal connection between speakers and things in the world, such as universals, qualities, particulars, etc. However, as we see with the Naiyāyika's remark about not distinguishing between universals and individuals when hearing words, the phenomenology of linguistic comprehension also plays a significant role in making meaning possible (and in considering what constitutes meaning).

There is yet another view about word meanings which was very influential, and which is important for Mukula's work. That is the earlier-mentioned Burst Theory of Bhartṛhari. While it's a matter of significant scholarly controversy what this thinker's final position is, one position he seems to hold is that words are merely abstractions from utterances. This approach prioritizes sentences—understood as a fundamentally unified sound—over words. Theories of word meaning may be useful to a certain degree, but they mistake the real nature of speech, which is to cause a moment of comprehension (a "flash" or *pratibhā*) that occurs in a unified burst (*sphoṭa*) and which is only analyzed into components from a later, abstract standpoint. In reality, we do not hear words and combine their meanings to constitute a sentence. Thus words, ultimately, are not meaning-bearing units, on this view. As we will see, Bhartṛhari's view is very influential for Mukula's own position, although he also incorporates the other theories just mentioned.

A final remark about theories of word meaning in Sanskritic philosophy. Despite sophisticated and early debates about theories of reference, one thing Indian thinkers seem to overlook, at least until the fifteenth century or so, is what contemporary philosophers call the "sense-reference distinction."[4] This distinction is, at its most basic, between what a word picks out and the way in which that object is picked out. To give a stock example, the word "Hesperus" is used for Venus appearing in the evening sky and "Phosphorus" for Venus appearing in the morning sky. The two words thus have the same reference (the object) but a different **sense** (way of conceiving the object). It's a matter of some scholarly debate whether Indian philosophers actually lack this distinction, but it's broadly accepted that they do not make heavy use of it, preferring to focus on reference. However, we will see in Mukula's work that, while it is not thematized explicitly, he makes use of the distinction between a word's referent and the ways in which that referent can be cognized, as a result of the same word type being tokened in different sentences. For instance, "Rāma" can be used to refer to the person Rāma, or to Rāma along with the cluster of properties he has in virtue of being the hero of the *Rāmayāṇa*. Whether a "sense-reference" distinction or not, Mukula is concerned with how words vary in the cognitions they bring about, given different contexts, while reference remains fixed. This phenomenon, however, does not occur at the level of the primary meaning, but what Indian thinkers call secondary meaning, to which we turn now.[5]

As we have said, for most Indian philosophers, primary word meaning is about reference. Under the right conditions, however, words convey meanings through a secondary function. This secondary function is given different names by different thinkers, all with varying connotations depending on the particular theory. Unless the specific term and distinctions are relevant, we will simply talk about "secondary meaning." Setting aside Bhartṛhari (whose commitment to the Burst Theory makes things more complicated), the conditions for secondary word meaning are as we said earlier: (1) when there is an obstacle in construing the primary meaning, and (2) when there is an appropriate relationship between the primary and a possible secondary meaning, and (3) when some warranting speaker intention is available, then secondary word meaning can function. Take for instance the English sentence

1 The newspaper called.

If we suppose that "newspaper" ordinarily refers to a physical object, then the result of the primary word meaning function is that the hearer entertains a cognition of this physical object. However, in context, there is a problem with this understanding. It is nonsensical given what we know about the world—newspapers aren't the kind of thing which can make phone calls. However, we can understand the secondary meaning "the editor of the newspaper" from the word "newspaper," if, fulfilling requirement (2) there is an associative relationship between newspapers and their editors, and, for requirement (3) there is a reason someone might speak this way, such as to emphasize the editor's standing in for the entire paper.[6] Examples similar to this typical English-language metonymy are found in Sanskrit texts, for instance

2 Feed the stick.

Here, the "stick" refers to the walking stick of a brahmin who goes around begging for alms, and since the two are associated together, we are able to understand the sentence as "Feed the *brahmin who has* the stick," because otherwise the sentence is nonsensical (sticks don't eat!) and to understand it this way is reasonable given how people ordinarily speak (for instance, to reduce people to their symbols).

Since Indian philosophers have different theories of word reference, and secondary meaning functions after the primary meaning, they will disagree over boundary between primary and secondary meaning. For instance, Bhāṭṭa Mīmāṃsā philosophers see secondary meaning at work in the sentence below, whereas others may not

3 The cow is to be sacrificially bound.

Here, since the primary referent of "cow" is a universal, there is an obstacle in understanding the utterance in this manner. We don't tie up COWHOOD. So, Bhāṭṭa Mīmāṃsakas argue, the kind of secondary meaning known as indication (*lakṣaṇā*) enables us to understand that a particular cow should be tied up to a post for the sacrifice. This is possible because there is a close relationship between universal and particular (Bhāṭṭa Mīmāṃsakas might say they are two aspects of the same thing).[7] However, the third requirement—speaker's intention—is not crucial for Mīmāṃsā except in human utterances. When dealing with Vedic commands, which have no speaker, all that's required is knowing that there is an obstacle and that there is an appropriate word meaning which, were it not accepted, would leave the obstacle in place. In contrast, Nyāya philosophers would be happy to accept that the word "cow" in sentence (3), given the right context, could have the primary meaning of an individual cow.

We might be tempted to call secondary meaning what Western philosophers call "pragmatics," since this kind of meaning focuses on what words mean beyond their ordinary referent, and the latter might be characterized as "semantics." However, the semantics-pragmatics distinction is often characterized as a contrast between words as types (abstracted from sentences) and words as tokens (used in utterances).[8] This is not the distinction here. The discussion of primary meanings focuses on how speakers understand words in particular contexts—these contexts of utterance, after all, are crucial for generating knowledge via testimony, which is a matter of agents entertaining veridical cognitions about the world. Likewise, the distinction between primary and secondary meaning is not necessarily that of literal and nonliteral meaning. On the Bhāṭṭa Mīmāṃsā view, the command "The cow is to be sacrificially bound," is not thought of as particularly nonliteral—at least certainly not in the sense of being figurative.

However, secondary meaning is also involved in what Western categorizing recognizes as figurative, sentences such as

4 Devadatta is a lion.

This kind of secondary meaning involves the attribution of shared properties between Devadatta and a lion. Just how this attribution occurs is a point of dispute, but the point is that, unlike the case of newspapers/editors, sticks/brahmins, COWHOOD/cows, the primary and secondary meanings have the relationship of being qualitatively similar. This sentence is an example of what

Western thought calls a "metaphor," although Sanskrit poetic theory makes a number of fine-grained conceptual and terminological distinctions within that broad category. Mukula himself identifies a number of distinctions within what Western thought might broadly call "metaphor."[9]

Again, as with the earlier cases of secondary meaning, there is an obstacle to understanding a word in its primary meaning. Here, the problem is with "lion," according to Indian thinkers—we cannot predicate being a lion of Devadatta, since it's a matter of common knowledge that "Devadatta" refers to a person, and lions are not people (here we set aside complications of theories of primary meaning, and whether "Devadatta" refers to a person or a universal inherent in a person). Unless we take "lion" as having a secondary meaning, the obstacle remains. Kumārila Bhaṭṭa argues that "lion" indicates a long list of properties that Devadatta and the lion both share. The reason one might speak this way rather than simply say "Devadatta is brave, strong, and etc." is that it is quicker to use this short expression. Here he appeals to speaker intention because this is an ordinary expression—but again, in the cases of Vedic figures of speech, there is no speaker to have an intention, so suitable interpretations are constrained by other considerations, such as the ordinary meaning of words, the discourse context, grammatical issues, and so on.

We will see Mukula identify a number of these constraints in his effort to identify the conditions under which the secondary function occurs. Although he differs with Bhāṭṭa thinkers in his fine-grained distinctions within secondary meaning, he chooses to quote both Śabara and his commentator, Kumārila, at crucial points in the *Fundamentals*. From them he borrows the claim that secondary meaning, although it goes beyond the primary, does so in a way which is restricted by convention and by some kind of connection to the primary meaning. He directly quotes or alludes to two other Bhāṭṭa Mīmāṃsā thinkers: Bhartṛmitra (living between Śabara and Kumārila's time) and Maṇḍana Miśra (c. eighth century CE). The first, a Mīmāṃsaka whose work is largely lost to us, provides Mukula with a typology of five relationships between primary and secondary meaning. The second is a thinker who writes works of Mīmāṃsā philosophy as well as another tradition, Advaita Vedānta. Mukula draws on a section of Maṇḍana's work in which he argues that people learn language not only through commands, but also assertions. While Mukula's point with the allusion is slightly different, we see the range of Mīmāṃsaka thinkers from which he is willing to draw.

Much discussion about secondary meaning and its relationship to primary meaning occurs in grammatical, philosophical, and poetic texts, though we have only touched on major views relevant to Mukula's text. As well, in early poetic and literary tradition of Alaṅkāra, we also find discussions of how to characterize secondary meanings with regard to poetry. We will discuss this aspect further in Section 4: Poetics and Linguistics.

Theories of sentence meaning

The standard position for Indian philosophers, as indeed for most modern Western philosophers, is that words on their own do not convey knowledge.[10] If a lookout on a watchtower shouts out, "Fire!" Indian thinkers would argue that the word "fire" is elliptical for a sentence like "There is fire!" While ellipsis is an important topic for Indian thinkers, our focus here is the various theories of sentence meaning which theories of ellipsis tend to presuppose. There are three main views of sentence meaning summarized in Mukula's text.[11] If we were to put these views as metaphors, we might say: in the first view words are building blocks, in the second view words are puzzle pieces, in the third view words are like a peacock's egg.

1 Connection of what is denoted (building block view)
2 Denotation through the connected (puzzle piece view)
3 Burst Theory (peacock's egg view)

The first view is defended by Bhāṭṭa Mīmāṃsakas. This theory of sentence meaning has it that words first fulfill their referential function. These resultant meanings are like the building blocks of sentences. After the blocks are established, then connection among meanings can occur, and this connection is in part due to the workings of the secondary word function, indication, which then connects the "blocks" together. On this view, we find both primary and secondary meaning implicated in nearly every sentence being uttered. Words convey their primary referents first, which are always universals. However, a sentence is not merely a list of universals, but it is a unity. The earlier sentence, "A cow is to be sacrificially bound," in Sanskrit is made up of two words: *gaur anubandhyaḥ*. The word *gaur* means COWHOOD in its primary meaning and, setting aside some complicated discussions of how verbs work, the word *anubandhyaḥ* means *tying up for sacrifice*. But the sentence is telling us something about a particular cow and that it is the object of the action of tying up. Bhāṭṭa Mīmāṃsā philosophers argue that it is the secondary word function, in its metonymical use, indication, that shifts the referent from the universal to the specific. Thus secondary meaning in some sense is necessary for any sentence. In a moment, we'll see what the other necessary elements are, but first let's turn to the second theory of sentence meaning.

The second view, in which words are like puzzle pieces, is defended by Prābhākara Mīmāṃsakas such as Śālikanātha Miśra (ninth century CE). On this theory, we might say each word is like a puzzle piece that has an empty slot and/or a tab. The word only conveys its meaning when it is successfully conjoined to a corresponding piece. (We have to be careful not to stretch the analogy too far, since puzzle pieces usually have only one match, but words can "match" to a number of other words.) On this view, words do not fulfill a referential function outside of the context of a sentence. For instance, the word "cow" does not invariably first refer to COWHOOD and then indicate something else, depending on the context. Rather, the word "cow" means something like __*cow* and would convey its meaning only when the right verb is connected. Likewise, "bring" would be *bring*__ and conveys its meaning only in combination with "cow."[12] For Prābhākara thinkers, words successfully refer only as part of a larger whole.

In contrast to both of these views, which presume that words exist as distinct entities and are paired in some way with meanings, Bhartṛhari's Burst Theory denies that sentences are constructed at all, whether of words-as-building blocks or words-as-puzzle pieces. Rather, as we saw earlier, words are hypothetical fictions which are abstracted from sentences. Instead of words composing sentences which cause us to have mental cognitions, Bhartṛhari reverses the priority: the sentences come first. He uses a metaphor to explain his understanding of the apparent relationship of parts and wholes, or words and sentences. Just like the egg of a peacock, which is an indivisible whole, opens to manifest a peacock which has divisions and colors, words "open" to manifest something radically different which seems to have divisions.

As for the meanings of sentences, we have already seen that for Bhartṛhari, the *sphoṭa* or "burst" is not susceptible to analysis. It is an indivisible whole. Sounds, which he characterizes as hypothetically divided in various ways—letters, words, sentences—reveal this *sphoṭa*, but they are not responsible for it in the way that the earlier thinkers believe words are responsible for meanings. Instead, like the bright circle that is seen when a torch is quickly swung in a circle, we understand meanings from words. The perception of a circle is not actually a perception of the torch moment-by-moment but a (unified) mental construction. But for Bhartṛhari, although the undivided circle of fire may be a mental construction, it represents what is most fundamentally real—a unity. He seems to be committed to the view that what is most real is a unified whole (although again, it is hard to determine what his final view is). The phenomenal world, with all its temporal and physical divisions, is not ultimately real. This monism informs his understanding of language (prioritizing whole over parts).

Despite their disagreements over how sentences come together from words to form a unified meaning, all of these theorists agreed on the importance of three concepts:

1 Expectation (*ākāṅkṣā*)
2 Semantic fit (*yogyatā*)
3 Contiguity (*sannidhi*)

When these three features are satisfied, a hearer forms a cognition on the basis of language. Put another way, an expression which satisfies each of these constitutes a sentence, since it is able to prompt a cognition of a state of affairs. While each of these features is grounded in facts (grammatical, semantic, and temporal), they are to do with a hearer's comprehension. Thus, **expectation (*ākāṅkṣā*)** is the sense of incompleteness one has when hearing a subject without a verb or vice versa. While which words have "expectancy" for other words is a matter of grammatical features, it is hearers which judge that an expression fails in its satisfaction of expectancy. So Indian thinkers can (and do) talk about expectation as a matter of language and of psychology. In the sentence "The cow is to be sacrificially bound," our noun phrase (which is a single word in Sanskrit) has the expectation of a verb phrase. In Sanskrit grammatical terms, there is an agent which has the expectation for an action. (Or, on some theories, it is the other way around—syntactical structure is an important issue for Sanskrit grammarians.) Since expectancy is satisfied, one of our criteria for the expression to be a sentence is completed.

But when we hear a sentence, we are not only concerned with grammatical structure, we are concerned with meaning. While a noun phrase may have expectation for a verb phrase, not just any phrase will do. When the right kind of words, from the standpoint of meaning, are in syntactic relationship, there is **semantic fit (*yogyatā*).** A frequent example of semantic fit's failure in Sanskrit texts is "One sprinkles the garden with fire." While it is perfectly grammatical, it is nonsensical: one does not sprinkle gardens with fire. Of course, we might object that perhaps you could metaphorically sprinkle with fire. This is true, and in fact, the failure of semantic fit is frequently the identified obstacle which triggers metaphorical, or more broadly, secondary interpretations. For instance, on the Bhāṭṭa theory of sentence meaning, it is the failure of semantic fit in the sentence "The cow is to be sacrificially bound," which prompts us to understand a particular cow from "cow," though this is metonymy and not metaphor. Prābhākara thinkers also require semantic fit, but since they argue that primary word meaning is relational in the first place, they would construe "cow" in whatever sense is necessary to be the object of "to be sacrificially bound."

Finally, **contiguity (*sannidhi*)** is the requirement that the words must be understood in relationship to one another, not just as discrete sounds. Indian thinkers sometimes talk about contiguity as something which happens mentally—we "put together" the word meanings when we understand a sentence. Other times, they talk about contiguity as the requirement that words are uttered in close temporal proximity (think of saying "the cow" on Wednesday and then "is to be tied up" on Friday—this is a failure of proximity). These ideas are related, of course, since in most cases, the fact that words are uttered in a temporally contiguous manner is part of how we construe them in close relationship to one another.

While Bhāṭṭa Mīmāṃsā thinkers admit that these three requirements are necessary for sentence meaning, they argue that words have referents independently first, apart from their being comprehended in tandem with other words in a sentence. There is then a second process, indication, in which comprehension of the particular contextual meanings occurs. Indication is a stage which employs these three features to determine the contextually appropriate meaning. In contrast, Prābhākara Mīmāṃsā denies the existence of two stages, arguing that we understand the particular contextual meanings directly from the word, in reliance upon the three necessary conditions of expectancy, semantic fit, and contiguity. Finally, while Bhartṛhari would deny that words and sentences exist ultimately, he still develops these three concepts at length in his *Treatise*, demonstrating that he accepts them at least in the provisional, ordinary level of analysis. Mukula himself will appeal to all three features at important points in his argument, and on his understanding, a failure of semantic fit often is the trigger for secondary meaning. This failure, which he spells out in some detail, is an incongruity which requires a new meaning for its resolution. Further, while he seems to be committed ultimately to the Bhartṛharian Burst Theory, on which sentences and their meanings are a unified whole, he also proposes a fourth view which he characterizes as a "combination" of the first and second theories. Since no historical correspondence for such a proposal has yet been found (although in the commentarial chapter I argue

Mukula draws historical inspiration from Naiyāyikas) we can conjecture this is Mukula's own contribution.

Poetics and linguistics

Ninth-century-CE Kashmiri thinker Ānandavardhana is one of the first thinkers to integrate the dramatic and poetic intellectual traditions into a unified theory.[13] However, while Ānandavardhana transformed poetic thought thereafter (the period beginning with his work is known as the Kashmiri Poetic Revolution), he built upon the foundation laid by Ālaṅkārikas, grammarians, and philosophers before him. While a great deal could be said about Ānandavardhana's influences, in what follows we restrict ourselves to the main influences relevant to the arguments which Mukula engages with in his text.

As we've said, in the *Light*, Ānanda contends that the main purpose of poetry is to create *rasa*, which was previously mostly understood in the context of dramaturgy. He argues that *rasa* is understood by a linguistic capacity called "suggestion" (*dhvani*).[14] The Sanskrit term *dhvani* was originally employed by grammarians to refer to the sounds of utterances, sounds which "reveal" their meaning. Ānandavardhana adopts this term for the suggestive capacity of language responsible for the subtleties of poetry (see 1.13l, 3.33m in Ingalls 1990). This capacity is in addition to the commonly accepted two explained above (primary and secondary meaning). Still, despite the name for this capacity coming from a grammatical context, this does not mean that Ānanda is committed to any particular grammarian's view of word or sentence meaning (in fact, he avoids taking too strong a theoretical position on anything apart from the existence of suggestion).

In addition to drawing on grammatical terminology, Ānandavardhana's theory of suggestion borrows conceptual resources from Mīmāṃsakas, especially the distinction between a meaning which is **intended to be expressed (*vivakṣita*)** and one which is not intended to be expressed (*avivakṣita*).[15] As we said above, Ānanda argues that *rasa* is the predominant aim of excellent poetry, but he does not wish to deny that other meanings are also communicated by the point in the course of conveying *rasa*. Instead, he distinguishes between the predominant aim of expression and other things which are expressed, but are not the main intention. In ordinary speech, when someone makes an assertion, like "Pārvatī is looking at the lotus flower in her hand," what is intended to be expressed is not some suggested meaning, but merely the fact of Pārvatī's attention. Even if something further were to be understood by the sentence (for instance, that Pārvatī is holding a lotus flower) that is not what the speaker intends to express. But in poetry, the further unsaid meanings are intended. Thus this distinction is central to Ānanda's case for suggestion. Mukula recognizes its importance and structures his competing theory around ways in which indication can convey both meanings that are intended to be expressed and not intended to be expressed.

Ānanda's theory emerges from the tradition of Alaṅkāra, which was previously primarily concerned with taxonomies of figures of speech and with practical advice on how to make poetry beautiful. While he brings together dramaturgy with Alaṅkāra, initially these had different aims: drama was aimed to inculcate a certain emotional and aesthetic state in the characters on stage: *rasa*, a word literally meaning "taste," "flavor," or "relish." A famous early verse in the *Treatise on Dramaturgy* says that "*Rasa* is brought about due to the combination of objects of emotions, manifestations of emotions, and temporary emotional moods."[16] Handbooks of drama instructed playwrights about how they could manifest *rasa* on stage. It's important to note that these plays were frequently performed within the context of days-long religious festivals, in which rehearsing well-known stories served to bring participants into the world of the sacred. Thus playwrights must incorporate appropriate plot devices, choreography, stage settings, and so on to manifest this world. So we see that from the start, Indian thinkers are not engaged in purely aesthetic reflection; art as a general phenomenon was not the concern, taken independently of its embodiment in drama and poetry. Eventually Ānandavardhana brings together these the two goals, the cultivation of dramatic *rasa* and the creation of poetic beauty into a unifying theory.

The *Treatise on Dramaturgy* compares the combination of emotive and bodily components needed to make *rasa* to a cook's recipe. When this recipe is followed properly and prepared for persons of culture it is gratifying. Thus there is a normative aspect to *rasa* in its creation (one must combine the elements appropriately) and in the requirement of a skillful audience member (not just anyone is satisfied by gourmet food without having a trained palate). Originally, theorists identified eight kinds of *rasa* (the comic, heroic, erotic, terrible, pathetic, compassionate, furious, wondrous), but eventually Ānanda adds a ninth to the list, the peaceful. What differs is the set of components leading to the experience. While the *Treatise on*

Dramaturgy does also discuss figures of speech in one of its thirty-six chapters, it surveys only four: simile (*upamā*), identification (*rūpaka*, referring specifically to the linguistic form "x is y"), parallelism (*dīpaka*), and twinning (*yamaka*). It is up to later writers to examine figures of speech in more detail, and in a strictly verbal context as opposed to dramatic.

In contrast to dramaturgy, early reflection on Sanskrit poetry focused on creating beautiful figures of speech. (The term for the kind of poetry they focused on is *kāvya* and it refers to courtly and epic poetry.) If the metaphor for a successful drama was a recipe, the metaphor for a good poem was a beautiful lady.

> The words and meanings which make up a poem are described as its "body" (*śarīra*), while those phonetic and semantic factors which, when introduced into poetic language, render it more beautiful are called "ornaments" (*alaṅkāras*).[17]

Emphasis in literature about poetics was on these ornaments, their kinds and relations to one another. Usually, two roughly contemporaneous thinkers mark the beginning of self-conscious literary analysis in Indian thought: Bhāmaha and Daṇḍin, both living circa 700 to 750 CE. Their respective priority is a matter of scholarly debate, but their importance is not. Bhāmaha's *Ornaments of Poetry* (*Kāvyâlaṃkāra*) and Daṇḍin's *Mirror on Poetry* (*Kāvya-darśa*) both define poetry and investigate its characteristic properties (*guṇas*), its figures (*alaṅkāras*) and the defects which threaten good poetry (*doṣas*).

Mukula, however, does not quote either Bhāmaha or Daṇḍin, nor does he explicitly refer to the *Treatise on Dramaturgy*, although one of his example expressions, "auspicious-faced one," may be drawn from use in plays, where it is an ironic address for low-brow persons. He does quote Udbhaṭa, though, who lived circa 800 CE, prior to Ānandavardhana. In his *Explanation* (*Vivaraṇa*), Udbhaṭa draws on Kumārila's Mīmāṃsā conception of secondary meaning to define the figure known as identification (*rūpaka*). Bronner (2016) argues this is evidence of a shift, earlier than Ānandavardhana, toward semantic theorizing—a focus on the meaningfulness of poetic expressions—and away from mere syntactic observation. While the relationship of Udbhaṭa's ideas to Ānandavardhana and the extent to which the former had a systemic account of figurative meaning are both subjects of scholarly debate, at minimum, we can speculate that Mukula must have had some purpose selecting Udbhaṭa as one of his interlocutors in the *Fundamentals*. A further intriguing historical fact is that Mukula's student,

Pratihāra Indurāja, wrote a lengthy commentary on Udbhaṭa's *Explanation* (the latter now unfortunately only available in fragments). Perhaps this is indirect evidence for the teacher's influence in, if not understanding of the text, its selection as an important work?

Mukula does not explicitly engage (by way of explicit quotation or obvious allusion) with other Ālaṅkārikas. He targets Ānandavardhana's theory, although never by name (only talking about the **sensitive critic (*sahṛdaya*)** who accepts suggestion) and primarily through structurally alluding to Ānanda, or choosing the same examples for different evaluation. By drawing on or engaging with thinkers from grammar, philosophy, and Alaṅkāra to construct his account of communication, Mukula demonstrates the presence of robust linguistic analysis in each of these sciences, and establishes himself as a thinker willing to draw on conceptual resources wherever they are found.

After Mukula

Mukula's criticisms of Ānandavardhana do not ultimately prevail. In fact, the theory of suggestion became so broadly accepted in Alaṅkāra science that eventually, critical energy goes primarily to competing approaches in applying suggestion, rather than to whether it ought to be accepted in the first place. However, before this shift, which has been identified by McCrea (2008) as solidifying around 1100 CE with Mammaṭa's *Illumination of Poetry* (*Kāvya-prakāśa*), there were several thinkers who followed Mukula in pushing back against the existence of a third linguistic capacity. (In grammar and philosophy, the situation is different—suggestion is not typically even taken up for discussion, except to briefly dismiss it, as in the work of Naiyāyika Jayanta Bhaṭṭa.)

Mukula's own student, who we discussed above in connection to Udbhaṭa, Pratīhāra Indurāja, discusses suggestion after the conclusion of his commentary on Udbhaṭa's other work, the *Synopsis of the Essentials of Poetic Ornaments* (*Kāvyâlaṁkāra-sāra-saṃgraha).* He argues that Udbhaṭa's structure of analysis can account for suggestion, especially through a particular kind of indirect expression (*paryāyôkta*).[18] Then, roughly contemporaneous with Pratīhāra Indurāja, the Ālaṅkārika Dhanika argues that suggestion could be included within another linguistic capacity known as sentence purport (*tātparya-vṛtti*). A bit later, Kuntaka, roughly 1000 CE, argues that something known as oblique speech (*vakrôkti*) is the basis for the kinds of phenomena which Ānandavardhana attributes to the work of suggestion. Whether Kuntaka, per Raja (1969) is an opponent of Ānandavardhana, is hard to establish, as McCrea (2008) argues, although he does seem to be modeling oblique speech on the structure of suggestion.

In contrast to Kuntaka, the last important critical figure we will mention is unambiguously an opponent of suggestion. Mahima Bhaṭṭa (c. 1100 CE) in his *Analysis of Suggestion* (*Vyakti-viveka*) argues that suggestion should be understood as the operation of inference. Like Mukula, he draws on existing epistemic theory to show that suggestion is unnecessary. Unlike Mukula, he takes the Buddhist philosopher Dharmakīrti as his main source of conceptual inspiration, though this does not exclude the use of Mīmāṃsā concepts as well. His *Analysis* is a much longer work than Mukula's *Fundamentals*, and delves more deeply into analysis of particular verses, as well as of the inferential structure of how poetic language is understood. While not explicitly positioning himself as an opponent of Mukula, he does take a stand on the existence of postulation, arguing that it is merely a special kind of inference (which is consistent with Dharmakīrti's own view). Thus while he might agree with Mukula in one sense, since both of them take suggested meanings to be grasped by a broadly inferential kind of reasoning, his particular account is distinct.

Much more could be said about the direction of Sanskrit linguistic theory after Mukula, its relationship to grammar and philosophy, and its relationship to Ānandavardhana's *Light on Suggestion*. However, for the sake of appreciating Mukula, perhaps only two other figures need be mentioned: Abhinavagupta and Mammaṭa. As already noted, Abhinavagupta is a highly influential commentator on the *Light* whose interpretation, which goes beyond Ānandavardhana's original conception of both suggestion and *rasa*, comes to dominate later poetic thought. In relationship to Mukula, however, there is an oddity in his work, which is that although Abhinavagupta expends significant effort in repudiating opponents of Ānandavardhana's theory, he does not explicitly refer to Mukula's theory. In the commentarial chapter, I have collected in footnotes instances where I believe Abhinavagupta may be implicitly responding to Mukula, but a more careful analysis of their possible relationship should be undertaken.

Finally, the towering figure of Mammaṭa (c. 1100 CE), although he is a strong proponent of Ānandavardhana's theory of suggestion, owes much to Mukula. In fact, he quotes large portions of Mukula's text verbatim in his *An Investigation into the Function of Speech* (*Śabda-vyāpāra-vicāra*), although in service of his own arguments that support suggestion. Further, Mammaṭa's focus on the linguistic capacities may be due to Mukula's own groundbreaking work in the *Fundamentals*, in that his is the first work of its kind to treat this as its own topic.[19] Thus while Mukula's criticisms may not have swayed his fellow Ālaṅkārikas to abandon the theory of suggestion, nor convinced philosophers of the importance of attending to poetic theory, his *Fundamentals* did influence the history of Indian linguistic philosophy for centuries to come. Perhaps it is time for his text to have a chance to influence a new generation of philosophers.

Further Reading by Topic

The recommendations below are not comprehensive, but a starting-point for further investigation. For more resources, readers should consult Karl Potter's online *Encyclopedia of Indian Philosophies Bibliography* (https://faculty.washington.edu/kpotter/) and, since this encyclopedia includes the textual traditions of grammar and philosophy but not Alaṅkāra, also consult Cahill (2001) for an annotated bibliography of Alaṅkāra.

Locating linguistic philosophy

For introductions to the (Sanskritic) Indian intellectual world generally, see Chapter 8 of Ganeri (2011) for a discussion of commentary as a philosophical genre along with Pollock (1985) for discussion of the concept of *śāstra*. Franco (2013) has helpful remarks on historiography of Indian thought. For a topical overview of the philosophical *darśana*s, see Perrett (2016) and see Frauwallner (1974) for a historical approach, though the latter should be read with Franco (2013) in mind. Gerow (1977), Lienhard (1984), and Pollock (2006) treat the history of Sanskrit poetics, and Pollock (2016) introduces the aesthetic problems surrounding *rasa* through primary texts in translation with accompanying analysis. Scharfe (1977) gives a historical overview of grammar, while the collection of essays in Staal (1972) delves more deeply into the linguistic problems discussed by grammarians. Coward and Raja (1990) summarize important grammatical works as well as introduce the textual tradition. Matilal (2001) and (2005) explores topics in language in both philosophical and grammatical literature, often making connections to modern analytic philosophy. Deshpande (2016) and Keating (2016) introduce linguistic analysis in encyclopedia entries aimed at philosophers, the former focusing on grammar and select philosophers, the latter on the division between primary and secondary meaning in all three *śāstra*s. Finally, Raja (1969) remains the most wide-ranging introduction to linguistic philosophy in India, including philosophy, Alaṅkāra, and grammar, though its extensive use of Sanskrit may prove difficult for novices.

Theories of word meaning

For a discussion of word meaning, Deshpande (1992) orients the reader to the debate and includes a translation of a Sanskrit grammarian's discussion of nouns (Kauṇḍabhaṭṭa's *Nāmârtha-nirṇaya*). Ganeri (2006) also includes some general introductory material, along with analysis, often in formal terms, of Nyāya philosophical positions. Scharf (1996) focuses on the debate in grammar, Nyāya, and Mīmāṃsā, over what generic terms refer to, including select translations of important texts. Some of the previously mentioned resources, such as Matilal (2001) and (2005) and Raja (1969) also delve into theories of word meaning in detail.

Theories of sentence meaning

Raja (1969) devotes a chapter to theories of sentence meaning and Siderits (1991) discusses it over several chapters, focusing on Mīmāṃsā theories as well as some Buddhist theories of meaning. Matilal and Sen (1988), Chakrabarti (1989), Taber (1989) and Siderits (1989) (reprinted in Siderits 2016) are the most important articles treating the discussion among Mīmāṃsā and Nyāya thinkers, all with reference to modern analytic philosophy. Graheli (2016) connects this debate, as discussed by Naiyāyika Jayanta Bhaṭṭa, with the work of Abhinavagupta, the early commentator on Ānandavardhana's *Light on Suggestion*. For work on Bhartṛhari's *sphoṭa* ("burst") theory, see the related chapters in Raja (1969), Matilal (2001), and book-length treatment by Coward (1980). Helpful articles for his philosophical approach include Bronkhorst (2001), and Desnitskaya (2006). Cardona (1999) is also an important overview in the context of a review of Houben (1995), which should be used to understand Bhartṛhari with those remarks in mind.

Poetics and linguistics

For understanding debates about theories of metaphor, see related chapter in Raja (1969) for an overview, and the introductory essay to Gerow (1971) which is a glossary of technical terms in Alaṅkāra. The introduction to Ingalls et al (1990) is also helpful for a brief historical and conceptual overview of Alaṅkāra, though it is focused primarily on Ānandavardhana and Abhinavagupta. Likewise, Pollock (2016) is useful as an overview, but it is focused on *rasa* and not Alaṅkāra more broadly. McCrea (2008) is a book-length treatment on Alaṅkāra in Kashmir which explores how Mīmāṃsā hermeneutics influences its conceptual development. Bronner (2010) is a book-length discussion of the treatment of poetry with multiple registers which includes some discussion of philosophical problems taken up in this context. While much work in Sanskrit poetics and aesthetics focuses on intellectual history and not on the first-order problems Sanskrit thinkers identified, Chakrabarti (2016) is an edited volume which includes some papers on the aesthetic problems raised within the tradition.

After Mukula

McCrea (2008) includes chapters on Kuntaka, Abhinavagupta, and Mahima Bhaṭṭa. Franco and Ratié (2013) collects papers on this time period as well. Rajendran (2003) treats Mahima Bhaṭṭa's *Analysis* in detail and Gnoli (1956) focuses on Abhinavagupta. Bronner (2002) and Tubb (2008) focus on later Sanskrit poetics and innovations in Alaṅkāra in the sixteenth and seventeenth centuries.

Part II

English Translation of "The Fundamentals of the Communicative Function"

About this Translation

This translation aims to make Mukula's text available in English for an audience which is unfamiliar with Sanskrit and Indian philosophy. Thus I've translated somewhat freely with regard to Sanskrit syntax, completing senses implicit in compounds, splitting apart lengthy sentences, making pronomial referents explicit, transforming passive into active voice, etc. I've tried to avoid parenthetical insertions entirely, unless absolutely necessary. For readers interested in looking at the corresponding Sanskrit text, in addition to the included transliteration, the translation has square brackets which indicate the corresponding page and line number in Dvivedi (1973). More information about the printed editions used for the translation can be found in the introduction to the transliterated Sanskrit text included in this volume. In the course of my own translation I have consulted the only complete English translation of Mukula's work Venugopalan (1977), as well as the portions translated by Lawrence McCrea in *The Teleology of Poetics in Medieval Kashmir* (2008). Johannes Bronkhorst also sent me an early (and partial) draft of his translation in 2016, which I read, but which I did not refer to in my own work. Verses, which are integrated into the text, are numbered when necessary as 2a, 2b, etc., corresponding to the metrical halves of a complete single verse in Sanskrit. Terms found in the glossary are marked in bold at their first occurrence, but not thereafter.

Two appendices after the translation guide the reader through the text. Appendix 1 is an analytical outline, which provides the structure of Mukula's argument. Appendix 2 is a list of examples which he uses, along with their location in the text and his analysis of the example. Just before this appendix, readers will find three cheerful illustrations of his examples, drawn by one of my Yale-NUS students, Sherice Ngaserin. These drawings bring alive the contrast between the primary and secondary meaning, depicting the nonsensical interpretation based on the primary meaning at left and the intended secondary meaning at right.

Introduction

[1.6] It is evident that, in this world, **ordinary linguistic practice** cannot come into existence without determinate **cognitions** of word **meanings** as well as determinate cognitions of their uses in obtaining the means to earthly pleasures and liberation from the world, and their uses in avoiding what prevents these. This is because all **epistemic instruments** which are the basis for objects of knowledge are knowledge-conducive[1] insofar as they give rise to determinate cognitions. And the understanding of word meanings, whose uses are obtaining the means to earthly pleasures and liberation from the world and avoiding what prevents these, have these epistemic instruments as their basis. Thus, determinate cognitions are necessarily connected with there being ordinary linguistic practices involving these words. And a determinate cognition brings about the cognition of a meaning as connected to its corresponding utterance. Further, speech causes the cognition of meaning, whether through its **primary** or **indicatory communicative function**. Therefore, in this work we engage in analysis regarding the communicative function which is primary and indicatory.

[2.14] Having raised the question, "But what is the primary and indicatory communicative function?" the author writes in order to delineate these two functions of words, that is, the primary and the indicatory functions, through an explanation of the topic.

Verses 1–15

Verse 1

The primary meaning is what is apprehended from the function of speech.
The indicated meaning is said to be ascertained further from that meaning.

[2.18] The primary meaning is the cognition which comes from the function of speech.[1] For, just as the face is seen before all the parts of the body like the hands (when a baby is born), in the same way the primary meaning is understood before the other meanings are conveyed. It is for this reason that, with the suffix *-ya* that is added to words like "branch" being added to the word "face," the word "primary" means "primary like a face."[2] An example of this primary meaning is "The cow is to be sacrificially bound up." Here, the **universal** is understood from the function of the word "cow." This universal is COWHOOD and it is a means to complete the sacrifice. Therefore, the primary meaning is understood from the primary function.

[2.24] Now, the indicatory function's meaning is understood by reflecting on the meaning conveyed from the primary word function. This is just like the earlier example ("A cow is to be sacrificially bound,") since a particular cow is understood. For this meaning is not understood from the primary word function. We know this from the maxim, "A communicative function cannot get at the property-bearer when it expends its capacity on the property," and because what directly follows from an uttered word is just a universal. But a universal without a particular cannot be understood as the means to complete a sacrifice. Thus, by force of the universal understood by speech, the particular cow, which is the universal's substratum, is **implied**. Therefore, in this case there is the indicatory function.

[3.2] In conclusion, this twofold communicative function of a word is explained by describing the meanings of the primary and indicatory functions, which are respectively: a meaning whose content is a direct meaning and a meaning which is based on an intermediary meaning.

[4.26] Now, we describe the four kinds of primary communicative function:

Verse 2

(2a) With regard to the primary and indicated meanings, the four distinctions among primary meanings are known because of distinctions among things like universals.

[4.28] Because of the distinctions among things like universals, there are four types of primary meanings among the primary and indicated meanings. The renowned author of the *Great Commentary*[3] delineates "The four uses of words: Words denoting **universals**, words denoting **properties**, words denoting **actions**, and words denoting **something contingent**." Accordingly, for all words whose uses aim to denote their meanings, their use is necessarily connected to **distinguishing features**, because their different contents are **semantically imbued** by the distinguishing features.

[5.3] And there are two kinds of distinguishing features: something stipulated by a speaker and a thing's **nature**. Sometimes a speaker just stipulates that something has a distinguishing feature, but other times, there is a property truly belonging to something. Among these two kinds of distinguishing features, something stipulated by a speaker is when the speaker wants to bring about the ability to denote some particular name-bearer, for instance, in words like "Ḍittha." In such cases, the word's nature, which is a sequence of phonemes whose temporal order has been dissolved, is grasped when the last phoneme in the word is heard. Here, the word's nature is stipulated as the distinguishing feature through the speaker's desire for the word to be able to denote something. Therefore, words such as "Ḍittha," denoting something contingent, are necessarily connected to distinguishing features.

[5.10] Now, take those who think that the nature of words like "Ḍittha," which is a sequence of phonemes whose temporal order has been dissolved, is not superimposed onto name-bearers. They hold this position because they think there is no such sequence of phonemes whose temporal order has been dissolved, but there is just the sound of individual phonemes like "ḍa." Even among these thinkers, it is completely acceptable that words like "Ḍittha" are words denoting something contingent. This is because the purpose of using words like "Ḍittha," which are conceptually constructed aggregates of phonemes, is to denote some name for some thing, according to various capacities brought about by the speaker's desires. Thus, what has been explained above is the distinguishing feature which, according to the view of Grammarians, is analyzed as a name whose nature is stipulated as a distinguishing feature by the speaker.

[5.16] Now, distinguishing features which belong to a thing's nature have two states, because there is a difference between distinguishing features yet to be established and distinguishing features already established. Words denoting actions have a necessary connection to a distinguishing feature that is yet to be established. This is like the example, "One cooks." But already established distinguishing features are subdivided into two, because of the difference between universals and properties. Now, sometimes, an already established distinguishing feature, such as a universal, brings about the existence of a word's object. For no objects ever obtain their particular nature without having a connection to a universal. This is what the *Treatise on Sentences and Words* says: "In fact, a cow is not a cow or a non-cow because of its particular nature, but it is a cow because of its relationship with COWHOOD."[4]

[5.22] On the other hand, sometimes an already established distinguishing feature is the basis for a verbal distinction about an object whose nature already exists. Take, for example, properties like white. An object like a cloth does not acquire its nature as a cloth by depending on the property white. Rather, it is just in virtue of the universal that the thing has acquired its particular nature of being a cloth. Therefore, in this case, a thing's having attained its nature is the basis for making a verbal distinction. Now, consider eternal properties referred to by words like "atomic." All of these properties are a single kind, because they share in the universal PROPERTY. In conclusion, a word which has a necessary connection to a distinguishing feature that brings about existence is a word denoting universals, like "cow." When the object the word conveys is the basis for verbal distinctions about something that already has a nature, the word is a word for properties, just like "white."

[8.25] (*Objection.*) This is not the case! Instead, all these words which are thought to be for properties, actions, and something contingent are necessarily connected to universals. For instance, words for properties, like the word "white," express a universal that inheres in various things whose properties are characterized as white, things like milk, shells, cranes, etc. Words denoting actions are the same, as it should be said that they only express universals. These universals inhere in actions like cooking, which is verbally distinguished as a single kind of action since it is differentiated from other actions on the basis of its object, which may be a ball of sugar, a sesame seed, a grain of rice, etc.

Now, with regard to words such as "Ḍittha" that denote something contingent, there is a universal which is BEING A ḌITTHA WORD. This universal inheres in various Ḍittha-words, in distinct utterances such as from a parrot, a mynah bird, or a human. And this universal is superimposed on name-bearers as is appropriate. Alternatively, there is something which unifies the various things called "Ḍittha" at different times, which are different things because of growth and perishing. Based on what is the same among these tokens of "Ḍittha, Ḍittha," there comes to be a cognition of something unified, free of internal contradictions. Taking things this way, it should be plausible there is a universal of ḌITTHA-NESS which really does inhere in things understood by words like "Ḍittha." And this universal is what is denoted by words like "Ḍittha." And, therefore, because words denoting properties, words denoting actions, and words denoting something contingent are actually words denoting universals, it is not correct to say the use of words is divided into four types.

[10.7] (*Response.*) To this we respond that, in fact, particular properties, actions, and words for names which have differences in virtue of various distinguishing features are grounded in a unitary cognition but not in a universal. This is the position of the revered author of the *Great Commentary*. For this is just like a single face is reflected in various ways in oil, a sword, water, or a mirror, since these are different sources of the reflection's perception. In the same way, what is in fact single, such as the particular property white, might appear as if it were multiplied. An instance of white might manifest itself in different ways because of the character of what it is dependent upon, such as a conch shell, which is produced according to various causal bundles in different places and times. And therefore words such as "white" are not words denoting universals because there is no universal corresponding to whiteness, since a universal has inherence in different substrata and white is a particular, single thing.

In a similar way, words like "cooks," words like "Ḍittha," and things with names like "Ḍittha" ought to be explained. For, too, in these cases, there is just one individual action of cooking, one individual "Ḍittha," and one name-bearer Ḍittha. Acts of cooking which manifest themselves sequentially are just like multiple utterances of "Ḍittha" and Ḍittha's particular stages of life, such as childhood. These each have a single nature that appears to be various different kinds of natures because of what is different in each case. Thus we have established that the primary meaning is divided into four kinds because what grounds the use of words is divided into four kinds.

[11.8] Now, the author continues in order to survey the indicatory function's two divisions.

Verse 2b

> Indication is considered to have two kinds because it lacks and involves transfer. (2b)

[11.20] **Indication** has two categories because there is one **which lacks transfer** and one **which involves transfer**. First, there is indication lacking transfer: "The village is on the Ganges." Here, the particular river is inappropriate as a foundation for a village. Therefore, the expression "on the Ganges" indicates the bank which is adjacent to that particular river, the particular river being the expression's natural denotation. Now, indication involving transfer is where one thing is transferred onto another thing, such as, "The Punjabi is an ox." In this case, since it is not possible to construe the word "ox" with the word "Punjabi" as having a common subject, the primary meaning is **blocked**. Properties like dullness and laziness, similar to properties of dullness and laziness understood in the ox, are transferred onto the Punjabi in virtue of their being defining properties of a Punjabi which are similar to those in an ox. This is indication involving transfer. In this way, since it both lacks and involves transfer, indication is said to be twofold.

[12.24] Now, the author demonstrates that there is also a twofold nature to indication lacking transfer.

Verse 3a

> Indication lacking transfer is thought to be of two kinds because of its having **inclusion** and **indirect expression** (3a)

[12.24] What is here explained as indication lacking transfer is said to be of two kinds. Now, in some cases indication works by inclusion of another meaning. But in other cases, it works by indirect expression of another meaning. So what is inclusion of another meaning or indirect expression of another meaning? Having raised this question, the author continues.

Verses 3b–4a

When another object is implied for the sake of a meaning's **being established**, that (3b) is inclusion. Now, indirect expression is thought to be the opposite of this (4a).

[13.3] Where another object is implied "for the sake of a meaning's being established," this is inclusion, as in the case, "The cow is to be sacrificially bound." For in this case, although COWHOOD (the primary meaning of "cow") is an instrumental means for the ritual, the word "cow" is not appropriate without implying an individual. Therefore, a particular is implied here in order to establish COWHOOD as a means for the ritual. And it is likewise for "Fat Devadatta does not eat during the day." Now in this case, Devadatta's being fat incorporates a cause into its meaning through implying there is eating at night, and through which his being fat is established. This is because fatness is an effect and it is being understood here as something which does not happen during the day. For it cannot be the case that his being fat is brought about by drinking something like an elixir. Because only when we can determine through another knowledge source that there is no elixir is this an example of indicated meaning. And because things like drinking an elixir are prevented as the cause of his being fat, and since his being fat is characterized here as something which does not happen during the day, and further, because there is the completion of an incomplete epistemic instrument (that is, testimony), in this case there is the implied phrase "eats at night." Let this be a matter of verbal postulation or postulation of just the cause, which is nighttime eating. Whichever is the case, inclusion is a suitable explanation because there is another, earlier, meaning implied for the sake of a meaning which needs to establish itself.

[13.15] In contrast, consider when another meaning is implied for the sake of an already accepted meaning by following a process opposite from inclusion which we've just explained.

Now, further, in such a case the word's **natural meaning** is given up in order to establish another meaning. In such a case there is indirect expression. This is just as in the earlier example, "The village is on the Ganges." Now in this case, since the riverbank supports the village, the word "Ganges" gives up its natural meaning for the sake of the riverbank, which is related to the action of supporting. Therefore, in order to understand the other meaning, which is *bank*, the word "Ganges," gives up what it usually expresses, which is the specific river. Thus, giving up the natural meaning is for the sake of establishing another meaning. And therefore, here, indirect expression is opposite from inclusion which was earlier discussed. Therefore, indication lacking transfer is subdivided into two kinds.

[15.27] Now, in order to delineate the four divisions of indication involving transfer, the author says:

Verses 4b-5a

> Indication involving transfer is divided into four kinds because each of its divisions, transfer of properties and transfer in general, are subdivided into superimposition and absorption (4b-5a).

[16.1] **Indication involving transfer** is divided into two: **transfer of properties** and **transfer in general**. There is transfer in general when one thing is transferred onto another through indication because of a relationship like cause and effect. This transfer occurs because indication involving properties similar to those in an **object of comparison** is impossible, since there is no relation of subject-object comparison, which is the relationship that is the foundation for such indication. This transfer in general is like the example "Ghee is long life." For in this **sentence**, given that life is the effect of ghee, and since the relationship of cause and effect is present, the effect, which is having life, and the word for this effect, "life," are both transferred through the aforementioned indication. Therefore this is transfer in general.

[16.1] In contrast, transfer of properties is where the word for the **subject of comparison** and its meaning are superimposed onto the object since those things are related as subject and object of comparison, which is the foundational relationship for such indication. This superimposition occurs when there has first been indication through connection with properties similar to the properties in the object of comparison. Now this transfer is denoted by the word "properties" since it is understood through properties, just as in the example, "The Punjabi is an ox." For in this case there is transfer of ox-nature as well as the word "ox" onto the peasant, because of the connection with things like dullness and laziness as being similar to the ox's properties, such as dullness and laziness. However, it is thought by some that when there is this transfer, it is not transfer of meaning, but only a transfer of words. This is incorrect. After all, transfer of words does not occur without transfer of meaning. Therefore, this transfer is said to have a twofold division into transfer of properties and transfer in general.

[18.1] And each category is subdivided into **superimposition** and **absorption**. Superimposition transfers one thing onto another without obscuring the difference between the two things subject to imposition. Where superimposition occurs, it is because the one thing which is being placed over another, or in other words, the one thing being made "super" onto another, has a way of imposing itself without obscuring the other's nature. This is just like the previously discussed example ("Ghee is long life"). For in this case, since ghee is understood just in terms of its ordinary nature, ghee is not understood as a cause in a way which includes its having a characteristic effect, that is, life. But due to its ordinary nature, since ghee is here being understood to cause life, it causes understanding of its being life. Therefore, this case is superimposition. It is the same thing, too, in the case of "The Punjabi is an ox" because the nature of the subject being compared (the Punjabi) with the object of comparison (the ox) is not obscured. Thus, where the nature of the subject is not obscured by whatever is being superimposed on it, in such a case there is superimposition.

[18.9] In contrast, there is absorption when the nature of the subject is obscured since there is an intention to express the subject as embedded within the object. Here is an example of absorption for transfer in general: "Pañcālas." For here the word "Pañcālas" is uttered as an **intermediated indirect expression**[5] for the Pañcāla people, based on the location where the Pañcāla descendants dwell. By "Pañcālas" is meant, through indication, first the descendants and then the location inhabited by the people's descendants. And in this case, there is no awareness of the object (the place Pañcāla) as distinct from that which is being transferred (the people Pañcālas). This is because the object (the place) is understood as really absorbed in the subject (the people). Thus, the expression's figurative character is characterized as lost through prevalent conventional use. Therefore, this is a case of transfer in general which includes absorption.

[18.16] Now for the case of transfer-involving properties, "ruler" is an example of absorption. For we observe in ordinary practice that the word "ruler" is used primarily for a member of the ruling class, a *kṣatriya*. When used for a servant class member, a *śūdra*, it is in virtue of properties, through the function of indication already described, that "ruler" refers to someone who guards a community just like a ruling class member guards a community. And here, the word "ruler" is not understood instantly as having a meaning based on properties, since this meaning is arrived at through careful reflection. Therefore, the meaning based on properties is not understood instantly since it has been lost, and it is rightly understood by careful reflection. In conclusion, then, this is a case of transfer-involving properties which includes absorption.

[18.23] Therefore there are four divisions of transfer. Since there is a fourfold division of transfer, along with the previously discussed two divisions of indication, indication should be described as having a total of six divisions.

[20.11] And this indication has three branches because there is indication lacking transfer, indication involving superimposition, and indication involving absorption. The branch of indication lacking transfer has two parts: inclusion and indirect expression, already discussed. The branches superimposition and absorption are respectively subdivided into two as just explained, because of transfer in general and transfer-involving properties. The author goes on in order to explain the differences in scope with regard to these three branches.

Verses 5b–6a

> In cases of extreme **distinction**, there is indication lacking transfer. But in cases where distinction is intermediate, it is superimposed (5b)
> In cases where the distinction is dissolved, indication is absorbed because of being conventional and closer in meaning (than the intermediate) (6a)

[20.17] Indication lacking transfer has two subdivisions since there is inclusion and indirect expression. What should be observed in this kind of indication is that the primary meaning which causes indication is understood as extremely distinct from what is indicated, because there is nothing semantically imbued from the primary meaning which causes indication. Take the example "The village is on the Ganges." When employing the word "Ganges" in the sense of "The village is on the Ganges, not the Vitastā," in this case, no semantic imbuing is understood by its use as connected to the indirect expression of the bank that is the supporting locus of the village. This is because this cognition of the bank is understood as extremely distinct (from the primary meaning). Thus the case of inclusion, as in the sentence

"Fat Devadatta does not eat during the day," should be described as extremely distinct in the same way.

[20.24] Now, there is superimposition in the earlier example, "The village is on the Ganges." This transfer occurs when the speaker wants to express the bank's nature without its being obscured by the specific river's semantic imbuing, since the bank is not far from that river denoted by the word "Ganges." Because the bank is understood as not being far from the specific river, therefore the village on the bank is understood to have the nature of that particular river.

[21.1] But when the sentence is used to make us understand the village as close to that river and the bank's nature has been obscured by being incorporated into the river, then the sentence is understood as "The village is on the Ganges itself directly and not anywhere else." And this is absorption.

[22.18] Now, just as the examples of superimposition based in indication lacking transfer and absorption and based in transfer in general have been discussed, we must also discuss transfer-involving properties, as in the sentence "The Punjabi is an ox" and "This ox!" Now in the first sentence, through connection with properties (of dullness and laziness) similar to the properties in an ox, there is superimposition of "oxness" onto the Punjabi, because of the desire to express that the Punjabi is not much different from an ox. But in the second sentence, since the properties (of dullness and laziness) in the ox are prominent, the Punjabi is absorbed into the ox-nature.

[22.23] And as the earlier cases of absorption were distinguished according to proximity, we distinguish conventional use in this same way. It is the same with the two examples seen earlier, "Pañcālas" and "ruler." Because of this it is said (in verse 6a): "Because of being conventional and closer in meaning." In other words, where the meaning has its distinction dissolved, because of being conventional and because of being closer in meaning, this would be a case of absorption.

[24.4] (*Objection.*) Your position is not correct. In the case of primary meaning, it is correct to say that the word is able to communicate meaning because there is a determinate relationship (between word and meaning). But this is not so in the case of the indicatory function, since its relationship is the opposite. For when discerning the relationship between word and meaning, the speaker and hearer first understand the use of words and their meaning grounded in the sentence and the sentence meaning taken as a whole, before they have awareness of cause and effect.

[24.8] And after this, from three or four observations involving **inference based upon positive and negative correlations**, the relationship of cause and effect is discerned, grounded in understanding the use of words and their meanings, an understanding which includes the distinction between sentence and sentence meaning. Then, at a later time, a relationship between word and meaning is understood, since what the speaker and hearer understand would be **incongruous** without it. And only the primary meaning is known, the four divisions among things like universals, but not as in the six kinds of indication. For a word does not have a relationship with its meaning through the indicatory function. This relationship is observed with the primary meaning function alone. Therefore, in this way, the relationship between word and meaning is only a primary one and not indicatory.

[24.15] Given this, we observe that the indicated meaning has a relationship with the primary meaning of the word. The understanding of the indicated meaning occurs through the primary meaning which comes from the word. This being said, it would then be the case that if the primary meaning independently communicates an indicated meaning by understanding the ordinary meaning, then that indicated meaning would always be understood. But the primary meaning communicates (the indicated meaning) contingently, so on what is it contingent?

[24.18] To this doubt, the author replies:

Verses 6b–7a

> From reflecting on the distinct natures of speaker, sentence, and expressed
> meaning (6b) six kinds of indication are able to be judged correctly by
> the thoughtful (7a)

[24.21] A speaker is one who utters a sentence for someone else's comprehension. A sentence is a combination which is a unified meaning made up of words with **syntactic expectancy**. The **expressed meaning** is that range of meaning which depends on the communicative function, either the primary or indicatory function of words.

[24.23] The six kinds of indication which are to be distinguished by the judgments of wise people have many divisions with this nature: these three, speaker, sentence, and expressed meaning, characterized individually or together, and taken in conjunction with, also either individually or together, place, time, state, and individuality. In this way, words which convey their own (primary) meanings through the meaning's relationship to the indicated meaning depend on this collection of factors of speaker, sentence, and expressed meaning, since this relationship depends on the ordinary linguistic practices of our predecessors. What has just been said is this:

> Words, whose relationship with the indicated meaning is unknown, cannot cause understanding of the indicated meaning. And neither is the relationship grasped directly. Then how do words communicate the indicated meaning? Through the intervention of the word's natural meaning, in dependence upon the collection of such things as the speaker, sentence, and expressed meaning, etc.

[25.5] What has been said by Ācārya Śabara Svāmin is: "How is one word used for another? We say: It is through the word's own meaning."[6] Now, what is said here is that words attach to the indicated meaning through their own meaning. And again, on this very topic, he says: "Further, indication is just customary speech." For what is said here is that in the case of the indicated meaning, the use of words is dependent on an ascertained relationship. For what is meant by the word "custom" is those epistemic instruments—perception and the like—which gain their status as proof through people's conventional use. This means that "just" custom is the "customary," understood as grounded in words whose relationship (with their meanings) has been grasped by their being understood in ordinary linguistic practice.

[25.12] This has been said by Kumārila Bhaṭṭa: "Some figures are **conventional** because they have a capacity like the primary denotation; some are newly created, some are even without power."[7]

[27.22] With respect to this passage, "figures (which) are conventional" are ones like "ruler." The "newly created" are ones which depend on such things as the linguistic use of our predecessors, the speaker, sentence, and expressed meaning. Their nature is like the types of figures observed in other cases, such as:

> Clouds with white cranes whirling extend across the sky,
> smeared with glistening dark color.
> Winds gently sprinkle water. The friends of the clouds cry out joyfully.
> Let all of this be. I am Rāma, whose heart is hardened. I can bear all this.
> But slender Sītā, how will she go on? Oh, alas, queen, stand firm![8]

[27.28] For here, the word "smeared" has its primary meaning blocked because the glistening dark-colored clouds are not really a means for smearing things like saffron. Therefore, the indicated meaning is *being covered up with glistening dark color*, because this is related to the property of slightly removing brilliance, which is similar to what the primary meaning of "smeared" communicates: the property of slightly removing brilliance. In this way, also, with the word "friends," the primary meaning of the word is blocked, as the non-sentient clouds have no relationship with friendship. In this case, properties like fondness understood by "friend" indicate peacocks whose faces are turned toward the clouds. The peacocks are related to properties like "fondness" since they have properties similar to those in friends.

[28.5] Moreover, because the word "Rāma" is so familiar to everyone, the mere referent of the name is blocked as the primary meaning of the word. Therefore, since the word has become part of a particular collection (speaker, sentence, expressed meaning), this word indicates certain properties, such as the loss of a kingdom, being a forest dweller, Sītā being kidnapped, or the death of a father. These properties are causes of (Rāma's) unique sorrow and are understood along with the primarily denoted meaning. Therefore, in this way cases of novel indication are to be explained.

[29.11] However, where cases of indication are not observed in the ordinary linguistic practices of our predecessors, nor are they like the word "ruler," and neither are they among the category of words like "smeared," then, since these cases of indication are without power, there is nothing being created. For example:

> From the middle of the ocean,
> its golden structures making the sky glow,
> breaking through the waters, it leaps up
> like the blazing sacrifice-carrier in the mouth of a beloved mare.[9]

[29.16] (*Objection.*) But in this verse, the words "sacrifice-carrier in the mouth of a beloved mare" mean by indication, "fire with the face of a horse."

[29.17] (*Reply.*) Now in this case, "fire with the face of a horse" is not a conventional figure. Further, the phrase "sacrifice-carrier in the mouth of a beloved mare" does not belong to the category of words like "smeared," as their meanings are known to be of that particular type insofar as they have become part of a particular collection (speaker, sentence, expressed meaning, etc.)

[29.20] (*Objection.*) From words such as "two-e's," by means of indication, a word like "bee" is understood, as it has two-e's.[10] Just as the word "two-e's" is used for a six-footed creature, why can't it be that, in the same way, the words "sacrifice-carrier in the mouth of a beloved mare," are used to mean "fire with the face of a horse" through indication based on the words "mare," "mouth," and "sacrifice-carrier"? For we know that there is indication of words in categories of words like "two-e's."

[29.24] (*Reply.*) This is not so. A word is accepted as able to indicate only when it is similar to the kinds of words known in the ordinary linguistic practices of our predecessors. A word is not able to indicate in all instances. Otherwise, we could be able to say about every single word that it is an indicating word, as there is some trace of general similarity between every word and every meaning. There would not be any word which could not convey any meaning! But when we make a distinction between content that is known or unknown in the linguistic practices of our predecessors, "sacrifice-carrier in the mouth of a beloved mare" is simply defective, lacking a motive. But when there is a motive—for example, the communication of a hidden meaning in speech—then, in contrast, these kinds of indication are not defective. This is because in this way, when the content is of such a kind, it is known as part of the ordinary linguistic practices of our predecessors.

[30.7] Thus this has been demonstrated about words which give up their natural meaning for another meaning: since they have become part of a particular collection (speaker, sentence, expressed meaning, etc.), they are indicators in the ordinary linguistic practices of our predecessors, either by their own character or by a word which is part of such a category.

[31.22] A case where indicated meaning is understood by a relationship with the speaker is in this example:

> Hey there neighbor, will you watch our house for a bit, as well?
> This child's father won't drink the tasteless well-water at all.
> I go now, all alone, from here to the forest stream full of tamala trees.
> Let the stiff, broken ends of the knotted reeds scratch my body.[11]

[31.27] Now in this stanza, a young woman wishing for an encounter with another woman's husband is going to an arranged location. This liaison is the motive for her utterance, as it supports her going to the particular arranged location which is for this encounter with another woman's husband. And as well, she suspects she will bear telling marks from the encounter, that is, scratches from teeth and fingernails. So, with the aim of concealing, she speaks like this: she is bringing drinkable water from the river fit to quench her husband's thirst and there will be marks of injury on her limbs caused by the hollow points of the dense reeds, broken and bent. And in this context, concealing is understood through the consideration that the speaker is unvirtuous. Concealing is by its nature communicating untrue things. And untruth has the capacity to convey the opposite of a true meaning. Therefore, by an untrue meaning, an uttered truth is implied since the untrue has another meaning which establishes itself. Therefore, here, understanding occurs from indication whose nature is inclusive of the true meaning, grasped by reflecting on the speaker's character. For certainly in this case, neither the sentence nor the expressed meaning has this expressive capacity. If the speaker were a virtuous woman, neither the sentence nor the expressed meaning would be able to imply this kind of meaning.

[33.9] In contrast, this example is one where an indicated meaning is understood through reflecting on the particular form of the sentence:

> "He has already taken Śrī, so why stir up pain by churning me?
> I cannot believe one so active would want to sleep like before.
> And why would he build a bridge again, when the lords of all the islands serve him?"
> The ocean's trembling when your Majesty marches near is like it has these doubts.

[31.17] For here, the king is addressed in poetic composition with a flattering verse. What is described hyperbolically as "trembling" is the ocean's disrupted state, which occurs because of the king's great army (marching on the shore). In this verse, this state is imagined as the cause of the ocean's having speculative doubts—"is like it has these doubts." And the content of the doubts are characterized as the specific actions of Lord Vāsudeva by such phrases as "he has already taken Śrī."[12] But since there is no identity between Lord Vāsudeva and the king, then how can there be doubt about the specific actions belonging to them? Therefore, in this case, though the ocean is not really trembling because of being crossed by a great army, because of similarity with the meaning of "trembling," trembling is superimposed upon the ocean.

Thus this case is superimposition which includes transfer of properties. Although the ocean is not really trembling, it has been superimposed with the meaning of "trembling." And therefore, this is said to be **hyperbole** where what really has a distinction is without distinction. A head-tremble is ordinarily seen in sentient beings because of doubt's influence. The nature of that trembling is transferred onto the ocean because it is similar to head-trembling caused by doubt in sentient beings. And thus, in this aspect, too, there is superimposition which includes transfer of properties.

[33.26] And as well, although these are two kinds of trembling, because of superimposition this is said to be a hyperbole where what really has a distinction is without distinction. That hyperbole is specifically connected with this **imagining**—"is like it has these doubts." Now, in this phrase, because of seeing the trembling, which is an effect, what is imagined is having doubts, which is a cause; and this imagining is a particular sort which is a false conception. And moreover, in this case, although the ocean does not actually have doubts, because this is explained by its having doubt, this is said to be hyperbole where what really has a distinction is without distinction.

[34.5] As has been said in the definition of imagining:

> When there is an intention to express similarity of natures, expressed by words such as "like," because there are no shared properties or actions, the figure of imagining is joined with hyperbole.[13]

Because of the "shared properties or actions" of what is being imagined, therefore, in this instance, too, there is "superimposition which includes transfer of properties." But it is implied that the king is Lord Vāsudeva in the use of the three lines, "He has already taken Śrī" which are three doubts about Lord Vāsudeva, as it's appropriate to take what is in these lines as reasons to exclude certain actions (of Vāsudeva). Therefore, in these lines, indication has the nature of inclusion. And because of the superimposition of the king as having Lord Vāsudeva's nature, there is superimposition which includes transfer of properties. And therefore, the syntactic relation of words employed in the sentence as a whole is understood to be incongruous otherwise. Therefore, indication is here grounded in the sentence.

[37.18] Now, indication grounded in an expressed meaning is as in this case:

> The flower-tipped arrows of the love-god are hard to avoid: spring blossoms everywhere.
> The bright moon's rays make my heart crazy and the cuckoos capture my mind.
> This young age, with these heavy breasts, is a hard burden to bear.
> These burdensome five fires—now, how can I endure them, my friend?

[37.23] For in these verses, the sentence meaning is the difficult nature of fire which has been superimposed onto the five things, which are the strikings of the love god's arrows (and so on). Therefore, this is the expressed meaning. And the ***rasa*** of love-in-separation is implied on account of reflecting on the sentential aim. Therefore indication grounded in the expressed meaning is inclusion. For in this case, apart from the words, there is no investigation of the speaker's nature. Neither is it impossible for the words to construe as a sentence without implying of love-in-separation. In this case, it is because we reflect on the character of what is being expressed, because it implies love-in-separation, that indication grounded in the expressed meaning is inclusion. And love-in-separation is predominant as the implied expressed meaning, despite its being implied, because it is implied as the predominant cause of refreshing the **sensitive critic's** heart.

[38.4] Now, concerning "makes the heart intoxicated," no letter *ī* (in *hṛdy-unmāda-karā*) is employed (to signify feminine gender) because there is an *aC*-affix, as in "the words *śiva*, *śama*, *riṣṭa* in the genitive when meaning 'he does,'" instead of a *Ṭa*-affix, although "moon's bright splendor" has a feminine gender. And for just this reason, where there is an intention to express such things as final causation, habitual action, or acquiescence, still, because there is no *Ṭa*-affix there is no grammatical fault.[14]

[40.26] Thus, by that relationship of each one to another—speaker, sentence meaning, and expressed meaning—there are three divisions, so much has been illustrated so far. And also, there are others. Combining the speaker with one or the other of them—speaker with sentence meaning and speaker with expressed meaning—just like combining sentence meaning with expressed meaning, there are three divisions, each division consisting of two factors. In the same way, there is the threefold division consisting of the triple: speaker, sentence meaning, expressed meaning, also by mutual combination—and therefore the triple is understood as one. And these divisions should be looked for in cases of indication taken in conjunction with, also either individually or together, place, time, state, and individuality. In this same way, the four divisions are delineated and are to be illustrated as within the scope of the six kinds of indication by the knowledgeable person's own understanding.

Verses 7b–9a

[42.9] Now, there is **connection-of-the-denoted**, there is **denotation-through-the-connected**, there is the combination of these views, there is the rejection of both views. The author continues in order to elucidate the range and structure of indication among these four alternative views.

> When there is **connection** among what is designated by words, indicated meaning is thought to be after that expressed meaning (7b)

When what is connected constitutes the expressed meaning, indicated meaning is at the stage preceding the expressed meaning (8a)
Now in the two-fold view, indication is in both stages. But for the unified whole view, the sentence is ultimately the bearer of meaning, and there is no indication (8b)
Now when the meaning is hypothetical, indication cannot be distinguished, as on the earlier views (9a)

[42.15] On this topic, some people think that when words have accomplished their own meanings this does not express the sentence meaning. Rather, sentence meaning is understood through the power of **semantic fit, contiguity**, and syntactic expectancy, applied to the meanings of words. The meanings of words are universals understood by the process of inference from positive and negative correlations. Sentence meaning is then understood further from what has been denoted, just like joy and sorrow—for this is like the examples: "O priest, your son is born," and "O priest, your unmarried daughter is pregnant." Although what is occasioned respectively by the birth of a son and the pregnancy of an unmarried daughter, joy and grief, is not denoted by the words, it is implied. It is implied from the state of affairs denoted by the words. Thus it should be observed that, although sentence meaning is implied by the word meanings, it is not denoted. And for those who think this way, from the denoted meanings coming into connection with each other at a later time, there is "connection-of-the-denoted."

[44.2] But others say: the understanding of the word meaning relationship comes from the ordinary linguistic practice of our predecessors. And this ordinary linguistic practice is characterized by using and refraining from using (words for objects). And use and refraining from use are grounded in objects as they are related together. Therefore, the word meaning relationship is determined to be about related objects. And thus, word meanings are already related entities, and there does not need to be further relationship among the word meanings. And thus, this is denotation-through-the-connected: there are interconnecting relationships between one constituent and another because these relationships are conveyed through words. Understanding these relationships happens because words have natural expressive capacities which are incorporated into a universal of some kind.

[45.15] But in the view of still others, words express a meaning which is a universal of some kind. However, sentence meaning is these word meanings in mutual connection with each other. This is connection-of-the-denoted, seen from the perspective of words, but it is denotation-through-the-connected from the perspective of the sentence. And thus, there is a combination of the two, connection-of-the-denoted and denotation-through-the-connected.

[46.17] In contrast, those who believe that sentence meaning is a unified whole say: suppose it is agreed that a sentence meaning involves related objects. Then a particular entity cannot come to be connected sententially, because a particular entity is opposed to a universal, since the universal has been given up in favor of the particular. It would be impossible to grasp this sentential connection through the word's expressive capacity, of particulars as having a nature characterized by the universal meaning, which is their real meaning. Therefore, because the sentence meaning and the sentence are an indivisible whole, what is ultimately meaningful is not connection-of-the-denoted, nor is it denotation-through-the-connected, and neither is it a combination of these brought together, because word meanings are unknown. Both views, since they depend on hypothetically posited word meanings, are themselves hypothetical, either separately or taken together (in the combined view).

[47.11] And in the case where there is connection-of-the-denoted, there is denotation of word meaning through the innate expressive abilities of words. Afterward, through the functions of syntactic expectancy, semantic fit, and contiguity, there comes to be an interconnecting relationship among these word meanings, a relationship which has the character of predicate-object. It is then that indication is to be found, when the sentence meaning is understood on account of the syntactic capacity of word meanings. The indication which is expressed is therefore "after" the word meanings which are universals.

[47.15] But on the denotation-through-the-connected view, what should be said is that what is expressed are word meanings which are already related as interconnected. And it is not true that there must be a relationship among word meanings which have previously been denoted as universals. On the view in question, when objects are coming into relationship, then, while this is happening, it is not possible for them to be word meanings. The (word) meaning we understand is what fits the sentence meaning taken as a whole, and it is based in a universal form that has a fixed relationship with the expressive capacity of words. If such a view is accepted, the six kinds of indication as distinguished here, as the content of various sentence meanings, would not appear in this process. Therefore, on the denotation-through-the-connected view, what is expressed involves the related word meanings which are the sentence meaning, and indication is "preceeding" this. Therefore, indication is situated in the causal stage prior to the expressed meaning.

[47.23] Now in the combined view of connection-of-the-denoted and denotation-through-the-connected, by the act of combining the two rules earlier described, we have, from the perspective of words, indication occurring at a time after the words express meaning. And from the perspective of sentences, it occurs after the sentence meaning and before there is an expressed meaning. Therefore it has been said: "In the two-fold view, indication is in two stages." "In the two-fold view" means being a combination of connection-of-the-denoted and denotation-through-the-connected. "Indication is of two kinds" means the indicated meaning occurs after and before there is an expressed meaning.

[48.3] Now in the case of the view that sentence meaning is undivided, there is no indication as far as the actual meaning. This is because, as far as what is really denoted, divisions among word meanings do not really exist. And indication depends on such divisions. However, indication is based in constituents which are to be distinguished by hypothesizing, as in the earlier views, connection-of-the-denoted, denotation-through-the-connected, or their combination, according to one's theoretical liking, in dependence on hypothetically posited word meanings. Such hypotheses exist because of the convention established by the speech community and by the factors of place and time which interact mutually one with another.

[48.8] In this way, the range and structure of indication in the four views, connection-of-the-denoted, and so on, has been explained.

[49.29] Now, this indication, given that there is a motive, has for its content which is something closely connected to the primary meaning. The author continues in order to present an illustration.

Verses 9b–10a

> Because of an incongruity in the primary meaning, because of its closeness to the primary meaning, (9b) because of established use or else a motive, that indication is found in ordinary linguistic practice (10a)

[50.3] And this indication, which has six kinds as previously discussed, occurs

1 Because of the primary meaning having an incongruity, since it is obstructed by some other epistemic instrument;

2 And because the meaning which is being indicated is close to the primary meaning;
3 And because there is a motive accompanying the other understood meaning.

[50.7] It is in this way that we observe indication in the ordinary linguistic practice of our predecessors, since it is grounded in a collection of conditions made up of three kinds of reasons.

[50.13] And the teacher Bhartṛmitra shows with this verse that there are five ways that indication has a close connection to the primary meaning:

> Indication is considered five-fold because of a close relationship with what is denoted, because of being similar, because of being associated, because of being opposed, and because of being joined to an action.[15]

[50.13] Why is motive further divided into two types?

[50.15] Now, in some cases, when a different meaning is grasped, it is because the meaning's nature follows what is established by the ordinary linguistic practice of our predecessors, which has no beginning. In these cases, the motive is to follow convention, as in the case of "thing with two-e's." For the term "thing with two-e's" follows convention since the word has been associated with something that has two-e's as it indicates the word "bee." In contrast, a motive different from following convention has been described earlier. Namely, a word communicates a specific meaning, one which does not have a particular term to communicate it, which is understood as another thing (than the primary meaning). This is as in the previous example, "I am Rāma." And therefore, when the primary meaning has an incongruity, then the indicated meaning is understood through the five kinds of relationships shown above, by close dependence upon the primary meaning. In such cases, two kinds of motive should be understood according to their contents.

[53.17] When there is indication based on a close relationship (with the primary meaning), it is as in the example, "The village is on the Ganges." For in this case, the primary meaning of the word is blocked, since the particular river denoted by the word "Ganges" is inappropriate as support for a village. Given that there is this obstacle, the close relationship, which is here specifically the relationship of contiguity, indicates the bank through its dependence on this relationship. And in this case, the motive of indication is to communicate things such as that bank's holiness and beauty without a particular term to communicate them, but which are inherent in things related to the Ganges. For the word "bank" cannot extend to things like holiness and beauty, since this would lead to an undesirable result, that of under and over-extending the word's application.

[53.26] Here is an example of indication by similarity:

> Bee, in all your buzzing about the spacious sky,
> Have you anywhere touched, seen, or heard
> —now speak unbiased truth—
> If there is a flower equal to the jasmine blossom?

[54.3] Now in this stanza, the words "bee" and "flower" indicate another meaning when their primary meaning is blocked, since the words would be incongruous otherwise as nouns in direct address, and so forth. They indicate this other meaning, which is associated with properties similar to the properties understood by "bee" and "flower," because of similarity to what has been denoted by the words. And here, the motive is to convey actions and properties which are without a particular term, but which are similar to actions and properties belonging to the bee and the flower.

[54.7] Indication by association is as in the example, "The umbrella-holders go." In this case, the primary meaning of the word "umbrella-holders" is blocked because of its being used the plural. For, in the case of a single umbrella-holder, the use of the plural is not appropriate. Therefore, in this case, where there is an action characterized as going along with the umbrella-holder, even the ones without an umbrella are understood by the word "umbrella-holders," through indication, by force of this association. And here, the motive is to communicate that all those who are lacking umbrellas trail after the royal person who is near the umbrella.

[56.6] Indication based on opposition is as in, "Auspicious-faced one," since in this case, not having an auspicious face is indicated due to the relationship of opposition, because what is expressed is the opposite of having an auspicious face. And here, indication's purpose is to communicate the truth in a hidden manner. For usually, speakers communicate the truth in a hidden manner on account of their having some particular aim.

[56.13] Indication based on being joined with an action is exemplified in, "You are the enemy-killer [Śatrughna] in the great battle."[16] For in this case, the primary meaning has an obstruction due to the use of the word *śatrughna* (enemy-killer) for someone who is not Śatrughna.[17] And the word *śatrughna* (enemy-killer) in the case of one who is not Śatrughna is said to indicate that the agent has a relationship with the action of killing an enemy. And here, the motive is to communicate that the one denoted by the word "Enemy-killer" has the king's nature. And in the same way, the one depicted as a king is being extolled as having kingliness after Śatrughna's nature:

You are Pṛthu in qualities. In glory you are Rāma,	You are great in qualities, you are beautiful in glory,
You are Nala and Bharata,	You are not attracted to greed,
You are Śatrughna in the great battle,	You are the enemy-killer in the great battle,
From your standing in the world, you are Janaka,	You are the one who causes stability,
Since by your good deeds you bear the names borne by the ancient kings	Since by your good deeds you bear renown borne by the ancient kings
How is it you are not lord Māndhātā,	How is it you will not support me,
From being victorious over the three worlds also?	Since you are victorious over the three worlds also?[18]

[56.13] In this way, it is stated that indication's function comes into existence from three causes.

[58.11] Now, when there are causes of indication which consist in the five kinds of relationship just described, in some cases the expressed meaning is entirely displaced, in some cases it is **intended to be expressed**, and in some cases it is not intended to be expressed. In this way there are the three kinds which the sensitive critic has observed. The author continues in order to show the classification of these meanings.

Verses 10b–12a

In cases of similarity and opposition, the expressed meaning is entirely displaced (10b)
There is intentional expression or unintentional expression in the two cases of connection and association (11a)
In the case of inclusion, there is intentional expression, but in the case of indirect expression, there is unintentional expression (11b)
In the case of connection to an action, there is displacement and sometimes its opposite (12a)

[58.18] In this verse, "Because of the close relationship with what is denoted"[19] what is said is that there are five kinds of relationship. With regard to these, when there is similarity or opposition, the expressed meaning is entirely displaced. For, in indication that depends upon similarity, the expressed meaning is entirely displaced. The expressed meaning, which is the subject of comparison (e.g., the moon), is entirely given up (in a sentence like "Her face is the moon"). The expressed meaning (of "moon") is a subject of comparison which aims at the compared object (her face) through the word expressing the subject of comparison (the moon). This is just like what has been shown already with "smeared by glistening dark color" and "friends of the clouds." Since in these cases, the words "smeared" and "friends" aim at the compared object through their own (primary) meanings, their own meanings are entirely unconnected to the matter at hand.

[58.24] As well, when opposition is the basis, the expressed meaning is entirely displaced because another meaning is applicable, one opposed to the expressed meaning. This is like "Auspicious-faced one." Now here, having an auspicious face is entirely displaced since the person has an inauspicious face. Thus in the cases of similarity and opposition, the expressed meaning is entirely displaced.

[59.28] But in connection with an action and association, the expressed meaning, whether it is intended to be expressed or is not intended to be expressed, is not entirely discarded. For in these cases when there is inclusive indication, given this inclusion, as there is the intention to convey the expressed meaning, the expressed meaning is intended to be expressed. It is because of such cases that sensitive readers have explained that the expressed meaning aims at expressing another intended meaning in the domain of poetry. But in the case of indirect expression, because the expressed meaning is transferred to another meaning, it is not intended.

[60.4] Now in this same way, when the expressed meaning is transferred to another meaning, as in inclusive indication based on close relationship with the denoted meaning, the expressed meaning is intentionally expressed, as shown in: "Fat Devadatta does not eat during the day." Now in this case, what is intended to be expressed is an effect, characterized as Devadatta's being fat. His being fat is intended to be expressed through the particular lack of daytime eating. In this case of indication based on close relationship, the meaning intended to be expressed implies the cause, eating at night, so that the meaning is able to establish itself.

[60.10] In the case of indication that depends upon association, when there is inclusion, the expressed meaning is intended, just as in "The umbrella-holders go." For here, "umbrella-holders," because of its being declined in the plural, also implies the umbrella-less people, since this meaning establishes the syntactic connection with the word's plural. Then, given that there is dependence on association, the people who are without umbrellas, being included, are intended to be expressed by the word "umbrella-holders." In this way, in two kinds of inclusive indication, that which depends on association and that which depends on connection, the expressed meaning is said to be intended to be expressed.

[63.17] Now there are two kinds of indication in which the expressed meaning is neither unintended nor entirely discarded. This is due to the indicated meaning having a relationship with action somehow, through what is being indicated. In cases of indication which are dependent upon close relationship with the denoted, there is unintentionally expressed meaning in the example, "I am Rāma." For in this case, what is expressed by the word "Rāma," which is being Daśaratha's son, is obstructed, since it is not used for its own meaning, because it is transformed into other manifested properties. Therefore, it is unintentionally expressed but it is not entirely discarded. This is because it has a unifying connection in some manner with the meaning of the sentence, through the properties being manifested. In the same way, "The village is on the Ganges" and others like it are to be explained.

[63.25] However, in the case of indication dependent on the association relationship, the same example "The umbrella-holders go," can be an unintentionally expressed meaning. For this occurs when the entire collection of people is included in possessing an umbrella, because otherwise there would be an incongruity as far as syntactic unity construed with the plural. In this case, then, because the collection is intended (by "umbrella-holders"), the expressed meaning is unintended. And in this way too, the umbrella-holder is also connected to the action and is in this manner easily understood along with the collection, since he is contained within it. And for precisely this reason, the expressed meaning is not entirely discarded, because it is connected with the action, as contained within the collection's boundaries. Thus it is shown that for the two kinds of indication which depend on the relationships of connection and association, the expressed meaning is intentionally expressed or unintentionally expressed, but is not entirely discarded.

[65.24] Now, in the case of indication that depends on connection with action, the meaning is being indicated based on the word's linguistic capacity, in conformity with the linguistic capacity of the word's constituent parts. And in this case, the expressed meaning is discarded, just as in, "The man is a man."[20] For here, since one word, "the man," means someone belonging to a class, the other word, "a man," takes on the meaning of being superior, in contrast. The other word does this by contrast with the word's own natural meaning, through indication which is dependent on connection with an action.

[65.29] But when, because of there being some cause for it, there is an intention to express the expressed meaning, a constituent of the overall meaning is transformed into another meaning, based on the word's having a different linguistic capacity. In such a case, there is the opposite of entirely giving up the expressed meaning, as "its opposite."[21] Here, it is certainly not the case that the expressed meaning is discarded. Instead, that meaning is intended, just as in the example "You are the enemy-killer in the great battle." For here, the word 'enemy-killer' (*śatru-ghna*), through indication connected with an action, makes known the actor whose action is killing (*ghna*) an enemy (*śatru*). As well, it communicates the word's own meaning, the thing being compared, namely, the son of Daśaratha. Therefore the word's own meaning is also intended.

[66.6] Now, suppose sensitive critics take this to be expressed meaning that is entirely discarded because the subject of comparison (the person Śatrughna) is used for the object of comparison (the king being an enemy-killer). But the expressed meaning is not displaced. This is because in the case of indication depending on an action, to the extent that the expressed meaning is made to be part of the subject of comparison (such as the person Śatrughna), there is no displacement of the expressed meaning. Therefore in this way, on the topic of dependence on connection with action, it is demonstrated that sometimes the expressed meaning is discarded but sometimes it is intended, on account of various meanings coming together.

[66.12] And, because there is much to be said, not everything is explained in this text. What is described here belongs to a deep understanding of the ways of indication, although it is considered by the sensitive critics to be a novel classification, **suggestion**. Therefore we give the general idea in order to open their eyes. And this should be investigated by wise persons with intellects sharp as the point of kuśa grass. But now, enough prolixity to avoid getting caught up in long-windedness.

[66.16] In conclusion, what has been shown is the classification of what is intended to be expressed and what is discarded in relationship to the expressed meaning.

Verses 12b–13a

[69.8] Now, when the language principle, being the unity among all sounds and words, manifests its nature threefold, like a rope mistaken for a snake, as speech, meanings, and their relationship, then this communicative function occurs in the ten kinds of ordinary linguistic behavior (that is, primary meaning and indication together). But the communicative function does not occur when the language principle aims at the nature of speech as a collected whole. To explain this, the author says,

> The nature of speech, when it is being made manifest, is analyzed as divided into ten kinds (12b).
> But when such differentiation is a sequence of phonemes whose temporal order has been dissolved, how can it be understood in this manner? (13a)

[69.14] The language principle, whose nature is unity among all the words, has a relationship with the tenfold communicative principle that has just been delineated. It has this through its fourfold nature of knower, epistemic instrument, object of knowledge, and knowledge-cognition, each of which participates in the multiplicity of the expressed meaning, the expression, and their relationship. In this way its diversification is like a rope mistaken for a snake. But when it is being made manifest it is distorted into concepts and descriptions that have parts not entirely given up, since unity is abandoned for sequence. In the case when the language principle is not being made manifest, how can the ten kinds of communicative function be understood? In that case, there certainly is no expression of the language principle. This is the meaning of the verse.

[72.3] Now the author summarizes the purpose of the work:

Verse 13b

> Therefore, the communicative function has been investigated here as a tenfold division.

[72.3] With regard to the communicative function's primary meaning, there are four divisions and there are six with regard to its indicative function. In this way the ten kinds of the communicative function have here been distinguished.

[72.13] Now the author shows the result of this investigation:

Verse 14

That communicative function is reflected in the sciences of words, sentence, and epistemic instruments.
For the one who employs it in composition, their words shine clearly.

[72.16] "Words" means Grammar because it is the means for understanding words. "Sentence" means Mīmāṃsā because it is the means for determining the sentential unity of sentences. "Epistemic instruments" means the tradition of Reasoning, because it is employed as a procedure for determining epistemic instruments. The reflection of the communicative function is divided into three kinds of subjects: Grammar, Mīmāṃsā, Reasoning. These are a means for understanding all of the four kinds of undertakings and all knowledge. This reflection has a nature which can be immediately ascertained through this collection of subjects. By completely understanding the entire tenfold communicative function of speech from its being employed in the four sciences of Grammar, Mīmāṃsā, Reasoning, and Composition, one becomes the lord of speech, whose speech progresses to shines clearly. From an undertaking of these four sciences, this reflection entirely pervades the whole of the world's ordinary linguistic behavior.

[73.1] This is because the tenfold communicative function entirely pervades the ongoing movement of speech, because it is usefully engaged in the four sciences—these being Grammar, Mīmāṃsā, Nyāya, and Composition—and because it stretches out among all these sciences which are the root of all ordinary linguistic practice. The tenfold communicative function which pervades the entirety of ordinary linguistic practice has been explained.

Verse 15

The fundamentals of the communicative function have been analyzed by Mukula, the son of Bhaṭṭa Kallaṭa, to enlighten the wise.

[73.7] Thus concludes the *Fundamentals of the Communicative Function*, written by Mukula Bhaṭṭa, son of Śrī Bhaṭṭa Kallaṭa, an inhabitant of the place sanctified by the grains of dust from Śārada's feet.

Appendix 1: Outline of the Fundamentals of the Communicative Function

1. [1.6] Reason for the investigation into the primary and indicatory communicative function: ordinary linguistic practice depends on determinate cognitions about the relationship between words and word meanings.
2. [2.14–3.2] Motivating and setting out the thesis: Words have two linguistic functions, namely the primary and indicatory function.
   2.1. [2.18] The primary function is understood directly from the uttered words.
   2.2. [2.24] The indicatory function is understood from the meaning of the primary function.
3. [4.26–10.7] There are four kinds of primary meanings which result from the primary function. These meanings are related to distinguishing features which are the basis for using different words and which semantically imbue their content.
   3.1.1. [5.3–5.10] Distinguishing features may be something a speaker stipulates to exist or something which is part of a thing's nature.
   3.1.1.1. [5.3] Words like "Ḍittha" are used to name things because the speaker wants the word to refer to some particular thing.
   3.1.1.1.1. [5.10] There is a controversy over whether words like "Ḍittha" involve a genuine sequence of phonemes or have a nature devoid of such sequence. On either view, these words name things based on speaker stipulation.
   3.1.1.2. [5.16–10.7] Distinguishing features which are part of a thing's nature may be features yet to be established or features already established. Already established features may be properties or universals.

3.1.1.2.1. [5.16] Words like "cooks" denote actions, which are yet to be established. Words like "cow" denote universals, which are already established. Universals are responsible for an object's nature.

3.1.1.2.2. [5.22] Words like "white" denote properties and not universals, because the white thing does not depend on being white for its nature.

3.1.1.2.3. [8.25–10.7] An objection is refuted: while some think words like "white," "cooks," and "Ḍittha" all refer to universals, this is not true. While "white" seems to denote a universal that manifests differently in various substrates, instead, there are individual, distinct natures which are conceived of as in a unitary way.

4. [11.8–20.11] Analysis of divisions of indication, based on transfer or lack of transfer.

4.1. [11.20] Indication involving transfer and lacking transfer is distinguished.

4.2. [12.24–15.27] Indication lacking transfer has two divisions: inclusion and indirect expression.

4.2.1. [13.3] Inclusion is when another meaning is indicated in order to make sense out of, justify, establish, the primary meaning.

4.2.2. [13.15] Indirect expression is when another meaning is indicated on the basis of a primary meaning which is then given up.

4.3. [15.27–20.11] Indication involving transfer has four divisions, each subdivided into two.

4.3.1. [16.1] Indication involving transfer may be transfer in general, where a relationship, like cause and effect, holds between the primary and indicated meaning.

4.3.2. [16.1] Indication involving transfer may be transfer of properties, where the properties of the primary meaning are similar to the properties of the indicated meaning, and the first are transferred to the second.

4.3.3. [18.1] Both kinds of transfer may involve superimposition or absorption. Superimposition involves transfer where the difference between primary and indicated meaning is retained in understanding.

4.3.4. [18.9] Absorption involves transfer where the difference between primary and indicated meaning is obscured in understanding.

4.3.5. [18.16] An example is given of transfer-involving properties which is absorption.

4.3.6. [18.23–20.11] Summary of the divisions of indication. These distinctions can be grouped according to three major kinds: indication lacking transfer, involving superimposition, and involving absorption, each of which is grounded in the difference between primary and indicated meaning.

4.4. [20.17–24.18] Analysis of divisions of indication, based on how distinct the primary and indicated meanings are. There are three categories of distinctness of meaning: extreme distinction, intermediate distinction, and dissolved distinction. These correspond to indication lacking transfer, involving superimposition, and involving absorption.

4.4.1. [20.17–21.1] Analysis of indication lacking transfer and having transfer in general.

4.4.1.1. [20.17] Indication lacking transfer is when the primary and indicated meanings are understood by the hearer as very different. They lack semantic imbuing.

4.4.2. [20.24] Indication involving superimposition is when there is some distinction between primary and indicated meanings, but they are understood in some relationship. There is semantic imbuing in these cases.

4.4.3. [21.2] Indication involving absorption is when the distinction between primary and indicated meanings is obscured.

4.4.4. [22.18–22.23] Analysis of indication involving transfer of properties is discussed.

4.4.4.1. [22.18] Transfer-involving properties may be either superimposition or absorption, depending on the expression and speaker's aims.

4.4.4.2. [22.23] Conventionally established indicated meanings which appear to be cases of primary meaning are cases of absorption.

4.4.5. [24.4–24.15] An objection is raised to the possibility of understanding indicated meaning. Indicated meanings are not always understood by the same word, unlike how the primary meaning is always understood. The objector asks what the indicated meaning is depended upon, such that it varies in different contexts.

4.5. [24.21–40.26] The answer to the objection is that indication depends on several factors, in various combinations: speaker, sentence, expressed meaning, place, time, state, and individuality. Many examples are given to illustrate these factors.

4.5.1. [24.23–30.7] Establishing that these factors exist. Earlier thinkers such as Bhartṛmitra, Śabara, and Kumārila have identified them. There are conventional figures of speech, ones which are novel, and ones which fail to act as figures of speech.

4.5.2. [27.22–30.7] Illustrating novel, poetic figures of speech. These cases of indication function based on problems understanding the meaning, and they indicate very particular meanings.

4.5.2.1. [29.11–30.7] Sometimes figures of speech fail to indicate, as in the example given here, from a poem. Mukula responds to a potential objection, explaining that there must be a constraint on the conditions under which words indicate new meanings.

4.5.3. [31.22–31.27] A case where the factor of speaker is what leads us to understand the indicated meaning.

4.5.4. [33.9–34.5] A case where the factor of sentence is what leads us to understand the indicated meaning.

4.5.5. [37.18–38.4] A case where the factor of expressed meaning is what leads us to understand the indicated meaning.

4.5.6. [40.26] There is a large number of possible combinations between these factors, since they may combine mutually.

4.6. [42.9–49.29] Discussion of four theories of sentential unity, and the stage at which the indicated meaning is understood.

4.6.1. [42.15] On the connection-of-the-denoted view, indication, along with semantic fit, contiguity, and syntactic expectancy, is responsible for the primary word meanings, which are universals, being construed together as a sentence.

4.6.2. [44.2] On the denotation-through-the-connected view, word meanings are construed together as a sentence as they are immediately understood, since word meanings are understood as related entities.

4.6.3. [45.15] On the combined view, words express universals and sentence meaning is comprised of mutually connected word meanings. The first two views are relative to the perspective of words and sentences.

4.6.4. [46.17] On the unified whole view, words are merely hypothetical constructions and sentences and their meanings are an indivisible whole. The first two views are merely hypothetical.

4.6.5. [42.15] On the connection-of-the-denoted view, indication is found at the stage when the sentence is understood as a unity, and it is after the word's expressed meanings, which are universals.

4.6.6. [44.2] On the denotation-through-the-connected view, indication occurs after word meanings as related come into combination as a sentence, but prior to the entire communicative act's expressed meaning.

4.6.7. [45.15] On the combined view, indication occurs after and prior to the expressed meaning (understood in the two senses above).

4.6.8. [46.17] On the unified whole view, indication does not actually occur, but is merely a useful hypothetical posit.

4.7. [49.9–56.13] There are three causes which lead to the functioning of indication: the primary meaning having an incongruity, a relationship between the primary and indicated meaning, and a motive.

4.7.1. [50.133–50.15] There are five kinds of relationship and two motives.

4.7.1.1. [50.15] One motive is convention. A second motive is being novel.

4.7.1.2. [53.17] The first kind of relationship is indicated meaning having a close relationship with the primary meaning. An example is given.

4.7.1.3. [53.26–54.3] The second kind of relationship is indicated meaning being similar to the primary meaning. An example is given.

4.7.1.4. [54.7] The third kind of relationship is indicated meaning being associated with the primary meaning. An example is given.

4.7.1.5. [56.6] The fourth kind of relationship is indicated meaning being opposite to the primary meaning. An example is given.

4.7.1.6. [56.13] The fifth kind of relationship is indicated meaning having a connection with action. An example is given.

4.7.2. [58.11–65.29] Depending on the relationship, the expressed meaning may be entirely displaced, intended to be expressed or not intended to be expressed.

4.7.2.1. [58.18–24] When there is similarity or opposition, the expressed meaning is entirely displaced.
4.7.2.2. [59.28] When there is connection or association, the expressed meaning may be intended to be expressed or not intended to be expressed.
4.7.2.3. [60.4] When there is a close relationship with the primary meaning, the expressed meaning is intended to be expressed.
4.7.2.4. [60.10] When there is association, given that there is inclusion, the expressed meaning is intended to be expressed.
4.7.2.5. [63.17] When there is close relationship with the primary meaning, the expressed meaning can be not intended to be expressed, though it is not entirely discarded.
4.7.2.6. [63.25] When there is association, it is also possible that the expressed meaning is not intended to be expressed. although it is not entirely discarded.
4.7.2.7. [65.24] When there is connection with an action, then in some cases there can be the discarding of the expressed meaning.
4.7.2.8. [65.29–66.6] However, there can also be connection with an action where the word's meaning is expressed and intended to be expressed, although it indicates another action. Reply to the sensitive critics that even though there is an implicit comparison in such cases, this does not mean the expressed meaning must be entirely discarded.

4.7.3. [66.12–16] Concluding remarks on divisions of indication. The work is only a schematic and further details should be investigated, but this demonstrates that suggestion is not a novel classification.

5. [69.8–69.14] The language principle is the underlying unity among language and concepts, and admits of no genuine divisions. However, in everyday use, such divisions are manifested as cognitive distortions and in this context we find the aforementioned divisions of the communicative principle.
6. [72.3–73.7] The purpose of this work has been to delineate the divisions of the communicative function which is involved in all pursuits of knowledge. People who understand this function will become clear in their speech and have mastery of the various disciplines.

The village is on the Ganges

Fat Devadatta does not eat during the day

The umbrella-holders go

Caption: In the images (above), at left we see an interpretation of the example sentence (printed below each image) based on the primary meaning. This interpretation prompts the proper, indicated meaning: villages cannot float on a river, a stout person must eat at some time, and there is only one person who holds an umbrella in a royal retinue.

Appendix 2: Linguistic Examples used by Mukula

Below are the examples Mukula uses to develop his theory of primary and indicated meaning, listed in order of appearance in the text. Each example is followed by the locations in the text according to the Dvivedi page and line numbers in brackets, along with its analysis according to Mukula's taxonomy.

1. The cow is to be sacrificially bound. 2.18, 2.24, 13.3
   - **a** Primary meaning function (as universal)
   - **b** Indicatory meaning function (as particular), inclusive variety
2. Ḍittha, 5.3–5.10, 8.25–10.7
   - **a** Word denoting a name-bearer
3. One cooks. 6.16
   - **a** Word denoting an action
4. white, 5.22
   - **a** Word denoting a property
5. cow, 5.22
   - **a** Word denoting a universal
6. The village is on the Ganges. 11.20, 13.15, 20.17, 20.24, 21.1, 53.17
   - **a** (general case) Indication lacking transfer, indirect expression
   - **b** (Vitastā) Indication with extreme distinction lacking semantic imbuing
   - **c** (holiness and beauty) Indication with intermediate distinction that has semantic imbuing, close relationship to primary meaning, motive to communicate things that lack a specific term to

communicate, expressed meaning unintentionally expressed and is not entirely discarded

d (directly on the Ganges) Indication with dissolved distinction, absorption

7 The Punjabi is an ox. 11.20, 16.1, 18.1, 22.18

a Indication involving transfer, transfer of properties, superimposition, intermediate distinction

8 Fat Devadatta does not eat during the day. 13.1, 60.4

a Indication lacking transfer, inclusion, expressed meaning is intended to be expressed

9 Ghee is long life. 16.1, 18.1

a Indication involving transfer in general (cause and effect), superimposition

10 Pañcālas, 18.9, 22.23

a Intermediated indirect expression, indication involving transfer in general, absorption, distinction dissolved

11 ruler, 18.16, 22.23, 27.22

a Indication involving transfer of properties, absorption, distinction dissolved, motive of following conventional use

12 This ox! 22.18

a Indication involving transfer of properties, absorption, distinction dissolved

13 smeared, friends of the clouds, 27.22, 58.18

a newly created figure, expressed meaning is entirely displaced

14 I am Rāma. 27.22, 63.17

a newly created figure, motive to communicate a specific meaning, close relationship to primary meaning, expressed meaning unintentionally expressed and is not entirely discarded

15 sacrifice-carrier in the mouth of a beloved mare, 29.11–30.7

a figure lacking indication

16 bee (*bhramara*), 29.29, 50.15

- **a** intermediated indirect indication, motive of following convention

17 Hey there neighbor . . . , 31.22–31.27

- **a** Indication understood by relationship with speaker, motive to communicate truth in hidden manner

18 He has already taken Śri . . . , 33.9–34.5

- **a** Indication understood by relationship with sentence, involves hyperbole, imagining, superimposition which includes transfer of properties

19 The flower-tipped arrows . . . , 37.18

- **a** Indication understood by relationship with expressed meaning, indication of *rasa*, predominant indicated meaning

20 Bee, in all your buzzing . . . , 53.26–54.3

- **a** Indication based on similarity, indication involving transfer of properties

21 The umbrella-holders go. 54.7, 60.10, 63.25

- **a** Indication based on association, expressed meaning is intended
- **b** Indication based on association, expressed meaning unintentionally expressed and is not entirely discarded

22 Auspicious-faced one, 56.6, 58.24

- **a** Indication based on opposition, motive to communicate truth in hidden manner, expressed meaning is entirely displaced

23 You are Śatrughna / the enemy-killer . . . , 56.13, 65.29

- **a** Indication based on being joined with an action, expressed meaning is intended

24 The man is a man. 65.24

- **a** Indication depends on being joined with an action, expressed meaning is discarded

Part III

Commentary on "The Fundamentals of the Communicative Function"

About this Commentary

The commentary is written so that it can be read along with the translation, although it presupposes acquaintance with the major figures and texts in the introduction. For readers who wish to read it along with the text, page references are given in parentheses, and the chapter is divided into sections corresponding to the verses, each section generally following the order of Mukula's own auto-commentary. Subsections are inserted to help readers follow the structure of Mukula's arguments. Overall, my aim is to clarify compressed arguments for the reader by filling out implicit assumptions. Sometimes this involves explaining the original context of a thinker whose work Mukula cites or alludes to, and sometimes it just involves developing the best reading of Mukula's ideas by thinking philosophically along with him.

This chapter is significantly indebted to, and informed by, two prior works on Mukula: Venugopalan (1977) and McCrea (2008). However, in contrast to my predecessors, who have been intentionally selective in their remarks, I have commented on every section of Mukula's work. In addition, I limit the use of Sanskrit terms in the commentary, preferring instead to use English, save for select technical terms. I will indicate Sanskrit in parentheses at the first instance of a term, for instance, suggestion (*dhvani*). The notes include citations and, when relevant, Sanskrit for the translations in the body of the essay. First uses of terms in the glossary are in bold. Finally, the commentarial chapter reproduces the verses so that a reader can find their way in the discussion, but the chapter explicates more than just these verses, discussing Mukula's auto-commentary in detail.

Introduction

The title of our work in Sanskrit is a compound of three words: *abhidhā-vṛtta-mātṛkā*, or "The Fundamentals of the Communicative Function." Its topic is how language communicates meaning, and its goal is to lay out the basics on this topic, the fundamentals. Like many works in the Sanskrit tradition, it is written in the form of a commentary, although Mukula is the author of the verses (*kārikā*s) as well as their commentary, making this an "auto-commentary." By participating in the conventions of the commentarial genre, Mukula is able to set out his principles in compact verse form and then to explicate them in what follows.[1] The explication may involve defining terms, making connections to previous thinkers, as well as raising and answering objections. This explicitly dialogical method allows Mukula to consider possible objections through the voice of opponents, ones whose positions may not always correspond to the view of a historical person. Before he enters into commentary on his own verses, Mukula opens the work by motivating its importance:

> It is evident that, in this world, **ordinary linguistic practice** cannot come into existence without determinate cognitions of word meanings as well as determinate cognitions of their uses in obtaining the means to earthly pleasures and liberation from the world, and their uses in avoiding what prevents these. (62)

His main point in this discussion is that successful language use requires confidence in language's ability to refer to things in the world. This is because we do things with language. Simply put, our ordinary linguistic practice (*vyavahāra*) is the way in which we pair utterances with actions.[2] Sometimes we speak in order to acquire things, and sometimes we speak in order to avoid things. This theme in Sanskrit linguistic analysis is seen clearly in the grammarian Patañjali, whose work, *The Great Commentary* (*Mahā-bhāṣya*), we will see Mukula cite several times:

> An object is cognized through a word's utterance: "Bring the cow," "Eat yogurt." The object is brought and the object is enjoyed.[3]

This kind of practice, though, is not possible unless we have determinate cognitions (*niścaya*) about what the objects of words, that is, in their **meaning** (***artha***).[4] Determinacy here involves both a sense of subjective confidence in the object and a sense of objective warrantedness in that confidence. Word meaning is thus understood in terms of a definite reference, or a word's relationship to some existing thing, like cows or yogurt. Hearing a word, we have a **cognition**, a mental state characterized by some content, of the cow or the yogurt. Mukula's point is that if we don't have confidence in our knowledge about what words refer to, when someone says "Bring the cow," we will not know how to act. This failure would have implications not only for our enjoyment of ordinary things like yogurt, but also for our possibility to attain liberation (*apavarga*) from ordinary life, which in the Indian religious-philosophical context broadly means the end to the cycle of reincarnation.

Mukula goes on to make more precise how word meanings are involved in our ordinary linguistic practices. They are known through **epistemic instruments (*pramāṇas*)**, knowledge-conducive processes such as perception and inference. Perception, for instance, is responsible for my knowing that there is a cow in the field. If my perception is a genuine one, then I have a determinate cognition. This is knowledge of which we can be confident, where "confidence" is a success term. That is, if someone has confidence, it is not merely a subjective sense which can be wrong, but a genuine determination that something is the case.

Now, the fact the word "cow" has the capacity to refer to a cow requires that, at some point in my acquisition of language, I genuinely see a cow and pair that perception with the utterance "cow."[5] So, Mukula observes that without this determinate knowledge, we don't understand "cow" as paired with a cow. But we use language in a wide range of ways. For instance, if I say, "The hired hands should go milk the cows," the phrase "hired hands" does not refer to hands which have been hired, but rather to *people with* hands, who have been hired. We talk this way all the time, and do so for ordinary and extraordinary purposes. We might say things like "I need coffee! It's my fuel," and thereby ask someone to get us a fresh cup. Religious examples of this kind of talk abound: in the Greek New Testament, Jesus instructs his disciples to eat bread, saying, "This is my body," and in Mukula's time there is much discussion about how to interpret Vedic sentences like "The grass bundle is the ritual's beneficiary." Mukula's stated purpose is to analyze how it is that we can utter such sentences and do so with determinate knowledge about their meanings.

What Mukula does not say explicitly, and will not until later on, is that his view about language is important because it forms a corrective to a new theory. Mukula says that there is a single **communicative function (*abhidhā*)** which has two aspects to it, a **primary (*mukhya*)** and **indicatory function (*lākṣaṇika*)**. He seems to be the first person to use the Sanskrit term *abhidhā* in this way, in contrast to previous thinkers who use the term as equivalent to primary (*mukhya*). His decision to use the term to cover both kinds of capacities is perhaps to emphasize that the confidence we have about the indicatory function is just as strong as the primary. Word choice aside, that there are two functions, or capacities of language, is widely accepted by thinkers up to Mukula's time. About a century before Mukula[6], Ānandavardhana, another thinker living in Kashmir, Mukula's home, challenges this orthodoxy by adding a third function, **suggestion (*dhvani, vjañjanā*)**[7]. In what follows, Mukula will argue that this third function is unnecessary, and that we can explain all of our linguistic practices with the primary and indicatory functions of communication. He will cast a wide net with regard to these practices: ordinary speech, religious speech, and poetic speech all come within his analysis, although the last category is crucial, since this is where Ānandavardhana thinks the existing analysis of language falls short.

Verses 1–15

Verse 1

The first verse defines two kinds of meaning, "primary" (*mukhya*) and "indicated" (*lākṣymāṇa*), stating that the primary meaning depends directly on the function of speech.

> The primary meaning is what is apprehended from the function of speech.
> The indicated meaning is said to be ascertained further from that meaning. (62)[1]

Put another way, the immediate result of uttering words is to convey, that is, to **denote**, this kind of meaning. (In this book, I use "denote" to mean the ability of linguistic expressions, whether words or sentences, to communicate a meaning, and I use "refer" for the more specific ability of a linguistic expression to relate to an object.) In contrast, the indicated meaning is not directly understood from linguistic utterances, but occurs at a second stage, understood from speech in a manner mediated by the primary meaning. For those philosophical traditions which accept the distinction between primary and some kind of additional meaning, Mukula's starting definition is uncontroversial. Although he will wade into some disputes, typically he presents his views so that almost any thinker could accept his position. This is because his aim is merely to show that Ānandavardhana's new kind of communicative function, suggestion, is unsatisfactory, and not to present a very novel theory of communication. Thus while, as we will see, Indian thinkers had a wide range of views on things like the referents of words, how words combine to create sentences, and the varieties of figurative language, Mukula wishes to avoid taking a controversial position while arguing against suggestion.

Although his focus is indication, as it is this function which he thinks will supplant the suggestive function, Mukula begins with the primary function. This is probably in part due to a concern with completeness, but also because the boundaries of indication depend upon how one understands primary meaning, which we will see in discussion of Verses 9 and 10.

Primary meaning

Having set out his basic position, Mukula turns to the etymology of the word "primary," explaining how it is derived from the Sanskrit word "face" (*mukha*). Understood etymologically, the word "primary" illustrates the priority of the primary meaning over the indicated meaning. Adding the affix *-ya* onto the word *mukha* results in the meaning "like a face," just as how when *-ya* is added to "branch" (*śākhā*), it results in "like a branch," or something which is branching, an example Mukula takes from Pāṇini's *Eight Chapters* (*Aṣṭâdhyāyī*) 5.3.103.[2] So, just like the face of a baby appears before its limbs when it is being born, the primary meaning appears before all of the other connected meanings, when we understand utterances. This analogy of the face is a common one for primary meaning, also being found in Kumārila Bhaṭṭa's *Exposition on Ritual Practice* (*Tantra-vārttika*) 3.2.1. We may not always be aware of this priority, however, and it requires sophisticated linguistic analysis for us to recover what is primary. Ordinary people aren't typically reflecting on this process of comprehension. In fact, without some motivation, the first case of primary meaning Mukula gives seems unusual. Thus, let us first introduce a more modern example. Suppose someone buying an item says to the cashier.

1 Put it on plastic.

Here she means, "Charge the purchase to my credit card." The word "plastic" can be used in many contexts to refer to things made of plastic, whether credit cards or something else. Its primary meaning is whatever all of these things have in common, being plastic. I can use the word "plastic" in many different contexts, and while it may work slightly different in each, we might think there needs to be some common contribution. This common contribution accounts for our ability to understand entirely new sentences. Each word contributes something fixed—its primary meaning. But in the context above, the word "plastic" has a secondary or indicated meaning, which is represented by the italicized words below (this is how we will distinguish primary from secondary meaning throughout the commentary).

2 Put it on *the card made of* plastic.

Because credit cards are made of plastic (or were up until the advent of payment apps on phones), we can understand that the speaker means a credit card. Mukula will eventually get to explaining how it is that we know what the indicated meaning is and discuss quite a number of varieties. The main point right now is just that we need two kinds of meaning functions in order to explain how words communicate something shared across contexts but yet convey slightly different things in contexts. While "plastic" might have the primary meaning of (let us say) *synthetic material which can be pressed into different shapes*, in some contexts, it can have an indicated meaning which is *card made of plastic*.

Let us now return to Mukula's illustration of primary meaning, which is an example from the Vedas.

3 A cow is to be sacrificially bound.

While a familiar example to Mukula's readers, it needs some explanation for modern readers. This injunction is part of a ritual, and it instructs a sacrificer to fasten a cow to a post. Mukula states that the primary meaning of "cow" is a universal, COWHOOD, and it is in virtue of this universal that the sacrifice can be completed. Implicit in Mukula's reasoning is the idea that unless you find something which is a cow (and not a horse or a goat), you have not obeyed the command. Thus "cow" tells us that we want something which is a cow, and it is universals which make things what they are (a point which will be emphasized again soon). Further, Patañjali's *Great Commentary* 1.2.64 points out the necessity for injunctions like this to be uttered in many different ritual contexts. If the word "cow" refers to a particular individual cow, then once that cow has been sacrificed, anyone else attempting to follow the injunction would actually be doing something other than what the injunction is ordering. In other words, "cow" is not the name of a cow, like "Bessie." Thus, what is meant needs to be something quite general, which is a universal. We will return to universals in more detail under Verse 2.

Indicated meaning

However, while the primary meaning is a universal, Mukula claims that a particular (*vyakti*) must be also communicated. This happens through the indicatory function, not the primary. This is because the primary function does only one thing, which is to refer to a universal. Mukula cites a maxim which gives a reason for this: "A communicative function cannot get at the property-bearer when it expends its capacity on the property" (63).[3] This principle individuates functions in terms of their results. Once a function has attained its result, there is nothing left for it to do. If we suppose that the primary function aims to denote universals, then, having done so, it is not possible for it also to denote an individual. This means that we must presume there is another function, at least if we think that the meaning of "The cow is to be sacrificially bound" includes more than just reference to a universal.

And it is an uncontroversial position that the utterance "The cow is to be sacrificially bound" must communicate someone's obligation to perform an action, which is in particular the action of fastening a cow to a post. All of the examples in Mukula's text, save perhaps one, are cases where the meaning is uncontroversial. We start with what we understand and then postulate the causes of that understanding. In this case, we know that the meaning of "cow" must include something general enough for the same sentence to be used in multiple contexts acceptably. Yet, now we recognize that the meaning must also be particular enough for the hearer in a specific context to follow the command.

Mukula argues that while COWHOOD is a means to complete the sacrifice, it is not so without our also understanding a particular cow. The way that we come to understand a particular cow is through reflecting on the first meaning, COWHOOD. While a universal makes a particular cow a cow (and not a horse or a goat), the sacrifice cannot be performed with just a universal. While Mukula does not get into the metaphysics of universals and particulars—of which there is much written—for all of the various realist

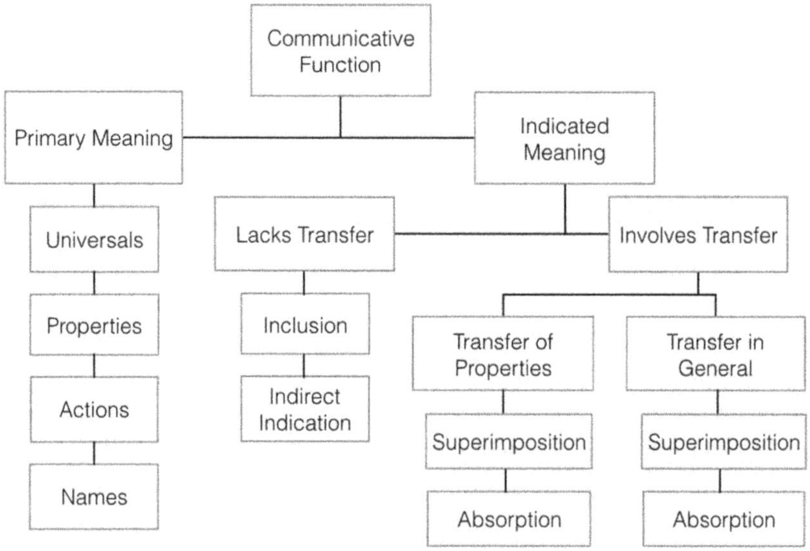

Figure 1 Mukula's analysis of the communicative function.

views, there is a close relationship between a universal and a particular. Whether it is inherence or some kind of identity, this close connection makes it easy to reflect on a universal and determine that what is meant is an individual.

Mukula has now set up his central distinction, between primary and indicated meanings, which are obtained by two functions, the primary and indicatory. The important difference between them is that the primary meaning is directly understood from an utterance, and the indicated meaning is understood from this primary meaning. Figure 1 shows all of varieties of meaning which Mukula will discuss in his text. As we progress, we will focus on specific aspects of this structure.

Verse 2a

Mukula now discusses the varieties of primary meaning and what it is that grounds their different uses.

(2a) With regard to the primary and indicated meanings, the four distinctions among primary meanings are known because of distinctions among things like universals. (64)[4]

When I say, "The cow is to be sacrificially bound," or "Put it on plastic," I use the words I do because I want my hearer to understand what particular things I'm talking about. These things, then, are the basis for my selecting certain words. Mukula calls such a basis a **distinguishing feature (*upādhi*)**.

Table 3 Analysis of primary meaning

Kind of primary meaning term	Kind of distinguishing feature	First analysis of distinguishing feature	Second analysis of distinguishing feature
Words denoting universals (Nouns)	Universal	Thing's nature	Already established
Words denoting properties (Adjectives)	Property		
Words denoting actions (Verbs)	Action		Yet to be established
Words denoting what is contingent (Names)	Word being used	Stipulated by a speaker	–

He identifies four different kinds of words which correspond to four different kinds of distinguishing features. Table 3 gives an overview of the analysis which follows.

In this section, Mukula follows Patañjali, whose *Great Commentary* he quotes again. Unlike Patañjali, whose discussion does not identify four grammatical categories that correspond to these four uses of words, in Mukula's text, a different grammatical category is the exemplar for each denotation. He uses nouns for universals, adjectives for properties, verbs for actions, and proper names for named things. On the principle he has introduced under Verse 1, once the primary function has denoted a universal, quality, action, or a name-bearing object, it has completed its purpose. It is after this that the indicatory function will operate, which is of course, the focus of Mukula's text. The boundaries of the primary function are thus important for identifying where the indicatory function begins.

Mukula's discussion of the primary meaning also gives us insight into some debates in Indian linguistic thought. As we have said, distinguishing features are whatever features demarcate the boundaries of linguistic use. The reason I use a word is that it refers to something which has a distinguishing feature. Conversely, if I use a word to refer to something that lacks the appropriate distinguishing feature, I have made an error. So distinguishing features have a normative dimension to them. In English one can't say "cow" and use it (in its primary meaning) as an adjective. Compare these sentences (the asterisk indicates an unacceptable sentence):

4 *That is a cow horse.
5 That is a brown horse.

Mukula says something else important in explaining this concept, using a term which will come up again at Verse 5b and 6a. He says that "[the word's] different contents are **semantically imbued** with the distinguishing features" (64). In other words, there is a way in which the distinguishing features, which are things in the world, influence the content of a meaning. This influence (the Sanskrit *uparakta* literally means "colored" or "shaded") will turn out to be an important concept for how indication is able to communicate so many different meanings. Distinguishing features contribute shades of meaning. At this point, however, Mukula's goal is to show that these four distinctions (universals, properties, actions, named things) can themselves be grouped into broader categories. He starts at the most general difference between distinguishing features.

Stipulation: Proper names

One kind of distinguishing feature is a speaker's stipulative aim, and another kind is the nature of things themselves. The only kind of word grounded in stipulation is a proper name. The term **something contingent (*yad-ṛcchā*)** is used for the object of a word which refers in virtue of extrinsically, contingently determined boundaries, in contrast to reference being fixed by intrinsic characteristics.[5]

Mukula's example of a word for something contingent is the word "Ḍittha," which is a Sanskrit name with no cultural associations or etymological constituents. Unlike many ordinary names such as "Devadatta" which can be analyzed into constituent parts (*deva-datta*) and can etymologically denote associated meanings ("god-given"), this name is purely stipulative. Thus it can illustrate a directly referential relationship between names and their objects, without the risk of suggesting that they function through some disguised descriptions or other meanings. It also avoids the history of famous people named "Devadatta," whose biographies might give rise to other connotations (Mukula discusses this along with etymological connotations later). It is the speaker's desire to label someone (or something) that makes the sound "Ḍittha" appropriate for that thing. The crucial point is that there is nothing about the thing called "Ḍittha" that makes it independently correct (or incorrect) to call it "Ḍittha," whereas in the other examples, there is some natural feature which determines when we should call it a "cow" or a "white" thing.

Mukula discusses the relationship between sound and meaning alongside of his explanation of the referential power of "Ḍittha." Here, the debate he is alluding to is probably between Grammarians and Mīmāṃsakas, although he only identifies the first explicitly. So we will talk about Grammarians and Phonemic Realists. At issue is how a collection of different sounds make a single word which communicates meaning: are words partless or made up of phonemes? This discussion is yet another attempt to show that his view is neutral with regard to important debates. Since Mukula seems sympathetic to the Grammarian view about how sounds come together to make up a word, someone who rejects that view might also wish to reject his claim about the primary meaning of proper names. He argues they need not. The reason they need not is that in both cases, proper names acquire their meaning in the same way, according to a speaker's stipulation.

The Grammarian's view is represented when Mukula says that "the word's character, which is a sequence of phonemes whose temporal order has been dissolved, is grasped when the last phoneme in the word is heard" (64).

What this means is that the word "Ḍittha" is heard by someone as /ḍit/ and /tha/, two sounds which take time to process. By the time one hears /tha/, the sound of /ḍit/ has gone. Yet, when we finish hearing /tha/ we somehow have a cognition of the meaning of the word in its entirety and also its meaning. According to a Grammarian like Bhartṛhari, words in their true nature are not made up of sounds, but sounds simply manifest words.[6] Sounds reveal the partless burst (*sphoṭa*) of meaning which exists independent of individual utterances. This is what we will call the Burst Theory. On this view, what has a genuine ontological status is the whole (the entire uttered sound) and not its parts (the phonemes).

In contrast to the Theory, on the Phonemic Realist's view, the individual phonemes /ḍit/ and /tha/ genuinely exist. Further, these are permanent entities. Consider how British and American speakers of English pronounce the "r" in "water"—Americans have a rhotic /r/ which is strongly pronounced, whereas most British speakers will often drop the letter or pronounce it as a schwa. Yet we might want to say that both cases of the word "water" involve the same "r" in some sense. The Phonemic Realist would say that British and English speakers are manifesting the "r" but not producing it, since the "r" which contributes to the meaning of "water" cannot vary, if we are going to explain the constancy of meaning. A word—again, understood as a **type**, the context-independent entity—is made up of phonemes, which are not tokens but instances of types (known as "occurrences"). Unlike the indivisible so-called "burst," a word type has parts. How do we understand what "Ḍittha" means? Even though each phoneme only lasts a short time, it creates a memory trace which, when the final sound is heard, we recall altogether in a sequence. This is how we understand the word "Ḍittha" on the Phonemic Realist's view.[7]

Mukula says that whether "Ḍittha" is a partless whole manifested by temporary phonemes or whether "Ḍittha" is composed of genuine phonemes, in either case it refers to the person Ḍittha just because the speaker has decided to use it in a certain way. What makes the use of "Ḍittha" bring about cognition of the person Ḍittha is nothing about the person, but everything to do with the word, which is the distinguishing feature. In contrast, there are distinguishing features which are not found in words, but in the world.

Nature of things: What is yet to be established (actions)

Mukula now turns to the other major category of distinguishing features: those based in the nature of things. This category is again subdivided: what is already established and what is yet to be established. Words for universals like "cow" and words for properties like "white" are based in distinguishing features that have already been established, whereas words for actions like "cooks" are yet to be established.

Mukula gives his analysis of action-denoting words using the example of the Sanskrit verb *pacati*, which means "He/she/it cooks." To explain in more detail—Sanskrit verbs are conjugated by adding affixes onto a verbal root (*dhātu*) which itself can be subject to changes. The changes to the verbal root and which affixes are added (these can be prefixes as well as suffixes) depend upon what morphological class the verbal root belongs to (Sanskrit has ten), as well as tense and inflection. Here, *pacati* is derived from the root *pac*, and as it belongs to the first class, one adds the letter *a* to the root, along with the ending *–ti*, which indicates that the action is performed by the third person in the singular.[8] This ending *-ti* is the verbal element which, along with the presence or lack of changes in the verbal root *pac*, conveys the particular action: one person cooks, two people cook, you have cooked, they continue cooking, etc. Although there is a significant debate over the definition of verbs and their role in sentences, Mukula is content to give this example and move on to the already established distinguishing feature. In choosing a simple transitive verb like "cook," he avoids the messy discussion about how to characterize intransitive verbs such as "is" (*asti*).

Nature of things: What is already established (universals and properties)

Those distinguishing features which are already established can be subdivided into two kinds: universals and properties. Mukula has already touched on universals in his discussion of primary meaning above. He underscores their importance by observing that universals are responsible for the objects in the world having their own particular nature and that "no objects ever obtain their particular nature without having a connection to a universal" (65). To support this claim, he gives a quote which he attributes to Bhartṛhari but which is not found in the *Treatise on Sentences and Words*, though the later thinker Mammaṭa also attributes it to Bhartṛhari. Thus we may have here a lost portion of the commentary on Bhartṛhari's text.[9] Again we see, as we have in his discussion of the Burst Theory of proper names, Mukula's preference for Grammarians. In what follows, we will also see him take the Grammarian's position in a debate about word meaning.

With regard to the word "white" (*śukla*), Mukula says its basis is an already existing property, but that unlike a universal, it is not responsible for the nature of an object. For instance, a white cloth depends on the universal of CLOTHNESS for its being a cloth, but not on a property like whiteness. A cloth has the nature of being a cloth not in virtue of its color—as cloths can be many colors and still count as cloths.[10] Mukula hints at the hierarchical nature of universals when he notes that the universal is the reason we can talk about an thing qua thing-hood. A cow is a living being, but it is also a cow. A cloth is an artifact, but it is also a cloth. Depending upon what aspect of the object is being described, different distinguishing features are the basis for our word use. Since it is generally accepted by Indian thinkers that multiple universals can inhere in the same individual, albeit in different manners, this raises questions about the basis of word use. When we say

6 The cloth is white.

it is the property of whiteness that is the basis for employing the word "white." But consider

7 The cloth is a thing.

Is it a universal (THINGNESS) or a property (being a thing) which is the basis for our use of "thing"? Mukula does not discuss a general theory for how to determine the answer. But he does raise this question for the word "atomic" (*paramāṇutva*).

On one analysis of ontological categories, that of Vaiśeṣika thinkers such as Kanada, atoms are eternal, imperceptible, particulars without color, shape, etc., and yet each individual atom is distinguishable from other atoms. Atoms, as the most basic and irreducible component of reality, constitute substances (earth, fire, air, water, etc.) through various combinations. Unlike being white, which is accidental to an object's nature, being atomic seems to be necessary for and logically prior to an object having any nature. On what Mukula has already said, we might think that being atomic is having a relationship to the universal ATOMIC.[11] This is reasonable, assuming that there is something which all atoms have in common, which is being the basic and irreducible stuff of reality. This would make "atomic" a universal-denoting word. However, according to Mukula, it is a property-denoting word.

The argument Mukula given for this position is compact: "All of these properties are a single kind, because they share in the universal PROPERTY" (66). Put in these terms, the argument seems to beg the question, since what is under dispute is whether atoms belong to the class of properties or not. We can reconstruct the motive behind Mukula's view, though: the difficulty with classifying atoms in the fourfold schema Mukula has given is that either of the two most attractive options—universals or an individual (which might make "atomic" a proper name)—collapses their ontological role.[12] They must be irreducibly particular, which means they cannot share in a universal. Yet, at the same time, they seem to have something in common, which is their foundational ontological role, so being the only contingently named individual doesn't capture this. The category of property comes closest to capturing the in-between status of atoms.

Objection to fourfold division

Having dealt with, however briefly, his fourfold schema, Mukula has an interlocutor object to the classificatory schema. Since he does not identify them explicitly, we will call them the Semantic Universalist. The Semantic Universalist argues that what are apparently words for properties, actions, and proper names are in fact words for universals. They take up each distinguishing feature in turn. Implicit in their argument is the worry that, unless we have something shared across the various different instances of things that we call "white," or "cooking," or "Ḍittha," our words will not be able to refer to all of the different references. Again, remembering Mukula's opening discussion of the role of language in action, we can see that unless we know what "white" refers to, and can use "white" appropriately in many different cases, we will fail in our ability to act. Being told to get the white cow, if "white" refers to a universal, then having learned what "white" means in the context of a white pot (which has the universal WHITE), I can understand that I am to look for the same thing, but in a cow.

The Semantic Universalist's first argument is that property words are grounded in universals since whiteness is what is common to different substances such as milk, shells, cranes, etc. Take the sentences

8 The crane is white.
9 The shell is white.

We can use "white" in different contexts successfully if there is something the properties of white have in common which form the basis of its appropriate use. What better candidate for commonality than a universal? The opponent applies the argument, *ceteris paribus*, to actions. While one may cook with sugar, sesame seeds, rice, or other objects, all of these actions are different than, say, the action of writing which takes objects like paper or parchment. So we should say there is a universal of cooking. The opponent then discusses "Ḍittha," the proper name, in significantly more detail.

To explain how it is that "Ḍittha" is applied to persons in virtue of a universal, the Semantic Universalist tries two approaches.[13] The first is to say that *the word itself* is something in which a universal inheres. The second is to say that there is a universal *in the object* which unifies what would otherwise be divided. Again, without being too precise about whose views (if any) may be represented here, the first option is neutral with regard to the ontology of substances. If one's ontology has it that substances are momentary and do not have relationships to universals, perhaps universals could still be found in the word. There is something that all utterances share, which is the sound /Ḍittha/.[14] The second option commits to the existence of a universal which makes the person Ḍittha the same person over his life, despite his changing from a baby to a young man to an old man.

Mukula responds to the objection by reiterating a point found in Patañjali's *Great Commentary*. Accepting that "white" picks out something which seems to be the same in multiple entities, Mukula argues that appearance need not require a universal for explanation. He illustrates with an analogy of a face being reflected in different materials. The reflection changes depending on whether it is in oil or a mirror, seen at different times and places in different ways. Likewise, the white in a conch shell and the white in a grain of rice are, respectively, each different instance of white, manifested (like the reflection) differently depending on the substrate. There is no white universal which is present in each substance. The point here is that a universal is, by definition, something unified which is shared among different substrata. We might think that there is a universal white which inheres in different substrata (and hence takes on slightly different presentation). But Mukula argues that this appearance of variegation, or multiplying, is just an appearance.

The same applies for cooking, the word "Ḍittha," and the person Ḍittha. In each case, what appears to be a single shared universal that unifies many instances should actually be understood as multiple instances of actions, words, or persons, having their own nature in each instance. To take cooking, the single act of cooking a pot of rice admits of multiple stages (getting the rice, rinsing it, boiling the water, etc.). This act should be understood as unified, despite the stages. However, it should not be understood as part of universal COOKING which belongs to other acts like cooking a chicken, cooking a casserole, etc. Likewise, when a parrot, a mynah bird, or a person says "Ḍittha," each word should be understood as having its own nature. And while Ḍittha is the same person from birth to old age, this is not because he has a relationship to ḌITTHA-HOOD, but because, despite his appearing differently throughout his life, he is still the same individual. Otherwise, each stage of his life would be analogous to a single cow in a field, which is a cow because it has a relationship to COWHOOD. Mukula does not offer detailed arguments for his position, but by appealing to Patañjali, he signals that these arguments are ones already found in his tradition—so interested readers can go elsewhere. His main purpose is to explain indication and how it makes suggestion an unnecessary postulate, which he begins to do now.

Verse 2b

Turning now to the indicatory function, Mukula distinguishes between two varieties: **indication lacking transfer (*śuddhôpacāra*)** and **indication with transfer (*upacāra-miśrā*).**

> Indication is thought to have two kinds due to its lacking and involving transfer. (2b)

This is the first major distinction he will make. Before moving on to discuss the distinction, let us pause to get an overview of Mukula's project. In Table 4, we can see the two major analyses of indication that Mukula will take up. He first focuses on the way in which the primary and indicated meanings are related: with or without transfer. He then focuses on how semantically distant the primary and indicated meanings are. These analyses take up the same examples (shown in italics). His ultimate goal is to demonstrate that, for those cases which Ānandavardhana thinks must be explained by suggestion, he can give an account of their meanings in terms of indication. The category of inclusion is the crucial place where this occurs, although this point is not explicit until later in his text.

In the text at hand, Mukula distinguishes between cases of indication which do and do not involve transfer (*upacāra*). The word *upacāra*, which derives from the verb *car* (move, go) and prefix *upa-* (toward), etymologically means "move toward." Essentially, what is being "moved" is one meaning "toward" another. In philosophical literature focusing on mental cognition,

Table 4 Mukula's first and second analysis, compared

First analysis		Kind of indication	Second analysis	
Indication's relationship with transfer	**Basis for transfer**	**Relationship between meanings**	**Relationship between meanings has . . .**	**Semantic distance is . . .**
Transfer-free		Indirect expression *Ganges*	No semantic imbuing	Total
		Inclusion *Cow* *Devadatta*	No semantic imbuing	
Transfer	Property-based	Superimposition *Peasant*	Semantic imbuing	Intermediate
		Absorption *Ruler*		
	Other than properties	Superimposition *Ghee*		Subsumed

upacāra is often used for perceptual errors such as the mistaking a rope for a snake, through superimposing the cognition of a snake onto a rope.[15] However, here, Mukula is not talking about complete (mis)identification. We will see as he develops his conception of transfer that he thinks it admits of different ways of understanding the relationship between primary and indicated meaning.

Indication lacking transfer

Mukula's first example of indication, to illustrate the variety lacking transfer, is a traditional example also discussed by Ānandavardhana:

10 The village is on the Ganges.[16]

The indicated meaning of this sentence is

11 The village is on *the bank of* the Ganges.

Mukula and Ānandavardhana agree that indication conveys "bank of the Ganges" because the river, which is the primary meaning of "Ganges," is not appropriate as a basis of support for a village. This example is important, since Mukula will use it again as part of his refutation of suggestion. We will wait to discuss this aspect of the example but pause to motivate it further. An analogous example of indication lacking transfer in English (paired with its explicit indicated meaning) would be

12 I had to go two streets over to find a parking meter.[17]
13 I had to go two streets over to find a *parking spot next to a* parking meter.

In this case of what is today called "spatial metonymy," the hearer understands that "parking meter" is not being meant in its primary meaning, since the speaker isn't interested in just looking for a meter. (Imagine if she found a meter which had been installed where there is no parking spot.) Rather she is looking for a parking spot that is adjacent to the meter. In fact, there may be a further instance of metonymy in this sentence—the word "I" refers to the person driving their car. She is not just walking around the city looking for a meter. We understand these meanings easily, and Mukula's claim is that these kinds of indication do not involve "carrying over" any content from the primary to the indicated meaning.

Indication involving transfer

What transfer is becomes clearer with the next example

14 The Punjabi is an ox.

This pejorative metaphor involves an obstacle for the primary meaning, as in the case of the Ganges river. A person is not an ox. Yet, we do not take our speaker as uttering nonsense or lying—rather, due to this obstacle we understand properties in the Punjabi which are similar to those belonging to the ox, namely dullness and laziness. These particular properties are the ones we understand because they are defining properties for a Punjabi, according to Mukula. So not just any and every property is understood, but only a particular set. As a similar example, we might take

15 George is a lapdog.[18]

In this case, since a lapdog is a particular kind of dog which has a life of canine luxury, enjoys pleasant surroundings, and so on, we might understand that from this example George is a spoiled rich person. Just which properties we ascribe to George and why are important questions in the analysis of what contemporary philosophy and linguistics calls "metaphor," which overlaps with what Mukula calls "indication involving transfer."

Verses 3a–4b

Having just explained indication lacking and involving transfer, Mukula focuses on the first category—lacking transfer.

> Indication lacking transfer is thought to be of two kinds because of its having **inclusion** and **indirect expression.** (3a)
> (3b) When another object is implied for the sake of a meaning that needs to establish itself, that (4a) is inclusion. Now, indirect expression is thought to be the opposite of this. (69)

The commentary he gives on Verse 3a is mostly a repetition and not very illuminating, simply pointing out that the two varieties are defined in terms of the relationship with another meaning. Thus he inserts a rhetorical question: what are these two types of indication? While this digression does not give much insight into the meanings of the newly introduced terms, the point of the rhetoric is to show the role of the first half of the verse, which is to introduce the division. The next half of the third verse and first half of the fourth together expand on the two terms.

Indication lacking transfer: Inclusion

Mukula defines **inclusion** as "another object is implied for the sake of a meaning's being established" and **indirect expression** as being its opposite (69). His explanation of inclusion involves the term "implied" (*ākṣepa*), which is influenced by philosophical literature. He does not use it in the sense that earlier aesthetic theorists like Bhāmaha and Daṇḍin do, which is as a particular figure of speech.[19] Rather, here, "implying" refers to a kind of reasoning which is often related to the epistemic instrument known of **postulation** (***arthāpatti***), which we will explain below. The term "imply" has already appeared earlier, in the explanation of how indication implies a particular cow from the primary meaning of COWHOOD. And, in fact, Mukula reminds us of this by now specifying that this previous example is a case of inclusion, where there is a particular which is implied.

Given the next example which Mukula gives to explain inclusion, it seems that he thinks there is a connection between implying, postulation, and indication. Further supporting this view, Mukula says that the same kind of inclusion which occurs in the case of the cow also occurs in the case of the sentence "Fat Devadatta does not eat during the day." This sentence is a stock example of postulation.[20] Postulation works by drawing a conclusion given an incongruity between newly acquired knowledge and something else already known.[21] More precisely, an incongruity arises because a new cognition, due to testimony or some other epistemic instrument, is in apparent conflict with another, already accepted cognition. The appropriate resolution is determined by conceptual connections. A schema below represents how postulation functions:

"*q*" (or *q*) is postulated from "*p*" and *m* if and only if
1 "*p*" is a testimonially given utterance and *m* is an already established fact.
2 The postulation of "*q*" (or *q*) is required to make "*p*" compatible with *m*.

There must be an incompatibility, an incongruity, between the linguistically given piece of knowledge ("*p*"), which is known through the epistemic instrument of testimony, and some other thing which is already known, *m*. The paradigmatic case of postulation based on hearing a sentence is that, on hearing "Fat Devadatta does not eat during the day," one will postulate and thereby come to know that Devadatta eats at night (or the sentence "Devadatta eats at night.") Whether you understand the sentence ("*q*") or simply the facts (*q*) depends on one's position on details of postulation—details which Mukula intentionally avoids, again, aiming to make his presentation amenable to everyone.[22]

Mukula's main point is that the phrase "eats at night" (or the fact that Devadatta eats at night) is necessary to complete an incomplete epistemic instrument. In other words, without the indicated meaning, the sentence is not testimonially adequate. Although he does not expand on why the sentence without its indicated meaning is not an incomplete means of knowledge, the reason is hinted at when he says that "fatness" must be established by its cause being implied. There must be a cause of being fat, and the sentence has just negated the usual cause—eating during the day. Further, it's part of the background of this case that we also know Devadatta isn't drinking an elixir (some kind of medicinal drink—today, we might think of someone drinking protein shakes instead). If we could see Devadatta, for instance, drinking elixir, we wouldn't need to postulate any additional meaning. We could simply look at him sipping his drink and say, "Fat Devadatta does not eat during the day." However, for this sentence to work as an example, Devadatta needs to be out of our perceptual range (and we also shouldn't be able to draw any inferences based on knowledge of his diet). So, here is how the case would go according to the schema above:

1 "Fat Devadatta does not eat during the day" is a testimonially given utterance and *that fatness has a cause* is an already established fact.
2 The postulation of "he eats at night" (or *he eats at night*) is required to make "Fat Devadatta does not eat during the day" compatible with the fact *that fatness has a cause.*

Putting things this way, we can see that (2) fails unless we make explicit that Devadatta does not drink during the day, that the cause of fatness includes eating and drinking, as well as that there are times during which eating and drinking can happen. With the assumption of a limited space of possible times for eating (day or night) and causes for being fat (eating or drinking), the negation of eating during the day and drinking during the day and night results in the conclusion that Devadatta eats at night.[23] This is how conceptual connections determine the resolution to postulation.

Finally, the structure of this example (and the case of the particular cow just previous) is important for understanding indirect expression which follows. When a particular cow is implied or indicated from the meaning of "cow" (COWHOOD), the relationship between the cow and COWHOOD is inherence—a particular cow has within itself the universal property. Thus, when referring to the particular cow, you are also referring to the universal. The universal is "included" within the particular. Likewise, on Mukula's understanding, the cause of fatness is "included" with the meaning of "fat." Here inclusion has a less metaphysical sense and is more conceptual—the idea is that the indicated meaning does not replace the primary meaning but augments it.[24] Again, in terms of postulation:

1 "The cow is to be sacrificially bound" is a testimonially given utterance and *that the sacrifice requires a means to be completed* is an already established fact.
2 The postulation of "particular cow" (or *a particular cow*) is required to make "The cow is to be sacrificially bound" compatible with the fact *that the sacrifice requires a means to be completed.*

As in the Devadatta example, there are further assumptions which must be involved for the indicated meaning to be a matter of postulation. We must assume that the meaning of "cow" is a universal, that a universal alone is not a means of completing a sacrifice, and then we must assume that there is a limited set of possibilities for the indicated meaning of cow. If the meaning is not (merely) the universal, then how do we know it is the particular (rather than a property, an action, etc.) Mukula will discuss the relationship between the primary and indicated meaning in more detail later.

At this point, though, it is important to recognize that this category of indication, that is, inclusion, which is grounded in the epistemic instrument postulation, does a lot of work in his argument against suggestion which will come later. Not only does inclusion allow the primary meaning to be retained as part of the indicated meaning, but inclusion turns on the idea that this primary meaning must be established—in a sense, *justified*, by the indicated meaning. There is a way in which, without the indicated meaning, the primary meaning is left incomplete, not making sense, not being used for its full purpose. And moreover, there is an instrumentality to the primary meaning: the utterance of "cow" is to bring about the cognition of a universal, which is not the final aim of the sentence, but is a means to bringing about a cognition of a particular cow. This idea, that the primary meaning has a subordinate relationship to the indicated meaning, will also be crucial for Mukula's argument against Ānandavardhana, who thinks that this dependence relationship is found between the primary meaning and the suggested meaning.

Indication lacking transfer: Indirect expression

In contrast to inclusion, rather than including a new meaning within the primary meaning, indirect expression replaces the primary meaning. Returning to the classic example "The village is on the Ganges," Mukula explains that the natural meaning—that is, the primary meaning—of "Ganges," which is the specific Ganges river, is replaced with the indicated meaning, the bank—the land adjacent to the river. The primary meaning cannot remain part of the indicated meaning or there will still be a problem as to how a village is supported by a river.

As for postulation, Mukula does not say anything about its relationship to indirect expression. In fact, there will be no more explicit discussion of postulation in the rest of the *Fundamentals*, although he continues to use the words for "implies" and "implying," which are here associated with postulation.[25] However, if we pay attention to the structure of indication on Mukula's account—it involves some incongruity which must be repaired by a further meaning—I think we can see that postulation underlies how he understands the interpretive process. Thus rather than speculatively identify some new function, suggestion, we can look to ordinary epistemic resources for an account of meaning:

1 "The village is on the Ganges" is a testimonially given utterance and *that Ganges does not support villages* is an already established fact.
2 The postulation of "the bank of" (or *the bank*) is required to make "The village is on the Ganges" compatible with the fact *that Ganges does not support villages.*

While the relationship between the primary and indicated meaning is not inclusion but rather indirect expression, we can see a possible role for postulation. We are not looking to establish "Ganges" in its primary meaning, but by postulating a closely related meaning, we can make sense out of the word's occurrence in the sentence. The basis for understanding "the bank of" is that this phrase (or its attendant meaning) is the one which will resolve the problem with the primary meaning.

Verses 4b–5a

Turning to the category of indication involving transfer, Mukula subdivides it into two varieties which are each themselves subdivided into two.

> Indication involving transfer is divided into four kinds because each of its divisions, transfer of properties and transfer in general, are subdivided into superimposition and absorption. (70)

Figure 2 illustrates the relationship between these subdivisions within indication involving transfer and the other major category, indication lacking transfer.

In the case of indication involving transfer, Mukula's focus is the relationship between the **subjects** and **objects of comparison**. To understand these terms, consider the sentence

16 Your face is the moon.

In this sentence (a common trope in Indian poetry), the face is the subject of comparison and the moon is the object. Whether there is a relationship between a subject and object of comparison determines the first major difference among cases of indication involving transfer. When there is such

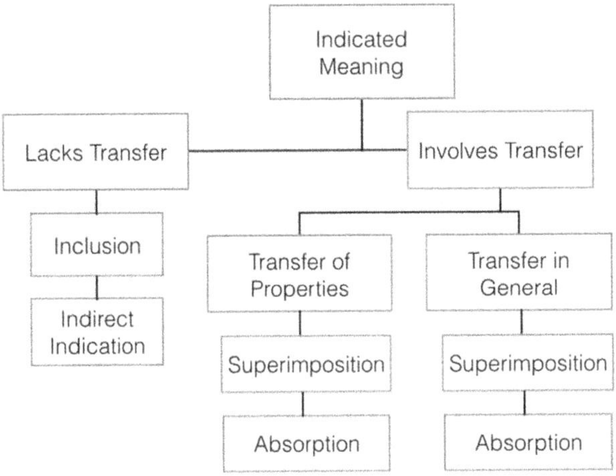

Figure 2 Indication involving transfer.

a relationship, we have **transfer of properties.** However, not all sentences have such a relationship, as we see in the category **of transfer in general**.

Further, whether or not there is this relationship, we can also distinguish ways in which we understand the referents of words. Does their ordinary nature remain in our awareness, or is it entirely obscured by the figurative meaning? Put another way, sometimes we talk about "frozen" metaphors where there is no sense that we are even talking metaphorically, because it has become so commonplace, such as

17 The hockey team was on fire this season.

In this sentence, the expression "on fire" does not mean that the hockey team was engulfed in flames, but that they were doing well. This expression perhaps originated because of the similarity between the way in which fire consumes energetically and people perform. Today, though, when using the expression, there is not typically a sense of its being figurative. In Mukula's terms, its figurative nature has been subject to **absorption**. In cases where there is not such absorption, but there is an apparent difference between, say, real fire and the indicated meaning of "fire," he calls these **superimposition**.

Indication involving transfer in general

Mukula defines indication involving transfer in general through contrast with transfer-involving properties. This is because what is transferred in this category may be anything other than a property. The key feature unifying these examples is that there is no relevant similarity between the referents of the words, understood in their primary nature.[26] Mukula argues that in an example like "Ghee is life" there are no properties which are taken to be similar between ghee and life. Ghee, a kind of clarified butter, is yellow, has a certain flavor, is a liquid, but none of these properties are similar to life. Rather, when eaten, ghee is the cause of long life, or at least is thought to be in Mukula's context. Because there is this relationship of cause and effect, "ghee" can be equated with long life. In the twenty-first century, with the ubiquity of coffee shops in the United States and elsewhere, one might say

18 Coffee is energy.

It is not coffee itself that is energy, nor is it that coffee is like energy in its properties (being a liquid, being sold at overpriced cafés, etc.). Rather, "coffee" is used to refer to the effects of coffee, its giving energy to a person.

Transfer of properties and an objection

Indication involving transfer of properties is closer to the paradigmatic sense of "metaphor" in Western rhetoric, as is clear with the example Mukula gives: "The Punjabi is an ox," discussed above. This section mostly reiterates what he has already said. His main point is just that in this variety of transfer there is similarity, and transfer occurs in virtue of these similarities already explained.

Mukula also brings up a potential objection. Perhaps, someone says, there is only transfer of words but not meaning. He doesn't identify the objector, and it is possible that the "some" here is only a rhetorical device intended to dispel a potential objection, but doesn't refer to any particular person. Mukula's main point in responding to the objection is that transfer of words and transfer of meaning are inseparable. But who would have thought they are not? One possibility is found in Bhartṛhari's discussion of the difference between primary and secondary meaning in the *Treatise on Sentences and Words*, starting at 2.250.[27] He distinguishes between transfer of words and transfer of meaning, using the same Sanskrit terminology as Mukula, using the example of "ox" for an actual ox and for a Punjabi. Transfer of a word means that the sound "ox" is used for two objects, an animal characterized by OXHOOD, and a Punjabi, who has some property (like dullness) that oxen also have. Transfer of meaning has two aspects for Bhartṛhari. The sound "ox," which we use as a word, has two meanings. The first is its nature (*sva-rūpa*) as a word. Put another way, this nature is what allows a particular sound to be used linguistically. It is the fact that "ox" is a type, or a sign, and not merely a sound. This nature is present in the use of "ox" for an actual ox as well as a Punjabi, since we are using the same word type in both cases. The second kind of meaning is known as the external object (*bāhyârtha*), which is COWHOOD. This meaning is also present in both cases, in some sense. The real ox certainly has it, and the Punjabi is characterized in a way that he is said to have something in common with things that have OXHOOD. Below is a schema of this view, using /ox/ to represent the sound and "ox" to represent the word type. Because in the secondary case, the same sound, the same word type, and the same external meaning are derivatively used for the Punjabi as in the primary case, this is transfer (subscripts show identity).

1 Primary meaning: $/ox/_1$→ $“ox”_1$ → OXHOOD_1 → real ox
2 Secondary meaning: $/ox/_1$ →$”ox”_1$ → OXHOOD_1 → Punjabi

However, Bhartṛhari argues that some thinkers (which he does not identify) deny the difference between primary and secondary meanings.[28] Instead, they argue that there is only the primary meaning. On this view, neither the real ox nor a Punjabi is the primary meaning associated with the sound /ox/. So there cannot be any "transfer" from a primary to a secondary meaning. However, if these thinkers believe that there is a single sound /ox/ which is applied in different ways (rather than arguing that there are differences in the sound /ox/ used for an ox and used for a Punjabi), then they will accept transfer of words. Their view would then be

1 Contextual meaning: $/ox/_1$→ $“ox”_1$ → OXHOOD → real ox
2 Contextual meaning: $/ox/_1$ →$”ox”_2$ → dullness, laziness → Punjabi

On this reconstruction, the same sound is used for a real cow and a Punjabi, but there is no transfer of meaning in either sense.[29] The ox is understood in the sense of having a universal and the Punjabi in a different sense, of being dull and lazy. Perhaps such a view could belong to some Prābhākara Mīmāṃsakas, whose views about sentence meaning we will encounter later. However, as Bhartṛhari is scant on details, and Mukula even more so, the reconstruction and historical identification are merely suggestive. However, if this understanding of the objection is correct, we can see why Mukula spends little time on it. His assumption throughout the text is that language has two functions, the primary and the indicatory. That view is fundamental to what he has to say is accepted by his interlocutor, Ānandavardhana, and even though there are some who might argue against it, this treatise is not the place to air that disagreement.

Absorption: Transfer in general

Mukula gives two examples of absorption, in which the difference between two meanings is concealed, one for transfer in general and one for transfer-involving properties. Absorption for transfer in general is exemplified by "Pañcālas."[30] In Mukula's time, the word *pañcālāḥ* (which is plural) was used to refer to the people living in the north where an earlier Vedic-era people lived. However, no one would have thought of this as a "figurative" or otherwise unusual use of the word, making it a case of absorption. It is akin to what we might call a "conventionalized" or "frozen" use of a word previously recognizably nonliteral, just like "on fire," earlier. Mukula explains this case as being **intermediated indirect expression**, in which there are two stages of indication. Traditionally, *dvi-repha* is an example of this, since the word literally means "word having two r's" and has come to mean "bee" because the Sanskrit for "bee" is *bhramara*, a word which has two r's. (The translation has *dvi-repha* as "two e's" because of the happy coincidence that "bee" in English has two "e"s.) Mukula identifies "Pañcālas" as a case of transfer in general, since the earliest people, the place, and the current people group are not related by similar properties, but by another relationship. That relationship is not cause and effect, as in the example "Ghee is life" but is, instead, association. Mukula's analysis of this kind of indication can be represented as below (where "p" refers to primary function and "i_1" and "i_2" to the two stages of indicatory function):

"Pañcālas" $_{p}\rightarrow$ Pañcāla people $_{i1}\rightarrow$ region Pañcālas lived $_{i2}\rightarrow$ Pañcāla descendants

An analogous case familiar to modern readers might be the frequent adaptation of place names derived from people's names to refer to their inhabitants, such as changing "Bolivia" to "Bolivian," although this involves a grammatical transformation (on which more below).

The connection between the two indicated meanings (the region and the people) is one of contiguity, so perhaps the closest example might be metonymies such as *Zhongnanhai*
for the government of China:

"*Zhongnanhai*" $_{p}\rightarrow$ a lake $_{i1}\rightarrow$ imperial garden next to lake $_{i2}\rightarrow$ government located where imperial garden used to be.

The fact that so many examples which come to mind (at least in English) involve obvious grammatical transformation ("Bolivia" to "Bolivian") points to another issue related to this case. There is a grammatical argument to take the word "Pañcālas" for the descendants as a different one than the word for the place. Mukula does not address this point, but the larger question here is when to consider two token utterances of a word as belonging to the same word type (as we saw in the discussion of transfer of word and meaning). Words are said to be **homonyms** when they have the same sound but are different word **types**. In contrast, the same word type which has different meanings is **polysemous.** Some cases are clear: "Bark" as an action of a dog and "bark" as the outside of a tree are homonyms. However, when word meanings are related, it is difficult to determine whether two-word **tokens** (i.e., particular uses in a context) belong to the same word type. Is "drive" in the sense of driving a vehicle the same word type (and thus polysemous) as "drive" used for driving a herd of cattle? Or are these two homonyms?

This distinction is important for the case at hand. Specific to Sanskrit here, to simplify over some complex grammatical discussion, there is a rule which allows the lengthened long *ā* to be deleted (in a process called *lup*, or elision).[31] The process is roughly as follows:

1 *pañcāla* + plural ending → *pañcāl**āḥ*** (the many Pañcāla people)
2 *pañcālāḥ* + derivative → ***pā**ñcālāḥ* (the home of the many Pañcāla people)
3 *pāñcālāḥ* - derivative → ***pa**ñcālāḥ* (the home of the many Pañcāla people)

Absorption: Transfer of properties

Transfer of properties where there is absorption is also exemplified by a word: "Ruler" (*rājan*). Mukula says that "ruler" is used in a secondary sense for members of the servant class (*śūdra*), whereas it is only applicable in a primary sense to members of the governing class, or *kṣatriya*. Whatever the actual historical development of these terms, on Mukula's explanation, "ruler" has a single primary application and other applications are derivative, or secondary, due to properties which others share with the primary referent. Here, as in other places, his example draws on points already made by Mīmāṃsakas, and it is in this context that we see the religious implications for Mukula's theory of communication (which he has emphasized from the outset). In *Exposition on Ritual Practice* 2.3.3, Kumārila explicitly addresses the question of whether the basis for using the term *rājan* is a Kṣatriya or simply someone who functions like a *rājan*.[32]

This question arises in considering who is authorized to perform a particular sacrifice (the *rāja-sūya*): only Kṣatriyas or others too? Mukula echoes the definition, verbatim, of *rājan* given by Kumārila's opponent, who thinks that more than just Kṣatriyas (though certainly not the low-caste Śūdra) should be allowed to perform the sacrifice. The opponent's reasoning is that there is a secondary meaning for *rājan* which includes them: someone who guards a community. While Kumārila agrees with that general point (broadly speaking—there are some nuanced disagreements about etymology and the role of local conventions) his point is that, in the context of the particular ritual, the primary meaning carries greater weight than the secondary. Even though Mukula does not take a position on the broader ritual question, here again we see the epistemological importance for knowing the referential relationship between about words and their objects, and understanding secondary meaning.

Finally, Mukula observes that the relationship between "ruler" and its original, primary meaning is arrived at through reflection. He doesn't say more about this reflection other than it should be "careful" (*vicāraṇa*). However, given the existence of a large literature dedicated to etymology, *nirukta*, which forms one of the "limbs" of Vedic study, Mukula need not reproduce these considerations here. His main point has been made: sometimes indicated meanings are not apparent to speakers and hearers as being secondary, but despite this, with sufficient analytical skill, it is possible to trace a relationship between the indicated and primary meaning.

Mukula now concludes the discussion of absorption and also the first analysis of indication as a whole. He has demonstrated that there are six kinds of indication, focusing upon several ways in which the indicated meaning is related to the primary meaning: whether related by similarity or not, and whether it obscures the primary meaning or not. He has also shown that the epistemic instrument of postulation can be involved in at least one category of indication. In what follows, he will shift his focus on these same six varieties of indication. From this point on, he will be looking at what we might call the "semantic distance" between primary and indicated meaning. How distinct are these meanings, and in what cases? He will distinguish between cases of indication where the indicated meaning is semantically imbued by the primary meaning and those cases which are not. This idea, originally introduced in the context of primary meanings being "semantically imbued" by their distinguishing features, will be crucial for Mukula in his arguments against Ānandavardhana.

Verses 5b–6a

Mukula starts his second analysis from the vantage point of three fundamental categories of indication: lacking transfer, transfer in general, transfer of properties.

> In cases of extreme **distinction**, there is indication lacking transfer. But in cases where distinction is intermediate, it is superimposed (5)
> In cases where the distinction is dissolved, indication is absorbed because of being conventional and closer in meaning (than the intermediate) (73)

His entire analysis in this second section can be connected to his first analysis, as in Table 5: Mukula's Complete Analysis of Indication (empty cells are places where his analysis is not stated explicitly). The purpose of this second analysis is to explain what happens to our understanding of the primary meaning in these cases. Since on Ānandavardhana's account, suggestion is present along with the primary meaning, and does not displace it, Mukula needs to show that indication is able to occur in the same way.

Table 5 Mukula's complete analysis of indication

First analysis		Kind of indication	Second analysis	
Indication's relationship with transfer	**Basis for transfer**	**Relationship between meanings**	**Relationship between meanings has . . .**	**Semantic distance is . . .**
Lacking transfer	None	Indirect expression *Ganges*	No semantic imbuing	Extreme
	None	Inclusion *Cow* *Devadatta*	No semantic imbuing	
Transfer	Properties	Superimposition *Peasant*	Semantic imbuing	Intermediate
		Absorption *Ruler*		
	General	Superimposition *Ghee*		Dissolved
		Absorption *Pañcālas* *That ox*		

Degrees of semantic distinctness: The village is on the Ganges

Mukula starts with the two varieties of indication lacking transfer: inclusion and indirect indication. He introduces a new way to distinguish between types of indication: whether the indicated meaning is "semantically imbued" (*uparakta*) or not by the primary meaning (what he calls here the "indicating meaning"). This term, as noted earlier in the context of word meanings, literally means "shaded" or "colored." It is not found in Ānandavardhana's discussion of suggestion. The idea may be, as much else is in Mukula, due to Bhartṛhari, who compares the way words communicate meanings to how a crystal takes on the colors of things it is put next to, such as a red flower. Bhartṛhari uses this image to explain how words take on meanings of other words in the context of a sentence—their meanings are, like a crystal, "tinged" by the meanings in their context.[33] Whether this particular simile is what Mukula has in mind or not, his concept of semantic imbuing allows him likewise to explain why words have different shades of meaning in different contexts.

However, having established that such semantic imbuing is at work in primary meanings, he now puts it to use in indication. In fact, he divides examples which do and do not have semantic imbuing into the same groups, respectively, as inclusion and indirect expression. Thus, examples which have semantic imbuing are also examples of inclusion. And cases of inclusion will be cases where Ānandavardhana has identified suggestion. Semantic imbuing is then a way for Mukula to explain the cognitive content, the meaning, that Ānandavardhana argues, is due to suggestion. It may be easier to understand cases without semantic imbuing through contrast with those cases which have them. Mukula offers the same sentence type, "The village is on the Ganges," as an example which can have or fail to have semantic imbuing in different contexts. The speaker's aim in uttering the sentence in each context is what distinguishes them. In a context when the speaker wants to refer to a village in virtue of its being nestled right up against the Ganges river, there is semantic imbuing.

The reason Mukula uses this single example in several ways is to illustrate how context and speaker intention impact meaning, which is relevant to Ānandavardhana's argument. Thus we need to consider Ānandavardhana's explanation of the primary and secondary functions of words, found in *Light on Suggestion* 3.33. In this section, Ānandavardhana is arguing that suggestion is different from the primary and secondary (what Mukula calls "indicatory") functions in two ways: in nature (*svarūpatā*) and in object (*viṣayata*).[34] Putting things in terms of set functions can make the argument clear. (Of course, we need to remember that Ānandavardhana is thinking in terms of *cognition* not simply formal mapping relationships.) The nature of these functions is the manner in which they are related to their meanings, their way of being a function or operation (*vṛtti*). The object is the result of the function, of the content of the resulting cognition.

Ānandavardhana has identified three functions—the primary, secondary, and suggestive—which, in contemporary terms, map members of one set to another.[35] One way to understand his argument is these functions do not have coextensive domains and the assignment functions do not map in the same way. In what follows, we will use the simple example of "The village is on the Ganges," and extrapolate how it might communicate a suggested meaning, even though Ānandavardhana himself never uses it to illustrate suggestion.[36] The primary function (Figure 3) maps words to meanings in a one-to-one manner, so that for every word, it is assigned to a single meaning. Thus its nature is directly assigning words to meanings and its object is meanings, which are things in the world. On the left is the domain of language, and on the right is the codomain of objects in the world.[37] The primary function maps "Ganges" onto the Ganges stream itself, and not the riverbank, the nearby village, or the property of holiness. The secondary meaning function, in contrast (Figure 4), does not map the word onto a meaning directly, but maps the Ganges stream onto the bank. Put another way, it takes the result of the first function as input and maps that to another object.[38] Thus it is a different function than the primary, even though it is related to the primary function (since it requires that output for its domain).[39] Finally, suggestion, or the suggestive function, (Figure 5) maps "Ganges" onto the property of holiness, rather than the Ganges stream or riverbank. Thus it has a different object than the primary meaning function and the secondary meaning function. But it is like the primary meaning in that it maps directly from the domain of words to objects, whereas the secondary meaning operates on meanings. Thus, Ānandavardhana concludes that since suggested meaning has a different object than primary meaning and a different nature than secondary meaning it cannot be reduced to either. In what follows, Mukula will argue that the object of the suggestive function can, in fact, also be attributed to the secondary function.[40]

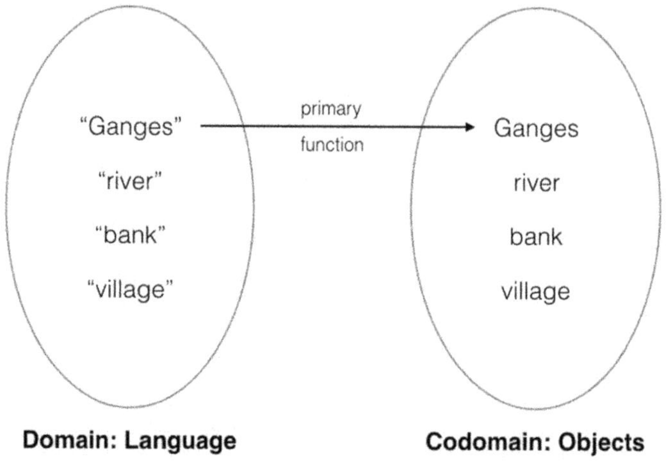

Figure 3 Ānandavardhana's primary function.

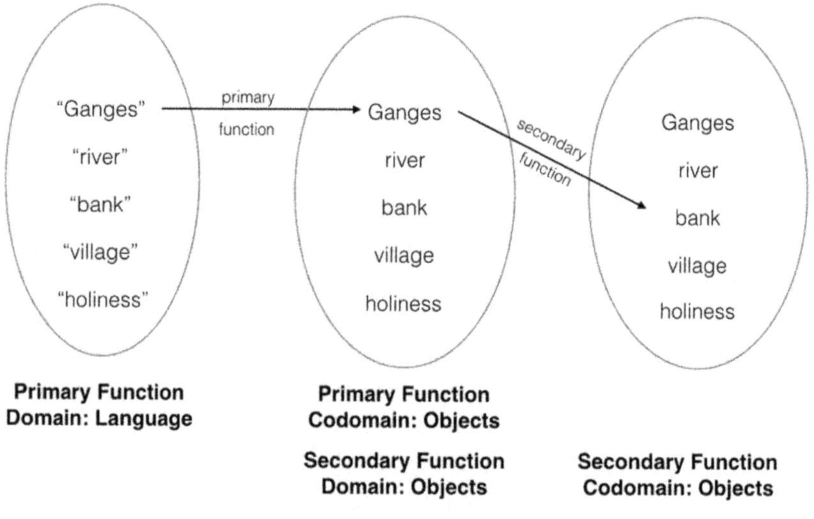

Figure 4 Ānandavardhana's secondary function.

Extreme distinction: Indication without transfer

Mukula's discussion of "The village is on the Ganges" proceeds by distinguishing between its meanings in different contexts. In the first case, the speaker's aim is to distinguish one village from another, when there is one village which is near the Ganges river and another village near

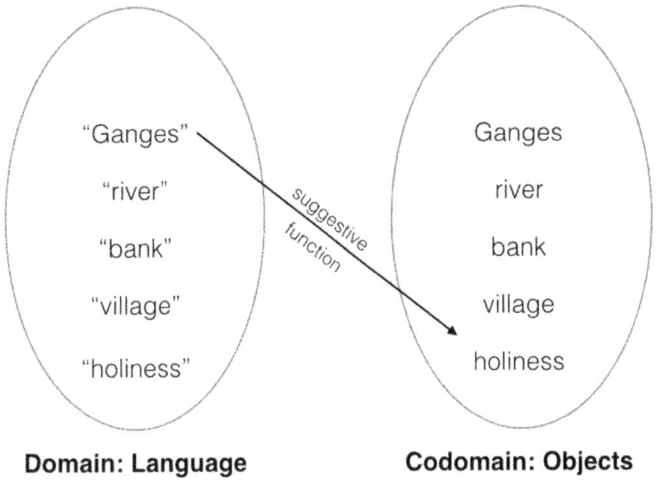

Figure 5 Ānandavardhana's suggestive function.

the Vitastā (modern-day Jhelum River, running between Pakistan and Kashmir). Because the intention is simply to point out where the first village is, there is no semantic imbuing. This is simply indication without transfer, as has been already explained. He notes that the earlier example of inclusion, "Fat Devadatta does not eat during the day," which is the other example of indication lacking transfer, works in the same way. In other words, the basis for the indicated meaning is not part of the meaning of what is indicated. A village being situated in a particular place does not involve the properties of the Ganges river, nor does eating at night involve a lack of daytime eating by a stout person. However, given the right context, the village or the eating at night can be understood by, respectively, the river or the lack of eating. Yet, we should not take Mukula to be saying that these two cases work precisely the same way, since the case of the Ganges is indirect expression and the case of Devadatta is inclusion. His point is merely that the indicated meanings in these cases do not involve semantic imbuing.

Intermediate and dissolved distinctions: Indication involving transfer

In contrast, when there is an intention to express a semantic imbuing, then the character of the river—in this case, the Ganges—does have an influence in how the hearer understands the indicated meaning of "bank."

Mukula will discuss this later when he directly takes up the crucial (and complex) role of speaker intention, but for now he simply notes that the river's nature is "not concealed." We might think of the difference between a server using "ham sandwich" to pick out the customer eating a ham sandwich and using the term to communicate some relationship between the sandwich and the customer. In the first case, a manager might say, "The ham sandwich is waiting for his check" to a distracted server. The sentence, on Mukula's understanding, would be an example of indirect expression, which is lacking transfer: "The person eating the ham sandwich is waiting for his check."

19a The ham sandwich is waiting for his check.
Indicated: The *person eating the* ham sandwich is waiting for his check.
Purpose: Pick out the customer eating the ham sandwich and not the turkey club.

Likewise, saying that the village is on the Ganges and not the Vitasta, is like pointing out the ham sandwich (and not the turkey club) wants their check. There is no semantic imbuing here.

20a The village is on the Ganges.
Indicated: The village is on the *bank of the* Ganges.
Purpose: Pick out the village on the Ganges and not the Vitasta.

A case—though unusual—where one might transfer properties from the meaning of "ham sandwich" could be as follows: the customer is an unusually charismatic and loud person, one who is often called a "ham." By saying "The ham sandwich is waiting for his check," the manager doesn't want to just pick out the customer, but also to communicate that he's waiting in a very dramatic manner (perhaps sighing and looking around the room). Something to do with the properties of the thing closely related to the ham sandwich shapes our understanding of the customer.[41]

19b The ham sandwich is waiting for his check.
Indicated: The *person who is loud and charismatic like a ham* is waiting for his check.
Purpose: Pick out the charismatic customer.

Mukula explains how in some situations, the properties of the Ganges river properties can semantically imbue the riverbank. He says that because the river and the village are close enough together, we can understand the bank as sharing in the properties. Later he will make explicit that these properties include holiness and beauty.

20b The village is on the Ganges.
Indicated: The village is on the *holy and beautiful bank of the* Ganges.
Purpose: Pick out the village which shares in the Ganges' properties.

Now we can see why semantic imbuing is important to Mukula's response to suggestion as a third linguistic function. In this example, though his full reasoning is yet to be developed, he claims that indication can sometimes communicate properties associated with the primary meaning of the word, by way of the indicated meaning. If true, this makes suggestion unnecessary. In order for his theory to be a true alternative to suggestion, he cannot simply be arguing that indication has two (unrelated) results, one being the bank, the other being holiness. This would mean that he's merely renamed a third function without truly reducing it. Instead, he argues that there is a way in which the bank itself is understood which leads us to conceive of it in a particular way. One way to represent this is that the concept *bank* is a structured entity, including at least a location and some properties (see Figure 6). In this context, the concept *bank* is understood as being located near to the Ganges river. Assuming that contiguity licenses property transfer, then bank is also understood as having some properties of the Ganges river, in particular its holiness. In contrast, in other contexts, *bank* is understood differently, for instance, not as near the Ganges (and

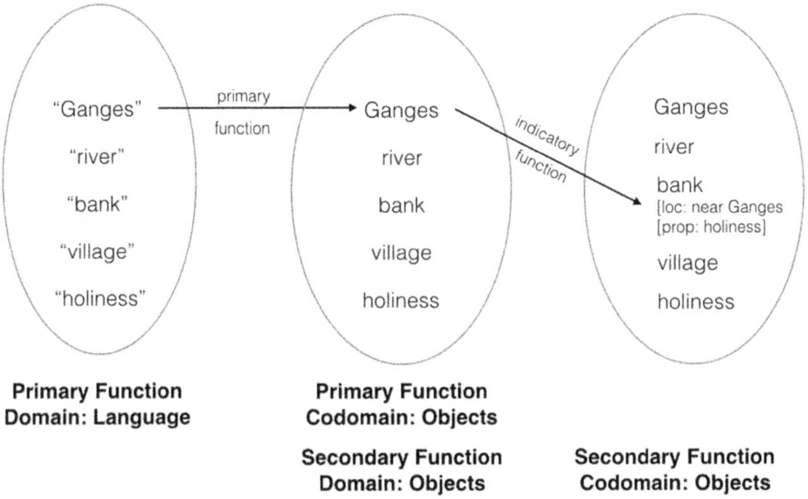

Figure 6 Mukula's indicatory function with semantic imbuing.

thus licensing property transfer) but as far from the Vitastā (which does not license transfer).[42]

Mukula's final analysis of the sentence type, "The village is on the Ganges," is that it can be a case of absorption. Consider the sandwich sentence again. Suppose that a customer eating a ham sandwich had an argument over dinner and, like the comedic pie-in-the-face trope, his dinner partner smushes the sandwich in his face. The customer sadly raises his hand and says, "check, please." Now, when the manager says, "The ham sandwich is waiting for his check," the sandwich and the customer are very closely related!

19d The ham sandwich is waiting for his check.
Indicated: The *customer with a ham sandwich on his face* is waiting for his check
Purpose: Pick out the customer who is closely related to the ham sandwich.

This example is like the final use of "The village is on the Ganges," where what is to be communicated is the very close relationship of the Ganges river and the riverbank. This is where a village is nestled right up against the Ganges, so close that it makes sense to simply say "the Ganges" and omit "the bank." In fact, Mukula says that the meaning which is understood by the hearer has no reference to the bank, since the bank has been "obscured" by the river.

20b The village is on the Ganges.
Indicated: The village is on the Ganges *directly*.
Purpose: Pick out the village which is directly right against the Ganges.

Mukula has now illustrated all three varieties defined in the verse—indication without transfer, indication with transfer, and absorption—by discussing a single sentence in different contexts. In the verse, he has identified cases which are "absorbed" as belonging to the category where a distinction is dissolved due to conventional use and closely related meanings. However, this last example of absorption does not refer to convention as an explanation, only the close proximity of the river and the bank (and thus the closeness of the meanings, in this case). This suggests that being conventional or being near in meaning can be the basis for absorption, and that both together are not necessary.

Degrees of semantic distinctness: Transfer of properties

Turning to indication involving transfer of properties, Mukula again returns to previous examples. Here, the insulting metaphor, "The Punjabi is an ox," along with a similar example, "This ox!" illustrates the semantic distance in cases where indication depends on resemblance. Again Mukula explains meaning in terms of a speaker's desire to express something. Here, in the first example, a speaker wants to communicate that a Punjabi is similar to an ox. This allows for transfer of an ox's qualities onto the Punjabi. However, in this sentence, the hearer doesn't mistake a Punjabi for an ox, or take the identification as complete.

In contrast, the second sentence, "This ox!" stresses the identity between the Punjabi and an ox. Mukula thinks that this allows for the properties of the Punjabi to be absorbed into the ox's properties. This sentence is different than the first illustration, which says "Punjabi" (*vāhīka*). Here, the speaker uses a demonstrative pronoun, "this" (*ayam*), perhaps to efface any difference which would be called to mind by using a word referring to human beings.[43] Mukula argues that the difference between the two sentences is that the properties in the ox are prominent (*utkaṭa*). The contrast between the cases is that in the second, by not referring to the Punjabi except through a pronoun, the ox-properties are linguistically brought to mind, but not the Punjabi's properties.

Rather than developing the previous examples of "Pañcālas" and "ruler," Mukula simply states that things are likewise, *ceteris paribus*, for them. That is, under the right circumstances, in which convention has made their use ordinary, or where meanings are very closely related, someone hearing these words used would have no cognition of any difference between a primary and indicated meaning. This explains why Mukula has said earlier that it requires reflection in order to ascertain the relationship between "ruler" used for a member of the warrior class and "ruler" used for other classes. When it has become conventionalized, the term "ruler" doesn't bring to mind any distinction between these uses.

Here we might consider the ham sandwich sentence again. When the restaurant has seen a customer (let's call him Bruce) regularly for a year, and he almost always eats a ham sandwich, it might be possible to say "The ham sandwich is waiting for his check," whether or not Bruce is at that moment actually eating one. This is a case of absorption due to convention. We could even imagine new servers being hired, after Bruce has decided to become a vegetarian, who call him "ham sandwich" despite never seeing him eat one, simply because that's how everyone in the restaurant refers to their regular.

19c The ham sandwich is waiting for his check.
Indicated: The *customer, Bruce,* is waiting for his check
Purpose: Pick out the customer who usually eats a ham sandwich.

Mukula doesn't explain the relationship of "being closer in meaning and being conventional." For the latter, there is no easy metric to determine when a meaning has become conventional. For the former, Mukula has given three discrete categories: extreme distinction, intermediate distinction, and dissolved distinction, claiming that at a certain point, two meanings become close enough to be categorized as "dissolved." However, Mukula gives no overriding principle for determining semantic distance, only particular exemplifying cases. This is another point in his account where he is content with the fact that there are paradigmatic cases, leaving ones on the boundaries for further investigation.

Objection to indicated meaning

However, this problem, which we might characterize as the "fuzzy boundaries" of secondary meaning, might give rise to some worries. Mukula thus introduces an unnamed opponent, one who seems to share some affinities with Mīmāṃsā philosophers, but who is difficult to entirely identify with any single viewpoint. Their argument relies on the following principles:

1. **Sentence primacy.** A hearer *H* understands the linguistic testimony of speaker *S* only through understanding her sentence meaning.
2. **Compositionality.** A syntactically and semantically unified combination of words (a sentence) causes there to be a sentence meaning.
3. **Derivation.** *H* understands the primary meaning of words through observing patterns of sentences in use.
4. **Fixity.** The word meanings able to be understood through *Derivation* have determinate relationships with their meanings.

The first principle, *Sentence Primacy,* is expressly laid out by Mīmāṃsakas such as Kumārila and Prabhākara. Sentences, not words, are the principle conveyers of meaning. Sentences communicate structured entities. Unlike words which (on the Bhāṭṭa Mīmāṃsā view) convey universals, sentences communicate a qualifier-qualified relationship. Even allowing for the three other kinds of meanings (qualities, actions, named things), none of these entities on their own are sufficient for communication. When a speaker wants to assert, she asserts something sentential. For instance, she asserts *a* is *F*, or *a* is qualified by *F*, where *a* is an individual and *F* is a universal, a property, etc.

Although sentences are the primary unit of communication, *Compositionality* requires that they are constituted by a combination of words, although precisely how composition occurs is the subject of debate, as we will see at Verses 7b–9a below. (The view that sentences are combinations of words is in contrast to Bhartṛhari, whom we will encounter later in Mukula's text, and other burst theorists, who claim that sentences are indivisible.) Word meanings, then, in order to be useful as the constituents of sentences, must have determinate relationships with their meanings. This relationship can be ascertained by watching a speaker utter several sentences in context, according to *Derivation*:

21 Bring the cow.
22 Bring the horse.
23 Feed the cow.
24 Feed the horse.

The relationship between the words "bring," "feed," "cow," and "horse" and their respective objects can then be isolated as the hearer observes the sentences in use.

Finally, given that word meanings have *Fixity* as well as *Compositionality*, we can combine words in a very large number of ways. Hearers need not learn a perhaps infinite number of sentence meanings, only a fixed vocabulary. However, if this is all right, then there is a problem about indicatory meaning. The interlocutor observes that on *Fixity*, words are able to communicate because of this determinate meaning-relationship. "Cow" always means COWHOOD, and "cook" always means the action of cooking, for instance.[44] The interlocutor here accepts four divisions of word meanings, but even four divisions is insufficient for the variability of indicatory meaning. Thus the opponent says that for indicatory meaning, the relationship is "the opposite" of primary meaning; it is variable and not determinate. Depending on the context, "cow" might mean a particular real cow, a clay cow, the metaphorical qualities associated with cows and so on. Thus, the opponent concludes, given that sentences need determinate word meanings to communicate, a hearer's cognition must be of primary meanings in combination, and not the indicatory meaning. The objector does not explain how their view accounts for the apparent phenomena of metaphor, metonymy, and the like. However, they do raise at least two problems for Mukula.

First, what accounts for learning indicatory meanings, if not the process of "positive and negative correlations" (the sentences above when cows and horses are and are not present)? Employing this process, we would come to learn that "Ganges" sometimes refers to a riverbank. One option would be to argue that words have a one-to-many relationship with primary meanings. Thus "Ganges" has at least two meanings: a current of water and a riverbank next to a current of water. However, this option appears to violate *Fixity*. The interlocutor doesn't explain how sentences like "The village is on the Ganges" work, but they do challenge Mukula to explain how we can come to understand such contextually variable meanings.

There is a second problem for Mukula. We have seen that (according to both interlocutor and Mukula) primary word meanings convey the same meaning invariably. Suppose Mukula were to reply that indicatory meaning operates in the same manner. Then, when the word "Ganges" is uttered, the primary function denotes the *Ganges river*, and the indicatory function indicates the *bank*. But if this is the explanation, then we have a problem with this sentence: "The boat is floating on the Ganges." Should we take this to mean "The boat is floating on *the bank of* the Ganges"? This would be a bad consequence, since it lacks semantic intelligibility (which we will discuss in detail later at Verses 7b–9a). However, in order to avoid such a result, the indicatory meaning must depend on something other than, or in addition to, the primary meaning. "Ganges" cannot invariably first mean *Ganges river* and subsequently always indicate *bank*. Otherwise, every time a speaker says "Ganges," no matter the context, she will communicate "bank of the Ganges." Mukula gives his response to this challenge in the next verse. At the same time, his response will continue to undermine reasons to posit a third putative linguistic capacity, suggestion.

Verses 6b–7a

Mukula now replies to the challenge of explaining how primary and indicated meanings are related in a way that allows for both creativity and constraint.

> From reflecting on the distinct natures of speaker, sentence, and expressed meaning. (6)
> six kinds of indication are able to be judged correctly by the thoughtful (6b).

The presence of a collection of factors (*samāgri*) will allow him to avoid the charge that a word must convey the same indicated meaning, if this meaning is to be related to the (context-invariant) denoted meaning. This section is where he begins his polemic against Ānandavardhana in earnest, illustrating how indication can account for poetic examples, a number of which were already analyzed in *Light on Suggestion*.

Six factors and convention

In order to explain what it is that indication depends on, in addition to the primary meaning of a word, Mukula introduces several factors: speaker, **sentence, expressed meaning**, place, time, state, and individuality. Since these seven factors can combine together in a number of ways, Mukula has more options than the two given by his interlocutor—that indication always comes along with the primary word meaning or never arises. The speaker, as we will see, can be not only a poet but also a character in the poem. The distinction between sentence and expressed meaning is important for Mukula, which we will see in more detail when he discusses theories of sentential unity. At this point, though, he defines sentence as "a combination which is a unified meaning made up of words with **syntactic expectancy**." On this definition, the primary meanings of words come together to yield a sentence based on the requirement that words construe together in appropriate grammatical relationships (syntactic expectancy). For instance, if a competent hearer anticipates a direct object based on the primary meaning of an action-denoting word (a verb) and it is lacking, then there fails to be a sentence. When there is such an obstacle to words construing together as a sentence, then the factor of sentence is relevant for indication. In contrast, the expressed meaning is defined as a "range of meaning which depends on the communicative function, either the primary or indicatory function of words." Expressed meaning here is broader than sentence meaning, in that indication may work to resolve problems other than acquiring sentential unity. We will see that indication can work on the basis of an expressed meaning which encompasses indication, for instance, that has worked to resolve problems with sentential unity. Indicated meanings can be input for another stage of the indicative function (as we have seen already with the *dvi-repha* example).

The next four factors are borrowed directly from Ānandavardhana at *Light on Suggestion* 4.7, who in turn is likely drawing on both Buddhist and dramaturgical thought.[45] By drawing directly from his interlocutor's words, Mukula aims to show that the analysis given in favor of suggestion actually supports indication. In his original use of these factors, Ānandavardhana is emphasizing the innumerable varieties of suggestion which depend on the innumerable varieties of the primary meaning. He says,

> An endlessness arises of the primary meaning, taken by itself, that is, even without regard to the suggested meaning, by its very nature. For the nature of things directly expressed, whether they are sentient or insentient, becomes endless from differences in state, differences in place, differences in time, and differences in individuality.[46]

His point is that even primary meaning itself can have innumerable varieties—so, since suggested meaning is dependent upon primary meaning, it, too, can be infinite. Mukula, however, takes this point and employs it in service of his own theory. The factors that explain varieties of primary meaning can explain the varieties of indication. If the primary meaning can be grounded in these factors and produce an innumerable variety of further meanings (erroneously identified as "suggestion"), given that the indicated meaning is closely connected to the primary meaning, we can use the same factors to understand indication.

Of these factors, the first, "state" (*avasthā*) is a term found in dramaturgy, in works such as Bharata's *Science of Dramaturgy* (*Nāṭya-śāstra*), which delineates five states of action within a play.[47] The idea, however, is wider in Ānandavardhana's text. It applies to any changes in a character, such as when Pārvatī appears in different manners throughout *The Origin of the Young God* (*Kumāra-saṃbhava*). We will see Mukula appeal to the notion of state in one of the examples which follows. This factor is frequently found mentioned along with other two factors, place and time (*deśa-kāla*), which are fairly self-evident, though they can be interpreted variously as well: we can distinguish between these factors as belonging to a speaker or else to a character within a poem or a play. "Time" might even refer to the tense of a verb, according to Ānandavardhana.[48] The last factor Ānandavardhana calls "individuality" (*svā-lakṣaṇya*).[49] While this factor receives no explicit discussion or exemplification in either Ānandavardhana or Mukula, it seems to refer to the particular individual nature of, for instance, a character in a poem, because of the unique cluster of properties they possess.[50] This collection of factors can be treated as a whole or each component could be viewed independently. The indicated meaning of a given word varies, depending on differences in these aspects.

In addition to these factors, there is another important element in grounding indication: the ordinary linguistic practice of our predecessors (*vṛddha-vyavahāra*). This is the first place in the text where this important term appears, although Mukula opens the book with a discussion of "ordinary linguistic practice" (*vyavahāra*) and its relationship with determinate cognitions about the relationship between words and their meanings. A crucial concept in linguistic philosophy, ordinary linguistic practice includes not just uttering words but also the behavior which accompanies our utterances. The addition of predecessors (elders, *vṛddha*) emphasizes the role of precedent in determining word meaning.

Summarizing his argument so far, Mukula concludes that the relationship between the primary meaning and the indicated meaning can only be understood because we know how other people before us have used a word. By observing the conditions under which others have used the word "Ganges" to mean bank, we can come to know the relationship between the word and its meaning. Thus our apprehension of the relationship between the primary and indicated meaning is mediated by this set of conditions, through our observing previous uses. This does not—as we will see—preclude new and creative poetic uses. If it did, then the project of responding to the suggestion theorists could not get off the ground. Rather, it introduces an intelligibility constraint. Our indicatory language use cannot be so alien to the usual customs as to preclude its being understood.

Mīmāṃsā Hermeneutics

At this point, Mukula returns to Mīmāṃsā hermeneutics, as he has before, to explain the relationship between indication and convention. Ānandavardhana himself, as McCrea (2008) has shown, makes use of Mīmāṃsā hermeneutics in developing his own theory. Here, Mukula turns this strategy against him, showing that this same framework is a powerful example of analyzing secondary meaning in a manner which preserves its status as an epistemic instrument. Mīmāṃsakas such as Śabara and his commentator, Kumārila, show that such meanings are not only intelligible in light of primary meaning and ordinary linguistic conventions, but these meanings also allow for a distinction between what is intended to be conveyed and what is only subsidiary to that aim. All of these features make Mīmāṃsā linguistic analysis powerful evidence for Mukula's contention that the wide variety of putatively suggested meanings can be accounted for by indication. Further, given that Bhāṭṭa Mīmāṃsakas in particular make heavy use of postulation in their account of secondary meaning, their theoretical apparatus is a natural fit for Mukula's own use of this epistemic instrument.

Mukula begins by quoting Śabara's commentary on Jaimini's aphorisms (abbreviated *MS*) 1.4.22 which identifies the basis for motivating speech (*artha-vāda*) such as "The ritual patron is the sacrificial grass-bed." This sentence, and others like it, uses figurative language to motivate ritual participants to follow Vedic injunctions. Such injunctions, like "Perform the New and Full moon ritual," are taken by Mīmāṃsakas to be testimonial epistemic instruments, conveying knowledge of what cannot be known by perception, inference, or other instruments. They convey knowledge of *dharma*, or human duty, especially with regard to Vedic ritual. Figurative language in the form of motivating speech is a supporting element of testimonial knowledge, and it is important for Śabara (and his later commentator Kumārila) that motivating speech be connected to testimonial knowledge. What Mukula quotes is an adaptation of a longer discussion in this context:

> How is a word used for something else? Now it is by a figurative statement. This is a statement which is due to properties. How is it that from speech which does not express properties, there comes to be properties? We say: it is through what is denoted by the word's own meaning.[51]

Here, Śabara is responding to a worry about how figurative language functions. Since words do not primarily refer to properties on his view, but to universals, how are they able to express properties, in sentences like "The ritual patron is the sacrificial grass-bed"? In that case, the figurative expression is supposed to convey that the ritual patron shares important properties with the sacrificial grass-bed—in particular, that both are central to the ritual. Śabara argues that there is a close relationship between the word's primary meaning and this figurative meaning. Mukula agrees with this emphasis on the primary meaning's role in secondary meaning. He argues that what Śabara is describing is the indicated meaning attaching itself to the primary, or the word's "own" meaning. This expression, "own meaning" (*svârtha*) which will from now on occur frequently in Mukula's text, is shorthand for the meaning which is directly a result of the word, or the primary meaning. In other words, the indicated meaning is closely related to the primary meaning.

Mukula also quotes another, earlier part of Śabara's commentary, at 1.2.22: "Further, indication is just customary speech."[52] This claim comes within the context of a longer discussion of sentences apart from motivating speech which support Vedic injunctions.[53] For Mukula's purposes, this claim supports his contention that there is a connection between indication and the ordinary linguistic practices of our predecessors. His discussion of Śabara's claim that indication is just customary (*laukika*) centers on the term from which "customary" is derived: *loka*, which can mean simply the world and its people, and by extension, what is ordinary. In Śabara's original context, this term is frequently opposed to "Vedic," since Vedic speech is importantly different from human or ordinary speech: it is unauthored. However, as Śabara would argue—and most likely also Mukula—Vedic speech is not an everyday kind of knowledge source, since it is not validated by our usual experiences.[54]

Indication, then, is speech grounded in the usual practices of speakers perceiving objects and naming them, using sentences to communicate desires, and so forth. Mukula goes on to refine the way in which indication works, quoting from Kumārila Bhaṭṭa's *Exposition on Ritual Practice* on *MS* 3.1.12.

> Some figures are conventional because they have a capacity like the primary denotation;
> Some are newly created, some are even without power.

Kumārila uses different examples than Mukula for the three categories. These, just as with Śabara's examples, are mostly drawn from Vedic ritual.[55] In contrast, Mukula focuses on poetry, since it is here that Ānandavardhana claims suggestion is necessary.

An important final point about Kumārila's discussion is relevant for what follows—Kumārila observes that the indicated meanings are not the point of the sentence. They are not intended to be expressed. This relationship between what is predominant and what is subsidiary appears toward the end of this section as Mukula tries to incorporate ***rasa***, which is according to Ānandavardhana the predominant aim of poetic language, into his account of indication. For Ānandavardhana, *rasa*, a term which literally means "flavor" or "sap," is a characteristic aesthetic mood found in the text of a play or poem. There are a number of such moods: the comic, heroic, erotic, terrible, pathetic, compassionate, furious, and wondrous. While the metaphysical status of *rasa* is subject to much discussion, especially after Ānandavardhana, he does not thematize it explicitly, preferring instead to refer to it in the course of analyzing texts. So for him, *rasa* is one of varieties of suggested meanings, and it is thus not an emotion found in the reader or actor. Ānandavardhana argues that *rasa* is the entire point of (excellent) poetry and when it is found in exemplary works, it will be the aim of the communicative act. Mukula, to show that indication can account for *rasa* and its predominant status, argues that some indicated meanings can also be the aim of the communicative act, that is, they can be intended to be what is expressed, and not merely subsidiary.

In the ensuing discussion, Mukula will provide the entire verse context even when treating a single word. This approach echoes Ānandavardhana's preferred method of analysis. But Mukula is not concerned just with individual words, he is also concerned with entire utterances. This, too, connects with Ānandavardhana—in particular, his arguments that suggestion arises at the level of the sentence, not only the word. In *Light on Suggestion*, among the many divisions of suggestion is the distinction between its basis: phonemes, words, sentences, and entire texts. Ānandavardhana argues that suggestion can be grounded in any one of these. As Mukula's focus here is suggestion, he thus sets conventional indication aside in a single sentence by noting simply that "ruler," previously discussed as an example of absorption, is a conventional figure.

Newly created figures

Mukula's first use of a poetic example occurs now, when he cites an anonymous verse also quoted in *Light on Suggestion*:[56]

> Clouds with white cranes whirling extend across the sky,
> smeared with glistening dark color.
> Winds gently sprinkle water. The friends of the clouds cry out joyfully.
> Let all of this be. I am Rāma, whose heart is hardened. I can bear all this.
> But slender Sītā, how will she go on? Oh, alas, queen, stand firm! (66)

Ānandavardhana describes this as an example of suggestion where the primary meaning of "Rāma" is shifted.[57] He identifies only "Rāma" as a word with suggested meaning, but Abhinavagupta's commentary, the *Eye,* discusses the other examples that Mukula analyzes: "Smeared" and "friends of the clouds." Since Abhinavagupta postdates Mukula, perhaps he is responding to Mukula's criticisms. In any case, according to Ānandavardhana, the suggested meaning of "Rāma" includes "various suggested properties."[58] The person speaking here is Rāma, but what is intended is not a tautologous claim ("I am me") but a reference to Rāma's character ("I am like this").

Ānandavardhana does not explain why this meaning is suggested and not indicated, but probably it is because he sees no obstacle in understanding the primary meaning, which is the person Rāma, since it is in fact the person Rāma who is speaking.

Mukula argues that this very fact is the obstacle. The name is immediately understandable to everyone as Rāma's name, meaning saying "I am Rāma" wouldn't be a very informative utterance on the narrator's part. Rather, by referring to himself, Rāma calls to mind the well-known events of his life, like his beloved Sītā's being kidnapped by Rāvaṇa, and other sorrowful situations recounted in the *Rāmayāna*. Mukula doesn't explain how it is that "Rāma" is part of the collection of factors he's introduced to us: speaker, sentence, expressed meaning, etc. His main point with this example is to illustrate the category of newly created indication. He uses other cases to illustrate these, in what follows, but we might surmise that here the important factor is the speaker. Since we know that he is Rāma, this is relevant to bringing about the indicated meaning.

Mukula explains two other words, in addition to "Rāma," which have newly created indicated meanings: "Smeared" and "cloud's friends." For these, as well as "Rāma," he emphasizes that the primary meaning is blocked. In the case of "smeared," he argues that the word in its primary meaning is used for smearing things like saffron paste. In the poetic context, however, the clouds are smearing their brilliant dark color across the sky. This occlusion of the sky's brightness (which partially leaks through the clouds, making them bright yet darkly shining) is similar to the way in which a smeared paint conceals. This similarity licenses indication. The "friends of the clouds" are peacocks, known for their happy bird-song and dancing when rains appear. This makes them, anthropomorphically, friends to the clouds which are harbingers of rain.

These motifs are typical in Sanskrit poetry as part of romantic poetry—the annual monsoons were a time for the well-off to stay indoors and enjoy the company of their lovers.[59] In this romantic atmosphere, Rāma's separation from Sītā (here the poet calls her "Vaidehī," which brings to mind her delicate figure) is made even more difficult. There is a contrast between the joyful cries of peacocks and the movement of the cranes and Rāma's hard heart, stolidly accepting the separation he must endure. Now, the well-known nature of the verses' background plays a role in understanding what is indicated. Mukula reasons that since everyone hearing the verses would know that the speaker is Rāma, there is no reason to think the poet is merely introducing Rāma to us. Rather, the poet wants us to think of all the events of Rāma's life which are sorrowful—just as is the separation from Sītā.

This makes the case of "Rāma" different from "smeared" and "cloud's friends." In the latter two, there is a straightforward problem of understanding the sentence, taken in its primary sense. The sentences would be, strictly speaking, false. Nothing is being smeared, nor are peacocks actually friends to inanimate objects. Thus we can reason to similar properties which are being conveyed. However, there is no problem with the primary sense of "I am Rāma." This sentence is, in fact, obviously true. It is the very obviousness which Mukula thinks triggers another meaning. Mukula is here aware that the manner of speech—it being too obvious on one interpretation—signals to us that we ought to understand it in a figurative way.

A figure without indicative power

Next, Mukula turns to the third of Kumārila's categories—cases which are not newly created indication, but which are without indicative power. He cites an excerpt from the epic poem, *The Killing of Śiśupāla* (*Śiśupālavadha*), written by Māgha, who lived in the seventh century CE.[60]

> From the middle of the ocean,
> its golden structures making the sky glow,
> breaking through the waters, Dvārakā leaps up
> like the blazing sacrifice-carrier in the mouth of a beloved mare. (78)

The surrounding context of the poem, from which the verse is taken, is describing Kṛṣṇa's home, Dvārakā, said to be on the west coast of modern-day India. Situated on the edge of the waters, the city seems to emerge out of the ocean, with golden buildings blazing in brilliance. Māgha compares the city to a famous underwater fire shaped like a horse's head. There are a number of origin stories about this fire, which is thought to emerge at the end of the age as part of floods and fire which engulf the world.[61] It is this fire which the poet alludes to with the words, "blazing sacrifice-carrier in the mouth of a beloved mare." Māgha's choice of language though, is unusual. For instance, the compound "sacrifice-carrier" (*havya-vāha*) refers to a Vedic ritual fire which carries burned offerings up to the gods.

> "sacrifice-carrier" (*havya-vāha*) → "fire" (*agni*) → fire
> "mouth" (*ānana*) → "face" (*mukha*) → face
> "beloved mare" (*turaṅga-kānta*) → "horse" (*vaḍava*) → horse

Mukula rejects this argument. His reasoning, which is important in explaining how indication functions, is that only certain words are capable of indicating, under certain conditions. Words have the ability to indicate only when they have some relationship to uses we have already observed. While it is true that there is a category of words like "two r's" that is able to indicate a word and thereby another meaning, this kind of indication has to be constrained. Otherwise, indicatory words would be able to communicate anything. We have seen people use "two r's" in this way, but we haven't seen people use "sacrifice-carrier with the mouth of a beloved mare" in such a manner. It is as if Shakespeare's Romeo had said, "Juliet is the gaseous orb at the center of the solar system." The word "gaseous orb" lacks the intertextual connotations that "sun" does, having a history of being used in comparisons, even if Shakespeare is employing it to new effect.

Perhaps in anticipation of the objection that surely a poet might be the first person to introduce a novel use (which might then become established convention), Mukula adds that one also needs a reason to think the poet intends such a second meaning. Without such a motive, it is reading too much into the verse for there to be such a hidden meaning. When we can ascribe motive to a poet, then we treat the use as part of our everyday practices. This is Mukula's first mention of motive, and he does not explain here, or elsewhere, how readers should understand motive. While modern readers might be tempted to look to the original poetic context of the verse, in Sanskrit poetics, the concept of "stray verses" (see footnote on page 164) meant that single verses, extracted from a work (or never belonging to one in the first place) were typically viewed as complete in their own.[62] And of course, even if we look into the broader context of *The Killing of Śiśupāla*, the hermeneutic puzzle remains, since to understand motive all we have are the poet's words, which themselves must be interpreted. Mukula doesn't focus on this puzzle, though whether this is because he thought it was not a puzzle or because it wasn't his primary purpose is hard to say.

Collection of factors for indication

At this point, having completed his remarks on Kumārila's tripartite distinction, Mukula returns to the main line of reasoning, which is to explain the conditions under which indication occurs. As a reminder, he

Table 6 Novel indication based on speaker, sentence, expressed meaning

Ānandavardhana's category	Mukula's corresponding example	Mukula's analysis
Suggested facts (*vastu-dhvani*)	Hey there neighbor . . .	Indication based on relationship with speaker
Suggested figures (*alaṅkāra-dhvani*)	He has already taken Śri . . .	Indication based on relationship with sentence
Suggested *rasa* (*rasa-dhvani*)	The flower-tipped arrows . . .	Indication based on relationship with expressed meaning

has mentioned a total of seven: speaker, sentence, expressed meaning, place, time, state, and individuality. His contention is that a word will convey an indicated meaning in virtue of particular collections of these features, in combination with the primary meaning. In what follows, he will focus on speaker, sentence, and expressed meaning, for each giving a stanza which exemplifies how the condition contributes to the indicated meaning (see Table 6). These are novel, or "newly created" cases of indication, in contrast to conventionally well-established ones which function just like the primary meaning. In these poetic cases we will see that Mukula is identifying examples which are parallel to, or sometimes identical to, examples that Ānandavardhana has explained as cases of suggestion, just as with the above verse involving "Rāma." As he proceeds, Mukula will not only give examples for sentence, speaker, and expressed meaning, but he will give examples which correspond to three major types of suggested meaning: suggested facts (*vastu-dhvani*), suggested figures (*alaṅkāra-dhvani*), and suggested *rasa* (*rasa-dhvani*). As was explained in the introduction, while Ānandavardhana thinks each of these types of suggestion can be found in poetry, it is the last category, of suggested *rasa*, that he thinks is essential to excellent poetry, and which is important to his contention that suggestion is a distinct linguistic capacity. While never mentioning these three categories explicitly, Mukula's choice of examples make the point for him. If he can account for all three of them with indication, then Ānandavardhana's proposed suggestive capacity is no longer necessary.

Relationship with the speaker

In a set of verses ascribed to the Sanskrit poet Vidyā (c. 650 CE), collected after Mukula in the twelfth-century poetic anthology, *The Treasury of*

Sparkling Single Stanza Jewels (*Subhāṣita-ratna-kośa*), a woman says she is going to go fetch water from the river.[63] In reality, though, she is going to meet an illicit lover and she is preparing an excuse:

> Hey there neighbor, will you watch our house for a bit, as well?
> This child's father won't drink the tasteless well-water at all.
> I go now, all alone, from here to the forest stream full of tamala trees.
> Let the stiff, broken ends of the knotted reeds scratch my body. (80)

This, says Mukula, is a case where "indicated meaning is understood by a relationship with the speaker." However, these verses alone do not tell us anything about the speaker. All we can tell from them, taken at face value, is that she has a neighbor, a husband, a child, and that she is planning to go to the river to get water but will come back scratched up due to the brush. Like a similar set of verses in Ānandavardhana's text, it is understood through genre conventions that the woman is "unvirtuous," and is planning a rendezvous. In *Light on Suggestion*, a similar poem reads

> Go your rounds freely, gentle monk
> the little dog is gone.
> Just today from the thickets by the Godā,
> came a fearsome lion and killed him.[64]

Ānandavardhana argues that this is a case where the primary meaning is an injunction, but a prohibition is suggested instead. Rather than "Go your rounds freely," what is suggested is "*Do not* go your rounds freely," presumably because the lion is more terrifying than the dog.[65] This is a case of "suggestion of a state of affairs" because it is an opposite state of affairs (a prohibition) which is understood from the primary meaning (an injunction). The term "state of affairs" (*vastu*) is broad, including cases of suggestion which do not involve figures of speech like metaphor nor *rasa* like a character's being in love.

Mukula's analogous case is one where the primary meaning takes on a somewhat opposed nature as well, though by indication. The state of affairs indicated is the woman's going to the stream for an affair. He argues in this way: first, we know that the woman is unvirtuous. Second, since we know that she is unvirtuous, we cannot take her words as being truthful. Rather, she is concealing something. This means she is telling us a lie, with the purpose of accounting for something else. So we try to ascertain what it is that her lie would account for. If this all follows, then the true meaning, what is implied, can be understood as being whatever would support the story she is telling. Put more simply: if we can figure out why she would say she's going to come back from the river with scratches—on the presumption that she's lying about them being due to the reeds—then we can understand what is being indicated. Mukula does not point out the contextual cues in this case that would help with this interpretation, even without the background knowledge that riverbanks are the usual location for a tryst in Sanskrit love poetry.[66] These might include things like the emphasis on going alone to the river and the fact that she describes her husband as the child's father, which is perhaps a distancing move.[67] However, without the supposition that the woman is unvirtuous (and hence aiming to mislead), these small details might not add up to the indication of an alternate meaning.

Mukula concludes by bringing together this indicated meaning with the prior taxonomy, saying that this is the kind of indication known as inclusion. The key point of commonality is that the primary meaning is established or justified by the indicated meaning. As with the case of "The cow is to be sacrificially bound" or "Fat Devadatta does not eat during the day," the indicated meaning is postulated in order to justify the sense of what has been given through the primary meaning. Unlike these two cases, though, we must reflect on the speaker. Previously, mere lexical knowledge seemed to be adequate for determining what was meant.

Relationship with the sentence

Mukula now moves on to a poetic example that illustrates indication related to the sentence. In this case, we will also see mention of another factor, state (*avasthā*), although it is not the primary focus of his analysis. The anonymous verse says:

> "He has already taken Śrī, so why stir up pain by churning me?
> I cannot believe one so active would want to sleep like before.
> And why would he build a bridge again, when the lords of all the islands serve him?"
> The ocean's trembling when your Majesty marches near is like it has these doubts. (81)

Just like the example involving the white cranes, this stanza is found in *Light on Suggestion*, where it is an example of a suggested figure. In particular, Ānandavardhana thinks that a specific figure of speech, an **identification** (***rūpaka***), is suggested here.[68] The first three lines of these verses written in praise of a king describe mythological actions performed by Viṣṇu, (here called "Lord Vāsudeva"). He withdrew his wife, the goddess Śrī, by churning the ocean's waters, he sleeps upon the ocean during the time in between creations of worlds, and he built a bridge over the ocean to Lankā, when he was incarnate as Rāma. In this stanza, the ocean is anthropomorphized as recalling each of these great feats when a king and his great army thunder across the nearby shore. It dismisses all of them as reasons for the king's worrying presence. Here the king is implicitly identified with Viṣṇu, but nowhere is Viṣṇu mentioned by name. Because of this, Ānandavardhana finds a suggested figure of speech, a metaphorical identification "The king is Viṣṇu," which is nowhere explicitly stated.

Like Ānandavardhana, Mukula finds figures of speech here, but he does not characterize them as being suggested. On his view, these are all explicable by indication. His general argument depends on the fact that the sentences in question would be incongruous, or fail to express anything as a syntactic-semantic unity, unless we understand the verse metaphorically. Thus the analysis of this case is along the same lines as our earlier instances of inclusion, which depend on postulation to resolve incongruity. The first sentential problem hinges on the word "trembling" (*kampaḥ*) which Mukula argues cannot be understood in its primary meaning. A second involves the reference to "your Majesty" and the three "doubts." Ordinarily, "trembling" refers to the action of people shaking their heads when they are in doubt. However, this verse describes the ocean as "trembling." Since oceans are insentient, and cannot have thoughts, let alone doubts, this application of the term must be taken in a secondary sense. So far, this is standard indication, of the kind where properties are ascribed or transferred from one thing to another, just like "The Punjabi is an ox." The rippling waves of the ocean are like the movement of a shaking head, and so we say the ocean is "trembling." Further, even though there are properties which are transferred, this is also a cause of superimposition, since the ocean's movements are understood as identified with trembling. (Why this is a case of superimposition we will understand more in a moment.)

In the meantime, there is still a further difficulty. The verse says that the ocean's trembling has or contains doubts, in particular a set of three doubts mentioned earlier, when the king goes by. In order for this sentence to make sense, there must be an intelligible relationship between these particular doubts, the king, and the trembling of the ocean. Recalling the sentence about fat Devadatta may help here. This is similar to that case, where the word "fat" doesn't make sense unless we can find a cause for the fatness, as the cause during the day has been denied. Here, Mukula observes that the trembling is an effect and the cause is the three doubts. While we are using "trembling" in a secondary way to refer to the ocean's movements, we still need to explain why these particular doubts cause the trembling. Everyone reading the poem knows that the actions that the ocean is "thinking" about are Viṣṇu's actions, but the ocean is ascribing these actions to the king, which we know by the phrase "your Majesty." Since the king is not Viṣṇu, unless we make sense out of the relationship between Viṣṇu and the king, we are left with an incongruity. Thus, we conclude that the poet is implying that the king, metaphorically speaking, is Viṣṇu.

While not the focus of this analysis, we can also notice that the feature of state (*avasthā*) is present in this case. Mukula talks about the ocean's trembling as being a "state," in explaining the relationship between the trembling heads of thinking beings and the rippling waters of an insentient body of water. Mukula does not anywhere explain how the triad of speaker, sentence, and expressed meaning is related to place, time, state, and individuality, although he will later observe that these features can be combined in a number of ways.

An aspect of Mukula's discussion in this section which we have not seen before is his discussion of types of poetic figures. This has not been his main purpose throughout, even though he has been developing his own taxonomy. As we have seen, this taxonomy has an explanatory purpose, and is not a mere catalog of rhetorical figures. Yet here he explains **hyperbole (*atiśayokti*)** and **imagining (*utprekṣā*)** in connection with his own taxonomy. In so doing, he chooses to appeal to Udbhaṭa, one of his predecessors in poetic theory who lived roughly in 800 CE.[69] While speculation about why he cites Udbhaṭa and not other thinkers cannot be conclusive, one possible motivation, which fits with his use of Mīmāṃsā, is that elsewhere Udbhaṭa has explained another figure, identification (*rūpaka*), in terms of secondary meaning and in terms of impossibility of the primary meaning.[70] Udbhaṭa's approach draws on Kumārila's method of analysis, and so would make him another ally in Mukula's attempt to show that previous linguistic analysis does, in fact, contain answers to Ānandavardhana's challenge.

Whatever his motivation, what Mukula argues is that this stanza exemplifies both hyperbole and imagining. First, hyperbole occurs when the word "trembling" is used for the ocean which does not actually tremble. Even though there is a difference between ocean waves and people's shaking heads, they are treated as if they are the same. Thus, we have "hyperbole where what really has a distinction is without distinction." As we've seen, this hyperbole happens because there are similar properties between the two states, so it is also a case of indication involving transfer of properties. Second, in the phrase "is like it has these doubts," there is a case of imagining (*utprekṣā*).[71] In imagining, a poet attributes properties of one thing to another, usually when it is physically impossible for the target of attribution to have such qualities (as in the case of anthropomorphizing inanimate objects). Further, there is not a complete identification of the two compared entities—the awareness that there is an imaginative act is part of its structure. Mukula quotes a definition for imagining when it is combined with hyperbole from Udbhaṭa's *Synopsis of the Essentials of Poetic Ornaments* (*Kāvyâl aṅkāra-sāra-saṃgraḥ*)

> When there is an intention to express similarity of natures, expressed by words such as "like," because there are no shared properties or actions, the figure of imagining is joined with hyperbole.

In this case, because the word "like" (*iva*) is present in the verse, and because there are no genuinely shared properties or actions (merely similarity) between the ocean's trembling and head-shaking, Mukula can conclude, on Udbhaṭa's definition, that imagining is joined with hyperbole. Thus Mukula has explained how a putative case of a suggested figure can be understood as an indicated figure. However, he has taken issue with Ānandavardhana's identification of the figure, arguing that rather than being a suggested metaphor, this is a case of hyperbole linked with imagining, and this hyperbole involves superimposition and transfer of properties.[72] Next he takes up indication based on expressed meaning, which will also form a rejoinder to Ānandavardhana's category of suggested *rasa*.

Relationship with the expressed meaning

The final poetic example in this section involves the expressed meaning.

> The flower-tipped arrows of the love-god are hard to avoid: spring
> blossoms everywhere.
> The bright moon's rays make my heart crazy and the cuckoos capture
> my mind.
> This young age, with these heavy breasts, is a hard burden to bear.
> These burdensome five fires—now, how can I endure them, my friend? (83)[73]

Mukula argues that this stanza indicates a *rasa*, making it a purported counter-example to the third major kind of suggestion, *rasa-dhvani*. As said earlier, for Ānandavardhana, when he finds *rasa* in poetry, it is always described as part of the text, by way of a character, and not in the reader's emotions. Thus *rasa* is a meaning, alongside of primary and secondary meaning.

Further, as explained in the introduction, this kind of suggested meaning is central to Ānandavardhana's account, and is exemplified in such verses as this one from Kālidāsa's *The Origin of the Young God* (6.84)

> While the heavenly visitor was speaking, Pārvatī,
> standing with lowered face beside her father,
> counted the petals of the lotus in her hand.[74]

In this example, Pārvatī shyly looks at a lotus in her hand while her betrothal to the god Śiva is discussed by her father and a messenger. There is no figure of speech involving an obstacle in understanding, only an ordinary description. But Ānandavardhana says that this case suggests the *rasa* of love (here by first suggesting shyness through Pārvatī's actions), and this *rasa* is not an incidental feature of the stanza, but its entire purpose. The poet nowhere says, "Pārvatī is shy" or "Pārvatī is in love," but they are understood regardless. Suggestion of *rasa* is predominant, at least when done well. We will see that Mukula's discussion of his own example focuses on the predominance of *rasa* as well as whether an obstacle is encountered.

Mukula argues that his example stanza, about the love god, indicates the *rasa* of love-in-separation, a *rasa* which captures the wistful longing between two lovers who are far apart, famously exemplified in poems like Kālidāsa's *The Cloud Messenger* (*Meghadhūta*). Here, the love god, known for shooting arrows whose tips are flowers, is doing his work in springtime. All of the natural signs of romance appear: flowers grow everywhere (implicitly compared to the deity's arrows), the moon is beautiful, the cuckoos are singing their song, and there are young women with large breasts. All of these are motifs in Sanskrit love poetry which typically signal love. The final sentence identifies these five things (arrows, blossoms, moon, cuckoos, youth) as being five fires. This results in indication which involves superimposition, since fire is identified with things which are not fires. Thus the stanza as a whole expresses a meaning which is figurative. This is the expressed meaning.

However, Mukula argues that there must be reason for this being the expressed meaning, which is to convey the *rasa* of love-in-separation. Here we have no knowledge about the speaker to help us understand why they speak in this way, unlike the case of the woman going to the river. And we have already appealed to superimposition in order to resolve any sentential difficulty between the "five fires" and the things which are not fires. So neither speaker nor sentence are the relevant factor. Rather, by considering why someone might want to speak in this way, we understand that it is to communicate love-in-separation. Thus we must reflect on the sentential aim (*tāt-parya*). Mukula does not develop this idea of sentential aim any further, though it is a controversial one in Sanskrit philosophy of language and poetics.[75] All he wants to say is that sentences have some final communicative aim, and we must keep this in mind as we understand what a speaker means. His reasoning here, as in the other two cases, again appeals to inclusion and (implicitly) an incongruity which is resolved by the indicated meaning.

Putting his reasoning more explicitly in line with the previous cases of poetic indication, we see that there is an incongruity in what is expressed unless we postulate that the main purpose of the stanza is to communicate love-in-separation. Since the five things compared to fire are ordinarily beautiful experiences, there is no purpose in comparing them to a trial by fire.[76] However, if we understand the main point of the stanza as communicating the pain of beautiful springtime love-reminders, then this incongruity is resolved. Further, this allows Mukula to claim that the indicated meaning of *rasa* is predominant. It not merely an after-thought, but it is the focal point of the stanza, and the only way in which it can be understood and appreciated by the sensitive reader or critic. As "sensitive critic" (*sahṛdaya*) is the term Ānandavardhana uses for literary critics and readers who are sensitive to the presence of suggestion, Mukula is indirectly saying that his analysis has displaced suggestion with indication. As we have seen, this requires that indication can occur in more than one stage, like the case of *dvi-repha* or "thing with two r's." Still, despite its having multiple stages, this does not mean the second stage must be suggestion, since incongruity remains crucial for its function.

Grammatical faults in poetry

Mukula takes a brief detour to explain an apparent poetic fault in the verses he's quoted, a fault from what seems like inappropriate grammar. Flouting Pāṇinian grammatical rules would ordinarily mean bad poetry, so Mukula spends some time explaining why the poet has not in actuality written a poem with bad grammar. This is the only time he does this kind of analysis in the text, making it curious—he does not seem to be making a larger point. Perhaps the purpose of this analysis is simply that he thinks that poetic language is subject to the same governing rules as ordinary language.[77]

The line in question is, "The moon's bright splendor makes the heart intoxicated," (*hṛdy-unmāda-karā śaśāṅka-rucīnām*). About this verse, Mukula says,

> Now, concerning "makes the heart intoxicated," no letter *ī* (in *hṛdy-unmāda-karā*) is employed (to signify feminine gender) because there is an *aC*-affix, as in "the words *śiva, śama, riṣṭa* in the genitive when meaning 'he does,'" instead of a *Ṭa*-affix, although "moon's bright splendor" has a feminine gender. And for just this reason, where there is an intention to express such things as final causation, habitual action, or acquiescence, still, because there is no *Ṭa*-affix there is no grammatical fault. (84)

The basic point of his argument is just that while we might think that the word *karā*, "makes," should be instead *kārī*, in order to match in gender the phrase "the moon's bright splendor," there is a grammatical justification for the present form. Readers uninterested in the details of the argument may skip to the next section, as the next several paragraphs delve into some technicalities of Sanskrit grammar and Pāṇini's *Eight Chapters*. Suffice it to say that the grounds for his conclusions are solid and attested by other Sanskrit grammarians interpreting the *Eight Chapters*.

What is translated in English as the phrase "makes the heart intoxicated" is in Sanskrit two words in compound: *unmāda-karā*. The compound appears to be what is called an *upapada tat-puruṣa*, in which one of the elements governs the other grammatically and the governed word never occurs on its own, outside of a compound.[78] Here, the word *karā* is derived from the verb root *kṛ* which means "make," and it takes as its object the compound *hṛdy-unmāda*, or the "heart which is intoxicated." The word *karā* appears to be an *upapada* or governed term—so not an independent word in its own right. What Mukula argues is that the compound is in fact, not of this sort, but instead is made up of two independent words. If this is the case, then the spelling *karā* is not a fault.

If this compound were an *upapada tat-puruṣa*, then certain grammatical rules would apply to the endings, ones which would require it to have a different ending—a long *ī*. These rules are found in two places, where certain affixes (*pratyaya*s) are identified as needing to be attached to the verb. Morphological rules for things such as vowel lengthening are identified by technical terms known as *pratyāhāra*s, and Mukula mentions two of them: *Ṭa* and *aṆ*. The lowercase letter represents a functional sound—it is added to the word in question. The capital letter is a convention used in transliteration to indicate something like an abbreviation (an *anubandha*). These letters tell us what morphological rules we should apply—even sometimes telling us that we should delete certain changes, so that they never occur in the final, spoken word.

There are two lines of reasoning here. First, Mukula argues that if we take this compound as an *upapada*, there are two options for how to transform *kṛ*. Neither of these options work, so he concludes the compound is not an *upapada*. Given that the compound isn't an *upapada*, we need to determine what rules actually apply, so as to justify the spelling which occurs. In each of steps, he is implicitly appealing to a rule (found in a *sūtra* or aphorism) in the *Eight Chapters*.

Mukula first alludes to rule 3.2.20, saying that there is no *Ṭa*-affix. Here he's taking one of the two options for transforming the verb root *kṛ* in an *upapada*. The reason he says there is no *Ṭa*-affix is implicit—in 3.2.20, Pāṇini explains what kinds of affixes should be used when certain semantic conditions are met in an *upapada*: when the object of the verb denotes final causation, habitual action, or acquiescence (*hetu-tāt-śīlyā-anulomyāneṣu*). If these conditions are met, then a *Ṭa*-affix is added (a short "*a*") and rule 4.1.15 is employed: the affix *NīP* is added, or a long "ī" which represents the feminine gender: *kārī*. Since Mukula says there is no *Ṭa*-affix, he is arguing that none of the three semantic conditions in 3.2.20 have been met. The final cause is not the moon's splendor—the moon's splendor is a reminder of the beloved's splendor, which is what makes the heart mad. Further, we might say that the moon's splendor isn't usually the cause of the heart's madness—there are other conditions involved (viz, the metaphorical "five fires" in the poem). Finally, the heart is not acquiescing to the moon by becoming mad, in the way that someone who obeys an order would acquiesce.

The other option to derive *kṛ* isn't explicitly mentioned by Mukula but is found in 3.2.1. Here, within an *upapada* compound, an *aṆ*-affix is added to the governed word, triggering one of the aforementioned morphological changes which aren't seen in the final result.[79] Again, if we follow 3.2.1, our next step is to follow the previously mentioned rule 4.1.15, which would generate *kārī*, in the feminine gender. However, Mukula is going to give us some positive reasons to think that the compound is not an *upapada* but involves two independently occurring words.

Mukula says that what we see is an *aC*-affix (and not a *Ṭa*-affix). Now, in 3.1.134, Pāṇini says that certain words occurring in a list take the *aC*-affix, or a long "ā" in the final position (as in *karā*.) This list of terms is referred to by the phrase *pacâdi*, or "*pac* and so on," since the verb root *pac* is the first in the list. If we look at the entire list of these terms, in 4.1.15, and we find *kṛ*, we would have a Pāṇinian justification for it taking a long *ā* ending. Unfortunately, it is not listed. However, there are two kinds of lists in Pāṇini, complete and partial, and if this list is a partial list, we might still be able to justify the form *karā*. Mukula does justify it, by quoting Pāṇini's own words in 4.4.143, when he uses a form of *kara* as its own word:

> The affix *tātil* comes in the Chandas after the words *śiva*, *śama*, *ariṣṭa*, in the sixth case (genitive) in construction when the sense is a condition (*kare*).[80]

So, even though there is no explicit rule allowing for *karā* as a feminine form for *kara*, that Pāṇini has used *kara* as an independent word—here in the locative, *kare*—means that it could be declined as *karā* (with the *aC*-affix), rather than the expected *kārī*, as within an *upapada* compound. Much later than Mukula, the seventeenth-century grammarian Bhaṭṭoji Dīkṣita, says as much. In his commentary, the *Illumination of the Established Position* (*Siddhānta-kaumudī*), he says on 4.4.143 that the word *kare* is formed from *kṛ* according to 3.1.134, showing that he thinks the word is implied to be part of the list.[81]

Finally, Mukula says that even if the poet were aiming to describe final causation, habitual action, or acquiescence, because this is not a governed term with a *Ṭa*-affix like in 3.2.20, there is no grammatical fault in using *karā*. (Recall that 3.2.20 functions only when one is describing one of these three as part of an *upapada*.) This observation is probably because the moon's bright splendor is regularly described as a cause of emotional distress in Sanskrit poetry, and so denying that it is a usual cause (*tāt-śilyā*) of madness is a strained interpretation.[82]

Conclusion to collection of factors

At this point, Mukula concludes his discussion of factors, observing that he has not given examples for all of their possible combinations. One could combine speaker with sentence meaning or with expressed meaning, for instance. As well, the four other factors (place, time, state, and individuality) can be analyzed in a number of combinations. The illustrations he has just given are merely examples to motivate further inquiry into indication's nature. He gives us a sense of different possible combinations in an explanation that we can represent as seven sets where a = speaker, b = sentence, and c = expressed meaning:

$\{a\}; \{b\}; \{c\}; \{a, b\}; \{a, c\}; \{b, c\}; \{a, b, c\}$

As he says, this makes three singles, three groups of two, and one group of three. While Mukula has only given examples where the indicated meaning is grounded in a single factor, (despite the fact that state seems to be involved in one) he claims there are cases where these other combinations are possible. Further, he notes that the four other factors are subject to the same kind of combination. Since listing all combinations of the seven factors, arranged singly or in groups of two through seven would involve representing 128 combinations (2^7), we agree with Mukula in leaving this exercise for the reader. His point, however, has now been made. Recall that the discussion of these factors in Ānandavardhana arises in part because he is explaining the incredible variety of suggested meanings possible. In his adaptation of these same factors for indication, Mukula has demonstrated the flexibility of his competing account. At the same time as these factors constrain what indicated meaning can be understood—so that it is not a free-for-all—they also allow indication of facts, figures, and *rasa*. The epistemic instrument of postulation, along with an expanded understanding of what kind of incongruity triggers indication, means that indicated meanings can be drawn out of poetic verses in an intelligible way (accounting for how we can actually come to know what poetry means) that nonetheless requires sophisticated attention to genre, word choice, grammatical rules, and so on.

At this point, Mukula seems to have made his case against Ānandavardhana quite well. However, he is only halfway through his treatise. In what follows, he will turn to the relationship between words and sentences, arguing that his account of indication is somewhat neutral among competing theories of sentence meaning. He will also focus on other distinctions which Ānandavardhana has made among kinds of suggested meaning, taking up the same strategy as seen in this section, in which he presents examples similar to those in Ānandavardhana's text, but explains the meaning as being indicated.

Verses 7b–9a

> When there is connection among what is designated by words, indicated meaning is thought to be after that expressed meaning. (7b)
> When what is connected constitutes the expressed meaning, indicated meaning is at the stage preceding the expressed meaning.

> Now in the two-fold view, indication is in both stages. But for the unified whole view, the sentence is ultimately the bearer of meaning, and there is no indication. (8)
> Now when the meaning is hypothetical, indication cannot be distinguished, as on the earlier views. (85)

Mukula now turns to theories of sentence meaning, as the discussion of poetic examples raises an issue about whether indication is a phenomenon which happens before the expressed meaning is understood or after. All the illustrations prior to the previous section, which treats poetry, have involved indication at the level of the individual word.[83] In contrast, in the last section, we have examples where the meaning is not indicated by a single word as part of a process of rectifying semantic incompatibility in order to yield an expressed meaning. The woman speaking to her neighbor does not indicate through a single word meaning being negated. Further, indicated meaning grounded in an expressed meaning, the third factor he discussed, is due to the overall meaning of the sentence, rather than a single word. While this allows Mukula's theory of indication to match Ānandavardhana's theory of suggestion—as both indication and the purported power of suggestion can be based in word or sentence, it raises a question. If indication is a matter of repairing semantic incompatibility, it necessarily is sentence-internal. If indication involves incompatibility between a speaker and a sentence, or an expressed meaning and the words composing the sentence, then it is sentence-external. Can it be both?

To answer, Mukula surveys four theories of sentential unity. He gives different accounts of what "expressed meaning" is, which enables him to identify precisely where indication occurs in each theory. In order of appearance of the verses, they are advocated by Bhāṭṭa Mīmāṃsakas, Prābhākara Mīmāṃsakas, possibly Naiyāyikas, and the grammarian Bhartṛhari. Mukula does not explicitly take a position on these theories, content to identify their implications for his analysis of indication. However, we can surmise, given what he has already said about word meaning under Verses 1–2a, that he cannot accept either the Bhāṭṭa or Prābhākara Mīmāṃsaka's viewpoint alone. For one thing, the latter view is at odds with the claim that words denote universals, properties, actions, and proper names. For Prābhākara thinkers, words denote things as related, not universals on their own. As for Bhāṭṭa thinkers, we have already seen Mukula disagree with them in other contexts, but here, the issue is that he needs indication to work on complete sentences, not only in a sentence-internal manner. Therefore, Mukula's own view may be either the combined view or the Bhartṛharian view. He will return to discuss Bhartṛhari's theory at the end of his monograph.

Bhāṭṭa: Connection of what is denoted

Mukula first describes the view espoused by Kumārila Bhaṭṭa and other Mīmāṃsākas who follow after him:

> When there is connection among what is designated by words, indicated meaning is thought to be after this expressed meaning. (85)

This theory of sentential unity is known as the **connection of what is denoted (*abhihitânvaya*)**. Recall that verbal cognitions—mental events that result from hearing sentences—are of relations between entities. Take the sentence Mukula uses early on, "The cow is to be sacrificially bound." The cognition which results from this injunction is of a cow characterized by the future action of tying up.[84] Bhāṭṭa Mīmāṃsakas argue that this relationship requires an understanding of the **connection (*anvaya*)** between the entities (cow, tying up), as well as of the entities themselves. Without presuming that words directly denote the connection and the meanings, how are we to make sense of the cognition that results from the sentence?

Further, as Mukula has discussed earlier, under Verses 5b and following, it seems as if we learn word meanings through "positive and negative correlations," or comparing sentences in context in order to ascertain the meanings of their component parts. However, as we are also already aware (from the discussion of the aforementioned cow-tying example), Bhāṭṭa thinkers are committed to universals rather than particulars as the primary denotation of words. Thus, no connection is possible between COWHOOD and the future action of tying up unless the meaning of a particular cow is indicated. This is all familiar so far, but now Mukula introduces new conditions to explain the relationship between word and sentence meaning:

> On this topic, some people think that when words have accomplished their own meanings this does not express the sentence meaning. Rather, sentence meaning is understood through the power of **semantic fit, contiguity**, and syntactic expectancy, applied to the meanings of words. The meanings of words are universals understood by the process of inference from positive and negative correlations. (85)

While words merely denote universals, sentence meaning arises as a result of three conditions **semantic fit (*yogyatā*)**, **contiguity (*sannidhi*)**, and syntactic expectancy (*ākāṅkṣā*) which apply to the word denotations. In other words, while there is a connection among the word meanings, this connection is not denoted, it is implied.

Mukula does not define the three conditions for sentential unity since they are well known by his time. The first, semantic fit, refers to the requirement that words have appropriate relationships with one another as far as their meaning. A common example where semantic fit fails is

25 He sprinkles the garden with fire.

Here, although the sentence is perfectly grammatical, the meaning of the Sanskrit verb "sprinkle" (verbal root *sic*) only makes sense applied to liquid things. (If a metaphorical interpretation seems readily available, this is accounted for on a common explanation for secondary meaning, which is that it is triggered by failure of semantic fit, prompting another meaning to be understood.) Hearers, in order to make sense out of words, make judgments about whether the words are appropriately related, judgments which are based in accepted use patterns. When they judge that words are being put together improperly on the basis of their meaning, then semantic fit is lacking. A similar sentence which has semantic fit would be

26 He sprinkles the garden with water.

This sentence makes perfect sense because "sprinkles" and "water" have semantic fit, as water is the instrument of sprinkling. In contrast to semantic fit, syntactic expectancy is the requirement that words construe together in appropriate grammatical relationships. Sentences which fail to have syntactic expectancy might be

27 *Water with sprinkles garden the he.
28 *cow elephant duck rabbit.

In fact, calling these "sentences" seems incorrect. They are lists of unconnected words. When present, syntactic expectancy, a psychological desire on the part of the hearer for appropriately connected words, allows the hearer to understand how the word meanings are related. While this expectancy is grounded in facts about grammar, it is, as with semantic fit, a matter of hearers making judgments in order to construe words together as related or as not.

Contiguity is the final requirement for such construal and the essential idea here is that words must be appropriately presented together in order for them to be taken as a unity. If I start speaking a sentence on Monday and utter a single word each day of the week, completing the sentence on Saturday, hearers will not be able to understand the sentence. On this view of sentence meaning, then, words first denote universals, and then those universals come to be more than just an unconnected list through semantic fit, contiguity, and syntactic expectancy. But we might wonder how we get from universals to the sort of thing which can be put into relationship.

Here we can return to Mukula's first paradigmatic case of indication, "A cow is to be sacrificially bound." First the words "cow" and "to be sacrificially bound" will convey their primary meanings, which are general: COWHOOD and the action of *being sacrificially bound*. But this is merely a list. Thus, Mukula says,

> Afterwards, through the functions of syntactic expectancy, semantic fit, and contiguity, there comes to be an interconnecting relationship among these word meanings, a relationship which has the character of predicate-object. It is then that indication is to be found, when the sentence meaning is understood on account of the syntactic capacity of word meanings. (87)

In other words, for Bhāṭṭa thinkers, indication is responsible for the transformation of COWHOOD into *particular cow*, so that being sacrificially bound can be predicated of a cow. This enables syntactic expectancy to be fulfilled (there is a verb and an object), semantic fit to be present (we can tie up particular cows, though we can't tie up universals), and of course the sentence is uttered at a single time, making these two features possible. Mukula argues that if we consider this primary meaning the "expressed meaning," then we would say that indication occurs after the expressed meaning. We can represent this with the schema below. The first arrow represents the denotation capacity (*d*) of the words which are uttered. The second arrow represents the indication process (*i*) which yields a predicate-object[85] relationship between the entities denoted by the words: entity_1 has a relationship (*R*) to entity_2.

$$\{\text{word}_1, \text{word}_2\} \rightarrow_d \{\text{entity}_1, \text{entity}_2\} \rightarrow_i \{\text{entity}_1 (R) \text{entity}_2\}$$

Mukula's conclusion is that sentence meaning is not denoted, but it is indicated, or implied. He uses an analogy to explain this:[86]

> Sentence meaning is instead understood further from what is denoted, just like joy and sorrow: for this is like the examples: "O priest, your son is born," and "O priest, your unmarried daughter is pregnant." Although what is occasioned respectively by the birth of a son and the pregnancy of an unmarried daughter, joy and grief, is not denoted by the words, it is implied. It is implied from the state of affairs denoted by the words. Thus, it should be observed that, although the sentence meaning is implied by the word meanings, it is not denoted. (85)

In Mukula's context, the birth of a son causes joy and an unmarried woman's pregnancy is grievous. The sentences themselves make no reference to joy or grief; it is the hearer's understanding of the state of affairs communicated by the sentence which brings about the emotional response. Analogously, the denotations of words themselves, being universals, do not bring about a predicate-object relationship. This is a further stage.

Finally, when Mukula states that the joy and grief are implied by the sentences, he uses the term "implied" (*ākṣipyate*) which he has used earlier, in several instances. We have seen that the individual cow is implied by the universal. Fat Devadatta's eating at night is implied from the sentence stating that he does not eat during the day. In the case of the unvirtuous woman, the true thing is implied by means of an untruth. The king's identity with Lord Viṣṇu is implied by the words of the poem in order to justify the ascription of the actions to the king (who has not performed them). And finally, the *rasa* of love-in-separation is implied as the predominant meaning in the poem about the arrows of passion. All of these uses of the verb "implied" are in cases where there is inclusive indication. One of these cases (Devadatta) is clearly an example of postulation employed in order to ascertain the indicated meaning. Arguably, the others also follow the same structure: the postulation of a meaning (identity with Viṣṇu, love-in-separation, etc.) in order to support or establish the plain meaning of the sentence. This case, where joy and grief are implied, is similar. On the theory of sentence meaning he has just explained, such implying is part of construing the sentence. However, he must also account for poetic cases when indication happens after a sentence is understood. So he turns to a second theory.

Prābhākara: Denotation through the connected

The second major theory of sentential unity, connection-through-the-denoted, is defended by followers of Prabhākara Miśra, such as Śālikanātha Miśra (c. 825 CE). Mukula introduces it in his verse this way:

> When what is connected constitutes the expressed meaning, indicated meaning is at the stage preceding the expressed meaning. (85)

Here, Mukula presents a different definition of "expressed meaning," one where indication occurs prior to what is expressed. On this view, sentence meaning consists in the relationship between meanings which are already connected. A major motivation for this position is the objection that Kumārila's view above does not account for how words actually contribute to sentence meaning, especially when we think of how people learn words. A natural conception of what children learn when they learn words like "cow" and "horse" (at least for Bhāṭṭa Mīmāṃsakas) is that they learn a single stable concept, like "cow" means COWHOOD. But thinkers such as Śālikanātha Miśra point out that when we learn words, we learn them in contexts, just as was discussed under Verses 5b–6a above:

1 Bring the cow.
2 Bring the horse.
3 Feed the cow.
4 Feed the horse.

We learn words associated with other words, not in isolation. This learning occurs through using and refraining from using words in certain situations, in particular when being commanded to do something. We apply words in some situations and not in others, and from these regularities can determine what words mean. Further, what we learn is that the meaning of a word is in relationship with other meanings. The word "cow" is related to bringing and feeding in (1) and (3), respectively. When we use a word in a sentence, we are not merely calling to mind a universal or remembering a prototype (the latter point is made explicitly by Śālikanātha in his *Exposition in Five Chapters*), but we are also conveying the relationship between the thing denoted by the word and other entities denoted by words.

One way to understand this claim, that a word meaning is not merely an entity, but involves relationship, is to say that the meaning of a word is a function.[87] In other words, what the word contributes to a sentence is a meaning with a syntactic expectancy for another meaning. For instance, a verb "expects" an object. Depending on the verb, it might require both a direct and an indirect object. A noun expects a verb. Thus we might say that "bring" denotes a function *bring*(*r*) where *r* is the input, a direct object which is the argument for the function. And "cow" denotes *F*(cow), where *F* is a function, or a verb, that takes *cow* as its argument. In the sentence "Bring the cow," these words combine in context to mean *bring*(*cow*), without any need for an additional semantic step which extracts or "implies" a meaning-in-relation. Further, whether a word meaning counts as a function or an argument depends on context and its relationship to other words.

Mukula concludes his explanation of the Prābhākara view by having the proponent admit that words must have some natural expressive capacity, but that these are not universals, though they are connected to universals.

> Understanding these relationships happens because words have natural expressive capacities which are incorporated with a universal of some kind. (86)

One explanation for the relationship between universals and word meaning, given by Śālikanātha, is that universals may be part of our memory, but they cannot be the full meaning of a word. In part, this view is motivated by the presupposition that memory is not an epistemic instrument, but testimony is. Therefore, remembering universals cannot be equated with word meaning, which is testimonial. However, there is still something general about our recollection of words, which is why we might say that word meanings express by their being incorporated into a universal for some thing. Another motivation seems to be that meaning is not simply reference, but that there is a certain way in which the referent of "cow," for instance, is brought to our mind.[88]

For Prābhākaras, while perhaps there is some core thing which is recalled by memory when someone utters the word "cow" in context, only those features of a cow which are relevantly similar are brought into relationship with the other words in a sentence. In this way, if the sentence is referring to generic features of all cows, those could be meant by "cow." A particular single cow could also be the meaning of "cow," again, given the relevant context. In contrast to the Bhāṭṭa schema above, the Prābhākara view can be represented as:

$$\{\text{word}_1, \text{word}_2\} \rightarrow_d \{\text{entity}_1 (R) \text{entity}_2\}$$

Here, words directly combine into relationship, without an intervening stage. Of course, as with the previous schema, more complex sentences than "Bring the cow" would need more nuanced representation. The general principle remains the same, however: every word meaning is either a function or an input to a function, a relating thing or a thing which admits of being related. Some may be both, but not with regard to the same word meaning (in "A black cow is to be tied up," the adjective *black* requires *cow*, while the noun *cow* requires a verb *tied up*).

Mukula says that on this view, his six-part division of indication does not appear at the stage when sentence meaning comes to be understood. This is because word meanings are not predetermined things (e.g., universals) but are determined in relationship to the sentence as a whole and the other words in the sentence. So there is no need for indication to act as an intermediary between universals and the meanings in relationship to one another. On this view, in cases involving only primary meaning, what is expressed is identical to the sentence meaning, which is just word meanings directly coming into relationship. However, in some cases, the entire sentence meaning is the basis for understanding something else which is indicated. For an example, take the earlier case where the ocean has its doubts about the king and his army. On this view, words have an innate expressive capacity to be understood in relationship, so there is no need to think that "ocean" first means OCEAN and then a particular ocean. Yet, even once the sentence meaning is understood, there is a further indicated meaning, because it is necessary to understand the sentences in question. So we can place indication as below:

$$\{\text{word}_1, \text{word}_2\} \rightarrow_d \{\text{entity}_1(R)\text{entity}_2\} \rightarrow_i \{\{\text{entity}_1(R)\text{entity}_2\}, \text{indicated meaning}\}$$

As it is unclear in Mukula's text precisely how, on this view, the sentence meaning and indicated meaning relate to constitute the expressed meaning, the representation simply puts them as a pair. However, this pair must have some unifying relationship in order to be a single expressed meaning. Before moving to the third and fourth view, a final diagram (Table 7 First and Second Sentence Theories, Compared) may help visualize the relationship between these two positions. In this table, the arrows simply represent movement from one stage of meaning comprehension (in italics) to another, where the functions are represented in boxes.

We can see that a crucial difference is in the understanding of "what is expressed," which on the first view is what is expressed by words (universals that are unrelated) and on the second view is what is expressed by the entire sentence in context (related meanings, plus any further indication).

Combined view: Having it both ways

The briefest discussion is reserved for the combined view, which essentially is the two earlier views, together.

> Now in the two-fold view, indication is in both stages. (85)

Mukula gives only the slightest hint as to how two theories, taken to be incommensurable by their proponents, can be synthesized.[89] He seems to have two points. One is the use of the names for the views. He appears to be saying that, depending on what phenomenon you wish to describe, you can use either term: "denotation-through-the-connected" or "connection-of-the-denoted." His second point is that in this combination view, indication occurs in two stages.

One way to make sense out of this view is to consider its likeliest proponents, historically speaking. While the use of "others" to point out proponents of a view is sometimes a rhetorical move, not intended to identify a particular thinker or textual tradition, since so far Mukula has been drawing intentionally on well-known thinkers (Patañjali, Śabara, Kumārila, etc.), we might consider if he has someone in mind here, too. The most likely possibility is a Naiyāyika. According to Gautama's *Aphorisms on Reasoning* (*Nyāya-sūtra*) 2.2.56 and following, words can mean an individual, a form, or a universal, depending on the particular context. Naiyāyika thinkers emphasized the flexibility of word meaning in their dialectics with Bhāṭṭa Mīmāṃsakas, denying that nouns invariably first convey a universal, but in dialectic with Buddhists who defend the "exclusion" (*apoha*) theory, they emphasize that words communicate something fixed, and positive, not a negation, like "not non-cow."[90]

In the work of the seventh-century CE Naiyāyika Uddyotakara, we find him defending his theory of word meaning against an interlocutor who denies that words aren't expressive—possibly representing a Prābhākara thinker who is committed to the (more subtle) thesis that words only express in the context of a sentence. Uddyotakara responds that, in fact, words are expressive—they express universals or genera while sentences express specificities.[91] He goes on to say that although words express universals, they do so in a way which is restricted or determined. Although nowhere does Uddyotakara say that his view is a "combined" position—he like other Naiyāyikas were presenting their view as opposed to both Bhāṭṭa and Prābhākara thinkers—it is possible to see why Mukula might understand him (or perhaps another Naiyāyika) as taking up an intermediate stance.

Thus, depending on how you want to understand denotation, there are two ways to characterize this (possibly) Nyāya-inspired position. If we ask whether words express anything, that is, to look "from the standpoint of words," then we find that yes, words contribute something fixed to the sentence, which is then brought into sentential connection. Thus there is connection-of-the-denoted. But if we consider things "from the standpoint of the sentence," which is a unified state of affairs (as Uddyotakara puts it, it is specific), then what a word expresses must be understood in that particular context. So whether "cow" means an individual cow, a clay cow, or cows in general depends on the sentence as a whole. Words have meanings in relationship to other words. Thus there is denotation-of-the-connected.[92]

Given this way of understanding Uddyotakara, let us now reconstruct Mukula's position— setting aside the historical question of whether, and to what degree, this might represent someone else's view (or their self-understanding of that view). We can combine the two previous diagrams into one, as shown in Table 8.

Table 8 distinguishes between what is expressed in a minimal sense of "expressed," which is unconnected meanings. After the first sort of indication operates along with syntactic expectancy, semantic fit, and contiguity, there is a sentence meaning. Based on this sentence meaning, additional indication happens, which works at a different level, that of the sentence, and taking into account such things as genre convention, background knowledge, etc. (what has been discussed in preceding section). Once this process occurs, then we have the maximal sense of what is "expressed." This distinction, between "minimal" and "maximal" is not found in Mukula but is my own way of making sense out of what he does say, which is that there are two ways of understanding what is expressed. Sometimes, if no further indication is necessary—we are speaking entirely in the ordinary sense of words, the "minimal" sentence meaning will be identical to the "maximal" utterance meaning. But in other cases, if the conditions are right—that is, if the collection of factors Mukula has identified are present—then a further indication is necessary.

Table 7 First and second sentence theories, compared

Connection of what is denoted	**Denotation through the connected**
Words uttered	*Words uttered*
↓	↓
Primary function (*mukhya*)	Primary function (*mukhya*)
↓	↓
What is expressed (*vācya*)	*Sentence meaning* (*vākya*)
↓	↓
Indicatory function (*lākṣanika*)	Indicatory function (*lākṣaṇika*)
↓	↓
Sentence meaning (*vākya*)	*What is expressed* (*vācya*)

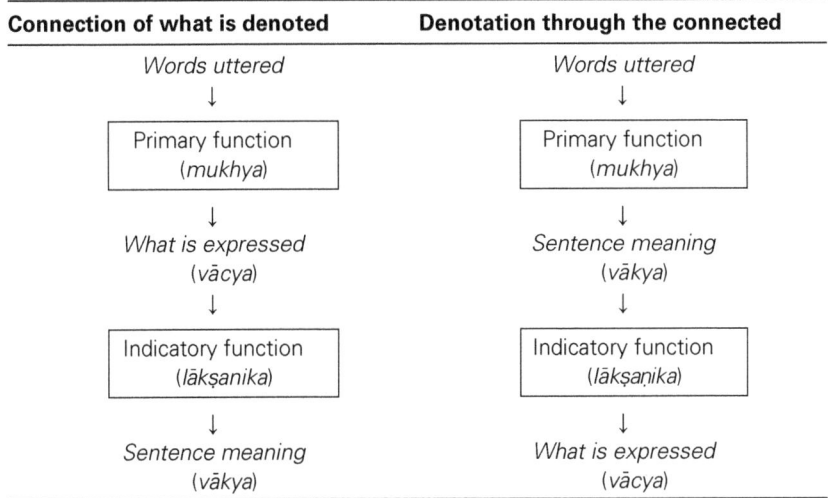

On this combined view, then, indication will naturally occur in two places, corresponding to where it appears in the two views being combined. Again, a historical note—Naiyāyikas did make room for secondary meaning, which they often called "transference" (*upacāra*). Gautama's *Aphorisms on Logic* 2.2.62 lists a number of examples, which are explained in terms of what grounds the transfer between denotation and secondary meaning. These examples are explained in terms of what grounds the transfer between primary and secondary meaning, grounds which include relationships like association. For instance, in "Feed the walking stick," the "walking stick" primarily refers to a brahmin's walking stick and secondarily to the associated brahmin himself. We will see Mukula take up such relationships in the very next section. But since Naiyāyikas also say things like "There is no rule about which of the three (individual, form, or universal) would be the meaning element that is predominant in a sentence," it is hard to make sense out of why they need to call the associated meaning *secondary*, if for them (as for Prābhākara thinkers) words attain their meaning in context.[93] However, on Mukula's Nyāya-inspired view, as we have reconstructed it, there is some indication which occurs at this stage (*pace* Prābhākaras) but perhaps it is automatic, or below our level of phenomenal awareness, being sub-sentential.

Thus indication may be subsequent to the minimal expressed (word) meaning or prior to the maximal expressed (sentence) meaning. The difference is whether indication is a sub-sentential process or a process acting on a completed sentence. Typically, when Indian thinkers talk about "indication," they mean the first process. This kind of indication is what Ānandavardhana, for instance, argues is inadequate to account for suggestion, since suggestion doesn't play a necessary role in sentential unity. However, Mukula seems to be arguing that the same structure is present in the sub-sentential and the post-sentential process, even if they operate on different contents (word meanings and sentence meanings). This insight is crucial to his entire argument against Ānandavardhana, as it allows him to account for suggestion.

Unified whole view: No word meaning

Given that the combined view so neatly provides a response to Ānandavardhana, why does Mukula go on to a fourth view? The main reason is that this is probably his own view. It is common for Indian writers to give the least favorable view first, then proceed until they conclude with their own view. Another reason may be that since, as we will see, the fourth view is in many ways compatible with the third, he is attempting to be theoretically neutral. Whether or not his readers accept the metaphysical implications in the fourth view, they can accept the third, most correct theory of sentence meaning. And that theory itself, rather than presenting the first and the second as flat-out-wrong, attempts to give a middle ground—saying that in a sense both are correct, depending upon perspective. Mukula's aim is thus theoretical neutrality of a sort—his displacement of suggestion does not entirely lean on a specific theory of sentence meaning. The final theory is:

> But for the unified whole view, the sentence is what is ultimately the bearer of meaning, and there is no indication.
> But when the meaning is hypothetical, indication cannot be distinguished, as on the earlier views. (85)

Here, Mukula presents a view represented most famously by Bhartṛhari: that sentence meaning is a unified whole and words (along with any other subdivisions such as prefixes) merely hypothetical abstractions, lacking any ultimate existence. The argument that Mukula gives for this view starts by assuming the Bhāṭṭa Mīmāṃsaka view for *reductio*. On this view, the primary word meaning is a universal, and it is given up in favor of a particular, as in the sentence "The cow is to be sacrificially bound." However, this means that it is not the word's expressive capacity that conveys the particular cow, but something at a further stage. This results in the unwanted consequence that sentence meaning is disconnected from word meaning. Mukula's argument here echoes closely what Bhartṛhari says in his *Treatise on Sentences and Words*

> If the particularized and the particular co-exist, there would be opposition between the two. If the meaning is abandoned, then the relation becomes impermanent.[94]

What Bhartṛhari concludes from his arguments, which take up eight different theories of sentence meaning, is difficult to conclude, and is the subject of much scholarly debate.[95] Happily for us, we need not adjudicate all of that here. Rather, we can look to Mukula's use of Bhartṛhari's work in this particular context, in which he draws on Bhartṛhari's claims such as "From the point of view of ultimate reality, there is no division in the sentence."[96] On this view, as Mukula puts it, the three views which have preceded still fall shy of the full truth. Rather, since there are problems for all

Table 8 Combined view of sentence meaning

Combined view
words uttered
↓
Primary function (*mukhya*)
↓
What is expressed$_{min}$ (*vācya*)
↓
Indicatory function (*lākṣanika*)
↓
Sentence meaning (*vākya*)
↓
Indicatory function (*lākṣaṇika*)
↓
What is expressed$_{max}$ (*vācya*)

the views on which sentences are made up of parts in combination, though he has focused just on the Bhāṭṭa Mīmāṃsakas, it is more fruitful to think of sentences as wholes which are only theoretically divided. Not only are sentences wholes (understood as the sound of an utterance, a sound usually divided into words), but sentence meanings are also wholes, and in such a way that they are unified with the sentence sound. This is known as the Burst Theory, which we encountered earlier. On this view, whose technical details are unessential to Mukula's argument, language is a burst, something like a flower bud opening or a popping bubble. Meaning appears in the mind of the hearer, prompted by this burst of sound.[97]

However, Mukula is careful to say that this holism is from the ultimate perspective. As Mukula says, in the unified whole view, we can still postulate word meaning for theoretical purposes. As long as we do not make the mistake of thinking that discrete words meanings are metaphysically necessary for comprehension, we can make use of them in our theorizing. Mukula will return to this approach at the end of his monograph, addressing the question of the theoretical fruitfulness of his proposed schema. After all, if Bhartṛhari is right, then ultimately speaking, neither Ānandavardhana nor

Mukula has a better purchase on language. Thus Mukula must address why it is that his framework should be preferred over Ānandavardhana's.

He hints at some reasons in his discussion of where indication would figure in the unified whole view. In terms of what actually exists, from the ultimate standpoint, there is no indication as there are no words or denoted word meanings. And from the outset, we have seen that Mukula's theory of indication depends upon the existence of both, as well as a particular position about what kinds of denoted word meanings one should accept. However, Mukula points out that there are at least three theories which one could employ. He has not rejected theorizing, so long as it is relativized. And, depending on one's theoretical preferences, indication would appear in different explanatory positions, as he has shown. Because our utterances take place in certain places and times, and are spoken by human beings with particular interpretive conventions in place, thus we might want to approach language from a more ordinary—and less ultimate—perspective. Given this aim, we would set aside (perhaps temporarily) the Bhartṛharian insight that language is a unified stream of sound which gives rise to a flash of comprehension. Depending upon our explanatory aim, we have a few theoretical choices for where indication occurs with regard to word and sentence meaning. However, for Mukula, the first two theories are incomplete, as they do not account for the full range of indication. So we must surmise that he is not committed to either of them. The third theory does account for indication as he understands it, but only at the level of the ordinary. Thus the fourth view is probably his own, as it accounts for indication but also preserves other, deeper metaphysical commitments.[98]

Verses 9b–10a

Having concluded his account of how indication is understood related to sentence meaning, Mukula returns to the main line of reasoning. For the remainder of the text, his focus is to demonstrate that indication can account for all varieties of nonprimary meaning, without remainder. He has already explained that some incongruity with the primary meaning must be involved in order to trigger indication. When there is an obstacle to understanding the ordinary meaning, then we may have license to interpret it in another way. However, an obstacle or incongruity is not alone sufficient for indicated meaning. There are in fact three requirements, each of which is individually necessary and all of which, together, are sufficient—and it is these requirements which Mukula introduces in his verse and elaborates on in the following section. Further important for this account is answering the question of how we move from the primary meaning to the indicated meaning. Mukula has already argued that certain conditions must be in place—and he will return to these again below—but now he will explain the relationship between primary and indicated meaning more precisely.

Mukula lays out the three requirements for understanding the indicated meaning, requirements broadly accepted by his predecessors and also found in Ānandavardhana's text:

> Because of an incongruity in the primary meaning, because of its closeness to the primary meaning, (9b) because of established use or else a motive, that indication is found in ordinary linguistic practice. (89)

In his discussion of this verse, Mukula makes clear that there are three conditions which are required for indication to occur:

1. We encounter an obstacle in understanding the primary meaning.
2. We identify some relationship between the primary meaning and an indicated meaning.
3. We attribute to the speaker some motive for understanding the expression in a nonprimary manner, which may be

    a A motive to follow an established convention, or
    b A motive to create some new, special meaning.

In his treatment of the conditions of speaker, sentence, and expressed meaning, Mukula has explained requirement (1) of an obstacle, in some detail. He has also treated (3), the motive, particularly in his explanation of poetic indication in the last section. He has not yet discussed (2) the relationship between primary and indicated meaning. Thus he presents five possible relationships, first introducing them through another thinker's work, and then subjecting those five categories to the same treatment of exemplification and analysis which has occurred earlier.

Here Mukula quotes Bhartṛmitra on indication, who is a Mīmāṃsā philosopher writing before Kumārila (c. 600–700 CE).[99] According to Bhartṛmitra,

> Indication is considered five-fold because of a close relationship with what is denoted, because of being similar, because of being associated, because of being opposed, and because of being joined to an action.

Although Mukula can cite Bhartṛmitra as an authority for his division of relationship into five kinds, we might wonder why he thinks there are two kinds of motive. Thus before explaining the five relationships, Mukula briefly returns to the question of the motive, where we get some repetition of what was discussed previously, explaining how *dvi-repha* ("two r's") is conventionally associated with the word for "bee," (*bhramara*). While the explanation may seem repetitive, in his discussion of the novel case, he introduces an important term which he will use in his subsequent explanations. He says that in the verse which says "I am Rāma," the word "Rāma" communicates a specific meaning, and this is a meaning which "does not have a particular term to communicate it."[100] The phrase "does not have a particular term to communicate it" is a translation of the compound *asaṃvijñāna-pada*, which is a technical term found in Bhartṛhari's *Treatise*. This term refers to those things which do not have particular words for them, but which we can understand in other ways.[101] (Ānandavardhana does not use this term but alludes to such a concept at 1.16.) In Bhartṛhari, the term is used to explain how the word "relation" (*saṃbhandha*) cannot refer to the variable and highly specific kinds of relationship that exist in the world. It can only get at the idea in a fairly general way, but not in its precise nature. So a specific relationship is *asaṃvijñānapada*, or it "does not have a particular term to communicate it." Likewise, Mukula seems to be arguing that one of the benefits of novel indication is that it is able to convey variable and highly specific meanings, which are contextually dependent, and which have no specific term for them. There is no ready-made term for the very particular manner in which Rāma suffered, and so using his name as an indication gives us access to them in an indirect manner. We will see this idea recur in what follows.

Now Mukula returns to the five relationships between primary and indicatory meaning. He will treat them in order of their occurrence in the quote from Bhartṛmitra's text. Table 9 shows these relationships along with their paradigmatic example in Mukula's text.

Indication based on close relationship with the primary meaning

The classic example of indication, "A village is on the Ganges," is Mukula's illustration of the first relationship, which is indication based on close relationship (*saṃbandha*) with the primary meaning (the denoted meaning). The term for "close relationship" is general, but Mukula observes that the relationship between the indicated meaning and the Ganges is a particular kind, contiguity between things. So we might suspect that other kinds of relationship might be subsumed under this category. This poses a puzzle, however, since Bhartṛmitra distinguishes between close relationship (*saṃbandha*) and association, (*samavāya*), though the latter term is also used to describe the inherence relationship between a substance and its qualities. In fact, close relationship (*saṃbandha*) often includes association (*samavāya*), as well as contact (*saṃyoga*), and identity (*sva-rūpa*). Further, all of the other items in the list—similarity, opposition, and being joined to an action—are kinds of relationship. So why distinguish them? One reason is that they all—except for the case of association—obviously involve different types of figures than the Ganges case. Mukula will explain simile, irony, and double meaning in terms of the underlying relationship. Thus subsuming them all under the category of close relationship would be to obscure these structural differences.

Another reason, perhaps, is that Mukula is still targeting Ānandavardhana's theory of suggestion, in which suggested properties can be conveyed by the primary meaning without the intermediary of indication. Here, Mukula argues that it is in virtue of its close relationship with the denoted meaning of "Ganges" that the indicated meaning, "bank," can indicate the properties of holiness which the village has, by its proximity. He is implicitly relying on the idea of semantic imbuing found in 5b–6a, where he has already argued that, depending on one's motive, a single expression can be used to different effect. Here the motive is a special one, to communicate holiness and beauty. The word "Ganges" does not primarily mean holiness, but the river does have those properties. Therefore, since the indicated meaning is closely connected to the primary meaning (the bank is adjacent to the river), the holiness of the Ganges is easily understood as being shared with what is nearby. For Ānandavardhana, properties such as this would be suggested from the primary meaning directly. By taking on board Bhartṛmitra's category of relationship with the primary meaning, Mukula can explain how these properties, which do belong only to the primary meaning, can be understood through indication. It is because this is a kind of indication which depends on a close relationship to the primary meaning. Further, these particular properties are, like those associated with "Rāma," communicated without a particular term to communicate them. Here, though, Mukula's point does not seem to be that the holiness and beauty found in the Ganges are so specific as to lack descriptive terms (after all he has just described them with two simple words) but that the word "Ganges" is not the particular term to communicate them. Thus these properties are communicated in an intermediate manner, not by their usual particular terms.

The reason that it must be the word "Ganges" which helps convey the properties is that the word "bank" cannot extend to things like holiness and beauty. That is, if we took "bank" as meaning *holy and beautiful*, there would be a formal flaw involved: the fault of under and over-extension (*avyāpty-ativyāpti-prasaṅga*). This fault is when a definition or a term applies to too few as well as too many things. For instance, defining a brahmin as "someone who carries a staff" would be under-extension because a brahmin might not have his staff on every occasion and over-extension because people other than brahmins might carry a staff. It would be under-extension if the word "bank" always meant *holy and beautiful*, since we might say "on the bank of the Mississippi river" which is not holy nor beautiful.[102] Likewise, attributing this meaning to "bank" would constitute over-extension since it is not just riverbanks which are holy and beautiful. Thus the word "bank" on its own cannot denote holiness and beauty, but only in virtue of its relationship, in this particular context, with the meaning of "Ganges."

Indication based on being similar

Mukula illustrates indication based on similarity (*sadṛśya*) with another stanza:

> Bee, in all your buzzing about the spacious sky,
> Have you anywhere touched, seen, or heard
> —now speak unbiased truth!—
> If there is a flower equal to the jasmine blossom? (90)

Mukula does not explain this stanza as he has explained others, and I have not been able to identify its source. However, the motifs are familiar to Sanskrit poetry. Jasmine flowers are frequently characterized as being favored by bees, and women are often compared to flowers which attract

Table 9 Relationships between primary and indicated meanings

Category of relationship	Example
Close relationship with primary meaning	A village is on the Ganges.
Being similar	Bee, in all your buzzing . . .
Being associated	The umbrella-holders are going
Being opposed	Auspicious-faced one
Being joined with an action	You are Śatrughna / you are the enemy-killer

bees. The bee is like a man who enjoys many women (which are the flowers) and the jasmine flower is an extremely beautiful woman. There is a problem with the word "bee" being in the vocative, or being a noun used for direct address, since bees can't reply when addressed. But there must be other problems, too, since "flower" is also an indicating word and it is not in the vocative case. Mukula alludes to this by his use of "and so forth" (*ādi*), but he does not explain the difficulty. The larger point must be that flowers and bees are being anthropomorphized.

Without identifying them, Mukula says that there are similar properties shared between the bee and the meaning that is being indicated. It is these similar properties which the poet wants to communicate, and so we conclude that the motive is a special poetic motive, not a matter of convention. Again, Mukula emphasizes that there is no specific term which we can readily use to bring to mind everything the poet wants to communicate. These actions and properties are what Ānandavardhana would likely consider to be suggested: the flitting from woman to woman like a bee moves from flower to flower, the particular way in which women are attractive to men as flowers are to bees, and so on. Mukula argues that, though these characteristics aren't easily described, they can be indicated through bringing our attention to similarity. We might add, this is why poetry's meaning is so difficult to put into explicit terms (and one reason, among others, why the Sanskrit intellectual tradition of poetic commentaries was so important).

However, despite this being a novel poetic motive, there obviously is "convention" in some sense here, in the trope of the bee. In the *Seven Hundred*, a collection of stanzas from Sanskrit poetry, there are numerous verses like this, in which the bee is the object of address and there are implicit similes involving both bee and the flower. For instance,

> O bee,
> One moment you hover above the lotuses,
> Then the next you brush against the mimosa,
> Then you stayed glued to the jasmine,
> Perhaps the trumpetflowers will cure you
> Of this fickleness.[103]

This sense of "convention," of an established poetic trope, is, however, different than Mukula's use of the term, which refers to figures of speech which are established in such a way as to be almost primary. And yet, we might think that the distinction between convention in this sense and a special poetic motive is not binary. After all, even the novel figures must have some warrant grounded in ordinary linguistic conventions. This is not a problem that Mukula raises, although a later critic of suggestion, Mahima Bhaṭṭa, does give some attention to how what we might think of as "background knowledge" allows us to understand the meanings of poetic figures. Drawing on ideas dating back to early dramaturgy but employing them in connection with the Buddhist Dharmakīrti's epistemology, he appeals to ordinary knowledge (*loka*), knowledge from intellectual traditions (*śāstra*), as well as one's own experience (*anubhāva*). These are what allow us to ascertain an invariable connection between words and their meanings, a connection which lets us use inference to understand the meaning.[104]

Mukula, in contrast, nowhere appeals to invariable connections or inference. The only epistemic instrument he's connected to poetic figures is postulation, explicitly in the case of "fat Devadatta," and implicitly elsewhere. However, postulation is also an epistemic instrument which, when employed properly, leads to knowledge. In the case of Devadatta, we know that if fatness has a cause, if that cause is eating, and if eating must happen either during the day or the night, then once we deny eating happens during the day, we must conclude that Devadatta's fatness is caused by eating at night. While constructing analogous postulations in cases like the stanza above is not an easy task, the presence of well-known poetic motifs allows a reader to begin with a set of background assumptions which function as the antecedents in the nested conditional above. In fact, Mukula's project throughout this text can be understood as making explicit what some of these background assumptions are.

Indication based on being associated

The third relationship which Mukula takes up is association (*samavāya*). To illustrate it, he gives the sentence, "The umbrella-holders are going." Here he shifts from a poetic example to an ordinary expression used to describe a royal retinue, moving perhaps in a procession down a street. This sentence, a stock example of indication also used by Śabara and others, describes a royal retinue in which the important person has an umbrella-holder to shield them from the sun. Following along in the procession are other, umbrella-less people. Therefore, there is only one umbrella-holder, despite the plural noun. Śabara says, "Due to the associated indicative sign, one word is employed for another. This is just like "The umbrella holders proceed," through which one umbrella-holder all of them are indicated."[105]

Because there is only a single umbrella—something which both Śabara and Mukula agree upon—it is inappropriate to say there are umbrella-holders, plural. This is the necessary incongruity. Agreeing with Śabara, Mukula says that all the others are indicated because they are associated with the umbrella-holder. While both Śabara and Mukula are explicit that there is only a single umbrella-holder, modern English-speaking commentators often describe this as a case of a crowd where some people have umbrellas and some do not.[106] This is understandable since, in English, it would be strange to say about a group of people following a single sign-holder, "The sign-holders are going." We might expect that use if there were a few people holding signs and others were not. However, here we encounter a case where the indication Mukula observes is grounded in the particular semantics of Sanskrit. This is likely an instance of what linguists call an "associative plural," which can be best understood in contrast to the "additive plural."[107] In English, "umbrella-holders" would refer to a group containing many umbrella-holders. This is the additive plural, in which one simply adds one or more of the same thing to yield a homogenous set. In contrast, the associative plural is a heterogeneous set, including the single umbrella-holder and the people associated with them.[108] Sanskrit is known for having associative plurals, especially in the dual number, like "fathers" (*pitarau*) which means the pair "father and mother." Thus for this case, we cannot construct a modern English example which easily motivates Mukula's point, since English doesn't allow for associative plurals in this manner.[109]

Given the contrast between associative and additive plural, we can use this to understand Mukula's reasoning about this example. Since he says that having only a single umbrella-holder constitutes an obstacle to the primary meaning, then this implies that the additive plural is the primary meaning of "umbrella-holders" for him. Normally, the addition of the plural marker simply means there is more than one of the same thing. However, when there is only one umbrella-holder, this makes the additive sense of the plural impossible, so it must be taken as an associative. The fact that such an understanding is possible rather than, as would be the case in English, a judgment of ungrammaticality, demonstrates that indication has some language-specific constraints. Mukula isn't explicit about whether the motive in this case is novel or to follow convention. He is only clear that the reason for using "umbrella-holders" in the plural is to include the associated retinue of people.

Finally, that Mukula focuses on the crowd as being close to the *royal person* who is near the umbrella, rather than simply the *umbrella-holder* himself, is an interesting detail—though he does not explain why it is this relationship which is important for the speaker's motive rather than the relationship to the umbrella-holder. The umbrella is often a metonym for royal authority, so perhaps there are two stages of indication here? Mukula will return to this example in the next section, giving us yet another variant on its meaning which depends on the speaker's motive.

Indication based on being opposed

In his discussion of the relationship of opposition, Mukula mentions irony for the first time in his treatise. He gives the example of "auspicious-faced one" which is used in the presence of a person who does not have an auspicious face. No particular poetic context is given here—the phrase is a common honorific used in daily life and also Sanskrit plays, so needs no special explanation.[110] According to Chapter 19 of the *Treatise on Dramaturgy* (*Nāṭya-śāstra*), this is one of the terms that a superior person should use to address an inferior person:

> The heir-apparent should be addressed as "sire," (*svāmi*) the other princes as "young masters," (*bhartṛ-dārakaḥ*) inferior people as "pleasing one" (*śaumya*) or "auspicious-faced one" (*bhadra-mukha*) and before these low people, "o" (*he*) ought to be spoken.[111]

However, here, Mukula ignores the presence of such a rule, arguing that since the person is not auspicious-faced, this constitutes an obstacle to understanding the ordinary meaning of the expression. Mukula says that the meaning indicated is that the person is not auspicious—further, they are the opposite of auspicious, we might think that they are low (according to Bharata, *adhamam*, sometimes connoting vile). In other words, the implication is not merely a distancing from the primary meaning (that person isn't particularly auspicious, but they might not be vile) but is the negation (they are inauspicious, and therefore, vile).

What Mukula says further is that the reason one might speak in this indirect way is to communicate a hidden meaning. He's said this earlier, in his commentary on Verses 6b–7a. After criticizing the underwater fire imagery from *The Killing of Śiśupāla*, he says that if there were a motive to communicate a hidden meaning, then such a figure might be acceptable. And the example of the woman going to the riverbank in the same section is, while not a case of irony, a case where a meaning is being hidden in some manner—perhaps from anyone who might overhear her plans. This raises the question of how these meanings are "hidden," if it is possible to understand them through indication. One way to think of the nature of this "hiding" is that it keeps the meaning from being on the plain surface of the words, giving the speaker plausible deniability. The insult to the not-so-auspicious person is veiled by way of a compliment. And whether the motive is an insult or something else Mukula also refrains from judging. There is some "particular aim" which we have when we use irony. Whether it is to insult, to say precisely the opposite, or merely to distance ourselves from the plain sense, he leaves open.

Indication based on being joined with an action

The final relationship which Mukula identifies is that of being joined with an action (*kriyā-yoga*). His examples, though, are what other Sanskrit thinkers would call bitextuality or double meaning (*śleṣa*). (This poetic figure is also sometimes translated as "punning," but it lacks triviality, which is connoted by that term in English.) Below are two versions of the same stanza. The different interpretations are possible in virtue of the range of meanings in Sanskrit for a single word as well as the ability to break words in different places. For instance, *nalobharatobhavān* could be *nalo bharato bhavān* or *na lobha-rato bhavān*, which would mean, respectively, "you are Nala and Bharata" or "you are not attracted to greed." The stanza (of which Mukula focuses only on a single sentence) is number 1417 from the previously mentioned *Treasury of Sparkling Single Stanza Jewels* (*Subhāṣita-ratna-kośa*), and is elsewhere used as an example of bitextuality, in Udbhaṭa's commentary on Bhāmaha's *Ornaments of Poetry*.

You are Pṛthu in qualities. In glory you are Rāma,	You are great in qualities, you are beautiful in glory,
You are Nala and Bharata,	You are not attracted to greed,
You are Śatrughna in the great battle,	You are the enemy-killer in the great battle,
From your standing in the world, you are Janaka,	You are the one who causes stability,
Since by your good deeds you bear the names borne by the ancient kings	Since by your good deeds you bear renown borne by the ancient kings
How is it you are not lord Māndhātā,	How is it you will not support me,
From being victorious over the three worlds also?	Since you are victorious over the three worlds also? (92)

Mukula says that since the poem is describing a king, and not Śatrughna, who is Rāma's youngest brother in the *Rāmayāṇa*, the third line must be understood in terms of the etymological meaning of *śatru-ghna*, which is "enemy-killer." This is the relationship with an action—the action of killing an enemy in this particular case. While describing double meaning as "connection with an action" seems inapt, McCrea (2008) points out that one might take action (*kriyā*) in a broad sense to mean "being and/or becoming" (297). Of course, he adds, whether this is how Bhartṛmitra understood the term is impossible to know without his original texts.

What we do know is that Mukula thinks that such multiple registers of meaning, like the other kinds of indication, must have a motive. Here, the motive is to communicate about the king's nature. The stanza says that the king is Śatrughna in the great battle—which could simply be comparing of the king's warring abilities to Śatrughna's abilities in killing the demon Lavaṇasūra. However, the name itself, as a pun, also communicates kingly qualities: killing enemies. When Mukula describes these two meanings, the person Śatrughna and the action of killing enemies, does he think they are related? Though our text is silent on these points, elsewhere in Sanskrit poetics, this question posed a significant topic for reflection.[112] Some thinkers argued that multiple registers of meaning had to be related by a broader relationship, like metaphor. Others argued that unrelated meanings could still be part of a bitextual poem. Here, we might think identifying of the king as Śatrughna is related to identifying the king as enemy-killer, because of Śatrughna's killing an enemy demon being similar to the king's killing his enemies. But Mukula does not stake out a position on this debate.

What maybe more difficult for Mukula's account is how to generalize his explanation of indication to all instances of double meaning. If the poem is read with the proper names as the primary meaning, then an incongruity with the king would arise. However, Sanskrit lacks capitalization which would force this as the first interpretation. The second version of the stanza above could be the first one understood. If so, then what incongruity would give reason for a different meaning to be indicated? Further, more complex registers are possible—some Sanskrit poetry, especially later *kāvya*, involves more than two meanings simultaneously. What triggers the search for a third, fourth, or further meaning? None of these are questions which Mukula seems interested in, perhaps because his primary goal is simply to demonstrate the explanatory sufficiency of indication over suggestion and Ānandavardhana has already had difficulty in accounting for bitextuality in his theory.[113]

Mukula stops his explication of the five relationships at this point. He has introduced four new examples to illustrate them, examples which he will return to in what follows. He has now explained all three of the required causes for indication to occur: an incongruity involving the primary meaning, the presence of a motive (conventional or novel), and a relationship between the primary and indicated meanings. Earlier, he had explained the way in which incongruity can be taken broadly, involving speaker, sentence, and expressed meaning. Given that indication then seems to occur at a sub-sentential and post-sentential level, he then explained how it is involved in sentential unity. And while earlier he had distinguished the two kinds of motive, he does so again in this context, emphasizing that indication can convey things for which we lack ready-made terms, especially in poetic contexts. This last point is especially important for his argument against Ānandavardhana, since it allows him to explain the subtle kinds of meanings which are accessible in an indirect manner, though associated with the primary meaning. He now turns to his last major discussion of indication, which also focuses on Ānandavardhana's suggestion. In Verses 10b–12a and the following auto-commentary, he will explain how sometimes indication does not require that the meaning expressed by the words is given up. The five relationships he has just introduced will form the structure for this next set of distinctions regarding what happens to the expressed meaning. As we will see, his understanding of this phenomenon directly contradicts Ānandavardhana's understanding of indication, and undermines one of his reasons for positing suggestion.

Verses 10b–12a

> In cases of similarity and opposition, the expressed meaning is entirely displaced. (10b)
> There is intentional expression or unintentional expression in the two cases of connection and association.
> In the case of inclusion, there is intentional expression, but in the case of indirect expression, there is unintentional expression. (11)
> In the case of connection to an action, there is displacement and sometimes its opposite. (93)

Mukula now turns to what happens to the expressed meaning in each of these relationships. "Expressed meaning" refers to whatever is directly communicated on any of the theories of sentence meaning above. Thus it could be the meaning expressed by a single word or the meaning expressed by a sentence, whether primary or indicated (recall the poem about the five fires). Whether the expressed meaning is displaced or expressed along with the indicated meaning is crucial for Mukula's efforts to explain suggestion in terms of indication. This is because, for Ānandavardhana, suggestion covers both of these major varieties:

> And there is such a thing as suggestion. And it is in general of two sorts: where the expressed meaning is not intentionally expressed and where the primary meaning is intentionally expressed in subordination to another meaning.[114]

Here again, a diagram may help with the distinctions. Shown in Figure 7 is how Ānandavardhana distinguishes between kinds of suggestion, in terms of the relationship between the expressed and suggested meanings.

In cases of suggestion where the expressed meaning is expressed intentionally, Ānandavardhana thinks it is also subordinate to another meaning (*vivakṣitânya-para-vācya*). In suggestion where the expressed meaning is not intended to be expressed (*avivakṣita-vācya*), there are two possibilities. It can include an expressed meaning that is shifted (*arthântara-saṅkramita-vācya*) or it can include an expressed meaning that is entirely displaced (*atyanta-tiraskṛta-vācya*). Here's how these categories work for Ānandavardhana. In the example we discussed earlier, of Pārvatī looking shyly at the lotus in her hand, the expressed meaning is intended. The poet uses all of the words in their ordinary, primary meanings. Yet, despite this, there is a suggestion of *rasa*. Here the expressed meaning does not include

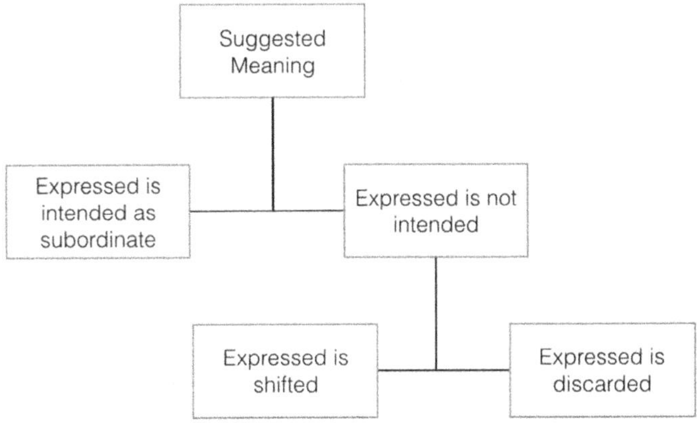

Figure 7 Ānandavardhana, suggestion, and intention to express.

indication. And yet there is suggestion. Thus, Ānandavardhana concludes that suggestion does not require indication. Further, the purpose of the expressed meaning is to suggest *rasa*, so it is subordinate to the suggested meaning. It plays an instrumental role in the hearer understanding suggestion, and so the expressed meaning isn't the aim of the verse, rather, suggestion is. For Ānandavardhana, this kind of suggestion is the best, aesthetically speaking, and it is the kind which is the most clearly, in his view, different from indication. When the expressed meaning is shifted, although it is not intended, we still understand the ordinary meaning of the word, but it comes to mean more than this. We'll see Mukula explain the same example that Ānandavardhana uses for this category, that of "Rāma," which primarily refers to the person Rāma but, in a poetic context, has a shift in meaning to also include the grievous actions that happened to him. Finally, when the expressed meaning is entirely displaced, not only does the poet not intend to express it, but we do not understand it at all. Ānandavardhana (at 2.1d) gives an example of uses the word "drunken" to characterize clouds moving through the sky. Since that word would ordinarily refer to a person's being intoxicated, this primary meaning cannot be what the poet intends to express here—and in fact, what we understand is something similar to drunkenness, here, the wild, erratic movements of clouds during a rainstorm.

Mukula, in contrast, argues that Ānandavardhana should not subdivide "unintended expression" as he has, but rather that indicated meaning (which, of course, replaces suggestion) admits of three different kinds, as shown in Figure 8. There are cases where the expressed meaning is intended to be conveyed, when it is not intended to be conveyed, and when it is entirely given up, in favor of another meaning.[115] This is far from mere taxonomic hair-splitting but goes directly to Ānandavardhana's claim about the impossibility of indication coexisting with the expressed meaning being intended. For example, in the case of Pārvatī and her lotus, Ānandavardhana would argue that since there is an intention to express the primary meaning, and not to shift it to another meaning or to give it up in favor of another meaning, there is no indication present.

However, Mukula would argue that in such cases, there is the variety of indication known as inclusion. In inclusion, the expressed meaning is intended to be communicated. It is not just a side effect, nor given up. However, along with that expressed meaning comes a second meaning, which is necessary to justify the first. Our earliest example of this category is, of course, "The cow is to be sacrificially bound up." Here, the primary

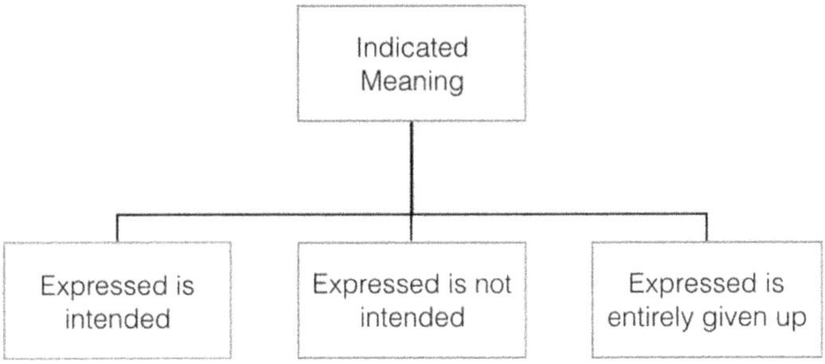

Figure 8 Mukula Bhaṭṭa, suggestion, and intention to express.

meaning of "cow," which is a universal, is intended to be expressed. However, a particular is indicated, as well. This same approach could be applied to the case of Pārvatī by arguing that, in order to justify the expressed meaning, which is intended, there must be an indicated meaning. Since Mukula does not actually take up this case, we have to extrapolate from what he says, but the account might be that, given what we know about human beings, when listening to someone address us, looking elsewhere (like at a flower) and not the speaker displays disinterest. But it would be incongruous with what we know about Pārvatī to attribute disinterest to her (she's marrying Śiva, a god), so we can conclude that the poet has written this stanza to convey her shyness.

Thus, again, the category of inclusion, functioning on the basis of postulation, plays a crucial role in rejecting Ānandavardhana's theory of suggestion. In the following section, we will see Mukula give examples which correspond to those in Ānandavardhana's text but explain them in terms of indication. He will argue that the five relationships just explained are useful in identifying what happens to the expressed meaning. In Figure 8, we can see how Mukula identifies some relationships as belonging to only one category of the three (expressed meaning is intended, not intended, or entirely given up) and others as belonging to two. For instance, depending on what kind of indication is involved, when there is a close relationship between the primary and indicated meaning, the expressed meaning may be either intended or unintended. The difference is whether indication is of the inclusive variety (e.g., fat Devadatta and the ocean's doubts) or indirect indication (e.g., the village on the Ganges). Here again, inclusion plays a central role in responding to Ānandavardhana, since, when indication is of the inclusive kind, the expressed meaning is intended. Figure 9 shows the way in which Mukula has organized the five kinds of relationships in terms

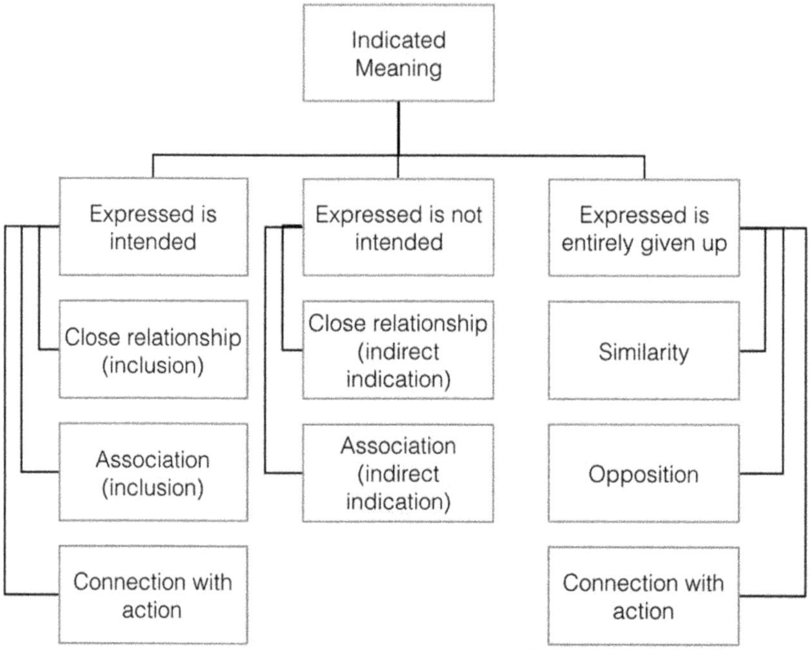

Figure 9 Mukula's varieties of relationship and intention to express.

Table 10 Five relationships in terms of expressed meaning

Category of relationship	Example	Analysis of expressed meaning
Close relationship with primary meaning	Fat Devadatta does not eat during the day	Expressed meaning is intended
	I am Rāma	Expressed meaning is not intended
Being similar	smeared, friends of the clouds	Expressed meaning is displaced
Being associated	The umbrella-holders go.	Expressed meaning is intended
	The umbrella-holders go.	Expressed meaning is not intended.
Being opposed	Auspicious-faced one	Expressed meaning is entirely displaced
Being joined with an action	The man is a man.	Expressed meaning is discarded
	You are Śatrughna . . . / you are the enemy-killer . . .	Expressed meaning is intended

of relationship to the expressed meaning. In the cases of close relationship to the primary meaning and association, if the kind of indication is inclusion, it enables the expressed meaning to be intended to be communicated.

Then in Table 10 we see how Mukula has used the five relationships to develop these distinctions.

Similarity and opposition

Mukula begins this discussion by showing how in either similarity or opposition, the expressed meaning is entirely displaced. He gives two examples for similarity: "Smeared by glistening dark color" and "friends of the clouds." He claims that the primary meaning of "smeared," spreading a substance, is displaced or set aside. The point of the figure is, as he has said earlier, to indicate the obscuring nature of the clouds. This new meaning supersedes the primary meaning. Likewise, "friends of the clouds," which would normally refer to actual (human) friends, in the context of the poem indicates the peacocks having friendly appearing attitudes toward the clouds. In neither case is there a close relationship between the primary meaning and the poem's narrative aims. The same goes for opposition, since in the ironic expression, "Auspicious-faced one," the speaker does not want to communicate "auspicious" but the opposite.

Close relationship and association

Turning to close relationship with what is denoted and to association, Mukula observes that, regardless of whether the expressed meaning is expressed intentionally or not, it is still *expressed* in some way. Recall that close relationship is exemplified by "A village is on the Ganges," where the indicated meaning "bank of" is inserted. This indication does not entirely replace the word "Ganges" or its meaning. After all, the bank is related to the Ganges river. Further, in the case of "The umbrella-holders are going," even though more than the single umbrella-holder is communicated—the entire retinue is being referred to—the umbrella-holder is still being referred to, along with the crowd. However, in both of these cases, although the expressed meaning is conveyed, there is a difference as to what the speaker is aiming to communicate. In the umbrella-holder case, the speaker wants to communicate the umbrella-holder and also the surrounding people. This is in contrast to the Ganges case, where a speaker uses "Ganges" as a shorthand for the bank of the Ganges. While the meaning of "Ganges" is not replaced, it isn't the speaker's main communicative aim, either.

Mukula now reminds us of the very important category of inclusion, which is exemplified by "A cow is to be sacrificially bound," and "Fat Devadatta does not eat during the day." This category by its very nature is said to include the original, primary meaning in what is indicated. Further, he says it works in the same way as how "sensitive critics," his term for suggestion theorists, think that suggestion works. The mistake, he insinuates, is to think that indication only works in the way that non-inclusive indicated meaning works. But while it's true that there is no intention to express the primary meaning in the Ganges case—which is often taken as paradigmatic case—such an intention does exist in inclusive indication.

Returning again to the case of Fat Devadatta, Mukula argues that what is intended by the speaker is that Devadatta is portly—and this characteristic, which is denoted primarily by the word "fat," is supported by the indicated meaning. Applying Bhartṛmitra's taxonomy to this case, he says that the kind of close relationship is cause and effect (which means that contiguity is not the only sort of relationship possible in this broad category). Because fatness is causally connected to eating, and, as is familiar by now, Devadatta does not eat during the day, eating at night is implied. Likewise, he concludes, the non-umbrella-holders, as said above, are included in the indicated meaning of "umbrella-holders," by virtue of association.

Sometimes the expressed meaning is not entirely set aside, as it is in the ironic utterance of "auspicious-faced one," but it is also not intended, as it is in "umbrella-holders." This is what happens in the example "I am Rāma," which is not used in the usual way of referring to Daśaratha's son, Rāma. The motive instead is to communicate actions associated with Rāma. As a result, while Rāma himself isn't the main communicative aim, he is still at some level necessary for the associated actions to be understood. So the primary meaning is expressed, but unintentionally. At the same time, there is a transformation or a shifting of focus to the story of Rāma.

Here, Mukula says something in Sanskrit that earlier translators and scholars have found puzzling. He says that these properties related to Rāma are "made manifest," using a term which is also translated as "suggested" (*vyaṅgya*) since it is used frequently by Ānandavardhana for his new linguistic capacity. But Mukula could not be suddenly and implicitly accepting Ānandavardhana's account of suggestion, as Venugopalan claims.[116] After all, he has been explicitly arguing that suggestion is identical to indication. There are, I think, two possible solutions for this use of the term, which as McCrea points out, does appear "odd and seemingly rather careless" if we understand it as "suggestion."[117] The first option is that, since he is here pointedly responding to the suggestion theorists, Mukula is self-consciously appropriating their own terminology, but gives an explanation in terms of indication. This would be to take the term in scare quotes. And since the phrase appears in Ānandavardhana's own discussion in this way, we can take Mukula as simply quoting him here, but not accepting the explanation.[118] However, Mukula has vocabulary for this, such as "apparent," (*abhāsa*), which was widely used in this kind of semantic distancing, as in "apparent" or "pseudo" inferential reasons, *hetv-abhāsa*.

Another option is that he is quoting Ānandavardhana but he is using the term in a broad sense—this would be to take the word as not yet having gained the conventionalized connotation of "suggestion" as Ānandavardhana's uses it. After all, even Ānandavardhana uses *vyaṅgya* in a broad sense compatible with how Mukula might be using it. The first use occurs at *Light* 3.33 in a discussion on the topic at issue here: how the expressed meaning is related to intention. Ānandavardhana is responding to the charge that in putative cases of suggestion which is unintended to be expressed, secondary meaning can account for it. The cases of secondary meaning here are the Ganges example and "The brahmin boy is fire," which would be analogous to our "The peasant is an ox." The objector argues that these seem to correspond to Ānandavardhana's categories of shifted and displaced unintended expression. In reply, Ānandavardhana distinguishes between *vyaṅgya* or a "suggested meaning" that is beautiful and *vyaṅgya* or a "manifested meaning" which is merely conveyed by secondary meaning. The second is what Ingalls, commenting on this dual use of *vyaṅgya*, calls a "wide meaning" of the term.[119] This is "manifested" not in the sense of being any new linguistic function, but just in the sense of revealing or making manifest a new meaning.

Of course, Mukula would not agree with Ānandavardhana that what is manifest by secondary meaning is ordinary and unbeautiful. He's given a range of examples, from the ordinary to the poetic, and this one, where he says the properties are made manifest (wide sense of *vyaṅgya*) is from a poem—one we should presume he finds beautiful. Ultimately, we may not be able to answer precisely what shades of meaning Mukula's original readers would find expressed—intentionally or unintentionally!—with *vyaṅgya*, but given that he is so close to Ānandavardhana, who himself uses the term in two senses, I think the second interpretation is plausible.

Let's return to the main line of reasoning. Mukula has now given us examples of unintentional expression and intentional expression. At this point, we might expect him to go on to cases where the expressed meaning is discarded. However, before he does, he again illustrates the flexibility of his analysis in terms of context. Just as "A village on the Ganges" can be classified in different ways depending on communicative context, so can "The umbrella-holders go." In the second case, while the relationship is still association, it is the converse association: the umbrella-holder is understood as part of the crowd. Here, because of plurality, what is indicated must be more than just one person, and so the crowd is primarily the target of indication. If we think in terms of the categories introduced earlier, the additive and associative plural, this is to take "umbrella-holders" in an additive sense, as illustrated in Figure 10. It primarily expresses many umbrella-holders. There are not, in fact, many umbrella-holders, so what is understood by indication is simply the sense of collectivity in the plural, of the crowd which is near a (single) umbrella-holder. However, because the umbrella-holder is associated with the crowd's movement, he becomes part of the indicated meaning. (In the figure, the shaded portion represents the meaning intended to be expressed in each case.) Mukula Bhaṭṭa's insight here is that speakers have nuanced ways of representing the same object, and while he does not spell this out explicitly, it seems clear that depending upon context, one or the other of these two interpretations might be made salient. For instance, one might say, "The umbrella-holders go and then disperse."

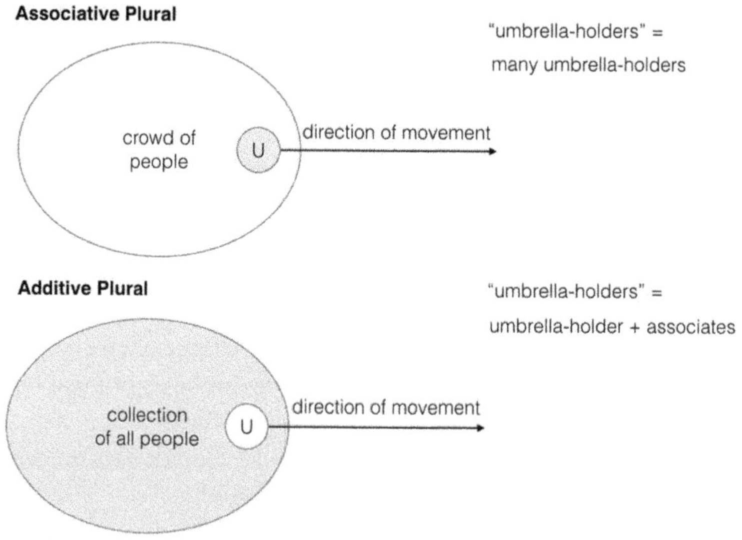

Figure 10 "The umbrella-holders go."

This shows more clearly that it is the crowd which is the primary target of indication.[120]

In either case, when we have the relationship of association, Mukula concludes that, when the association or connection relationship undergirds the relationship between indication and the primary meaning, then the expressed meaning is not entirely displaced.

Connection with action

Speech with multiple registers posed a problem for Sanskrit poetic theorists. It does not neatly fit into preexisting taxonomies and, indeed may challenge some of the presuppositions undergirding those taxonomies. Mukula, like other theorists before him (and after) reflects on this aspect of figurative meaning. He takes up two kinds of bitextual speech. The first is where the indicated meaning involves two tokens of a single word type, each one with a different intended meaning. The second, in contrast, involves a single word with two simultaneous different meanings.

The first case, which he says involves the word (token's) linguistic capacity, is "Such a man is a man." This may be an excerpt from a larger verse by Hemacandra. If so, the wider context is

> A hero who moves in battle, at the forefront, killing a great many enemies: that man ('*puruṣa*') is like a *puruṣa* ("one who goes in front," "one who protects").[121]

If this is right, then the second occurrence of *puruṣa* is to be taken in an etymological sense, an agentive form either of the verb root *pṛ*, "to protect," or *pur*, "to go in front." Thus what "word's linguistic capacity" means here is the etymological capacity—as Mukula says, "with the linguistic capacity of the word's constituent parts." This means that the second occurrence does not express the meaning which the first one does—and the double meaning only works with both meanings in place. Strictly speaking, this is "twinning," (*yamaka*) where the same word appears in sequence, and the poem trades on multiple meanings.[122] A more modern example of such a play on words might be this sentence, said of a widely watched television show: "That broadcast was a real *broad*cast."[123] Here, while "broadcast" has come to just mean any televised program, in its etymological sense, it refers to something with a wide reach. The repetition, typically combined with appropriate stress to indicate a different reading, would lead hearers to understand two meanings. Since in the second occurrence of the word we understand the etymological meaning and not the ordinary meaning, Mukula would explain such a case as one where the expressed meaning is discarded.

In contrast, Ānandavardhana gives a similar example of twinning, arguing that it involves a shift in the expressed meaning:

> When admired by sensitive critics, excellent qualities blossom;
> When admired by the sun's rays, a lotus becomes a lotus.[124]

This stanza plays on how excellent qualities that blossom or grow appear under the gaze of a sensitive critic (qualities or properties, which can then be set into poetry) and how a lotus flower, under the admiring "gaze" of the sun, becomes more than just a lotus—its qualities are characteristically associated with a beautiful woman. So the second "lotus" becomes more than the lotus, like the case of Rāma it includes all the qualities characteristic of that poetic trope. Ānandavardhana argues that this is a case where the expressed meaning is not intended, and it is shifted, but not entirely discarded. His point is that in the twinning form "x is x" the second tokened x has a different meaning than the first, but the ordinary meaning is not discarded in the entire expression. In contrast, when Mukula says that the meaning is discarded, he seems to be focusing on only the second token. In that case, it is true that the ordinary meaning is discarded, and the etymological meaning is the one conveyed. What is especially important here is that Mukula will go on to show that this same kind of relationship—connection with an action—also undergirds cases where the expressed meaning is intended.

The expressed meaning is intended in a second kind of double meaning known as bitextuality, often called "punning" (*śleṣa*). Unlike twinning, it involves simultaneous understanding of the meanings. (Or at least, both meanings are understood as resulting from the same word token—whether they are comprehended simultaneously was a difficult question addressed in the poetic tradition.) This is the example previously discussed: "Śatru-ghna," or "enemy-killer." Mukula argues that the expressed meaning in this case cannot be discarded—the reason is because the purpose of the wordplay is to bring to mind both the person Śatrughna and the king who is an enemy-killer. Further, these two registers are being compared with one another. Here, although he does not develop the idea, Mukula echoes theorists who relate simile (*upamā*) and bitextuality (*śleṣa*). The point of the wordplay is not to convey two distinct sets of meanings, but a further figure.

For Ānandavardhana, when a single-tokened word yields two different meanings which are unrelated, and originate because of some obvious verbal trigger, he is happy to say that this phenomenon is due to the secondary function of words.[125] In his discussion at 2.21, he argues that this is a case of implication, just as Mukula would say (they both use *ākṣipta* for "implication," which is equal to indication for Mukula). Ānandavardhana thinks that any further suggested comparison or a further suggested *rasa* is a case of suggestion, and it cannot be explained by implication/indication. This is because there is no verbal trigger in the ordinary meanings of the words to bring about this dual meaning. He gives an example of a case where a comparison is suggested, at 2.27 (the double meaning is printed in square brackets)

> Where young men with their wives enjoyed
> covered terraces with sloping eaves
> [covered terraces with curving folds at the waist]
> decked with banners to give them beauty
> [winning fame because they were beautiful]
> and stirring passion by their privacy.
> [and stirring passion by their adornment.][126]

Ānandavardhana argues that the ordinary sense of the stanza is just that young men enjoyed the terraces of their homes with their wives, terraces that were covered with beautiful banners and were private for the young lovers. However, the second meaning, in brackets above, describes the terraces in terms appropriate for women, having curving folds at their waists, being beautiful, and being adorned (with jewelry). This second meaning, though, is not independent. It is a simile: the terraces are like wives. Ānandavardhana argues that this second meaning, understood as related to the first, occurs through a capacity which is not related to the primary meaning. In other words, there is no comparative word such as "like" in the stanza. And we do not need the second meaning to complete the stanza—it could be read entirely as a naturalistic description of men and women sitting together on terraces. Thus Ānandavardhana argues that the second meaning understood as related to the primary meaning has to be due to suggestion.[127]

For some reason, Mukula does not discuss this example or directly respond to Ānandavardhana's position. Instead, what he says is that sensitive critics might explain cases like Śatrughna as when the expressed sense is entirely discarded. As Venugopalan notes, there does not seem to be any evidence that Ānandavardhana took this position, so this seems to be Mukula's imagined response on his behalf.[128] On this view, the main point is that "You are Śatrughna in the great battle" involves similarity. Recall that in cases like "friends of the clouds," the ordinary meaning (human friends) is given up and instead what is meant is something similar (peacocks). There is a comparison between human friends and peacocks. Likewise, here, the sensitive critic's position is that the word *śatrughna* is used only to convey what is like Śatrughna, which is being an enemy-killer. So this would be like the other cases of similarity, which we have already said involve the ordinary meaning being entirely given up.

Mukula, however, thinks that postulation and inclusive indication are responsible for the way that two related meanings are understood from a single word. He argues that, in the case of "Śatrughna," since both meanings are intended, and the ordinary meaning is included in the overall meaning, this is a case of inclusion. Understood in its primary sense as a name, "Śatrughna" picks out a person, the son of Daśaratha. Understood in its indicated sense, etymologically, it communicates someone who kills an enemy. Finally, the king, through his heroic actions of killing is being compared to Śatrughna (also someone who kills an enemy). Since the primary meaning is included in the indicated meaning, which is understood as a comparison, this is inclusion. Now, Mukula does not, as he has before, explain what incongruity might give rise to this inclusive indicated meaning. He simply says that this happens when there is a cause for it. We are meant to understand that in a situation with the right kinds of conditions in terms of speaker, sentence, expressed meaning, place, time, such double meanings can occur. Perhaps here, knowing that the speaker is addressing a king who is not Śatrughna might be the relevant incongruity which requires postulation of a second meaning. Whatever the particular explanation, for Mukula, cases of bitextual registers such as this, where there is an implicit comparison, do not need to be explained by suggestion, but are again accounted for by postulation and inclusive indication.

In twinning, as in "The man is a man," the expressed meaning is discarded in one of the occurrences. And Mukula does not explicitly connect this case to inclusive indication and postulation. So not all double meanings require that the expressed meaning is intended. Still, on Mukula's view, for either kind of case, there is no need to appeal to suggestion.

Closing reflections on Mukula's argument

Mukula has now argued that indication is a powerful explanation for a wide range of meanings, an explanation which does not need augmentation by a novel linguistic capacity. He has only given a general sense—details are left out, but the argument and attendant taxonomy is now complete, with indication having been investigated from a number of perspectives. He closes his treatise by emphasizing the need for "wise persons" with sharp intellects—as sharp as the point of *kuśa* grass, in fact, to reflect further on these relationships.

In the spirit of investigating indication, let us close with a few remarks on his choice of closing imagery: "This is to be investigated by wise persons with intellects sharp as the point of *kuśa* grass." This kind of grass was used in Vedic rituals, woven into mats on which sacrificial objects would be placed. The grass was also thick and difficult to cut—Mammaṭa points out that the phrase *karmaṇi kuśalaḥ* means "skillful actions." This is because a person who cuts *kuśa* grass needs to have skill to avoid being cut.[129] By Mammaṭa's time, circa 1100 CE, this was a conventional figure, and probably was for Mukula as well.

So Mukula's meaning in this sentence could be analyzed, on his view, in this way: there is an incongruity in calling someone's intellect as sharp as *kuśa* grass, since the sharpness of an intellect is not the (physical) sharpness of a blade of grass. The motive here is either to follow an established conventional use, in which case "sharp" is a matter of absorption, or to communicate the adeptness needed by those thinkers who would investigate indication. Whether the motive is conventional or not, there is a relationship between the primary meaning (sharp as in cutting) and the indicated meaning (sharp as in skillful). The relationship here would be similarity, just as in the case of "bee" and "flower." That is, the ability of *kuśa* to physically cut is similar to the ability of a wise person to distinguish, to separate categories. Finally, where Ānandavardhana might think that the holiness of the *kuśa* grass was responsible for some suggestion that the wise person is not merely intelligent but morally upstanding, Mukula might attribute this to semantic imbuing (of the sort discussed under 5b–6a). In this case, the figure would need to be superimposed and not absorbed. Thus, for such an effect to result, this instance of indication would need to be superimposition of properties, based on the relationship of similarity, which means that the expressed meaning is entirely displaced.

We have seen that the same expression can be interpreted in different ways (e.g., "umbrella-holders" and "Ganges"), so we have no way of knowing for certain if Mukula would agree with this interpretation. However, the possible moves have now been mapped out for us, so that we have a way to cut through the thicket of language. Still, Mukula is not quite finished with his treatise. He opened the work with a discussion of the importance of language use and linguistic reference in relationship to ordinary and religious aims. He will close the work by returning to this theme, picking up earlier threads as he does, especially from the discussion of sentence meaning and Bhartṛhari's Burst Theory.

Verses 12b–13a

Mukula now returns to the nature of language in general. He alludes to Bhartṛhari in his use of crucial Sanskrit terms: "Manifesting" (*vivarta*) and "language principle" (*śabda-tattva*).

> The nature of speech, when it is being made manifest, is analyzed as divided into ten kinds. (12)
> But when such differentiation is a sequence of phonemes whose temporal order has been dissolved, how can it be understood in this manner? (98)

As Mukula explains in the auto-commentary, by "language principle" he means whatever it is gives unity among all sounds and words (*sakala-śabdâvibhāgâtmaka*). Here, "sounds and words" translates the single term *śabda* in its broad sense, which includes the sounds that are understood as words as well as the words which are understood as referring to meanings. The language principle is that which allows such connection between speech-as-sound, and speech-as-word, and speech-as-meaning. Whatever this language principle is—and Mukula does not give us much insight into any metaphysical commitments he might have—in some important sense it is a unified whole.[130] While it manifests itself as speech, meanings, and their relationship, this manifestation is like a "rope mistaken for a snake." This image is a paradigmatic example in Indian thought of cognitive error. Mukula's use of the simile in this context is to illustrate that only when the language principle takes on this apparent (but ultimately unreal) differentiation do we use it in our ordinary practices. The language principle's differentiation is what enables communication. This is because language requires differentiation between word and meaning. And it is in this context that Mukula's previous discussion about the varieties of primary meaning and indication (which total ten) is appropriate.

In contrast, we can understand the language principle in the context of the *sphoṭa or* Burst Theory of meaning, in which meaning is merely "manifested" by sounds which do not genuinely admit of parts. As he discussed first in the context of word meanings and again in the context of sentence theories, on this view, any distinctions between words or parts of words are theoretical, and not grounded in corresponding real distinctions in uttered sound. Thus when we understand language from this perspective, there is no communicative function divided into ten kinds, as those divisions depend on other divisions (between words, parts of words, and so on). This is Mukula's main point, which he explains concisely in the verse, by using language we saw earlier at Verse 2 which describes an aspect of the *sphoṭa* theory: "A sequence of phonemes whose temporal order has been dissolved." In fact, when the language principle is manifested, it is distorted, because there is sequence, as Bhartṛhari himself says in the *Treatise* at 3.56–57, using similar language. Language and concepts, which both carve out distinctions, are cognitive distortions, like the rope-snake error, but these distinctions are the only way for there to be ten varieties of the communicative function.

There are other distinctions, in addition to word, meaning, and relationship, which are necessary in order for communication to occur. There must be a person who hears speech, who is a knower. The speech itself constitutes an epistemic instrument, as when people speak they do so in order to convey knowledge. What they wish to communicate with speech is thus an object of knowledge, and when the hearer successfully understands what is spoken, they entertain a knowledge-cognition. These divisions, along with the division between word, meaning, and relationship, are crucial for Mukula's account of the communicative function (as well as any other linguistic philosopher engaged in the same project). But, as we have already noted, such divisions have the metaphysical status of a perception of a rope.

Mukula's use of the word translated here as "manifestation" (*vivartamāna*) would remind his reader of Bhartṛhari's use of the term in connection to the language principle. As with "language principle," this term is difficult to interpret in Bhartṛhari's context, as the range of scholarly interpretations shows. Relevant for Mukula's context, though, is the opening of the *Treatise on Sentences and Words* which identifies this language principle with Brahman:

> Beginningless and endless Brahman which, as the imperishable language principle (*śabda-tattva*), behaves in various ways (*vivartate*) as the thing-meant; by virtue of which the world proceeds
>
> .... Of this Brahman, the Veda is the means of attainment and the image, the Veda which is handed down by the great seers in different, separate ways as having numerous paths, though it is actually one.[131]

Later, in the Chapter on Relation (*saṃbandha-samuddeśa*), Bhartṛhari again refers to the process of behaving in various ways or manifesting by which something which is unified comes to have parts:

> Very wonderful indeed is this process: that partless, that without sequence, the real individuality of previously non-existent things manifests itself.[132]

How to make sense of Bhartṛhari's idea(s) of existence, and the relationship between language and metaphysics is difficult. However, while Mukula clearly is alluding to this text and the Burst Theory of language, he nowhere mentions Brahman nor explicitly takes a stance on Bhartṛhari's metaphysics. His main point is just that there are two ways to see the relationship between language and the world, one of which involves diversity and one of which does not. The unified perspective is the ultimate, but this does not preclude making distinctions in the realm of the hypothetical. And these hypothetical distinctions, he concludes, are the purpose of his work.

Verse 13b

> Therefore, the communicative function has here been investigated as a tenfold division.

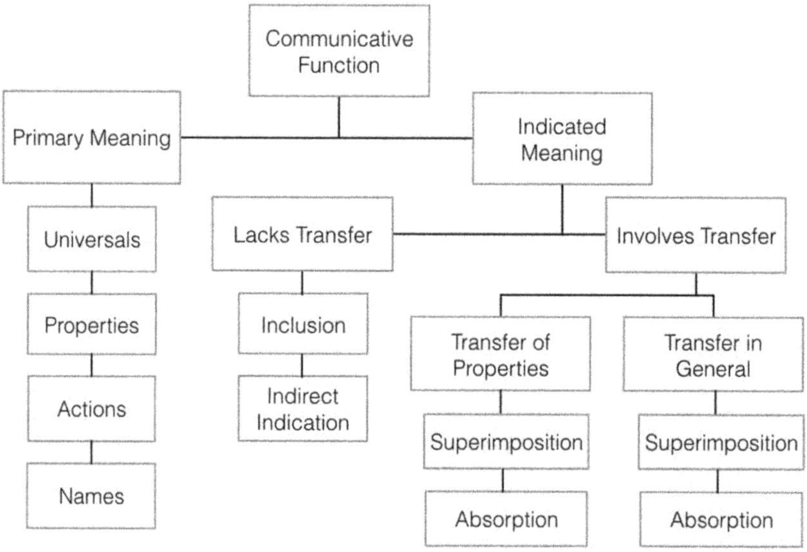

Figure 11 Mukula's analysis of the communicative function.

The ten divisions, once again, are, four within primary meaning and six within the indicatory meaning, as shown in Figure 11.

Mukula merely reiterates that he has shown these ten kinds to exist. He makes no attempt to synthesize the multiple perspectives from which he has analyzed the various examples. As he has said above, he wants to avoid prolixity, and leaves further analysis for those who wish to hone their skills.

Verse 14

In conclusion, Mukula emphasizes the epistemological role of the communicative function. It is reflected in epistemic instruments (*pramāṇas*) as well as words and sentences.

> That communicative function is reflected in the sciences of words, sentence, and epistemic instruments
> For the one who employs it in composition, their words shine clearly. (99)

Perhaps the choice of "reflected" (*pratibimba*) is another allusion to Bhartṛhari, for whom the term connotes the unfolding differentiation of sound from the language principle.[133] The image of a reflection is certainly present in the next line in which Mukula says that using the communicative function in composition (*sāhitya*), a word associated with poetry (*kāvya*), makes one's words clear (*prasīdati*), which I have translated as "shine clearly" to pick up on the idea of reflection. Here, "shine clearly" may be a final response to Ānandavardhana, although the term is common enough that this is not definite. For Ānandavardhana, clarity (*prasāda*) is the capacity for a poem to convey any *rasa* whatsoever, a capacity which isn't limited to a particular kind of *rasa*.[134] Mukula attributes this capability to the tenfold communicative function, in contrast to Ānandavardhana, who restricts it to being related to suggestion. After all, if a poem is to make something known (*jñeya*) to a reader, we must be in the realm of language and also epistemology.

This last point is reinforced in his auto-commentary on this verse, when Mukula explains "the science of words, sentence, and epistemic instruments." He says that "words" refers to the science of Grammar (*vyākaraṇa*), since it is through grammar that we understand words. We have seen him make use of Pāṇini, Patañjali, and Bhartṛhari, evidence of the relevance of grammar for his own undertaking. "Sentences" refers to Mīmāṃsā, also known as the science of sentences (*vākya-śāstra*). We have also seen him draw from Bhāṭṭa and Prābhākara Mīmāṃsā throughout the text, despite sometimes siding with the Grammarians on certain issues, such as word and sentence meaning. Finally, "knowledge sources" means Reasoning (*tarka*), a term which can be taken specifically or more generally. In its specific sense, it would mean something like counterfactual reasoning. More generally, it could refer to reasoning in general, including the knowledge source of inference (*anumāna*). It can also refer to the philosophical traditions, such as Nyāya and Buddhism, which focus on epistemology, thus being a way of referring to "philosophy" in general. This formulation, or something like it, is used after Mukula as a way to identify the major three sciences or *śāstras*.[135] These three sciences are useful for understanding humanity's aim, traditionally numbered as four.[136] Again, Mukula emphasizes the human context for the communicative function, which is found in Grammar, Mīmāṃsā, and Reasoning. Without these three, all human undertaking would be confused. Likewise, all knowledge pursuits (*sarva-vidyā*) require correct application of these three foundational disciplines.

The communicative function (which we have seen above has an ultimately unreal nature) is here compared to a reflection. While not going so far as to identify the reflection of the communicative function with the language principle, Mukula is again emphasizing that there is a distinction between appearance and reality. While sounds exist as a stream, flowing uninterrupted, our theorizing carves this unity into distinct aspects. Analysis is essential for understanding speech—which, as he has said, is not merely human speech, but is the ground of all being. Not only is analysis important to master, meaning Grammar, Mīmāṃsā, and Reasoning but also Composition, which is a science of putting together (*sāhitya*). The imagery here is of taking apart and reconstituting, even if this process is merely playing with a reflection. This reflection, Mukula reiterates, is what constitutes the ordinary practices of the world.

Mastering this communicative function—in theory and practice—results in one who is the lord of speech (*vāg-īśvaraḥ*). The phrase "lord of speech" could be read simply as referring to someone who is skilled in composition, in putting words together clearly in a particular structure.[137] Although it will take a process, mastery of these disciplines eventually yields clarity—the ability to say precisely what you want with your words. Hence we have a final reason we might think indication is preferable to suggestion: it allows such precision because there are clear conditions under which indicated meanings arise from the primary meaning, in contrast to the mysterious nature of suggestion.

Verse 15

In his closing line, Mukula identifies himself as the son of Bhaṭṭa Kallaṭa, who is a commentator on a Kashmiri Śaivite text, *Verses on Vibration* (*Spanda-kārika*).

> The fundamentals of the communicative function have been analyzed by Mukula, the son of Bhaṭṭa Kallaṭa, to enlighten the wise.

He closes with an homage to the goddess Sarasvatī, the goddess of speech and learning, also known as Śāradā, who is identified with Kashmir, Mukula's home. In his short text he has given wise people a positive account of how communication functions, explained its epistemological role in ordinary and religious life, and accounted for its relationship to the broader disciplines of educated people. At the same time, he has argued against a novel theory of communication, the suggestion theory of poetic meaning put forward by Ānandavardhana, in part by marshaling a range of luminaries as allies in his defense. He has argued that poetic language must be connected to the ordinary meanings of words and sentences, and that the existing theory of indication does this. In explaining how indication can account for suggested meaning, Mukula has given an account of what sorts of motives allow for non-ordinary meaning and what relationships connect primary and indicated meaning. The epistemic instrument of postulation is crucial to his explanation. With its reliance on resolving an apparent incongruity, postulation enables indication to work at both the sub-sentential and post-sentential level. While future thinkers do not follow Mukula in his particular approach, others, like him, will take issue with Ānandavardhana. This includes Mukula's student, Pratīhāra Indurāja, as well as Mahima Bhaṭṭa, Bhaṭṭa Nāyaka, and others. While eventually, in the realm of poetic and aesthetic theory, Ānandavardhana's view, especially understood through the lens of his commentator Abhinavagupta, becomes predominant, the challenge initially laid out by Mukula remains relevant to this day.

Part IV

Sanskrit Text of the Abhidhāvṛttamātṛkā

Transliteration Conventions

The following transliteration uses the Dvivedi (1973) edition as its basis, checked against a few other printed editions and one hand-copied version of a manuscript. In this transliteration, hyphens indicate compounds: *avagati-nibandhana* not *avagatinibandhana*. This is the case unless there is compound-internal vowel *sandhi* at word boundaries, in which case a circumflex marks the joining: *padârthānām* not *pada-arthānām*. I have broken *sandhi* at word boundaries but have generally not restored vowel changes, especially in cases of semi-vowels: so *ity etat* not *iti etat* but *sa eva* in place of *saiva*. If *sandhi* is not present in the Dvivedi edition, I have not emended the transliteration: where the text read *nyāyāt śabdasya* I have not corrected it to *nyāyāc chabdasya*. There is no sentence-internal punctuation provided, even if present in the printed editions. Footnotes indicate select alternate readings based on printed editions and major emendations and do not break sandhi, insert hyphens, or use circumflexes. Not all variants among editions are included in the notes. In the main text, numbers in square brackets refer to the Dvivedi edition: page number followed by line number. Abbreviations for editions used:

A = *Abhidhāvṛttamātṛkā* (1977), eds. Brahmitra Avasthi and Indu Avasthi, Delhi: Indu Prakashan.

D = *Abhidhāvṛttamātṛkā* (1973), ed. R. Prasada Dvivedi, Varanasi: Vidhyābhāvan Saṃskṛta Granthamāla No. 165.

F = *Abhidhāvṛttimātṛka* (2016), hand-copied version of No. 63 of 1873–1874 manuscript in the Government Manuscript Library at the Bhandarkar Oriental Research Institute Poona No. 4, India. Print on demand, SN Books World.

M = *Abhidhāvṛttimātrkā* (2008), in *Abhidhāvṛttimātrkā with Subodhini first Sanskrit commentary and Sangamani Hindi commentary*, ed. Sugyan Kumar Mahanty, Varanasi: Caukhamba Saṃskṛta Akadami.

V = *Abhidhāvṛttimātṛkā* (1977), ed. and transl. K. Venugopalan, *Journal of Indian Philosophy*, 4:203-264.

Introduction[1]

[1.6] iha khalu bhogâpavarga-sādhana-bhūtānāṃ tad-viparyaya-parivarjana-prayojanānāṃ ca padârthānām niścayam antareṇa vyavahārôpārohitā na upapadyate. tathā hi sarvāṇi pramāṇāni prameyâvagati-nibandhana-bhūtāni niścaya-paryavasāyitayā prāmāṇyaṃ[2] bhajante. pramāṇa-nibandhanā ca bhogâpavarga-sādhana-bhūtānāṃ tad-viparyaya-parivarjana-prajojanānāṃ ca padârthānām avagatiḥ. ato niścaya eva teṣāṃ padârthānāṃ vyavahārôparohe[3] nibandhanam. niścayaś ca śabda-sambhedena arthaṃ go-carī-karoti. śabdasya ca mukhyena lākṣaṇikena vā abhidhā-vyāpārāreṇa arthâvagati-hetutvam iti mukhya-lākṣaṇikayor abhidhā-vyāpārayor atra vivekaḥ kriyate.

[2.14] kaḥ punar mukhyo lākṣaṇiko vā abhidhā-vyāpāra ity āśaṅkya viṣayôpadarśana-dvāreṇa mukhya-lākṣaṇikau śabda-vyāpārav upavarṇayitum āha

Verses 1–15

Verse 1

śabda-vyāpārato yasya pratītis tasya mukyatā |
arthâvaseyasya punar lakṣyamāṇatvam ucyate || 1 ||

[2.18] śabda-vyāpārād yasya avagatis tasya mukhyatvam. sa hi yathā sarvebhyo hastâdibyo 'vayavebhyaḥ pūrvaṃ mukham avalokyate tad-vad eva sarvebhyaḥ pratīyamānebhyo 'rthântarebhyaḥ pūrvam avagamyate. tasmān mukham iva mukhya iti śākhâdi-yād-antena[1] mukhya-śabdena abhidhīyate. tasya udāharaṇaṃ gaur anubandhya iti. atra hi go-śabda-vyāpārād yāga-sādhana-bhūtā gotva-lakṣaṇā jātir avagamyate. atas tasya mukhyatā. tad evaṃ śabda-vyāpāra-gamyo mukhyo 'rthaḥ.

[2.24] yasya tu śabda-vyāpāra-gamyârtha-paryālocanayā avagatis tasya lākṣaṇikatvam. yathā[2] pūrvasminn eva udāharaṇe vyakteḥ. sā hi na śabda-vyāpārād avasīyāte viśeṣyaṃ na abhidhā gacchet kṣīṇa-śaktir viśeṣaṇe iti nyāyāt śabdasya jāti-mātra-paryavasitatvāt. jātis tu vyaktim antareṇa yāga-sādhana-bhāvaṃ na pratipadyate iti śabda-pratyāyita-jāti-sāmarthyād atra jāter āśraya-bhūtā vyaktir ākṣipyate. tena asau lākṣaṇikī.

[3.2] evam ayaṃ mukhya-lākṣaṇikâtmaka-viṣayôpavarṇana-dvāreṇa śabdasya abhidhā-vyāpāro dvividhaḥ pratipādito nirantarârtha-viṣayaḥ sântarârtha-niṣṭhaś ca.

[4.26] samprati mukhyâbhidhā-vyāpārasya cātur-vidhyam abhidhīyate

Verse 2a

tatra mukhyaś catur-bhedo jñeyo jāty-ādi-bhedataḥ |

[4.28] tayor mukhya-lākṣaṇikayor arthayor madhyān mukhyasya arthasya cat-vāro bhedāḥ jāty-ādi-bhedāt. catuṣṭayī hi śabdānāṃ pravṛttir bhagavatā mahā-bhāṣya-kāreṇa upavarṇitā jāti-śabdā guṇa-śabdāḥ kriyā-śabdā yad-ṛcchā-śabdāś ce 'ti. tathā hi sarveṣāṃ śabdānāṃ svârthâbhidhānāya pravartamānānām upādhy-uparañjita-viṣaya-vivekatvād upādhi-nibandhanā pravṛttiḥ.

[5.3] upādhiś ca dvividhaḥ vaktṛ-sanniveśito vastu-dharmaś ca. kaścit khalu vaktrā tasmiṃs tasmin vastuny-upādhitayā sanniveśyate kaścit tu vastu-dharma eva. tatra yo vaktrā yad-ṛcchayā tat-tat-saṃjñi-viṣaya-śakty-abhivya kti-dvāreṇa tasmiṃs tasmin saṃjñini saṃniveśyate sa vaktṛ-saṃniveśitaḥ yathā ḍittâdīnāṃ śabdānām anty-abuddhi-nirgrāhyaṃ saṃhṛta-kramaṃ sva-rūpam. tat khalu tāṃ tām-abhidhā-śaktim abhivyañjayatā vaktrā yad-ṛcchayā tasmiṃs tasmin saṃjñini upādhitayā saṃniveśyate. atas tan-nibandhanā yad-ṛcchā-śabdā ḍitthâdayaḥ.

[5.10] yeṣām api ca ḍa-kārâdi-varṇa-vyatirikta-saṃhṛta-sva-rūpâbh āvān na ḍitthâdi-sva-rūpaṃ saṃhṛta-kramaṃ saṃjñiṣv adhyasyate iti darśanaṃ teṣām api vaktṛ-yad-ṛcchâbhivyajyamāna-śakti-bhedânusāreṇa kālpanika-samudāya-rūpasya ḍitthâdeḥ śabdasya tat-tat-saṃjñâbhidhānāya pravartamānatvād yad-ṛcchā-śabdatvaṃ ḍitthâdīnām upapadyata eva. tad evaṃ pūrvam upadarśito yo vaiyākaraṇanayaḥ tad-āśrayeṇa upādhir vaktṛ-saṃniveśita-sva-rūpâkhyo vyākhyātaḥ.

[5.16] yasya tu vastu-dharmatvena upādher avasthānaṃ tasya api dvai-vidhyaṃ sādhya-siddhatâbhedāt. tatra sādhyôpādhi-nibandhanāḥ kriyā-śabdāḥ yathā pacati iti. siddhyasya tu upādhi-dvai-vidhyaṃ jāti-guṇa-bhedāt. kasya-cit khalu siddhasya upādhiḥ padârthasya prāṇa-pradatā yathā jāteḥ. na hi kaścit padârtho jāti-saṃbandham antareṇa sva-rūpaṃ pratilabhate. yad uktaṃ vākya-padīya gaur iti na hi gauḥ sva-rūpeṇa gauḥ na apy agauḥ gotvâbhisambandhāt tu gauḥ iti.

[5.22] kaścit punar upādhir labdha-sva-rūpasya vastuno viśeṣâdhāna-hetuḥ yathā śuklâdir guṇaḥ. na hi śuklâder guṇasya paṭâdi-vastu-sva-rūpa-pra tilambha-nibandhanatvam jāti-mahimna eva tasya vastunaḥ pratilabdha-sva-rūpatvāt. ato 'sau labdha-sva-rūpasya vastuno viśeṣâdhāna-hetuḥ. ye 'pi ca nityāḥ[3] paramāṇutvâdayo guṇās teṣām api sarveṣāṃ guṇa-jātīyatvād evaṃ prakāratvam eva. tad evaṃ prāṇa-pradôpādhi-nibandhanatvaṃ yasya śabdasya sa jāti-śabdo yathā gavâdiḥ. yasmāl labdha-sva-rūpasya vastuno viśeṣâdhāna-hetur arthaḥ pratīyate sa guṇa-śabdo yathā śuklâdiḥ.

[8.25] nanu[4] sarveṣām api guṇa-kriyā-yad-ṛcchā-śabdâbhimatānāṃ jāti-nibandhanatvam. tathā hi guṇa-śabdānāṃ tāvac chuklâdīnāṃ payaḥ-śaṅkha-balākâdy-āśraya-samavetā ye śuklâdi-lakṣaṇā guṇā vibhinnās tat-samaveta-sāmānya-vācinaḥ. evaṃ kriyā-śabdānām api guḍa-tila-taṇḍulâdi-dravyâśritā ye pākâdayo 'nyonyam anyatvena avasthithāḥ kriyāviśeṣāḥ tat-samavetaṃ tāsām sāmānyam eva vācyam. yad-ṛcchā-śabdānāṃ tu ḍitthâdīnāṃ śuka-sārikā-manuṣy-ādy-udīriteṣu bhinneṣu ḍitthâdi-śabdeṣu samavetaṃ ḍittha-śabdatvâdikaṃ sāmānyam eva yathā-yogaṃ saṃjñiṣv adhyastam avaseyam. yadi ca upacayâpacaya-yogitayā ḍitthâdau saṃjñini pratikālaṃ bhidyamāneṣu abhidyamāno yan-mahimnā ḍittho ḍittha ity-evam-ādi-rūpatvena abhinnâkāraḥ pratyayo bādha-śūnyaḥ saṃjāyate taiḥ tathā-bhūtaṃ ḍitthâdi-śabdâvaseya-vastu-samavetam eva ḍitthatvâdi-sāmānyam eṣṭavyam. tac ca ḍitthâdi-śabdair abhidhīyate. ataś ca guṇa-kriyā-yad-ṛcchā-śabdānām api jāti-śabdatvāc catuṣṭayī śabdānām pravṛttir na upapadyate.

[10.7] atra abhidhīyate guṇa-kriyā-śabda-saṃjñā[5]-vyaktīnām eva tat-tad-upādhi-nibandhana-bheda-juṣām ekâkārâvagati-nibandhanatvam na tu jāter iti bhagavato mahā-bhāṣya kārasya atra abhimatam. yathā hi ekam eva mukhaṃ taila-khaḍ-godakâdarśâdīnāṃ pratibimbâvagati-nibandhanānāṃ bhedān na anākāratvena pratyavabhāsate tathā eka eva śuklâdi-vyaktir deśa-kālâvacchinnā tat-tat-kāraṇa-sāmagry-upajanita-śaṅkhâdy-āśraya-v iśeṣa-vaśena na anārūpatayā abhivyaktim āsādayantī vicitrā iva syād iti.[6] ataś ca tasyāḥ śuklâdi-vyakter ekatvāj jāteś ca bhinnâśraya-samavetatvāt śulkatvâdi-jāty-abhāvān na śuklâdi-śabdānāṃ jāti-śabdatvam. evaṃ pacati ity-ādau ḍittha-śabdâdau ḍitthâdau ca saṃjñini vācyam. atra apy ekasyā eva pākâdi-kriyâvyakteḥ ḍitthâdi-śabda-vyakteḥ ḍitthâdeś ca saṃjñino yathā kramam abhivyañjakānāṃ pākâdīnāṃ tathā dhvanīnām vayo 'vastha-viśeṣānām kaumārâdīnāṃ ca yo bhedas tad-vaśena na anāvidhena rūpeṇa avabhāsamānatvāt. sthitham etac chabda-pravṛtti-nimittānāṃ catuṣṭvān mukhyaḥ śabdârthaś catur-vidha iti.

Verse 2b

[11.8] adhunā lākṣaṇikasya dvi-bhedatvam upadarśayitum āha.

śuddhôpacāra-miśratvāl lakṣaṇā dvi-vidhā matā || 2 ||

[11.20] lakṣaṇāyā dvi-prakāratvam śuddhatvād upacāra-miśratvāc ca. śuddhā tāval lakṣaṇā gaṅgāyāṃ ghoṣa iti. atra hi ghoṣaṃ prati sroto-viśeṣasya adhāratā na upapadyate iti gaṅgā-śabdaḥ svâbhidheyasya sroto-viśeṣasya yaḥ samīpa-bhūtas taṭaḥ taṃ lakṣaṇayā avagamayati. upacāra-miśrā tu yatra vastv-antaraṃ vastv-antare upacaryate yathā gaur vāhīka iti. atra hi go-śabdo vāhīka-śabdena anupapadyamāna-sāmānâdhikaraṇyād bādhita-mukhyârthaḥ san go-gatā ye jāḍya-māndyâdayo guṇāḥ tat-sadṛśa-vāhīka-gata-jāḍya-māndyâdi-guṇa-lakṣaṇā-dvāreṇa go-gata-jāḍya-māndyâdi-guṇa-sadṛśa-jāḍya-māndyâdi-guṇôpete vāhīka upacaritaḥ. tena ayam upacāra-miśrā lakṣaṇā. evam śuddhôpacāra-miśratva-bhedena lakṣaṇāyāṃ dvai-vidhyam uktam.

[12.24] idānīṃ tu śuddhāyā api lakṣaṇāyā dvai-vidhyaṃ darśayati.

Verse 3a

upādānāl lakṣaṇāc ca śuddhā sā dvividhôditā |

[12.26] yā iyaṃ lakṣaṇā śuddhā pratipāditā sā dvividhôktā. kvacit khalv arthântarôpādānena lakṣaṇā pravartate kvacit tu arthântara-lakṣaṇena. kiṃ punar arthântarasya upādānaṃ kiṃ vā tasya lakṣaṇam ity āśaṅkya āha.

Verses 3b–4a

sva-siddhy-arthatayā ākṣepo yatra vastv-antarasya tat. || 3 ||
upādānaṃ lakṣaṇaṃ tu tad-viparyâsato matam |

[13.3] yatra sva-siddhy-arthatayā vastv-antarasya ākṣepo bhavati tatra upādānam yathā gaur anubandhya iti. atra hi gotvasya yāgaṃ prati sādhanatvaṃ śābdaṃ vyakty-ākṣepam antareṇa na upapadyata iti tat-siddhy-arthatayā vyakter ākṣepaḥ. yathā ca pīno devadatto divā na bhuṅkte iti. atra hi pīnatvaṃ dinâdhikaraṇa-bhojanâbhāva-viśiṣṭatayā avagamyamānam eva kāryatvāt sva-siddhy-arthatvena kāraṇa-bhūtaṃ rātri-bhojanam ākṣẹpād abhyantarī-karoti. na hi pīnatvasya rasāyan-ādy-upayoga-janyatā pramānântareṇa tad-abhāvâvasāye saty etasya udāharaṇatvāt. pīnatvasya ca atra dinâdhikaraṇa-bhojanâbhāva-viśiṣṭatvena rasāyan-ādy-upayoga-bādha-hetutvāt. atra ca rātrau bhuṅkta ity etac chabdâkṣepa-pūrvakatayā pramāṇasya aparipūrṇasya paripūraṇāt śrutârthâpattitvaṃ bhavatu atha-vā kāraṇasya eva rātri-bhojanasya ākṣepa iti. sarvathā sva-siddhy-arthatvena arthântarasya ākṣepa-pūrvakatayā antar-bhāvanād upādānatvam upapadyate.

[13.15] yatra tu pūrvôditôpādāna-rūpa-viparyāsa-saṃśrayān na svârtha-siddhy-arthatayā arthântarasya ākṣepaḥ api tv arthântara-siddhy-arthatvena svârtha-samarpaṇaṃ tatra lakṣaṇaṃ yathā pūrvam udāhṛtaṃ gaṇgāyāṃ ghoṣa iti. atra hi taṭasya ghoṣâdhāratayā dhāraṇa-kriyânvitasya gaṅgā-śabdena sva-samarpaṇaṃ kriyate. ato 'rthântara-bhūtaṃ taṭam avagamayituṃ gaṅgā-śabdena sva-vācya-bhūtaḥ sroto-viśeṣo 'tra samarpyate ity arthântara-siddhy-arthatvena svârtha-samarpaṇam. evaṃ ca atra pūrvôditôpādāna-rūpa-viparyāsāl lakṣaṇatvam. evaṃ śuddhā lakṣaṇā dvi-vidhā pravibhaktā.

[15.27] idānīm upacāra-miśrāṃ catur-bhedatvena nirūpayitum āha

Verses 4b–5a

> āropâdhyavasānābhyāṃ śuddha-gauṇôpacārayoḥ || 4 ||
> pratyekaṃ bhidyamānatvād upacāraś catur-vidhaḥ. |

[16.1] dvividhaḥ upacāraḥ śuddho gauṇaś ca. tatra śuddho yatra mūla-bhūtasya upamānôpameya-bhāvasya abhāvena upamāna-gata-guṇa-sadṛśa-guṇa-yoga-lakṣaṇâsaṃbhavāt kārya-kāraṇa-bhāvâdi-saṃbhandāl lakṣaṇayā vastv-antare vastv-antaram upacaryate yathā āyur ghṛtam iti. atra hy āyuṣaḥ kāraṇe ghṛte tad-gata-kārya-kāraṇa-bhāvāl[7] lakṣaṇā-pūrvakatvena ayuṣṭvaṃ kāryaṃ tac-chabdaś ca ity ubhayam upacaritam. tasmāc chuddho 'yam upacāraḥ.

[16.6] gauṇaḥ punar upacāro yatra mūla-bhūtôpamānôpameya-bhāva-samāśrayeṇa upamāna-gata-guṇa-sadṛśa-guṇa-yoga-lakṣaṇāṃ puras-sarī-kṛtyôpameya upamāna-śabas tad-arthaś ca adhyâropyate. sa hi guṇebhya āgatatvād gauṇa-śabdena ābhidhīyate yathā gaur vāhīka iti. atra hi go-ga ta-jāḍya-māndyâdi-guṇa-sadṛśya-jāḍya-māndyâdi-yogād vāhīke go-śabda-gotvayor upacāraḥ. kecit tu upacāre śabdôpacāram eva manyante na arthôpacāram. tad ayuktam. śabdôpacārasya arthôpacārâvinā-bhāvitvāt. evam ayam upacāraḥ śuddha-gauṇa-bhedena dvividho 'bhihitaḥ.

[18.1] tasya ca praty-ekam dvai-vidhyam adhyâropâdyavasānābhyām. yatra adhyāropa-viṣayayor bhedam anapahnutyā eva vastv-antare vastv-antaram upacaryate tatra anapahnuta-sva-rūpa eva vastv-antare vastv-antarasya ādhikasya āropyamāṇatvād adhyâropaḥ. yathā pūrvôktayor udāharaṇayoḥ. tathā hi āyur ghṛtam ity atra na āyur-lakṣaṇa-kāryântar-līnatayā kāraṇa-bhūtasya ghṛtasya pratipattiḥ sva-rūpena eva tasya pratipatteḥ. sva-rūpeṇa eva tu tasya pratīyamānasya āyuḥ-kāraṇatvād āyuṣṭvaṃ pratīyate. tena atra ādhyâropaḥ. evaṃ gaur vāhīka iti atra api upamānôpameya-svarūpânapahnavāt. tad evaṃ yatrôpacaryamāṇena upacaryamāṇa-viṣayasya sva-rūpaṃ na apahnūyate tatra ādhyâropaḥ.

[18.9] yatra tu upacaryamāṇa-viṣayasya upacaryamāṇe 'ntar-līnatayā vivakṣistatvāt sva-rūpâpahnavaḥ kriyate tatra adhyavasānam. tatra śuddhôpacāre 'dhyavasānasya udāraṇaṃ pañcālā iti. atra hi pañcālâpatyāni-vāsâdhikaraṇatvāj jana-pade lakṣita-lakṣaṇayā pañcāla-śabdaḥ prayujyate. pañcālena apatyānāṃ lakṣaṇād apatyaiś ca sva-nivāsâdhikaraṇasya jana-padasya. na ca atra upacaryamāṇârtha-viṣayasya upacaryamāṇād bhedena pṛatipattiḥ. upacaryamāṇârtha-nigīrṇatayā eva tasya pratipatteḥ. tena atra upacāratvaṃ rūḍhi-māhātmyād bhraṣṭam iva lakṣyate. ato 'tra ādhyavasāna-garbhaḥ śuddha upacāraḥ.

[18.16] gauṇôpcāre tu adhyavasānasya udāharaṇaṃ rāje 'ti. rāja-śabdo hy atra prayoga-darśanāt kṣatriye mukhyayā vṛttyā prayuktaḥ san śūdrâdau kṣatriya-gata-jana-pada[8]-pari-pālana-sadṛśa-jana-pada-paripālana-yoga-lakṣaṇā pūrvakatayā gauṇa-vṛttyā prayujyate. na ca atra jhagity eva gauṇatvasya avagatiḥ. vicāraṇâvyavasthāpyatvāt. tena atra gauṇatvaṃ jhagity eva apratīyamānatvād bhraṣṭaṃ sad vicāraṇayā samadhi-gamyate. ato 'tra ādhyavasāna-garbho gauṇa upacāraḥ. tad evam upacāraś catur-vidhaḥ pravibhaktaḥ.

[18.23] etena catur-vidhena upacārena saha pūrvôktau dvau lakṣaṇā bhedau saṃkalayya ṣaṭ-prakārā lakṣaṇā vaktavyā.

[20.11] eṣā ca lakṣaṇā tri-skandhā śuddhatvād adhyâropād adhyavasānāc ca. tatra śuddha-skandhasya dvai-vidhyam upādāna-lakṣaṇābhyām uktam adhyâropâdhyavasāna-skandhayor api praty-ekaṃ dvi-prabhedatā śuddha-gauṇôpacāra-miśratvāt. tatra eteṣāṃ trayāṇāṃ skandhānāṃ viṣaya-vibhāgaṃ pradarśayitum āha.

Verses 5b–6a

> taṭasthe lakṣaṇā śuddhā syād āropas tv adūrage || 5 ||
> nigīrṇe 'dhyavasānaṃ tu rūḍhy-āsannataratvataḥ |

[20.17] yā eṣā lakṣaṇā śuddhā upādāna-lakṣaṇâtmakatvena dvi-prabhedā pratipāditā sā lakṣakârthânuparaktatvāt taṭasthatayā pratīyamāne lakṣye 'rthe draṣṭavyā. na hi tatra lakṣakârthôparaktatayā lakṣyasya arthasya avagatiḥ. tathā hi gaṅgāyāṃ ghoṣa ity atra ghoṣâdhikaraṇa-bhūta-taṭô palakṣaṇâbhisaṃdhānena gaṅgāyāṃ ghoṣo na vitastāyām iti gaṅgā-śabde prayujyamāne taṭasya sroto-viśeṣeṇa upalakṣakatva-mātrôpayuktatvena uparāgo na pratīyate taṭasthatvena eva tasya taṭasya pratyayāt. evam upādāne 'pi vācyam yathā pīno devadatto divā na bhuṅkta iti.

[20.24] yadā tu gaṅgā-śabdâbhidheyasya sroto-viśeṣasya avidūra-varttitayā taṭam anapahnuta-sva-rūpaṃ sroto-viśeṣôparaktatayā vivakṣitaṃ bhavati tadā pūrvasminn udāharaṇe 'dhyāropo bhavati. sroto-viśeṣôparaktasya taṭasya pratīteḥ sroto-viśeṣâvidūra-varttitvāt sroto-viśeṣa-rūpe taṭe ghoṣa iti.

[21.1] yadā tv atyantam āsannatāṃ ghoṣaṃ prati sroto-viśeṣasya pratipādayitum etad vākyaṃ sroto-viśeṣa-nigīrṇatayā taṭam apahnutya prayujyate gaṅgāyām eva sākṣād ghoṣaḥ na tv anyatre 'ti tad-ādhyavasānam.

[22.18] yathā ca etac chuddhôpacāra-niṣṭhatayâdhyāropâdhyavasānayor udāharaṇam uktaṃ tathā gauṇe 'py upacāre vācyam gaur vāhīka iti gaur eva ayaṃ sākṣād iti ca. atra api yathā-kramaṃ go-gata-guṇa-sadṛśa-guṇa-yoga-dvāreṇa gor avidūratvena vāhīkasya vivakṣitatvād gotvâdyāropaḥ go-gatānāṃ tu guṇānām utkaṭatvena vāhīkasya gotvâdhyavasānam.

[22.23] yathā ca āsannataratvena ādhyavasānaṃ pūrvaṃ pravibhaktaṃ tathā rūḍhitvena api pravibhaktavam yathā pūrvôpadarśitayor udāharaṇayoḥ pañcālā iti tathā rāje 'ti. tad idam uktaṃ rūdhy-āsannataratvata iti. rūdhitvād āsannataratvāc ca nigīrṇe 'rthe 'dhyavasānaṃ syād ity arthaḥ.

[24.4] nanu mukhyârthe śabdasya saṃbandhâvadhāraṇāt pratipādakatvam upapadyate na tu lākṣaṇike tad-viparyayāt. tathā hi saṃbandhâvadhāraṇa-samaye vyavahartṛ-gatayos tāvat śabda-prayogârtha-pratipattyor avibhaktôd deśa-vākya-vākyârtha-niṣṭhatayā pūrvaṃ hetu-phala-bhāvâvasāyo bhavati.

[24.8] tad-anantaraṃ ca tri-catur-ādi-darśanebhyo 'nvaya-vyatirekābhyāṃ vākya-vākyârthôddeśa-pravibhāga-gate ye śabda-prayogârtha-pratipattī tan-niṣṭha-kārya-kāraṇa-bhāvâvadhāraṇam. tad-uttara-kālaṃ ca vyava hartṛ-gatârtha-pratipatty-anyathânupapattyā śabdârtha-saṃbandhâvagatiḥ. sā ca mukhya eva arthe jāty-ādau catur-vidhe na tu lākṣaṇike ṣaṭ-prakāre. na hi lākṣaṇikena arthena saha śabdasya saṃbandhaḥ. mukhyena eva arthena paridṛśyate. tathā bhave sati tasya mukhyatvam eva syānn na lākṣaṇikatvam.

[24.15] atha śabdasya mukhyo yo 'sāv arthas tena saha saṃbandho lakṣyamāṇasya arthasya dṛṣṭa iti tad-dvāreṇa śabdāt tasya avagatir ity abhidhīyate evaṃ sati yadi nirapekṣaḥ svârtha-pratipādana-dvāreṇa lakṣyamāṇam artham avagamayati tadā sarvadā tam artham avagamyet atha sâpekṣaḥ kiṃ tasya āpekṣaṇīyam.

[24.18] ity āśaṅkhya āha

Verses 6b–7a

> vaktur vākyasya vācyasya rūpa-bhedâvadhāraṇāt || 6 ||
> lakṣaṇā ṣaṭ-prakārā eṣā vivektavyā manīṣibhiḥ |

[24.21] yaḥ parapratipattaye vākyam uccārayati sa vaktā. sâkaṅkṣāṇāṃ padānām ekârthaḥ samūho vākyam. śabdena mukhyaṃ lākṣaṇikaṃ vā abhidhā-vyāpāram āśritya yad go-carī kriyate tad vācyam.

[24.23] eteṣāṃ trayāṇāṃ vaktrâdīnāṃ vyasta-samasta-bheda-bhinnānāṃ deśa-kālâvasthā-vailakṣaṇya-gata-samasta-vyasta-bheda-saṃyojitānāṃ yaḥ sva-bhāva-bheda-prapañcaḥ tata eṣā ṣaṭ-prakārā lakṣaṇā parāmarśa-kuśalair vivecanīyā. tathā vidha-vaktrâdi-sāmagry-apekṣaya eva śabdānām svârtham avagamayatāṃ svârtha-dvāreṇa lakṣyamāṇârtha-saṃbandhasya vṛddha-vyavahāreṇa avadhāritatvāt. etad uktaṃ bhavati. na śabdānām anavadhārita-lākṣaṇikârtha-saṃbandhānāṃ lākṣaṇikam arthaṃ prati gamakatvam na api ca tatra sākṣāt saṃbandha-grahaṇam kiṃ tarhi vaktrâdi-sāmagry-apakeṣayā svârtha-vyavadhānena iti.

[25.5] yad uktam ācārya-śabara-svāminā. kathaṃ punaḥ para-śabdaḥ paratra varttate svârthâbhidhānena iti brūmaḥ iti. atra hi svârtha-dvāreṇa lakṣyamāṇârthâbhiniveśitā śabdānām uktā. punaś ca asāv eva āha lakṣaṇā āpi hi laukiky eva iti. atra hi saṃbandhâvadhāraṇa-sâpekṣāṇāṃ śabdānāṃ lakṣyamāṇe 'rthe pravṛttir uktā. vyavahārôpārūḍhāni hi pratyakṣâdīni pramāṇāni loka-śabdena ābhidhīyante. loka eva viditā laukikī vyavahārâvagamyā parigṛhīta-saṃbandha-śabda-niṣṭhā ity-arthaḥ.

[25.12] tad uktaṃ bhaṭṭa-kumārilena

> nirūḍhā lakṣaṇāḥ kāścit sāmarthyād abhidhānavat |
> kriyante sāṃprataṃ kāścit kāścin na eva tv aśāktitaḥ || iti ||

[27.22] tatra nirūḍhā lakṣaṇā rāja-ity-ādikāḥ. sāmprataṃ kriyante ya vṛddha-vyavahāra-vaktrâdy-apekṣayā tathā vidhe 'nyatra viṣaye paridṛṣṭa-sva-bhāvāḥ. yathā

> snigdha-śyāmala-kānti-lipta-viyato vellad-balākā ghanā |
> vātāḥ sīkariṇaḥ payod-suhṛdām ānanda-kekāḥ kalāḥ ||
> kāmaṃ santu dṛḍhaṃ kaṭhora-hṛdayo rāmo 'smi sarvaṃ sahe |
> vaidehī tu kathaṃ bhaviṣyati ha hā hā devi dhīrā bhave 'ti ||

[27.28] atra hi lipta-śabdaḥ kānteḥ kuṅkumâdival lepana-sādhanatvâbhāvād bādhita-mukhyârthaḥ atas tena svârtha-gato yo 'sāv īṣat-tirodhīyamānatvâdidharmaḥ pratipāditaḥ tat-sadṛśeṣat-tirodhīyamānatvâdi-dharma-yogāt kānti-saṃpṛkto 'rtho lakṣyate. evaṃ suhṛc-chabdena api payodānām acetanatvena maitrī-saṃbandhâbhāvān mukhya-śabdârtha-bādhe sati suhṛd-gatā ye te te sāṃ-mukhyâdayo dharmāḥ tat-sadṛśa-sāṃ-mukhyâdi-dharma-yogataḥ payodâbhimukhā mayūrā lakṣyante.

[28.5] rāma-śabdasya api pratipannatvāt saṃjñino mukhya-śabdârtha-bādhaḥ. atas tena api rājya-bhraṃśa-vana-vāsa-sītâpanayana-pitṛ-maraṇâda yaḥ svâbhidheya-bhūtârtha-eka-gāmino 'sādhāraṇa-duḥka-hetavo dharmā viśiṣṭa-sāmagry-anupraviṣṭena lakṣitāḥ. tat evam-ādīnāṃ lakṣaṇānāṃ sāmpratam kriyamāṇatā.

[29.11] yāsāṃ tu lakṣaṇānāṃ na vṛddha-vyavahāre dṛṣtatā na ca tasmin śabde rāja-śabdavad darśanaṃ na api ca taj-jātīyeṣu śabdântareṣu liptâdi-śabdavat tāsām aśakyatvād akriyamāṇatvam eva. yathā

> madhye samudraṃ kukubhaḥ piśaṅgīr yā kurvatī kāñcana-bhūmī-bhāsā |
> turaṅga-kāntânana-havya-vāha-jvāleva bhittvā jalam ullalāsa || iti ||

[29.16] atra hi turaṅga-kāntânana-havya-vāha-śabdo vaḍavâmukhâgnau lakṣaṇayā prayuktaḥ.

[29.17] na ca asau vaḍavâmukhâgnau nirūḍhaḥ na api ca taj-jātīyaḥ śabdo viśiṣṭa-sāmagry-anupraviṣṭatayā tathā vidhârthâvagāhitvena[9] paridṛṣṭaḥ.

[29.20] nanu dvi-rephâdīnāṃ śabdānāṃ repha-dvitayā anugata-bramarâdi-śabda-lakṣaṇā-dvāreṇa yathā ṣaṭ-padâdau pravṛttiḥ tathā turaṅga-kāntânana-havya-vāha-śabadsya api vaḍavâmukhâgnau vaḍavâdi-śabda-lakṣaṇā-dvāreṇa kathaṃ pravṛttir na syāt taj-jātīye dvi-rephâdau śabda-lakṣaṇāyāḥ paridṛṣṭatvāt.

[29.24] na etat. yato vṛddha-vyavahārâbhyanujñāteṣv eva śabdeṣu taj-jātīya-śabda-darśanāt lakṣaṇātvam abhyupagamyate na tu sarvatra. anyathā sarveṣām eva śabdānāṃ yena kenacij jātileśena sarvān arthān prati lakṣaṇā-śabdatvasya vaktuṃ śakyatvāt.

[30.2] na kaścic chabdaḥ kaṃcid-arthaṃ pratyavagamakaḥ syāt. vṛddh a-vyavahārâbhyanujñānânabhyuanujñāyāṃ tu viṣaya-vibhāge kriyamāṇẹ turaṅga-kāntânana-havya-vāhêty-ādinām asati prayojane duṣṭatvam eva sati tu guptârtha-pratipādanâdi-prayojana-saṃbhave evaṃ vidhānām api lakṣaṇānām aduṣṭatvam. tathā vidha-viṣaye vṛddha-vyavahāreṇa tāsām abhyanujñātatvāt. tad evaṃ vaktrâdi-sāmagry-anupraveśena śabdānāṃ svârtham arpayatām arthântaraṃ prati vṛddha-vyavahāre sva-rūpadvāreṇa sa-jātīya-śabda-dvāreṇa vā gamakatayâvadhāritānāṃ lakṣakatvam iti sthitam.

[31.22] tatra vaktṛ-nibandhanatvena yatra lākṣaṇiko 'rtho 'vagamyate tatra udāharaṇam.

dṛṣṭiṃ he prativeśini kṣaṇam iha api asmad-gṛhe dāsyasi
prāyo na eṣa śiśoḥ pitā 'sya virasāḥ kaupīr apaḥ pāsyati |
ekâkiny api yāmi tad varam itaḥ srotas tamālā-kulaṃ
nīrandhrā vapur ālikhantu jaraṭhac-chedā nala-granthayaḥ || iti ||

[31.27] atra hi para-puruṣa-saṃbhogânubhavec-chayā saṃketa-sthānaṃ yuvatir vrajantī sva-pravṛtti-prayojanaṃ viśiṣta-saṃketa-sthānâdhāraṃ para-puruṣa-saṃbhogâtmakaṃ tathā saṃbhoga-cihnāni nakha-daśana-kṣatāni gātra-saṃlagnatayā śaṅkyamānā-virbhāvāṇi yathā-kramaṃ bhartṛ-pipāsā-nivṛtti-kṣama-nādeya-sarasa-pānīyânayanena cirac-chinna-nala-granthi-paruṣa-jarjara-prānta-janayiṣyamāṇena ca gātra-gata-vikāra-viśeṣôdgamena apahnutyâbhidhatte. sā ca atra apahnutir asādhyā vaktṛtvaṃ paryālocyâvagamyate. apahnavasya ca alīka-vastv-abhidhānâtmakatvād alīkasya ca satyârtha-viparyāsa-kāritvād alīkena arthena atra satyôrthaḥ[10] sva-siddhyârthatvena ākṣipyate. tena atra vaktṛ-viśeṣa-paryālocanayā satyârthe niṣṭhāyā upādānâtmikāyā lakṣaṇāyāḥ pratipattiḥ. na hy atra vākya-vācyayoḥ sāmarthyam. sādhvyā vaktṛtve sati tayor evaṃ vidhârthâkṣepâsamarthatvāt.

[33.9] vākya-gata-rūpa-viśeṣa-paryālocanayā tu yatra lākṣaṇikârtha-parigrahaḥ tatra udāharaṇam.

prāpta-śrīr eṣa kasmāt punar api mayi taṃ mantha-khedaṃ vidadhyā-
nnidrām apy asya pūrvām analasamanaso na eva saṃbhāvayāmi |
setuṃ badhnāti bhūyaḥ kim iti ca sakala-dvīpa-nāthânuyata-
stv ayyāyāte vitārkān iti dadhata iva abhāti kampaḥ payodheḥ || iti ||

[33.15] atra hi ca aṭuślokena upaślokyate yo nṛpatis tadīya-bala-bhara-kṣobhyamāṇa-svâvasthasya samudrasya yaḥ kampaḥ atiśayôktyôpavarṇitaḥ tasya samudra-kartṛka-vitarka-dhāraṇa-hetukatvam atra utprekṣatam iti vitarkān dadhata ive 'ti.

[33.17] te ca vitarkāḥ prāpta-śrīr-ity-ādinā bhagavad-vāsudevasya vyāpāra-viśeṣa-viṣayāḥ. yāvac ca tasya nṛpater bhagavad-vāsudevatā na samasti tāvat kathaṃ tadīyeṣu vyāpāra-viśeṣeṣu saṃśayaḥ samupajāyate. ato 'tra yad etad bala-bharâkrantatvena samudrasya akampamānasya api kampamānârtha-sādṛśyāt kampamānatvam adhyavasitam tatra adhyavasāna-garbha-gauna-upacāraḥ akampamānasya api tasya kampamānârthatvena ādhyavasitatvāt.

ata eva ca iyaṃ bhede 'py abheda ity-evam-ātmikâtiśayôktiḥ. vikalpavaśād yaś cetanānāṃ mūrdha-kampo bāhulyena paridṛśyate cetana-gata-saṃśaya-hetuka-mūrdha-kampa-sādṛśyāt tad-bhāvo 'sya kampasya upacaryate. evaṃ ca atra apy adhyavasāna-garbho gauṇa upacāraḥ.

[33.26] iyam api ca vibhinnayor api kampayor abhedena adhyavasānāt bhede 'py abheda ity-evam-ātmikâtiśayôktiḥ. tan nibandhana eva ca iyam utprekṣā iti vitarkān dadhata ive 'ti. atra hi kārya-bhūta-kampa-darśanāt kārana-bhūtaṃ vitarka-dhāraṇaṃ mithyâjñāna-sva-rūpayôtprekṣaya utprekṣyate. atra api ca vitarkān adhārayato 'pi payodheḥ vitarka-dhāraṇôpanibandhād bhede 'py abheda ity-evam-ātmikâtiśayôktir garbhī-kṛtā.

[34.5] tad uktam utprekṣā-lakṣaṇe.

sāmya-rūpa-vivakṣāyāṃ vācyevâdyātmabhiḥ[11] padaiḥ |
atad-guṇa-kriyā-yogād utprekṣā-atiśayânvitā || iti ||

[34.8] saṃbhāvyamānasya guṇa-kriyā-yogāt tena atra api adhyvasāna-garbho gauṇa upacāraḥ. prāpta-śrīr-iti-ādiṣu tu triṣu vitarkeṣu bhagavad-vāsudeva-viṣayeṣu yathā-yogaṃ tat-tat-kārya-nirākaraṇa-hetu-garbhatayā pravarttamāneṣu nṛpater bhagavad-vāsu-devatā 'kṣiptā. tena atra upādānâtmikā lakṣanā. bhagavad-vāsudeva-rūpatayā ca atra nṛpater adhyavasānād adhyavasāna-garbho gauṇa upacāraḥ. etac ca atra sarva-vāky ôpātta-pada-samanvayânyathânupapattyā avagamyata iti vākya-nibandhanā atra lakṣaṇā.

[37.18] vācya nibandhanā tu yathā

durvārā madaneṣavo diśi diśi vyājṛmbhate mādhavo
hṛdy-unmādakarāḥ śaśāṅka-rucayaś cetôharāḥ kokilāḥ |
uttuṅga-stana-bhāra-durdharam idaṃ pratyagram anyad vayaḥ
soḍhavyāḥ sakhi sāṃprataṃ katham amī pañcâgnayo duḥsahāḥ || iti ||

[37.23] atra hi smara-śwara-prabhṛtīnāṃ pañcāna-madhyâropita-vahni-bhāvānām asahyatvaṃ vākyârthī-bhūtam atas tasya vācyatā. tāt-paryā-locana-sāmarthyāc ca vipralambha-śṛṅgārasya ākṣepa ity-upādānâtmikā lakṣaṇā vācya-nibandhanā. na hy atra vaktṛ-sva-bhāva-pariśīlanasya śabda-rahitasya upayogaḥ na api ca vākye padānāṃ vipralambha-śṛṅgārâkṣepam antareṇa anvayôpapattiḥ. vācya-sva-rūpa-vicāreṇa tatra vipralambha-śṛṅgārâkṣepād upādānâtmikā lakṣaṇā vācya-nibandhanā. vipralambha-śṛṅgārasya ca ākṣipyamāṇasya api vācyâpekṣayā prādhānyam sahṛdaya-hṛdayâhlāda-hetutayā prādhānyena ākṣepāt.

[38.4] hṛdy-unmāda-karā ity atra saty api śaśāṅka-rucīnāṃ strītve hetutāc chīlyânulobyānām avivakṣitatvāṭ ṭa-pratyayâbhāvena ac-pratyayântatvād ī-kārâbhāvaḥ. pūrvaṃ ca atra karma-saṃbandhasya avivakṣaṇāt aṇ-pratyayasya abhāva iti ac-pratyayaḥ śiva-śama-riṣṭasya kare itivat. ata eva hetv-ādi-viviakṣāyām api ṭa-pratyayâbhāvād adoṣaḥ.

[40.26] evaṃ vaktṛ-vākya-vācyānam ekaika-samāśrayeṇa ye trayo bhedā bhavanti te tāvad-udāhṛtāḥ anye 'pi ca ye vaktāraṃ vākya-vācyayor anyatareṇa saṃyujya, tathā vākyaṃ vācyena saha samuccitya dvika-bhedās trayaḥ tathā tat-trika-bhedāś ca vaktṛ-vākya-vācyānāṃ trayāṇam api paraspara-saṃyojanayā ca eka ity-evaṃ cat-vāro bhedā dṛśyante te sva-buddhyā ṣaṭ-prakāra-lakṣaṇā viṣayatvena manīṣibhir udāhāryāḥ. teṣām ca deśa-kālâvasthā-svā-lakṣaṇya-gata-samasta-vyasta-bheda-prapañca-yojanā lakṣye 'nveṣaṇīyā.

[41.3] tad evaṃ catur-vidho mukhyo 'rtho nirṇītaḥ. lakṣaṇayā tu ṣaṭ-prakārā uktāḥ.

[42.9] idānīm abhihitânvayo 'nvitâbhidhānaṃ tat-samuccayaḥ tad-ubhayâbhāvaś ca ity evaṃ ye cat-vāraḥ pakṣās teṣu lakṣaṇāyāḥ kakṣā-vibhāgaṃ darśayitum āha.

Verses 7b–9a

anvaye 'bhihitānāṃ sā vācyatvād ūrdhvam iṣyate || 7 ||
anvitānāṃ tu vācyatve vācyatvasya puraḥ sthitā |
dvaye dvam akhaṇḍe tu vākyârtha-paramârthaḥ || 8 ||
na asty asau kalpite 'rthe tu pūrvavat pravibhajyate |

[42.15] iha keṣāṃ-cid anvaya-vyatirekâvaseya-sāmānya-bhūta-svârtha-mātra-viśrānteṣu padeṣu padârthâkāṅkṣā-sannidhi-yogyatā-mahimnā vākyârthasya anabhidheya-bhūtasya harṣa-śokâdivad-avaseyatvam eva. yathā hi brāhmaṇa putras tejātaḥ brāhmaṇa kanyā te garbhi-ṇīti iti yathā-kramaṃ putra-janma-kanyâgarbhi-nītva-nimittau harṣa-śokau sva-śabdena anabhihitāv api śabdâbhidheya-bhūta-vastu-sāmarthyād ākṣipyete evaṃ vākyârthasya anabhidheya-bhūtasya eva padârthâkṣepyatve draṣṭavyam. eṣāṃ ca evaṃ vādināṃ matena arthānām abhihitānām uttara-kālaṃ paras-parânvayād abhihitânvayaḥ.

[44.2] apare tv āhuḥ vṛddha-vyavahārāc chabdârtha-saṃbandhâvasāyaḥ. sa ca vṛddha-vyavahāraḥ pravṛtti-nivṛtti-rūpaḥ. pravṛtti-nivṛttī ca viśiṣṭârthaniṣṭhe. ato viśiṣṭa eva arthe padānāṃ saṃbandhāv adhṛtiḥ. tataś ca viśiṣṭā eva padârthāḥ na tu padârthānāṃ vaiśiṣṭyam. evaṃ ca parasparânvitānāṃ tat-tat-sāmānyâvacchāditatvena gṛhīta-sva-vācaka-saṃbandhānāṃ padaiḥ pratyāyanād anvitâbhidhānām iti.

[45.15] anyeṣāṃ tu mate-padānāṃ tat-tat-sāmānya-bhūto vācyo ʻrthaḥ vākyasya tu parasparânvitāḥ padârthā iti padâpekṣayâbhihitānvayaḥ vākyâpekṣayā tu anvitâbhidhānam. evaṃ ca etayor abhihitânvayânvitâbhidhānayoḥ samuccayaḥ iti.

[46.17] akhaṇḍa-vākyârtha-vādinas tv āhuḥ viśiṣṭasya vastuno vākyârthatve ʻbhyupagamyamāne viśeṣasya ananvitatvena tad-viparīta-sāmānya-viruddhatvān na paramârtha-sva-bhāva-sāmānya-bhūtârthâvacchādita-r ūpatayā viśeṣāṇāṃ sva-vācakaiḥ saṃbandha-grahaṇam upapadyate. ataḥ paramârthato vākya-vākyârthayor akhaṇḍatvān na abhihitânvayo na apy anvitâbhidhānam na ca tat-samuccayo yujyate padârthânabhividyamānatvāt kalpita-padârtha-niṣṭhatvena ubhayam api vyasta-samasta-rūpatayā kalpyata iti.

[47.11] tatra ca yadā tāvad abhihitânvayaḥ tadā sva-vācakair abhihitānāṃ padârthānām abhihitôttara-kālam ākāṅkṣā-yogyatā-saṃnidhi-māhâtmyād viśeṣaṇa-viśeṣya-bhāvâtmake parasparam-anvaye sati sā lakṣaṇā padârthānāṃ sāmānya-bhūtānāṃ yad vācyatvaṃ tasmād ūrdhvaṃ vākyârthe padârtha-sāmārthyād avagamyamāne sati iṣyate.

[47.15] anvitâbhidhāna-pakṣe tv anvitānāṃ viśiṣṭānām eva padârthānāṃ vācyatvam abhidheyatvam na tu padârthānāṃ sāmānya-bhūtatvena abhihitānāṃ vaiśiṣṭyam. tatra viśiṣyamāṇānāṃ vastūnāṃ padârthatvaṃ tāvan na ghaṭate yāvat sakala-vākyârthânuyāyitayā pratipannasya avyabhicarita-sva-vācaka-sambandhasya sāmānya-rūpasya nimitta-bhūtasya arthasya saṃpratyaye sati tat-tad-vākyârtha-viṣayatayā yathā viṣayaṃ ṣaṭ-prakārā lakṣaṇā na avirbhavati. ato ʻnvitâbhidhāne viśiṣṭānāṃ padârthānāṃ vākyârtha-sva-bhāvānāṃ yad vācyatvaṃ tasya puraḥ tasmāt pūrvaṃ nimittâvasthāyāṃ lakṣaṇâvasthatā.

[47.23] abhihitânvayânvitâbhidhāna-samuccaye tu pūrvôdita-nyāya-dvitaya-saṃkala-nayā padâpekṣayā vācyatvôttara-kāla-bhāvinī lakṣaṇā bhavati vākyâpekṣayā ca[12] vākyârthôttara-kālaṃ tasyāḥ[13] pūrvam avasthānam. tad idam uktaṃ dvaye dvayam iti. dvaye abhihitânvayânv itâbhidhāna-samuccayâtmake dvayaṃ vācyatvād ūrdhvam prāg-bhāvaś ca lakṣaṇāyā ity-arthaḥ.

[48.3] akhaṇḍe tu vākyârthe 'sau lakṣaṇā paramârthena na asti. bhinnānāṃ padârthānām paramârthato 'bhidheya-bhāvasya anupapadyamānatvāt tad-āśritatvāc ca lakṣaṇāyāḥ. kalpita-padârtha-āśrayeṇa tu sā lakṣaṇā yathā-ruci pūrvavad-abhihitânvayânvitâbhidhāna-tat-samuccaya-kalpanayā vibhaktavya-bhāge niveśyā parasparasya deśa-kālâvacchedena aśeṣavya-vahartṛ-niṣṭhatayā rūḍhatvāt.

[48.8] evam abhihitânvayâdi-pakṣa-catuṣṭaye lakṣaṇāyāḥ kakṣā-vibhāgo nirūpitaḥ.

[48.29] idānīm etasyā[14] yatra mukhyârthâsaṃbhavas tatra mukhyârthâsanna-vastu-viṣayāṃ sati prayojane pravṛttim upadarśayitum āha

Verses 9b–10a

mukhyârthâsaṃbhavāt sā iyaṃ mukhyârthâsatti-hetukā || 9 ||
rūḍheḥ prayojanād vā api vyavahāre vilokyate |

[50.3] yā ca iyaṃ ṣaṭ-prakārā lakṣaṇā pūrvam uktā sā

1 mukhyâsya arthasya pramāṇântara-bādhitatvena asaṃbhavāt
2 lakṣyamāṇasya ca arthasya mukhyârthaṃ pratyāsannatvāt[15]
3 sântarârtha-grahaṇasya ca sa-prayojanatvāt

[50.7] ity evaṃ vidhakāraṇa-tritayâtmaka-sāmagrī-samāśrayaṇena vṛddha-vyavahāre paridṛśyate. yac ca tat mukhyârthâsannatvam tat pañca-prakāratayā ācārya-bhartṛmitreṇa pradarśitam

abhidheyena saṃbandhāt sādṛśyāt samavāyataḥ |
vaiparītyāt kriyā-yogāl lakṣaṇā pañcadhā matā ||

[50.13] iti ślokena. kena[16] prayojanasya api dvai-vidhyam.

[50.15] kiñcid hi sântarârtha-parigrahe prayojanam anādi-vṛddha-vy avahāra-prasiddhy-anusaraṇâtmakatvād rūḍhy-anuvṛtti-sva-bhāvam yathā dvi-rephâdau. dvi-repha-śabdena hi repha-dvitaya-yogitayā bhramara-śabda-lakṣaṇā-dvareṇa rūḍhy-anuvṛttir eva kriyate. aparaṃ tu rūḍhy-anusaraṇâtmakaṃ yat prayojanam uktam tad-vyatiriktaṃ[17] vastv-antara-gatasyaasaṃvijñāna-padasya[18]rūpa-viśeṣa-pratipādanaṃnāmayathāpūrvam udāhṛtaṃ rāmo 'smîti. etac ca prayojana-dvitayaṃ mukhyârthâsaṃbhave sati mukhyârtha-pratyāsannatayā pūrvôpadarśitena saṃbandha-pañcakena avagamyamāne lākṣaṇike 'rthe yathā-viṣayam anusarttavyam.

[53.17] tatra sambandha-lakṣaṇā yathā gaṅgāyāṃ ghoṣa iti. atra hi gaṅga-śabdâbhidheyasya sroto-viśeṣasya ghoṣâdhikaraṇatvânupapattyā mukhya-śabdârtha-bādhe sati yo 'sau samīpa-samīpi-bhāvâtmakaḥ saṃbandhaḥ tad-āśrayeṇa taṭaṃ lakṣayati. atra ca lakṣaṇāyāḥ prayojanaṃ taṭasya gaṅgātva ekârtha-samavetâsaṃvijñāna-pada-puṇyatva-manoharatvâdi-pratipādan am. na hi tat puṇyatva-manoharatvâdi sva-śabdaiḥ spraṣṭuṃ śakyate avyāpty-ativyāpti-prasaṅgāt. [53.26] sādṛśya-lakṣaṇāyām udāharaṇam

bhamara bhramatā dig-antarāṇi kvacid-āsāditaṃ īkṣitaṃ śrutaṃ vā |
vad satyam apāsya pakṣa-pātaṃ yadi jātī-kusumânukāri puṣpam ||

[54.3] atra hi bhramara-puṣpa-śabdau saṃbodhanâdy[19]-anyathânupapattyā bādhita-mukhyârthāv abhidheya-sādṛśyāt tad-gata-guṇa-sadṛśya-guṇa-prayuktam arthântaraṃ lakṣaṇayâvagamayataḥ. prayojanaṃ ca atra bhram aratva-puṣpatvaîkârtha-samaveta-kriyā-guṇa-sadṛśānām asaṃvijñāna-padānāṃ kriyā-guṇānāṃ pratipādanam.

[54.7] samavāyato lakṣaṇā yathā chatriṇo yānti iti. atra bahu-vacana-prayogān mukhya-śabdârtha-bādhaḥ. na hy ekasmiṃś chatriṇi bahu-vacanasya prayoga upapadyate ato 'tra gamana-lakṣaṇāyāṃ kriyāyāṃ chatriṇā saha yo 'sau chatra-śūnyānām samavāyaḥ sāha-caryam tad-vaśāt chatri-śabdena chatra-śūnyā api lakṣaṇayā 'vagamyante. prayojanaṃ ca atra chatra-śūnyānāṃ sarvâtmanā chatrôpeta-svâmy-anuyāyitayā pratipādanam.

[56.6] vaiparītyāl lakṣaṇā yathā bhadra-mukha iti. atra hi bhadra-mukha-śabdasya abhadra-mukhe prayogāt svârtha-bādhaḥ ato 'sau vācya-bhūta-bhadra-mukhatva-viparītatvād abhadra-mukhatvaṃ viparīta-nibandhanayā lakṣaṇayā pratyāyati. atra ca lakṣaṇā-prayojanaṃ guptâsatyârtha-pratipattiḥ. gupto hy asatyo 'rthaḥ tat-tad-abhiprāya-vaśena prāyeṇa prayôktṛbhiḥ pratipādyate.

[56.13] kriyā-yogāl lakṣaṇāyām udāharaṇaṃ yathā mahati samare śatru-ghnas tvam iti. atra hi aśatrughne śatru-ghna-śabda-prayogān mukhya-śabdârtha-bādhaḥ. śatru-ghna-śabdaś ca aśatrughne śatruhan anakriyā-kartṛtva-yogāl lakṣaṇayôktaḥ. prayojanaṃ ca atra śatru-ghna-śabdâbhidheye nṛpati-rūpatā pratipādanam. tathā ca

pṛthr asi guṇaiḥ kīrttyā rāmo nalo bharato bhavān
mahati samare śatru-ghnas tvaṃ kṣitau janakaḥ sthiteḥ |
iti sucaritaiḥ khyāti bibhrac-cirantana-bhūbhṛtāṃ
katham asi na māṃdhātā deva tri-loka-vijayy api || iti ||

[56.13] śatru-ghna-rūpatayā nṛpatitvaṃ upaślokyamānasya rajño varṇitam. tad evaṃ nibandhana-tritaya-samudbhavatā lakṣaṇā vṛttasya utkā.[20]

[58.11] idānīṃ pañca-vidha-saṃbandha-nibandhanāyām āsattau pūrvôpavarṇitāyāṃ kvacid vācyasya atitiraskāraḥ kvacid vivakṣitatvaṃ kvacic ca avivakṣitatvam ity evaṃ vidhaṃ trayaṃ yat sahṛdair upadarśitaṃ tasya viṣaya-vibhāgam upadarśayitum āha.

Verses 10b–12a

sādṛśye vaiparītye ca vācyasya atitiraskriyā || 10b ||
vivakṣā vā[21] avivakṣā ca saṃbandha-samavāyayoḥ. |
upādāne vivakṣā atra lakṣaṇe tv avivakṣaṇam || 11 ||
tiraskriyā kriyā-yoge kvacit tad-viparītatā |

[58.18] abhidheyena saṃbandhād ity atra yad āsatti-rūpaṃ pañcam uktaṃ tatra sādṛśye vaiparītye ca vācyasya atyantaṃ tiraskāraḥ. tathā hi sādṛśya-nibandhanāyāṃ lakṣaṇāyām upamāna-vācinaḥ padasya upameya-paratvam upamānâtmakaṃ vācyam atyantaṃ tiraskriyate. yathā upadarśitaṃ snigdha-śyāmala-kānti-liptā iti payoda-suhṛdām iti ca. atra lipta-suhṛc-chabdayoḥ svârthôpamita-vastu-paratvāt svârthasya atyantaṃ kārye 'nanvitatvam.

[58.24] vaiparītya-samāśaryāyām api tasyām arthântarasya vācya-viparītasya upādeyatvād vācyasya atyantaṃ tiraskāraḥ yathā bhadra-mukhyā iti. atra hi bhadra-mukhatvam abhadra-mukhatvād atyantaṃ tiraskṛtam. evaṃ sādṛśya-vaiparītyayor atyanta-tiraskṛta-vācyatā.

[59.28] saṃbandha-samavāyayos tu vācyasya vivakṣitatvâvivakṣitatvena tasya na atyaṅtaṃ[22] tiraskāraḥ. tatra[23] hi upādānâtmikāyāṃ lakṣaṇāyām upādāne[24] vācya-vivakṣāyāṃ vācyasya vivakṣitatvam. tathā hi tatra vivakṣitānyaparatā[25] sahṛdayaiḥ kāvya-vartmani nirūpitā. lakṣaṇe tu vācyasya avivakṣitatvaṃ tasya arthântara-saṅkramitatvāt.[26]

[60.4] tathā hi yatra arthântara-saṃkramita-vācyatā tatra saṃbandha-nibandhanāyāṃ lakṣaṇāyām upādāne vācya-vivakṣāyām upadāharaṇam pīno devadatto divā na bhuṅkte iti. atra hi dinâdhikaraṇa-bhojanâbhāva-viśiṣṭatayā pīnatva-lakṣaṇaṃ kāryaṃ vivakṣitam eva sat sva-siddhy-arthatvena saṃbandha-nibandhanāyāṃ lakṣaṇāyāṃ rātri-bhojanâtmakaṃ kāraṇam ākṣipati.

[60.10] samavāya-nibandhanāyāṃ tasyām upādane vācyasya vivakṣitatvaṃ yathā chatriṇo yānti iti. atra hi yadā chatrī bahutvôpetatvāt sva-gata-bahutv ânvaya-saṃsiddhy-arthatvena chatra-śūnyān api ākṣipati tadā samavāya-nibandhane chatra-śunyānām upādāne kriyamāṇe vācyaś chatrī vivakṣitaḥ. tad evaṃ saṃbandha-samavāya-nibandhanayor upādānâtmakayor lakṣaṇayor vācyasya vivakṣitatvam uktam.

[63.17] lakṣaṇâtmakayos tu tayor vācyasya avivakṣitatvam na tv atyantaṃ tiraskāraḥ lakṣyamāṇa-dvāreṇa kathaṃcit kārye 'nvitatvāt. tatra sambandha-nibandhanāyāṃ lakṣaṇāyām avivakṣita-vācyatva udāharaṇaṃ rāmo 'smi iti. atra hi rāma-śabda-vācyaṃ dāśa-rathi-rūpaṃ vyaṅgya-dharmântara-pariṇatatvāt sva-paratvena anupāttam tasmād avivakṣitam na tv atyaṇtaṃ tiraskṛtam vyaṅgya-dharma-dvāreṇa vākyârthe kathaṃcid anvitatvāt. evaṃ gaṅgāyāṃ ghoṣa ity-ādāv apy unneyam.

[63.25] samavāya-sambandha-nibandhanāyāṃ tu lakṣaṇāyām avivakṣita-vācyatā chatrino yānti ity atra eva udāhāryā. tathā hi yadā chatritvaṃ bahutvânvayânyathânupapattyā samudāya-paratayā upādīyate tadā atra samudāyasya vivakṣitatvād vācyasya avivakṣā. evam api ca samudāyântar-bhūtatvāt samudāya-dvāreṇa chatrino 'pi kriyânvayaḥ sulabha eva. ata eva ca atra vācyasya na atyantaṃ tiraskāraḥ samudāya-rūpântar-bhūtatvena kriyânvitatvāt. tad evaṃ sambandha-samavāya-nibandhanayor lakṣaṇayor vācyasya vivakṣitatvam avivakṣitatvaṃ ca na tv atyanta-tiraskāra iti sthitam.

[65.24] kriyā-yoga-nibandhanāyāṃ tu lakṣaṇāyāṃ śabda-gatâvayava-śakty-anusaraṇe śabda-śakti-mūlatā lakṣyamāṇasya arthasya. tatra ca vācyasya arthasya tiraskṛiyā yathā puruṣaḥ puruṣa iti. atra hy ekena puruṣa-śabdena viśiṣṭa-jātīyasya arthasya upāttatvād aparaḥ puruṣa-śabdaḥ sva-vācya-vyatirekeṇa eva kriyā-yoga-nibandhanayā lakṣaṇayā punar atiśayitṛtvam upādatte.

[65.29] yatra tu nimitta-sad-bhāvād vācye 'rthe vivakṣita eva tasya arthântarasya śabda-śakty-antara-mūlatayā vyavasthitasya 'vyavāyaḥ kriyate tatra tad-viparītatayā vācyârtha-tiraskriyâvaiparītyam. na khalv atra vācyasya arthasya tiraskriyā api tu vivakṣitatvam eva yathā mahati samare śatru-ghnas tvam iti. atra hi śatru-ghna-śabdaḥ śatru-hanana-kriyāyāḥ kartṛtvaṃ kriyā-yoga-nibandhanayā lakṣaṇayā avagamayann api svârthaṃ daśa-rathim upamānatayā api pratipādayati. tena tasya vivakṣitasya svârthatā api.

[66.6] yady api ca upameya-paratvena upamānasya upādānād evaṃ vidhe viṣaye 'tyanta-tiraskṛta-vācyatā sahṛdair aṅgī-kriyate tathâpi kriyā-yoga-nibandhana-lakṣaṇâvasare tāvad vācyasya upamānatvena aṅgī-kṛtatvād atiraskṛta-vācyatā api bhavati. tad evaṃ kriyā-yoga-nibandhanāyām antaḥ-saṃkrānta-nānârtha-vaśataḥ kvacid vācyaṃ tiraskriyate kvacit tu vivakṣyata iti sthitam.

[66.12] etac ca sarvaṃ bahu-vaktavyatvād iha na nirūpyate. lakṣaṇā-mārgâvagāhitvaṃ tu dhvaneḥ sahṛdair nūtanatayôpavarṇitasya vidyata iti diśam unmīlayitum idam atra uktam. etac ca vidvadbhiḥ kuśâgrīyayā buddhyā nirūpaṇīyam na tu jhagaty eva asūyativyam ity alam atiprasaṅgena.

[66.16] tad evaṃ vācyasya tiraskṛta-vivakṣāyāṃ viṣaya-vibhāgo nirūpitaḥ.

Verses 12b–13a

[69.8] idāṇīṃ sakala-śabdâvibhāgâtmakasya śabda-tattvasya yadā śabdârtha-sambandha-triya-rūpatayā rajju-sarpatayā vivarttamānatvaṃ tadā etad abhidhāvṛttaṃ daśa-vidha-vyavahārôpārohitayā upapadyate na tu saṃhṛta-krama[27]-vākta-tattva-viṣayataye 'ti darśayitum āha

vivarttamānaṃ vāk-tattvaṃ daśadhā evaṃ vilokyate || 12 ||
saṃhṛta-krama-bhede tu tasmiṃs teṣāṃ kuto gātiḥ |

[69.14] sakala-śabdâvibhāgâtmanaḥ śabda-tattvasya pramātṛ-pramāṇa-prameya-pramiti-rūpeṇa prakāra-catuṣṭayena pratyekaṃ vācya-vācaka-tat-saṃbandha-prapañca-bhājo rajju-sarpavad vivartamānasya nirūpitā evaṃ vidha-daśa-vidhâbhidhā-vṛtta-sambandhitvam. apratyastamita-sakal a-vikalpôllekhôpaplavatve tu krama-bheda-saṃhāreṇa tasmin vāktatve avivarttamāne[28] teṣāṃ daśānām abhidhā-vṛttānāṃ kuto gatiḥ na eva prasara ity-arthaḥ.

Verse 13b

[72.1] idānīṃ prakaraṇârtham upasaṃharati

ity-etad abhidhā-vṛttaṃ daśadhā 'tra vivecitam || 13 ||

[72.3] mukhyasya abhidhā-vṛttasya prakārāś cat-vāraḥ lākṣaṇikasya tu ṣaḍ-ity-evaṃ daśa-prakāram abhidhā-vṛttam atra vivecitam.

Verse 14

[72.13] adhunā phalam etasya darśayati

pada-vākya-pramāṇeṣu tad-etat pratibimbitam |
yo yojayati sāhitye tasya vāṇī prasīdati || 14 ||

[72.16] padâvagati-hetutvāt padaṃ vyākaraṇam. vākya-samanvayâvasāya-hetutvād vākyaṃ mīmāṃsā. pramāṇa-pratipatti-kāritvāt pramāṇaṃ tarkaḥ. eteṣu pada-vākya-pramāṇa-śāstreṣu catur-vargôpayogi-sarva-vidyâdhigam ôpāya-bhūteṣu triṣu pravibhidyamāneṣu saṃkrāntânantara-nirūpita-sva-rūpa[29]-pratibimbaṃ daśa[30]-vidham abhidhā-vṛttaṃ yaḥ sāhityâdau[31] sakala-loka-vyavahāra-darpaṇa-prakhye[32] saṃcārayati sa vāci krameṇa prasīdantyāṃ vāg-īśvaro bhavati.

[73.1] daśa-vidhena anena abhidhā-vṛttena samagrasya vāk-parispandasya vyāptatvād anena vyākaraṇa-mīmāṃsā-tarka-sāhityâtmakeṣu caturṣu śāstreṣu upayogāt tad-dvāreṇa ca sarvāsu vidyāsu sakala-vyavahāra-mūla-bhūtāsu prasāraṇâdasya daśa-vidhasya abhidhā-vṛttasya sakala-vyavahāra-vyāpitvam ākhyātam.

Verse 15

bhaṭṭa-kallaṭa-putreṇa mukulena nirūpitā
sūri-prabodhanāyeyam abhidhā-ṿrtta[33]-mātṛkā. || 15 ||

[73.7] iti śāradā-caraṇa-rajaḥ-kaṇa-pavitrita-sthala-vāstavya-śrī-kallaṭâtma-ja-bhaṭṭa-mukula-viracitā abhidhā-vṛtta[34]-mātṛkā samāptā.

Part V

Mukula and Contemporary Linguistic Philosophy

Mukula Bhaṭṭa on Sentence Meaning and the Semantics-Pragmatics Distinction

In his *Fundamentals of the Communicative Function* (*Abhidhā-vṛtta-mātṛkā*), Mukula Bhaṭṭa argues that linguistic comprehension involves several stages. His treatise sketches a theory of how hearers understand the full range of what speakers express, beyond just the ordinary meanings of words. An important aspect of his argument is the distinction between the primary (*mukhya*) and indicatory (*lākṣaṇika*) functions of speech. The primary function is referential in nature, and directly conveys one of four types of entities: universals, actions, properties, or a contingently named thing.[1] On the basis of the results of the primary function, the indicatory function operates, when certain conditions are present, to convey some further meaning. However, rather than a two-stage process, from primary to secondary meaning, Mukula seems to be committed to a four-stage process, which he calls the combined view of sentence meaning (*samuccaya*) in which there are two kinds of indicatory functions. In contemporary terms, we might say that one of these indicatory functions is semantic, and the other is pragmatic, although this division turns out to be too simple as we will see. Mukula's view is not attested elsewhere, that is, he does not seem to be drawing on a four-stage view explained in detail by a previous thinker.[2] Further, his treatise does not develop the view in detail, so part of this chapter's goal is to reconstruct a possible understanding of his view. A secondary goal is to identify some analogies with contemporary positions regarding the semantics-pragmatics distinction, with the further goal of setting an agenda for future research.

The following chapter introduces Mukula's project, his reasons for understanding the indicatory function as he does, and the two views of sentence meaning he wishes to reconcile. Then it briefly introduces the problem of the "semantics-pragmatics" distinction in contemporary philosophy and one solution, which François Recanati (2004) has called

"The Syncretic View." Subsequently it draws some connections between Mukula's combined view and Recanati's syncretic view, noting points where the two positions have different commitments or arrive at the same conclusions through different arguments. Finally, the chapter identifies some general lessons from this approach, including points for further research into Indian treatment of the semantics-pragmatics boundary, on the presumption that comparative work is a starting point for inquiry into first-order questions about the topics being compared.[3]

Mukula Bhaṭṭa on Primary and Secondary Meaning

Like many thinkers in the Indian philosophical traditions, Mukula Bhaṭṭa distinguishes between two functions (*vyāpāra*) or powers (*śakti*) of words: the primary (*mukhya*) and the secondary or "indicatory" (*lākṣaṇika*). Toward the beginning of his treatise, Mukula Bhaṭṭa defines them in this way:

> The primary meaning is what is apprehended from the function of speech.
>
> The indicated meaning is said to be ascertained further from that meaning. (63)[1]

According to Mukula, when the power of speech is "expended" by denoting its referent (which can be a universal, a property, an action, or a contingently named thing), the power of indication comes into operation if there is still work to be done. In other words, linguistic powers are demarcated based upon their effects. The primary function's effect is the cognition of a referent by a hearer. The indicatory function causes some further cognition. As well, the primary and indicatory functions are distinguished based upon their domains. In the verse above, they are different not only because they perform different functions, but because they operate on different entities. The primary function is said to be the function of speech (*śabda-vyāpara*); indication functions on the meaning resulting from this first function, thus it works indirectly whereas the primary function works directly. Mukula's focus is how these two functions result in a cognition caused by speech (*śabda-bodha*). Specifically, he wishes to explain how speech-cognitions come about from everyday language as well as poetry, explaining the full range of human communication.

However, while the primary-indicatory function distinction at the outset of his treatise appears to involve just two stages of comprehension, by the end of his text, it is clear that this cannot be the full story. In what I will call "sentence-internal indication," indication is involved in construing a set of uttered words as a complete, syntactically unified sentence. In what I will call "post-sentential indication," indication is involved in understanding what a speaker means to say with a particular sentence. Further complicating

Mukula's account is his attempt to reconcile two theories of sentential unity which were historically taken to be incompatible.

Mukula exemplifies sentence-internal indication with a case which depends on his particular four-type semantic theory, on which nouns refer to universals through the primary function. In the utterance

1 The cow is to be sacrificially bound (*gaur anubandhyaḥ*)

the word "cow" (*gaur*) refers to the universal, COWHOOD. While Mukula does not say so explicitly, probably the Sanskrit gerundive *anubandhyaḥ*, translated as "to be sacrificially bound," refers to an action, although he does not discuss its semantics in detail.[2] What he does say is that "although COWHOOD (the primary meaning of 'cow') is an instrumental means for the ritual, the word 'cow' is not appropriate without implying an individual" (70). In other words, there is an interpretive issue with the use of "cow" if taken in its primary meaning in this context. To complete the action of tying a cow to a stake, it is necessary to find an animal which is a cow, and thus the universal is said to be "instrumental." However, we cannot bind abstracta to stakes, and thus we must understand "cow" to have a second, indicated meaning: a particular cow.[3] Here, indication is necessary in order to interpret the utterance as an intelligible sentence. This requirement of intelligibility is called "semantic fit" (*yogyatā*) by Indian thinkers, and when it fails with relationship to the primary meaning, hearers understand another, second meaning, instead (or in addition). While this particular case depends on Mukula's semantics of nouns as referring to universals, we could construct an analogous example if we allow nouns to refer to particulars.

2 The newspaper called.

In this case, if we suppose that "newspaper" refers to a physical object, a paper, then there is a failure of semantic fit, given that papers are unable to make telephone calls. However, what Mukula would say is that, given this failure, the indicatory function enables hearers to understand something which is related to the newspaper-as-physical-object: the publisher of the newspaper. In the case of "cow," there is a close relationship between a universal and a particular, which enables the secondary understanding on the part of the hearer. Likewise, in the case of "newspaper," there is a close relationship (perhaps ownership, production, etc.) between the physical object and the understood indicated meaning, which modern linguists would call metonymical. In both (1) and (2), indication is necessary in order to understand the utterance as a sentence having semantic fit. For Mukula and other Indian thinkers, semantic fit is one of the necessary features for an utterance to constitute a sentence, in addition to its being grammatically constructed. So sentence-internal indication in (1) and (2) is not optional, but required.

Mukula also gives a number of poetic examples which involve indication throughout his treatise, explaining the conditions under which hearers understand the indicated meaning, as well as identifying those meanings. It is in poetic cases that we encounter post-sentential indication. For instance, he gives the example of a stanza in which indicated meaning is based upon the expressed meaning (*vācya*). We will have time to investigate expressed meaning in more detail below, but first we will discuss post-sentential indication.

3 The flower-tipped arrows of the love-god are hard to avoid: spring blossoms everywhere.
The bright moon's rays make my heart crazy and the cuckoos capture my mind.
This young age, with these heavy breasts, is a hard burden to bear.
These burdensome five fires—now, how can I endure them, my friend? (84)

In this stanza, Mukula identifies the indicated meaning as "the *rasa* of love-in-separation." *Rasa* is a technical term in Indian poetics and dramaturgy referring to an aesthetic mood, such as the comic, heroic, erotic, etc. The *rasa* of love-in-separation is the painful longing a lover experiences while away from their beloved, understood as a longing worthy of aesthetic appreciation. Mukula argues that the poet (or narrator—this distinction is not explicit here) expresses with this stanza a specific *rasa,* love-in-separation.[4] However, this is not communicated through the primary word meanings in the verse, as the phrase "love-in-separation" nowhere appears. Further, he says, it is not "impossible for the words to construe as a sentence without implying of love-in-separation" (84). That is, while sentence-internal indication may be necessary (some of the nouns would need to indicate particulars, for instance), the stanza is grammatical and intelligible without understanding that the poet is experiencing love-in-separation. Rather, post-sentential indication occurs because a hearer reflects on the point or the sentential aim (*tātparya*) of the poetic utterance.[5] The poet has described beautiful motifs of love: the love-god's arrows, beautiful flowers, bright moon rays singing birds, and youth. However, they have characterized these things as burdens to be endured. Through indication that considers the aim of a complete sentence, a hearer understands that the poet speaks this way to communicate that they are experiencing love-in-separation.

From just these two examples, we can see that Mukula thinks indication occurs at two stages in utterance comprehension, sentence-internal and post-sentential. He makes this explicit when he treats two Indian theories of sentence meaning in relationship to this topic. Mukula's discussion of sentence meaning in the *Fundamentals* has not received much attention even by those few scholars who have written on his work. Perhaps this is because it seems to simply reiterate three well-known theories of sentential unity and to add little to the purpose of his treatise, which is to argue for indication's sufficiency as an explanation of the range of communicated meanings. For instance, Nandi (2002:14-15) gives only a brief summary and McCrea (2008) omits it entirely. However, Mukula's account succeeds only if indication can occur at both sentence-internal and post-sentential stages, and it appears that this depends on having a novel view about sentence meaning. It is no accident, then, that the discussion of sentence meaning occurs just after he has explained the example of indication based on the expressed meaning, the poetic example (3).

Mukula presents four theories of sentence meaning, or how it is that utterances are comprehended by hearers in a way that generates a unified cognition and not merely a string of sounds or disconnected meanings. The fourth theory, on which words are merely useful fictions and there is, at some metaphysically ultimate level, no such thing as indication, is probably his own view, but we will set it aside for simplicity's sake.[6] After all, Mukula himself distinguishes between a theoretical stance in which divisions are helpful and a stance in which we are doing ultimate metaphysics. Since our concern is theoretical divisions, we will leave ultimate metaphysics for another time.

The first two theories of sentence meaning which Mukula summarizes are found in the works of Mīmāṃsā philosophers belonging to the Bhāṭṭa and Prābhākara intellectual traditions, respectively.[7] The first, the connection-of-the-denoted (*abhihitânvaya*) view, I will call the "word independence" view, and it is argued for by thinkers who tend to follow seventh-century-CE Kumārila Bhaṭṭa's understanding of Mīmāṃsā principles. On this view, a word can refer to an entity independently of the capacity of the other words in a sentence. The second, the denotation-through-the-connected (*anvayâbhidhāna*) view, I will call the "word dependence" view, and it is found in thinkers who follow Prabhākara Miśra's approach to Mīmāṃsā. On the second view, words do not refer independently of their relationship with other words in a sentence, and what they refer to is not only an entity, but an entity as related to another entity.

Mukula argues that on the word independence view, indication occurs at a stage after the word has expressed its primary meaning, but before the complete sentence is understood. (See Table 11 for a visual representation of these two views.) He argues that on the word dependence view, in contrast, indication occurs at a stage after the sentence has been construed in its complete meaning, but before the complete utterance meaning, in the sense of the full range of the speaker's aim, is understood. He further argues that we can therefore distinguish between two senses of "what is expressed" (*vācya*). On the word independence view, what is expressed is the primary meaning of a word, such as when "cow" expresses COWHOOD. Sentence-internal indication works after this primary function, as we have seen, to construe "cow" in the sense of a particular. On the word dependence view, what the word "cow" means is a contextually appropriate meaning in relationship to the other words in the sentence. But this is not "what is expressed." In fact, there is no single primary meaning for "cow," even though word dependence theorists might admit that some kind of universal or paradigmatic conception of a cow is part of our learning on how to use the term. Since "cow" in its primary function can mean a wide range of things (the universal COWHOOD, a clay cow, an individual cow, etc.), there is no need for indication at this stage. But even though indication isn't necessary at the sentence-internal stage, in order to understand what is expressed in poetic cases like example (3), sometimes we need indication which is post-sentential. Table 11 contrasts the positions of the word independence and word dependence views. The arrows indicate input to and output from the

Table 11 Word independence and word dependence theories

Word independence	***Word dependence***
Words uttered	*Words uttered*
↓	↓
Primary function (*mukhya*)	Primary function (*mukhya*)
↓	↓
What is expressed (*vācya*)	*Sentence meaning* (*vākya*)
↓	↓
Indicatory function (*lākṣanika*)	Indicatory function (*lākṣanika*)
↓	↓
Sentence meaning (*vākya*)	*What is expressed* (*vācya*)

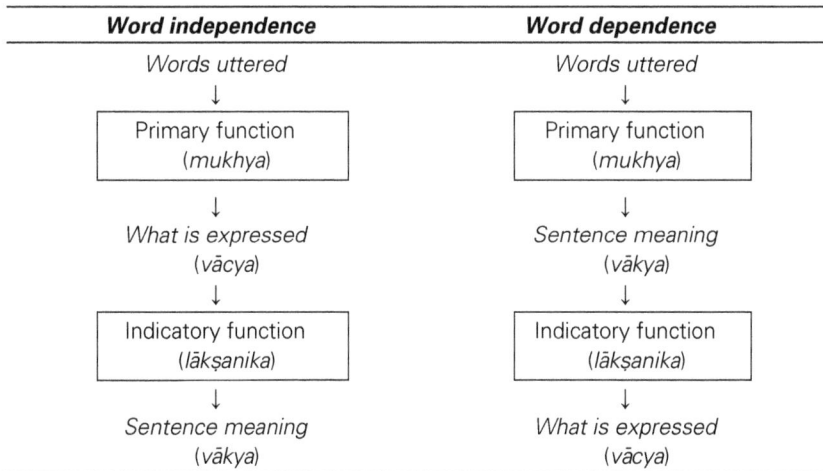

functions, marked by boxes. Input and output, the content which is cognized by the hearer, is in italics.

Since Mukula claims there is indication in cases like (1) as well as cases like (3), he cannot accept the word independence or the word dependence theory alone. These two philosophical positions were historically taken to be in opposition, since they force a choice between whether words refer to a discrete entity or to entities in relation to one another. Mukula implicitly argues for a third view by stating explicitly that on this view, the combination view, indication occurs in two places, both before and after the expressed meaning, depending on how we characterize "what is expressed." No Indian philosopher before Mukula's time, that I am aware of, presented a theory of sentence meaning called the "combination view," suggesting that this is his own innovation. It has two main commitments

1 The scope of our theorizing (words or sentences) will impact our description of the processes involved in utterance comprehension.
2 Indication is involved in utterance comprehension both after words express meaning and again after a complete sentence meaning.

Mukula does not develop the first point in detail, but says

> This is connection-of-the-denoted, *seen from the perspective of words*, but it is denotation-through-the-connected *from perspective of the sentence*, (87)

and again

> Now in the combined view of connection-of-the-denoted and denotation-through-the-connected, by the act of combining the two rules earlier described, we have, *from the perspective of words*, indication occurring at a time after the words express meaning. And *from the perspective of sentences*, it occurs after the sentence meaning and before there is an expressed meaning. (89)

What he means by "perspective" (*apekṣayā*) is left implicit, but one way to understand his point is that there are different explanatory concerns in each theory.[8] The word independence theorists are concerned to explain, among other things, the possibility of interpreting new sentences. Unless there is a context-invariant contribution on the part of the component word, the word independence theorist sees no way to account for the possibility of understanding new combinations of words. Thus their focus is on what words contribute, which is the "perspective" of words.

In contrast, the word dependence theorist focuses on the process of language acquisition. They argue that we always learn word meanings by their use in sentences, and thus we acquire not just a single referent, but a range of possible connections (along with rules about what combinations are inappropriate). Even though we can isolate words from within sentences, a word that is not in a sentence will not refer to anything, but at most remind us of an associated memory.[9] So the word dependence theorist prioritizes how sentences constrain the particular word meaning of "cow" in a certain context, which is the "perspective" of sentences.

Mukula's own perspective is that both explanations are necessary. We must explain what words contribute in common across multiple contexts. But we must also explain how a sentence constrains the understanding of its component words. He claims that on the combined view, indication happens in two stages, by his refusal to adjudicate between the word dependence and word independence theories, signaling that he believes the debate is misguided. We can represent Mukula's position in a diagram as in Table 12.

On this view, there is a minimal sense of what is expressed, which is what words express, as well as a maximal sense of what is expressed, corresponding to what the speaker expresses with the utterance as a whole. Sentence-internal indication operates on the minimal sense of what is expressed, whereas post-sentential indication operates on the sentence meaning as a whole. Sometimes indication is a matter only of construing a sentence

Table 12 Combined view

Combined view
Words uttered
↓
Primary function (*mukhya*)
↓
What is expressed$_{min}$ (*vācya*)
↓
Indicatory function (*lākṣanika*)
↓
Sentence meaning (*vākya*)
↓
Indicatory function (*lākṣaṇika*)
↓
What is expressed$_{max}$ (*vācya*)

meaning, although this kind of indication seems mandatory, given that it is responsible for sentential unity on the first account. Other times, indication makes sense out of what a speaker means with a complete sentence, although this kind of indication seems optional, as Mukula gives multiple examples of indication which are only at the sentence-internal level. Thus his original distinction between primary and indicatory meaning must be nuanced:

> The primary meaning is what is apprehended from the function of speech.
> The indicated meaning is said to be ascertained further from that meaning.
> Indication is necessary to understand sentences as unified syntactic wholes.
> And sometimes indication is required to understand what a speaker means by a sentence.

A Contemporary Approach to What is Said: François Recanati

Like Mukula Bhaṭṭa one thousand years earlier, contemporary philosopher François Recanati is concerned to explain the full range of human communication. In his work, he argues for a contextualist understanding of communication, on which there are no principled grounds for distinguishing between what a speaker literally says and what a speaker means in speaking literally.[1] As part of his project, Recanati has set out systematic representations of the competing views on offer, attempting to characterize families of views in terms of their major shared commitments. In what follows, I sketch out these views in part according to Recanati's discussions in *Literal Meaning*, though I also refer to more recent work to fill out the positions he characterizes. While proponents of the positions he has described have given some critical responses to his analysis, my concern is primarily with Recanati's formulation of what he calls the syncretic view in relationship to two competing theories of meaning, and, the ways his approach may or may not track Mukula's own syncretic approach.

Recanati groups a number of philosophers together as defending what he calls minimalism, in order to contrast them with the availability view.[2] On the minimalist approach to meaning, there is a distinction between what is literally said and what just seems to be said. Take the sentence

1 I have had breakfast

uttered at 10 a.m. on a Monday morning. What seems to be said by the speaker is

2 I have had breakfast *today*.

However, on a minimalist account, sentence (4) does not express (5) but only the more minimal content

3 I have had breakfast *before the time of this utterance.*

This makes the sentence likely to be true in most contexts, assuming the speaker has ever eaten breakfast. However, when answering the question of whether they would like to have some food, the speaker is not intending to communicate (6), but instead (5). On the minimalist account, the speaker has said (6), although she communicates (5). According to Bach (1994), this minimal content of what is said is subject to expansion, so that the speaker's full intention is understood by what he calls "impliciture" (in contrast to Gricean implic*a*ture which works on a complete sentence). Bach's (2001) definition of impliciture is

> In implic-i-ture, one says something but does not mean that; rather, what one means includes an implicit qualification on what one says, something that one could have made explicit but didn't (252).[3]

Another proponent of minimalism, Emma Borg (2012), puts the view this way:

> According to minimal semantics, natural language sentences mean things, the things they mean are in some sense complete (that is to say, they are propositional, truth-evaluable contents), and these literal meanings are determined entirely as a function of the lexical elements a sentence contains together with its syntactic form. (3)

She argues that while context can influence the semantic content of a sentence, it does so in a very constrained manner, so that words like "I," (indexicals) do require contextual input because it is syntactically required, but words like "red" would not, even though we might want to know whether a speaker means red on the inside or red on the outside. The first kind of content is semantic and strictly necessary for a sentence—in the sense of something which is truth-conditional or which is propositional—and the second kind of content is pragmatic and depends upon things like speaker intention.[4] Thus, on minimalism, roughly, we distinguish between what is said by a sentence and what is said by a speaker, where the first is semantic and the latter is pragmatic.

Recanati contrasts this approach with availability, on which what is said is understood based on what is consciously available to the interpreter, and involves pragmatic processes. He explains the methodology here (in a way reminiscent of Mukula's emphasis on standpoints) by saying

> Instead of looking at things from the linguistic side and equating "what is said" with the minimal proposition one arrives at through saturation, we can take a more psychological stance and equate what is said with (the semantic

> content of) the conscious output of the complex train of processing which underlies comprehension.[5]

On availability, "what is said" is not a "bottom-up" process, in the sense that it is not a matter of the compositional components of the sentence (whether words or unarticulated constituents). Rather, a wider set of pragmatic processes are involved in determining what is said. To take the example of (4) "I have had breakfast," what is said is indeed expressed by our paraphrase (5) "I have had breakfast *today*," and this expanded content is dependent on the broader discourse context. For instance, the fact that it is an answer to the inquiry, "Do you want to eat breakfast?" would influence what is said. Recanati calls this "free enrichment," a pragmatic process that constrains interpretation to something more specific than the ordinary, conventional meaning. Here, free enrichment works on the temporal scope of having had breakfast.

Beyond the role that context would play in expanding what is said by (4), Recanati argues that on availability, there are other, secondary pragmatic processes involved in understanding the communicative act, ones that depend on what is said. These include Gricean implicatures, which he characterizes as inferences from what is said (in the above pragmatic sense) to what the speaker intends to convey, based on general communicative norms[6]. For instance, when responding to the question, "Do you want to eat breakfast?" a speaker who says "I have had breakfast" is merely implicating that her answer is no. However, the speaker has not said "no," Instead, her implicature is understood on the basis of what she has said. On availability, since this implicature is worked out on the basis of (5) "I've had breakfast

Table 13 Minimalism and availability

Minimalism	**Availability**
Sentence meaning	*Sentence meaning*
↓	↓
Saturation	Primary pragmatic processes (saturation & free enrichment)
↓	↓
What is said$_{min}$	*What is said$_{prag}$*
↓	↓
Optional processes	Secondary pragmatic processes
↓	↓
What is communicated	*What is communicated*

today" and not (6) "I've had breakfast before the time of this utterance," this is evidence that what is said is not the minimal proposition (or, indeed, something schematic and sub-propositional) but rather something which has certain "pragmatic" processes already employed. In Table 13, I adapt Recanati's diagrams (page 21) to illustrate the difference between these views.

Recanati argues that a third intermediate position is also available, citing Nathan Salmon (1991) and Scott Soames (2002) as possible proponents of such a reconciliation, and Kent Bach (1994) as a kind of fourth intermediate position, with an additional level. This syncretic view is characterized by minimalism about "what is said in the strict and literal sense" and being more maximal about "what the speaker asserts."[7] On this view, there are two ways to characterize what is said. There is something said which is strict, that is understood in terms only of necessary processes like "saturation," in which indexicals determine their reference through contextually completed arguments. Only those processes which are mandatory in order for the sentence to express a proposition are involved in this sense of what is sentence-said. In contrast, once this minimal proposition is available, then what is speaker-said is determined by pragmatic processes like free enrichment.

Returning to (4) "I have had breakfast," on this view, the minimal proposition expressed by (6) "I have had breakfast before the time of this

Table 14 Syncretic view

Syncretic view
Words uttered
↓
Semantic interpretation
↓
Sentence meaning
↓
Saturation
↓
What is said$_{min}$
↓
Other primary pragmatic processes
↓
What is said$_{prag}$
↓
Secondary pragmatic processes
↓
What is communicated

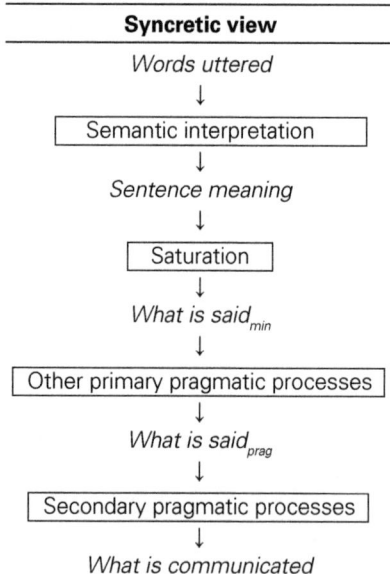

utterance" is attained by necessary processes like saturation. The fuller sense of what is said (by the speaker) is the proposition expressed by (5) "I have had breakfast today," and it involves free enrichment. Finally, with what the speaker says, she is able to communicate something further, by optional or "secondary" pragmatic processes. This is the implicature that she does not want to eat. Table 14 is my adaptation of Recanati's diagram for the syncretic view (page 52).[8]

Ultimately, Recanati rejects all three views in favor of contextualism, on which words do not have a context-independent meaning, although they may be learned by association with some abstract schema or concrete situations. However, his arguments for contextualism depend upon the distinctions he has made between mandatory linguistic processes (saturation) and pragmatic processes, whether primary or secondary.

What is Said, What is Expressed

The preceding sketch of theories of sentence meaning in classical Indian and contemporary analytic philosophy is just that, a sketch. The main positions involved, word dependence theory and word independence theory, minimalism and availability, etc., cannot entirely be divorced from their particular presentation in specific philosophers. This is true for both groups of philosophers. However, it is possible to make some general observations about shared commitments among individual thinkers so that we can speak of these theories in abstraction. Further, it is possible to make some general observations about the commitments of Indian and analytic philosophers, to see whether what appear to be structurally analogous debates are indeed running along the same conceptual lines. To date, most comparative discussion of Indian theories of sentence meaning have taken debate over Frege's context principle as a starting point. Chakrabarti (1989), Ganeri (1999), Matilal and Sen (1988), Siderits (1991) all primarily discuss the context principle and sense/reference distinction, often adding Quine, Russell, and other seminal figures of twentieth-century philosophy to the mix. Taber (1989) focuses on applying theories of sentence meaning to the problem of words changing meaning in different contexts. Still, as Siderits (2016) points out in his reprint of Siderits (1986), little has been done since these papers. He adds that, in light of the discussion of semantic contextualism in contemporary philosophy, it might be "useful to compare this debate with the Indian debate over word- and sentence-meaning" (180). The remarks which follow are a starting point for this comparison, although, as we will see in Section 4, the purpose is not simply a list of similarities and differences, but to understand more clearly what projects Indian and contemporary philosophers are engaged in, before considering whether these projects are commensurable, and what new questions might emerge from their careful investigation.[1]

One of the first observations we might make about the two groups is that Indian philosophers are considered with cognitions (*jñāna*, *bodha*) in the context of epistemological questions, whereas many analytic philosophers and contemporary linguists are concerned with formal semantics, understood as what our best theory of grammar delivers, but not what human beings actually mentally entertain. For instance, Soames (1984) argues that we can (and should) distinguish between theories of natural language, understood as a formal system, and theories of language users, understood as the psychology of conscious and subconscious processes. Even if there is no consensus among analytic philosophers (and linguists) about the precise relationship between psychology and linguistic theory, it is an explicit point of debate as to what the relationship is between facts about language use and our best semantic theories.[2] Now, such a distinction is not unknown to Indian philosophers, but as Siderits (1991) points out, those working on sentence meaning did not attempt to unify together Pāṇini's (abstract) grammatical system with (cognitive) theories of sentence meaning.[3] Rather, theories of sentence meaning are taken to explain how human language users come to have certain mental states with certain contents in virtue of hearing a string of sounds. Characteristic of this is Mukula's concern with functions or processes (*vyāpāra*s) which result in cognitions. Within the Indian debate on sentence meaning, all parties are concerned about speech-cognitions.

That said, even those contemporary philosophers such as Soames who argue for the conceptual distinctness of semantic analysis from analysis of language use admit that psychological facts play a constraining role in theorizing about language (where the latter is understood as a formal system of rules). For instance, Soames (1984) argues that facts about language acquisition could help constrain the range of possible rules that are actually employed by language users (163). And one fact about language competence that informs contemporary theory is the fact of linguistic productivity: human beings can understand new sentences which they have never previously heard, which is arguably due to the fact that they understand smaller component parts of these sentences. Such a principle also informs Indian theorizing. Mukula has an objector put forward a standard view of language acquisition, which is that that people acquire competence with the word meaning relationship through a process of inference. By hearing words being used in certain contexts and not hearing them used in others, speakers come to know the relationship between word and meaning, since linguistic competence does not make sense unless we assume such knowledge.[4]

One problem—for both Mukula and contemporary thinkers—is that it seems human beings are able to both produce and interpret a wide range of meanings which go beyond a core set of stable word meaning pairs that would form the basis of such competence. For instance, a simple theory might have it that one acquires competence with the word "red" by learning to associate the word with a red patch, or a range of red patches of different shades. But when using "red" in context, what must hold for a table, a bird, and a crystal to be red are not the same.[5] (A table is "red" if it is painted red on the outside, but not red in material underneath; a bird is "red" when its wings and body are red in color, but not when it is painted red; a red crystal is "red" throughout its entire material.) The way this difficulty is characterized in Recanati and other contemporary work, however, is frequently in terms of truth-conditions. Different truth-conditions are found to correlate to different meanings of "red," for instance. And in the example we have seen already, minimalists argue that the truth-conditions for the sentence meaning of "I have had breakfast" are different than the truth-conditions for what the speaker meaning is, which would include the narrower temporal scope for when breakfast would have been had.

Such a distinction is not explicitly found in Mukula's treatment of theories of sentence meaning, nor in such a way in the thinkers from which he is drawing. This is not to say that Indian philosophers are unconcerned with truth—far from it. Rather, the issue is that Mīmāṃsā philosophers (whom Mukula is drawing on) begin not with assertions but with commands, and so for them, truth-conditions are not the primary focus. Further, because of some presuppositions which would take us too far afield to delve into, Mīmāṃsā thinkers explain the force of many commands (those found in the Vedic texts) not in terms of a speaker's intention, but through appeal to the syntactic and semantic features of the expression.[6] Thus the distinction between sentence meaning and speaker meaning is not the one at play in the Mīmāṃsā context, and assertions are not the paradigmatic kind of expression for linguistic theorizing. However, in his discussion at Verses 5b to 6a of how different sentence tokens of the same type, "The village is on the Ganges," have different meanings, Mukula gets close to Recanati's point about truth-conditions. If "Ganges" contributes the same thing in every sentence, then why can we use "The village is on the Ganges" in one case to say that the village is right up against the Ganges river and in another, to say that the village is near the Ganges and not near the Vitastā? These two cases do involve different truth-conditions, although Mukula does not put things in this manner.

Finally, there is a crucial assumption about pragmatic interpretation in contemporary philosophy which is probably not shared by Mukula, although to what extent it may be shared by other Indian thinkers needs to be investigated. This is the idea that pragmatic interpretation is defeasible. Recanati (2004) calls defeasibility a "distinguishing characteristic" of pragmatic interpretation (54) and he, like others, explains pragmatic interpretation in terms of inference to the best explanation (91). On this view, interpretation of what the speaker means is the best explanation of the sentence meaning in context. Such an inference is a hypothesis, and while it is a possible explanation of why the speaker has said what she has, it is possible to override it with further information. While there is a range of possible models—some prefer Bayesian inference, for instance—a large chunk of pragmatic interpretation is thought to involve conclusions which are likely or are the strongest explanation, rather than following necessarily and algorithmically from semantic structures.

However, there is no precise analog to such defeasible reasoning about sentence meaning even in Mukula and others who emphasize the role of a kind of reasoning known as postulation (*arthāpatti*). While some such as Siderits (1991:41) have equated postulation to inference to the best explanation, it is plausible that, at least in Mukula's context (and probably others), postulation derives an interpretation based on syntax, semantics, and background knowledge. To what extent it is defeasible is a question for investigation.[7] Even though Mukula is engaging in poetic interpretation, if my hypothesis is correct—that he does think an epistemic instrument is responsible for coming to know the meanings of poetry—then, when everything is working correctly (we have all relevant facts and our reasoning processes are functioning), such knowledge cannot be overturned. Once the context is fixed, we must conclude that the sentence "Fat Devadatta does not eat during the day," gives rise to the further meaning, "he eats at night." If we know the relevant additional facts that Devadatta does not drink during the day or night, and that fatness is caused by eating or drinking, it is an inescapable conclusion. And interpretation of poetic stanzas involving figures of speech and hidden meanings involve the same structure.

Against this background, let us look at Mukula's combined view and Recanati's syncretic view (comparison in Table 15).

We can see some structural analogies between Recanati's construal of the syncretic view and Mukula's construal of the combined view. Both take it that the process responsible for deriving sentence meaning from the uttered words is one which is determined by what we might call "semantics," in Recanati's case, something that is "deductive" (probably meaning "algorithmic" as Bach 2007 surmises), and in Mukula's case, based on the

Table 15 Combined view versus syncretic view

Mukula's combined view	Recanati's syncretic view
Words uttered	*Words uttered*
↓	↓
Primary function (*mukhya*)	Semantic interpretation
↓	↓
What is expressed$_{min}$ (*vācya*)	*Sentence meaning*
↓	↓
Indicatory function$_{word}$ (*lākṣanika*)	Saturation
↓	↓
Sentence meaning (*vākya*)	*What is said$_{min}$*
↓	↓
Indicatory function$_{sent}$ (*lākṣaṇika*)	Other primary pragmatic processes
↓	↓
What is expressed$_{max}$ (*vācya*)	*What is said$_{prag}$*
	↓
	Secondary pragmatic processes
	↓
	What is communicated

primary function. However, for many minimalists, this first step leads to something truth-evaluable or propositional. In contrast, when Mukula says that something is expressed at this point, he is meaning that the individual words express their referents. The sentential connection (*anvaya*) between these individual meanings requires indication, another process. Perhaps, then, of the Syncretists Recanati surveys, most analogous is Bach's view, on which there is sometimes first a "propositional radical" (not truth-evaluable) before the minimal proposition of "what is said."

The first stage of indication on Mukula's combined view works on individual word meanings in order to, in Recanati's terminology, "modulate" them to suit the context. For instance, in COWHOOD, the primary meaning of "cow" is shifted (freely enriched) to the narrower sense of a particular cow. This seems to fit with the way in which Recanati talks about primary pragmatic processes. However, Mukula's explanation of this first stage of indication characterizes it as functioning along with syntactic expectancy, semantic fit, and contiguity, in order for a unified sentence meaning to be understood. Syntactic expectancy (*ākāṅkṣā*), the psychological desire on the part of hearers that sentences be syntactically well constructed, depends on grammatical features. It thus looks like it fits more properly at the level of the necessary processes of semantic interpretation, in Recanati's terms.

Finally, secondary pragmatic processes are those Recanati thinks require a complete sentence meaning (fully propositional) which are the results of the primary pragmatic processes and saturation. These processes tell us what the speaker says, using defeasible pragmatic interpretation, and reflection on a wide range of contextual information. Anything could be relevant, not merely what is necessary for understanding indexicals, for instance, as on semantic interpretation. The input to these processes is *what is said*$_{prag}$ which is available to our intuitions as ordinary interpreters.[8] In a way, this level seems to fit what Mukula characterizes as indication that involves reflection on sentential aim (*tātparya*). At this stage, after we resolve any possible incongruities internal to the sentence, which might involve metonymy or metaphor, we then reflect on why the speaker has said what she has. In Mukula's text, in contrast to the Bhāṭṭa and Prābhākara concerns with Vedic hermeneutics, he is dealing with human speech. Thus he has room for reflection on the speaker. However, it is unclear in his presentation just how speaker motive should be incorporated into the functioning of indication.[9]

Lessons and Future Inquiry

These three possibilities (minimalism, availability, and the syncretic view) are not the only possible points of comparison for theories of sentence meaning in Indian philosophy in Recanati's work. For instance, contextualism (defended by Recanati as well as others) and the word dependence view of Prābhākara thinkers might, as Siderits (2006) suggests, be a fruitful point of contact to explore. And of course, the various theories of Naiyāyikas on sentence meaning, many of which do incorporate speaker intention, are potential points of inquiry as well. However, this (very!) brief summary of some of the positions and starting points in analytic philosophy of language illustrates the challenge in locating non-arbitrary points of engagement. Apparent structural analogies, when investigated, may turn out to be less analogous than initially thought.

Further, Recanati's reconstruction of the semantics-pragmatics debate is not without controversy. For the sake of space, and because of the way his discussion seems to pick up on some themes in Mukula, I have limited myself primarily to explicating his view, but the literature on this topic is large, and there are those who would disagree with his way of carving up the conceptual space. In fact, another reason for selecting Recanati as an interlocutor is one recurring criticism of his work that strikes me as worth pausing to consider. This is the claim, put neatly by Bach (2007), that he tends to "to psychologize semantics and to semanticize psychology."[1] Now, the evaluation of Recanati's work, and whether what he has done is confused, requires attention to details which are beyond my scope here. However, given the psychological emphasis in Indian philosophy on the cognitive processes involved in sentence comprehension, we might wonder whether this aspect of his work is a flaw. It could be that he is unknowingly converging in some ways with the projects that Mukula and other Indian philosophers are engaged in. Certainly he is, with Mukula, concerned with what Indian thinkers call *vyavahāra*, or ordinary linguistic behavior, the "activity of saying things" (2) in the sense of emphasizing speech as an action, not just a formal structure abstracted from contexts of utterance.

What I argue below is that, if Indian philosophy of language is to be brought further into conversation with contemporary philosophy of language, it is important that not only the philosophical disciplines (*darśanas*) such as Buddhism, Nyāya, and Mīmāṃsā, be investigated, or even the study of grammar (*vyākaraṇa*), which has been a subject for linguists for decades, but also the textual tradition which Mukula is part of, known as Alaṅkāra-śāstra (poetic and aesthetic reflection), since it is at the intersection of syntax, semantics, and pragmatics. In particular, the literature in Alaṅkāra which focuses on the functions of speech (*śabda-vyāpara* and *śabda-vṛtti*) is an important point for inquiry. Ālaṅkārikas such as Mahima Bhaṭṭa have received treatment typically within the methodologies of intellectual history and Sanskrit, which is crucial if philosophical investigation is to be grounded in what these thinkers have written rather than confabulations. However, there is as yet little, if any, inquiry into how these thinkers can help our understanding of first-order philosophical questions. To take Mahima Bhaṭṭa as an example, his treatise, the *Analysis of Suggestion* (*Vyakti-viveka*), which is significantly longer and more detailed than Mukula's, gives an account of how we understand poetic meanings by inference, which he understands in a manner indebted to the Buddhist thinker Dharmakīrti. His work is sophisticated and wide-ranging, taking up many of the same topics as Mukula, plus more (for instance, he discusses the semantics of disquotation, which Rajendran (2000) summarizes).

There is an important aspect of Alaṅkāra literature which makes it worth investigation in light of the observations above. Thinkers in this tradition are explicitly drawing on Pāṇinian syntax as well as philosophical theories of meaning to account for speech beyond the paradigmatic literal assertion or Vedic injunction. Both of these kinds of speech form the core of inquiry in philosophical texts, given that the aims were to explain the way in which human linguistic testimony is knowledge-conducive or Vedic scriptures are obligatory and also knowledge-conducive, with regard to what ought to be done. However, despite concern with metonymy and metaphor in both cases, the typical examples are standard, conventional expressions. In Alaṅkāra literature, although these cases are also found, we also encounter a wide range of poetic examples. These cases, as we have seen with Mukula's "five fires" poem, account for a range of linguistic phenomena not focused on in philosophical or grammatical contexts. In conclusion, several central questions seem worth further investigation in this context:

1 What is the relationship between psychology, syntax, semantics, and pragmatics in Indian linguistic philosophy? Are there thinkers who bring these together in a systematic way, and reflect on methodology as they do?

2 To what extent do theoretical starting points (e.g., assertions vs. commands, human speech vs. unauthored speech) inform theories of meaning? What does the appropriation of, for instance, Mīmāṃsā hermeneutics for poetic pragmatics tell us about what aspects of these theories were seen as necessarily connected and which could be abandoned?
3 What is the relationship between epistemic instruments such as inference and postulation and the psychological reality of linguistic interpretation? To what extent are interpretive processes understood as consciously available and to what extent are they reconstructions, justifications for the interpretive result?

At present, many of these questions are being explored in the context of the philosophical "systems" (*darśanas*) such as Buddhism, Nyāya, and Mīmāṃsā, as well as the grammatical-philosophical work of Bhartṛhari and others. However, I hope that this brief investigation into the work of a thinker who does not explicitly align himself with any of these traditions demonstrates the philosophical richness of Alaṅkāra. Much philological, let alone philosophical, work remains to be done in order for this tradition to be brought into robust conversation with contemporary linguistic thought, but if Mukula's small work is any indication, the effort will be well worth it.

Part VI

Study Resources

Glossary

English translations or English terms appear first, with Sanskrit in parentheses where applicable. Cross-references within a glossary entry appear in bold.

Absorption (*adhyavasāna*). Indication where a word's primary meaning is concealed due to the subject of superimposition being merged, together with the object that is being superimposed. A subvariety of qualitative superimposition and quality-free superimposition.

Action (*kriyā*). Actions are subject to significant theorizing in Indian philosophy, but broadly can be understood as the meaning of a verb. They are typically inter-distinguished by relationships to an agent, an instrument, a method, and an aim.

Being established (*siddhi*). A meaning which is established is one which is justified in a context, that is, which makes sense. The category of **inclusion (*upādāna*)** indicates a second meaning in order to establish the first, primary meaning, which is retained (and thus **intended to be expressed, *vivakṣita***) but the primary meaning is subordinate to the indicated meaning.

Blocked (*bādhita*). The cognitive obstacle which prevents a hearer from understanding a word or expression in its primary meaning.

Cognition (*avagati, bodha*). Broad category for mental content which an agent entertains. Typically in Mukula's context, it is a meaning which a hearer understands. It is mental in that it is entertained by an agent but it is also a structured content. For instance, there can be a cognition that a cow is red from the words "The cow is red." When such a cognition is settled, or underwritten by an **epistemic instrument**, it is said to be determinate (*niścaya*).

Communicative function (*abhidhā-vyāpāra*). The entire communicative function of language, including two subvarieties: primary and indicatory. In contrast to other authors who often use *abhidhā* to refer to denotation or literal meaning alone, Mukula uses the term to include indication (*lakṣaṇā*).

Connection (*anvaya*). The syntactic-semantic relationship between word meanings which enables them to form a sentence.

Connection-of-the-denoted (*abhihitânvaya*). A theory about sentential unity which emphasizes compositionality. Sentences are constituted by word meanings first denoting through the primary function. At a second stage, indication allows a shift from, for instance, universals to particulars.

Contiguity (*sannidhi*). The proximity of words in a sentence—this is understood variously. It may be either psychological proximity (closely related cognitions) or phonetic—temporal (words uttered in close sequence).

Conventional (*nirūḍha*). Secondary expressions whose nature as figurative is not immediately available to ordinary speaker intuitions.

Denotation. The ability of a linguistic expression, whether word or a sentence, to communicate a meaning. Denotation in this sense is a broader concept than **reference**.

Denotation-through-the-connected (*anvitâbhidhāna*). A theory about sentential unity which emphasizes context. Sentences are constituted by the combination of word meanings, where word meanings are understood to be related to one another. Words do not denote first entities such as universals and then shift to particulars, but denote entities-as-related.

Distinction (*taṭastha, adūraga, nigīrṇa*). The difference between the primary and indicated meanings. Distinction can be extreme (*tatastha*), when there is no content from the primary understood in the indicated meaning, intermediate (*adūraga*), when there is some content from the primary understood in the indicated meaning, or dissolved (*nigīrṇa*), when the two meanings are not cognized as distinct at all.

Distinguishing feature (*upādhi*). Whatever features, taken together, sufficiently and necessarily demarcate the boundaries of linguistic use. These features set the application conditions for word use. Mukula identifies four: **universals**, **actions, properties**, and **something contingent** that is stipulated by the speaker, or a proper name.

Epistemic instrument (*pramāṇa*). Epistemic instruments are the means by which human beings acquire knowledge. Perception and inference are two commonly accepted epistemic instruments.

Expectation (*ākāṅkṣā*). A requirement for sentence meaning. Words which, in virtue of their grammatical roles, must be paired with other words (such as subject and predicate), are said to have expectation.

Expressed meaning (*vācya*). Mukula typically uses this to mean what is said in a given context, including both primary and indicated meaning. It is contrasted with **sentence meaning**. However, he notes also that the term can be used to mean what is expressed by words before they are sententially unified.

Function of speech (*śabda-vyāpāra*). The capacity of speech, whether by words or sentences, to cause a corresponding cognition in a hearer.

Homonym. A word which has the same spelling or sound as another word but has a different meaning that is not etymologically connected, like the “bark” of a tree and the “bark” of a dog.

Hyperbole (*atiśaya*). Literally "excellence," or "superiority," this figure involves exaggeration of properties actually present in an object.

Identification (*rūpaka*). A figure where two objects are identified together through grammatical constructions such as compounds ("face-moon," a face which is a moon) or predicate constructions ("Her face is the moon").

Imagining (*utprekṣā*). A figure where two objects are compared, explicitly or implicitly, despite no realistic basis for resemblance.

Implied (*ākṣepa*). A reasoning process often closely related to **postulation (*arthāpatti*)** on which something is presumed which is lacking, for explanatory purposes or to resolve what is incongruous otherwise.

Inclusion (*upādāna*). A subvariety of superimposition-free indication. Where a meaning is implied to make sense of, or establish, the primary meaning, and the primary meaning is incorporated into the new, implied meaning.

Indication lacking transfer (*śuddhôpacāra*). One half of the first binary division within indication, where there is no attribution of properties from subject to the object of comparison.

Indication with transfer (*upacāra-miśra*). One half of the first binary division within indication, where properties from the object of comparison are attributed to the subject of comparison. Also simply transfer, *upacāra*.

Indicatory function (*lākṣaṇika-vyāpāra*), indication (*lakṣaṇā*), indicated meaning (*lakṣyârtha*). The communicative function which is at one step removed from the **primary function**, but which follows from it. It is responsible for metonymy, metaphor, irony, hyperbole, and a host of other indirect meanings. The function or operation is either "indication" or the "indicatory function," whereas the resultant meaning is "indicated."

Indirect expression (*lakṣaṇa-lakṣaṇā*). A subvariety of **indication lacking transfer**. Defined as the opposite of **inclusion**, this variety is where the **natural meaning**, or **primary meaning**, is given up and replaced by another meaning.

Inference based upon positive and negative correlations (*anvaya-vyatireka*). A process used in determining word meanings by their appearance and non-appearance in various contexts.

Intended to be expressed meaning (*vivakṣita-vācya*). When the **expressed meaning (*vācya*)** is intended to be expressed (*vivakṣita*). It is an important condition for the suggested meaning in Ānandavardhana that the speaker does not intend to express the primary meaning; Mukula thinks such an intention can exist in the cases Ānandavardhana identifies.

Intermediated indirect indication (*lakṣita-lakṣaṇā*). Where the primary meaning and the secondary meaning are related via an intermediate word or concept. Traditionally, *dvi-repha* is an example of this, since the word literally means "word having two r's" and has come to mean "bee" because the Sanskrit for "bee" is *bhramara*.

Meaning (*artha*). The meaning of a linguistic expression is usually understood in terms of **reference**. Meanings of words are objects, and meanings of sentences are states of affairs.

Natural meaning (*svârtha*). Literally, "own meaning," that is the meaning which directly belongs to the word. Another word for the **primary meaning** which is understood from the **primary function**.

Nature (*sva-rūpa*). This term can refer to the nature of a thing or of a word. When used for a word, it can refer to the word's ordinary meaning, that is, before indication, or the word's nature as a type in contrast to a token. For instance, the own nature of the word "cow" is what all utterances of "cow" have in common. When used for an object, it refers to the object's essential character.

Object of comparison (*upameya*). In figurative comparison such as "Your face is the moon," the moon is the object of comparison. It is, strictly speaking, not identical to the face (the subject of comparison) but its properties are in some way related or similar to the properties in the subject.

Ordinary linguistic practice (*vyavahāra*). Human behavior associated with language. We use certain words at certain times and not others to prompt action, convey ideas, and etc. Sometimes also characterized as ordinary linguistic practices of our predecessors (literally, "elders") (*vṛdda-vyavahāra*), which are linguistic practices with prior acceptance in the linguistic community.

Otherwise incongruous (*anyathā anupapattyā*). Something having an obstacle which would, without something being indicated or implied or postulated etc., otherwise cause an epistemic fault.

Polysemous. When a word has multiple related meanings, such as "newspaper" in the sense of a physical paper and "newspaper" in the sense of the company producing such items.

Postulation (*arthāpatti*). An **epistemic instrument** which involves reasoning based on an incongruity between a previously known fact and a newly acquired fact. What is postulated is what is necessary to resolve the incongruity.

Primary function (*mukhya-vyāpāra*). The communicative function responsible for word denotation. For Mukula, there are four kinds of referents which words denote: universals, properties, actions, and contingently denoted things. Related: **primary meaning, *mukhya*.**

Property (*guṇa*). Repeatable instances which characterize a particular thing (*dravya*). For instance, shape, color, size, and so on. Properties are distinguished from **universals (*jāti*)** in that they are particular instances, in contrast to a universal, which is a unity found in many substances.

***Rasa*.** An aesthetic mood in a poem or play. There are nine: the comic, heroic, erotic, terrible, pathetic, compassionate, furious, wondrous, the peaceful.

Reference. The relationship between a word or other linguistic expression and its object. For example, the referent of "cow" might be a particular cow in a field or it might be a **universal (*jāti*)** such as COWHOOD. There are competing theories of reference in Indian philosophy.

Semantically imbued (*uparakta*). The term literally means "colored" or "darkened," but Mukula uses it to refer to how one meaning influences another, thus a semantic "shade," as in a "shade of meaning."

Semantic fit (*yogyatā*). The mutual appropriateness of word meanings in sentence context, with regard to meaning and not syntax. The word "sprinkle" has semantic fit in the sentence "The gardener sprinkles the flower with water" but not in "The gardener sprinkles the flower with fire."

Sense. A linguistic expression's conceptual content. On theories which distinguish between sense and **reference**, a word (here a name) such as "Superman" might have a different sense than "Clark Kent" despite having the same referent.

Sensitive critic (*sahṛdaya*). A word literally meaning "like-hearted," it refers to poetic theorists who agree with Ānandavardhana that there is a third linguistic capacity, suggestion.

Sentence (*vākya*). A syntactical unity comprised of a number of words in context. There are different theories of sentence composition, leading also to different theories of **expressed meaning**.

Something contingent (*yad-ṛcchā*). The bearer of a proper name. A word for something contingent is a proper name, which refers in virtue of the speaker's desire to use the word that way and not in virtue of a property in the object such as a property, action, or universal.

Subject of comparison (*upamāna*). In figurative comparison such as "Your face is the moon," the face is the subject of comparison. It is, strictly speaking, not identical to the moon (the object of comparison) but the moon's properties are being emphasized to emphasize certain the properties in the subject.

Superimposition (*adhyâropa* or *āropa*). Indication where there is superimposition of one object onto another, but with awareness of the difference between the subject and object of comparison.

Suggestion (*dhvani*). The communicative function which, according to Ānandavardhana, is responsible for conveying meanings that are not **primary** or **indicatory**. There are three major kinds of suggested content: facts (*vastu*), figures (*alaṅkāra*), and ***rasa***.

Syntactic expectancy (*ākāṅkṣā*). The need for a word in a sentence to have a corresponding word present. For instance, a transitive verb has expectancy for a direct object. This expectancy can be understood strictly syntactically or as the hearer's expectation based on pragmatic needs.

Transfer of properties (*gauṇôpacāra*). A subvariety of **indication with transfer**. The subject of comparison is superimposed onto the object of comparison because of similarity between the properties of the two.

Transfer in general (*śuddôpacāra*). A subvariety of **indication with transfer**. The subject of comparison is superimposed onto the object of comparison but not because of similar properties. The reason could be a relationship of cause-and-effect or association, etc. Subdivided into **superimposition** and **absorption.**

Type-token distinction. Phonemes, words, and sentences can be distinguished into types and tokens. A **type** is an abstracta, whereas a **token** is a concrete particular. The sentence type "The village is on the Ganges" may be tokened in different contexts, specific times, and places. Likewise the word type "village" may be tokened in different contexts. Finally, the phonemic type "v" may be tokened in different contexts. (But note: a sentence type contains occurrences of word tokens, not the tokens themselves, *ceteris paribus* for other types.)

Universal (*jāti, sāmānya*). The single, permanent thing which wholly exists in multiple individuals and in virtue of its presence makes that thing what it is. Represented with small capital letters in the text. For instance, COWHOOD is the universal which makes a cow a cow. Other universals may inhere in the same entity, such as SUBSTANCEHOOD, ANIMALHOOD, etc.

Sanskrit Pronunciation

In this book, Sanskrit words are written using the International Alphabet of Sanskrit Transliteration (IAST) so that English-speaking readers who do not know other scripts (such as Devanāgarī) can read them. A complete guide to such diacritical marks and pronunciation can be found in a number of resources, both online and in print, such as the video resources at Cambridge University Press (2017) and the Sanskrit textbook by Goldman and Goldman (2004). To help the novice, a few important principles follow.

1. Vowels in Sanskrit are distinguished between long and short with a macron, as in *a* and *ā*. So while *a*, *i*, *u*, *e*, and *o* approximate English pronunciations, *ā*, *ī*, *ū* are long (like "father," "police," and "rune").
2. Consonants can be aspirated, or pronounced with a breath after them. These are marked with an *h* after, as in *bh*, *ph*, *th*, and so on. So a *th* is pronounced like the *th* in "warthog" and never like the *th* in "the."
3. Sibilants *ś* and *ṣ* are pronounced slightly differently, the first with the back of the tongue against the soft palate, and the second with the tip at the roof of the mouth, but are roughly the *sh* sound as in "wish."
4. Two other common letters: *ṛ* and *ṃ*. The first is pronounced with the tongue rolled a bit back, as "Rita" or "fiber." The second is a nasalized sound whose proper pronunciation varies in context, but sounds roughly like the "n" in "hang."
5. Stress in Sanskrit typically falls on the penultimate syllable. If the penultimate syllable is not long (that is, if it does not contain a vowel with a macron), the stress falls on the preceding long syllable. So "Him**ā**laya" and "Ved**ā**nta."

Chronology of Important Figures and Dates

All dates are rough estimates, rounded to the nearest century unless more precision is possible. Dates which are very controversial are marked with a question mark. Readers interested in more historical detail should consult sources in the bibliography and introduction.

Name	Date	Major works
Jaimini	400–200 BCE (?)	*Aphorisms on Exegesis* (*Mīmāṃsā-sūtra*)
Bhartṛhari	450 BCE	*Treatise on Sentences and Words* (*Vākya-padīya*)
Pāṇini	400 BCE	*Eight Chapters* (*Aṣṭâdhyāyī*)
Patañjali	150 BCE	*Great Commentary* (*Mahā-bhāṣya*, Commentary on *Aṣṭâdhyāyī*)
attributed to Akṣapāda Gautama	200 CE (?)	*Aphorisms on Logic* (*Nyāya-sūtra*)
Śabara Miśra	200–400 CE (?)	*Commentary on the Aphorisms on Exegesis* (*Śābara-bhāṣya*)
Dharmakīrti	625 CE	*Commentary on Epistemic Instruments* (*Pramāṇa-vārttika*)
Kumārila Bhaṭṭa	660 CE	*Commentary in Verse* (*Śloka-vārttika*), *Exposition on Ritual* (*Tantra-vārttika*)
Prabhākara Miśra	700 CE	*Vast Commentary* (*Bṛhatī*, Commentary on *Mīmāṃsā-sūtra*)
Ānandavardhana	850 CE	*Light on Suggestion* (*Dhvanyâloka*)
Śālikanātha Miśra	850 CE	*Monograph in Five Chapters* (*Prakaraṇa-pañcikā*)
Jayanta Bhaṭṭa	875 CE	*Garland of Logic* (*Nyāya-mañjarī*)
Mukula Bhaṭṭa	950 CE	*Fundamentals of the Communicative Function* (*Abhidhā-vṛtta-mātṛkā*)
Abhinavagupta	990 CE	*The Eye* (*Locana*, Commentary on *Dhvanyâloka*)
Mahima Bhaṭṭa	1000 CE	*Analysis of Suggestion* (*Vyakti-viveka*)
Mammaṭa	1100 CE	*Illumination of Poetry* (*Kāvya-prakāśa*)

Indices

Mukula quotes from a range of thinkers. Below is an index of the first line of citations in English, along with the original text in Sanskrit. Subsequent is an index with the first lines in Sanskrit (alphabetized according to Sanskrit) with English translation in parentheses. When possible to provide, the original text and author follow. A subject and name index follows, ordered according to the English alphabet.

Index of first lines (English)

Bee, in all your buzzing about the spacious sky, Have you anywhere touched, seen, or heard . . . (*bhamara bhramatā digantarāṇi kvacid-āsāditam īkṣitaṃ śrutaṃ vā*) 68

Clouds with white cranes whirling extend across the sky, smeared with glistening dark color . . . (*snigdha-śyāmala-kānti-lipta-viyato vellad-balākā ghanā*) 58

From the middle of the ocean, its golden structures making the sky glow . . . (*madhye samudraṃ kukubhaḥ piśaṅgīr yā kurvatī kāñcana-bhūmī-bhāsā*) *Śiśupalavādha*, Māgha 59

Further, indication is just customary speech. (*punaś ca asāv eva āha lakṣaṇā āpi hi laukiky eva*) *Mīmāṃsā-sūtra-bhāṣya*, Śabara 58

He has already taken Śrī, so why stir up pain by churning me? (*prapta-śrīḥ eṣa kasmāt punar api mayi mantha-khedam vidadhyā...*) 61

Hey there neighbor, will you watch our house for a bit, as well? . . . (*dṛṣṭiṃ he prativeśini kṣaṇam iha api asmad-gṛhe dāsyasi*) 60

How is one word used for another? We say: It is through the word's own meaning. (*kathaṃ punaḥ para-śabdaḥ paratra varttate svârthâbhidhānena iti brūmaḥ*) *Mīmāṃsā-sūtra-bhāṣya*, Śabara 58

Indication is considered fivefold because of a close relationship with what is denoted . . . (*abhidheyena saṃbandhāt sādṛśyāt samavāyataḥ*), Bhartṛmitra 67

In fact, a cow is not a cow or non-cow because of its particular nature, but it is a cow because of its relationship with COWHOOD. (*gaur iti na hi gauḥ sva-rūpeṇa gauḥ na apy agauḥ gotvâbhisambandhāt tu gauḥ*) *Vākya-padīya*, Bhartṛhari 49

Some figures are conventional because they have a capacity like the primary denotation; Some are newly created, some are even without power. (*nirūḍhā lakṣaṇāḥ kāścit sāmarthyād abhidhānavat. kriyante sāṃpratam kāścit kāścin na eva tv aśāktitaḥ*) *Tantra-vārttika*, Kumārila Bhaṭṭa 58

The flower-tipped arrows of the love-god are hard to avoid: spring blossoms everywhere . . . (*durvārā madaneṣavo diśi diśi vyājṛmbhate mādhavo . . .*) 62

The words *śiva, śama, riṣṭa* in the genitive when meaning "he does" . . . (*śiva-śama-riṣṭasya kare...*), *Aṣṭâdhyāyī*, Pāṇini 63

There are four uses of words: words denoting universals, words denoting properties, words denoting actions, and words denoting something contingent. (*catuṣṭayī śabdānām pravṛttiḥ. jāti-śabdā guṇaśabdāḥ kriyāśabdā yad-ṛcchāśabdāś caturthāḥ.*) *Mahā-bhāṣya*, Patañjali. 48

When there is an intention to express similarity of natures, expressed by words such as "like," . . . (*sāmya-rūpa-vivakṣāyāṃ vācye vācya-ātmabhiḥ padaiḥ*) *Kāvyâlaṅkāra-saṃgraha*, Udbhaṭa 62

You are Pṛthu in properties. In glory you are Rāma, You are Nala and Bharata . . . (*pṛthur asi guṇaiḥ kīrttyā rāmo nalo bharato bhavān . . .*) 69

Index of first lines (Sanskrit)

abhidheyena saṃbandhāt sādṛśyāt samavāyataḥ . . . (Indication is considered fivefold because of a close relationship with what is denoted . . .) Bhartṛmitra 67

kathaṃ punaḥ para-śabdaḥ paratra varttate svârthâbhidhānena iti brūmaḥ. (How is one word used for another? We say: It is through the word's own meaning.) *Mīmāṃsā-sūtra-bhāṣya*, Śabara 58

gaur iti na hi gauḥ sva-rūpeṇa gauḥ na apy agauḥ gotvâbhisambandhāt tu gauḥ (In fact, a cow is not a cow or non-cow because of its particular nature, but it is a cow because of its relationship with COWHOOD.) *Vākya-padīya*, Bhartṛhari 49

catuṣṭayī śabdānām pravṛttiḥ. jāti-śabdā guṇaśabdāḥ kriyāśabdā yad-ṛcchāśabdāś caturthāḥ. (There are four uses of words: words denoting universals, words denoting properties, words denoting actions, and words denoting something contingent.) *Mahā-bhāṣya*, Patañjali 48

madhye samudraṃ kukubhaḥ piśaṅgīr yā kurvatī kāñcana-bhūmī-bhāsā . . . (From the middle of the ocean, its golden structures making the sky glow . . .) *Śiśupala-vādha*, Māgha 59

durvārā madaneṣavo diśi diśi vyājṛmbhate mādhavo . . . (The flower-tipped arrows of the love-god are hard to avoid: spring blossoms everywhere . . .) 62

dṛṣṭiṃ he prativeśini kṣaṇam iha api asmad-gṛhe dāsyasi . . . (Hey there neighbor, will you watch our house for a bit, as well?) 60

nirūḍhā lakṣaṇāḥ kāścit sāmarthyād abhidhānavat. kriyante sāṃprataṃ kāścit kāścin na eva tv aśāktitaḥ (Some figures are conventional because they have a capacity like the primary denotation; Some are newly created, some are even without power.) *Tantra-vārttika*, Kumārila Bhaṭṭa 58

punaś ca asāv eva āha lakṣaṇā āpi hi laukiky eva. (Further, indication is just customary speech.) *Mīmāṃsā-sūtra-bhāṣya*, Śabara 58

pṛthur asi guṇaiḥ kīrttyā rāmo nalo bharato bhavān . . . (You are Pṛthu in properties. In glory you are Rāma, You are Nala and Bharata . . .) 69

prapta-śrīḥ eṣa kasmāt punar api mayi mantha-khedam vidadhyā (He has already taken Śrī, so why stir up pain by churning me?) 61

bhamara bhramatā digantarāṇi kvacid-āsāditam īkṣitaṃ śrutaṃ vā . . . (Bee, in all your buzzing about the spacious sky, Have you anywhere touched, seen, or heard . . .) 68

sāmya-rūpa-vivakṣāyāṃ vācye vācya-ātmabhiḥ padaiḥ (When there is an intention to express similarity of natures, expressed by words such as "like," . . .) *Kāvyâlaṅkāra-saṃgraha*, Udbhaṭa 62

snigdha-śyāmala-kānti-lipta-viyato vellad-balākā ghanā . . . (Clouds with white cranes whirling extend across the sky, smeared with glistening dark color . . .) 58

Notes

Part I

Introduction

1 Shakespeare (1997).
2 In analytic philosophy and contemporary linguistics, the literature on metaphor comprehension and related questions is quite large. Davidson (1978) is a classic treatment, as is Grice (1989), each representing two broad, and divergent, trends in the understanding of metaphor's relationship to so-called "literal" speech. Some recent collections provide a helpful introduction to the literature, including Ezcurdia and Stainton (2013), Ritchie (2013), and Semino and Demjén (2017).
3 For expediency, I follow others who shorten Ānandavardhana's name to "Ānanda," although readers should note that "-vardhana" is not a title like "Bhaṭṭa" (which probably means "lord" or "honored one"), but part of his name.
4 For the question of how universal the *dhvani* theory is and the possibility of employing it to other cultural art forms, see Ashton and Tanner (2016), Gerow (2002), and Patankar (1980), for instance.

Why did Mukula Bhaṭṭa Write the *Fundamentals?*

1 Ānandavardhana's work is typically read alongside of the very influential commentary, the *Eye on Suggestion* (*Locana*), written by Abhinavagupta in the late tenth or early eleventh centuries CE. However, Abhinavagupta, who comes after Mukula, extends Ānanda's arguments in some innovative ways. To understand Mukula's concerns, we should refrain from reading this interpretation back into the original text. Thus I do not discuss Abhinavagupta's interpretation of Ānanda here. For discussion of the relationship between these two thinkers, see McCrea (2008) and Pollock (2012).
2 For a recent discussion of the relationships between metaphor and plausible deniability, see Camp (2017).

3 Translation Ingalls (1990:311), *Light on Suggestion* (henceforth *DL*) 2.22.
4 *DL* 1.4c, Ingalls (1990: 98).
5 *DL* 2.27a, Ingalls (1990: 331).

Indication and Resolving Incongruity: Mukula's Response

1 This position is different than one of the more common views in contemporary linguistics and philosophy of language, which is that a false or nonsensical sentence is understood, and then a second meaning is understood by the hearer, a meaning called an "implicature." See Grice (1989) and Gricean-inspired modifications by Searle (1979). Relevance theorists such as Bezuidenhout (2001), Carston (2010), and Carston and Wilson (2006), modify Gricean approaches even further. Even those who reject a broadly Gricean implicature view, such as Donald Davidson think that it is possible to understand the original sentence in its false sense. See Davidson (1978) and Lepore and Stone (2010).
2 See page 80 for translation in context.
3 This case, though, raises an important question: Who is the speaker in a poem? Is it the fictional character or the poet? Here, if the speaker is the fictional character, then, setting aside problems about fictional intentions, we might worry that the woman isn't trying to communicate the hidden meaning to her neighbor. But if the speaker is the poet communicating this hidden intention to us, the reader, then facts about the neighbor are no longer facts about the speaker.
4 In this he is unlike the later thinker Mahima Bhaṭṭa (twelfth century CE), who is explicit that suggestion is explained by another epistemic instrument, inference.
5 And in fact, shyness, shame, or modesty (*lajjā*) is an important concept in Sanskrit poetics and its presence in women is a contributing factor to the presence of the *rasa* of love, or the erotic.
6 Although it is sometimes characterized as inference to the best explanation as in Siderits (1991:41) or some other non-necessary inference as in Roodbergen (2008:53) , this is only one interpretation of its structure, which others argue is analytic or *a priori* in nature, as in Guha (2016).
7 Ānandavardhana says "In the area of poetry an inquiry into the truth or falsity of suggestions is useless; so the testing of the suggestive operation by other epistemic instruments [like inference] is a laughable occupation" and commenting on this Abhinavagupta goes even further, arguing that someone investigating poetry in this way "has a heart so hardened by his efforts at

logic that he cannot understand pleasure." *DL* 3.33p, Ingalls (1990:591-592) The logicians, though, respond with equal scorn to the suggestion theorists, as Jayanta Bhaṭṭa, bringing up suggestion in the context of his own discussion of postulation, facetiously characterizes its defender as "one who thinks himself as a scholar" (*paṇḍitaṃmanyaḥ*), implying he is not really one.

Understanding Mukula's Context

1 What I translate as "postulation" is also translated as "implication," "presumption," or "supposition," none of which has become standard.

2 For discussion of how epistemology of testimony in India relates to modern analytic epistemology, see Matilal and Chakrabarti (1994). Both traditions discuss the problem of whether testimony can be reduced to inference, and in what sense, for instance, as well as problems of testimonial transmission and what constitutes speaker reliability. However, in the Indian context, there is attention to the possibility that testimony can be an epistemic instrument without a speaker, which is explored in Billimoria (1988) in a way that resonates with contemporary work such as Lackey (2008).

3 Prabhākara is a roughly contemporaneous rival to Kumārila, also dedicated to Vedic orthopraxy, but differing over some important epistemological details, which need not concern us here. But see the introduction to Freschi (2012) for discussion.

4 Ganeri (2006:130-158) argues that the fifteenth-century philosopher Vardhamāna employs something like this distinction.

5 In fact, the primary/secondary distinction gets complicated in the theories put forward by Prābhākaras, for which see the commentarial chapter as well as Appendix 2.

6 Metonymy has received increasing attention in recent years in the work of cognitive linguists who are concerned with the relationship between metaphor and metonymy. For instance, see Dirven and Pörings (2000). For some recent remarks the relationship between Indian and "Western" thinking on this point, see Gerow (2010).

7 For discussion of the "difference in non-difference" (*bhedâbheda*) theory of the universal in Kumārila, see Dravid (2001) as well as Taber (2017).

8 In fact, the semantics-pragmatics distinction is contentious in analytic philosophy, both in terms of what it might be and where it might lie. There are number of ways to characterize it, beyond our scope here. Some introductions to this wide-ranging debate include Depraetere and Salkie (2017), Jaszczolt (2002), and Ezcurdia and Stainton (2013).

9 See also the introduction to Gerow (1971) for a discussion of the varieties of "metaphorical" figurative speech.

10 But see Stainton (2006) for a competing view.
11 Mukula also proposes a fourth view, which is a combination of the first and second, and which is discussed in more detail in the commentarial chapter. Note that these three views are presented in broad contour, in Mukula's text and in this introduction. Nyāya philosophers proposed their own theories in contrast to the three presented here, and increasingly sophisticated alternative views are proposed by all parties which do not neatly fit into these categories.
12 See Siderits (1991). As he points out, however, Prābhākara thinkers would not entirely agree with this representation, as incomplete (unsaturated) entities are not part of their ontology.
13 As Bronner (2016) has convincingly argued, Ānandavardhana was not the first to write on poetry and drama together, nor to theorize somewhat systematically about the importance of *rasa*.
14 As with most technical terms in Sanskrit, translation of *dhvani* varies, although "suggestion" is fairly common, as in Ingalls (1990). McCrea (2017) uses "resonance," trading on the term's literal sense of a reverberating sound. Recently Pollock (2016) has proposed "implicature" though this is imprecise, (as he does admit), and possibly, given its technical sense in analytic philosophy which requires the possibility of inferential calculation—something Ānandavardhana would strenuously reject.
15 See McCrea (2008) for more on the relationship between Ānandavardhana and Mīmāṃsā philosophy.
16 *vibhāvânubhāva-vyabhicāri-saṃyogād rasa-niṣpattiḥ* Bharata (1926:274).
17 Translation McCrea (2008:35-36).
18 McCrea (2008) and Bronner (2016).
19 McCrea (2008:266).

Part II

Introduction

1 In printed editions, the word I translate as "knowledge-conducive" (*prāmāṇyam*) has a variant reading, *prādhānyam*. However, some printed editions such as Venugopalan (1977) correct it to *prāmāṇyam*, meaning "epistemically authoritative" or "knowledge-conducive." For detailed discussion of this and other textual variants, see the transliteration.

Verses 1–15

1 Throughout his work, Mukula frequently begins his auto-commentary on a verse with a paraphrase of the verse. This repetition is part of the commentarial style, which seeks to elucidate an author's verses. See commentarial chapter for discussion of this genre.
2 The Sanskrit term for primary meaning is *mukhya*, which is derived by adding the suffix *-ya* to *mukha* ("face"). As *–ya* means "like," the etymological meaning of *mukhya* is "like a face." Mukula illustrates this grammatical change with the word *śākhā* ("branch") which, with the suffix *–ya* becomes *śākhyā* or "like a branch."
3 This refers to Patañjali, who writes the *Great Commentary* (*Mahābhāṣya*) on Pāṇini's *Eight Chapters* (*Aṣṭâdhyāyī*).
4 Ascribed to Bhartṛhari's *Treatise on Sentences and Words* (*Vākyapadīya*), but the quote is not found in the text. It may belong to a lost portion of the commentary (*vṛtti*) on the text.
5 This is a well-known kind of indication which involves two stages. See glossary.
6 *Commentary on the Mīmāṃsā Sūtras* on *MS* 1.4.22.
7 *Exposition on Ritual Practice* on *MS* 3.1.12.
8 Anonymous verse collected in several places.
9 Verse from Māgha's *Killing of Śiśupāla* (*Śiśupālavadha*) 3.33. The last line, which Mukula finds too strained to be a meaningful figure of speech, reads in Sanskrit: *turaṅga-kāntânana-havya-vāha-jvāla iva.* See the commentary for more detailed discussion, but essentially, the image is of a fire erupting from the waters, in the shape of a horse's head.
10 Literally, the text refers to the word "two-r's" (*dvi-repha*) by which the word for a bee is understood (*bhramara*).
11 Anonymous verse ascribed to Vidyā. Warder (1983: 425).
12 The stanza refers to three great feats of Viṣṇu, whom Mukula calls by the name "Vāsudeva." The first is his churning the ocean and taking out of it the goddess Śrī. The second is his sleeping on the ocean during the times in between the world's cyclic destruction and recreation. The third is his building a bridge to Laṅkā while incarnate as Rāma.
13 Udbhaṭa, *Synopsis of the Essentials of Poetic Ornaments* (*Kāvyâlaṅkāra-sāra-saṃgraḥ*).
14 See commentary for discussion of the Sanskrit grammatical terms in this section. Mukula is defending the stanza from the charge of a grammatical error, based on some principles found in Pāṇini's *Eight Chapters.*
15 Quote is from a lost text of Bhartṛmitra, a Mīmāṃsaka thinker circa 600–700 CE.

16 The square brackets indicate a double meaning for the word. The proper name Śatrughna, which is a compound (*śatru-ghna*), etymologically means "enemy-killer."
17 Śatrughna is Rāma's youngest brother in the *Rāmayāṇa*.
18 The two columns represent two distinct readings of the poem due to breaking word boundaries differently and multiple word meanings. See commentary for more discussion.
19 Quotation refers to commentary on verse 9b above, the quote from Bhartṛmitra.
20 The Sanskrit phrase is two identical words, *puruṣaḥ puruṣaḥ*, probably taken from a verse by Hemacandra, though this version includes "just as" (*yathā*): A hero who moves in battle, at the forefront, killing a great many enemies: that man [*puruṣaḥ*] is like a *puruṣaḥ* ["one who goes in front," "one who protects."] Translation adapted from McCrea (2008:307). The word *puruṣaḥ* as a noun means "man," but could also be taken as an agentive form of a verb root, either *pṛ* ("to protect"), or *pur* ("to go in front"). This would make the second occurrence either "one who protects" or "one who leads." See commentary for more discussion.
21 Mukula is quoting from the verses above.

Part III

Introduction

1 For more details on Sanskrit commentarial genres, see Tubb and Boose (2007) and the Chapter, "Commentary and Creativity" in Ganeri (2011).
2 Sometimes the term is simply translated as "verbal communication," though as we will see, the activity of language is an important aspect of this concept, and indeed, sometimes the term just means behavior.
3 *śabdena uccaritena artho gamyate. gām ānaya dadhy aśāna ity artha ānīyate 'rthaś ca bhujate*. Keilhorn and Abyankar (2005:175). Unless otherwise noted, translations are mine.
4 For a discussion of how the term for word meanings, *artha* is used in Sanskrit grammar and philosophy, see the introduction to Deshpande (1992).
5 Of course, perception is not the only epistemic instrument we can use to learn the referents of words. Some things are beyond perception and known only by inference or testimony.
6 See Chronology of Important Figures and Dates.

7 The term "suggestion" is ambiguous between suggestion as a meaning and suggestion as a function (which generates the meaning). Thus I will often talk about "the suggestive function" and "suggested meanings" in order to make the distinction explicit if the context does not make it clear. Also, while this is not crucial for understanding Mukula, for Ānandavardhana, *dhvani* is a special case of *vyañjanā*, as it is suggestion when it is the main point of the poem or stanza.

Verses 1–15

1 While I include verses for reference, readers should look back at the main text for details, since this chapter is not just a commentary on the verses, but on Mukula's auto-commentary.

2 "The affix *yat* is used after 'branch' and similar words." Sanskrit: *śākhâdibhyaḥ yat* (1897:976).

3 Mukula does not identify its author, although the phrase is quoted elsewhere by other Ālaṅkārikas. Possibly they are from a lost work of Kumārila's, according to McCrea (2008:269, n. 17).

4 The verses are split into a and b where they form two halves of a metrical unit.

5 The term *yad-ṛcchā-śabda,* for a word which denotes something contingent is often translated as "arbitrary name" by Ganeri (1999) or "arbitrary word" in Venugopalan (1977). Though the distinction is slight, "arbitrary" connotes a decision without any purpose or rationale, while "contingent" is contingent upon something—in this case, the speaker's desire.

6 In fact, Bhartṛhari goes even further, as we will see when we get to discussion of sentence meaning, since he thinks that sentences are not really made up of words. Here, though, we are assuming a one-word utterance, so the distinction between sentence and word isn't strictly relevant.

7 For a Mīmāṃsaka analysis of this, see Śabara's *Commentary* at *MS* 1.1.5, translated in Jha (1933:19 to 20, Vol 1). Here we see a proponent of the "burst" theory argue against the phonemic realist view.

8 In fact, there is also a change to the verbal root, which is that it takes a strengthening known as *guṇa*. However, applying *guṇa* to *a* results in *a,* so that this change is imperceptible but is an essential part of the morphology of conjugation in the first class. For more, see Chapter 4, "Conjugation" in Macdonell (1974).

9 See Bronkhorst (1998) for discussion. While Venugopalan (1997:248-49, n. 18) cites a similar remark in Helārāja's commentary as a source, since Helārāja postdates Mukula (he dates to the eleventh century CE), it is likely that Mukula was citing a lost portion of the commentary, as Bronkhorst suggests.

10 Whether Mukula would, with some Indian thinkers, distinguish between natural kinds and artifacts is unclear—are cow-universals, horse-universals, and so on the same kind of thing as cloth-universals, chair-universals? For instance, Uddyotakara, a Naiyāyika thinker around the sixth century CE, argued that while there is a genuine universal in virtue of which we can categorize all things that are cows, when we talk about all people who are cooks, there is no such universal. For a book-length overview of some views on universals in Indian philosophy, see Dravid (2001).

11 This is what Gautama argues in the *Aphorisms on Logic* (*Nyāya-sutra*) at 2.1.33–37.

12 For more discussion of Vaiśeṣika thinkers on metaphysics, see Halbfass (1992). He makes the point about atoms this way: "Without ultimate particularity, the whole edifice of distinct, enumerable entities would not have a secure basis" and yet "the ultimate, permanent substances have an irreducible numerical identity which is at the same time generic identity" (273).

13 The Buddhist philosopher Kamalaśīla, circa eighth century CE, speaks in his *Detailed Explanation of the Compendium of Truth* (*Tattva-saṃgraha-pañcikā*) at verse 1266 in a way that sounds like Mukula's Semantic Universalist:

"Words like 'Ḍittha' are known as 'words for something contingent.' They take as their meaning a universal, one which inheres in entities which are restricted by boundaries of temporal duration. This is because it is impossible for proper names to convey an object which is divided into different moments without any common feature, whilst continuing to follow the object from birth until the moment of death. Otherwise, when used to denote the portion of the object as delimited by the state of childhood, how could it denote the object as having its condition the state of old age? . . . So even for proper names a universal has to be admitted." Translation adapted from Ganeri (1999: 196).

Here, Kamalaśīla argues that the name "Ḍittha" cannot refer directly to the individual person Ḍittha, say, by being associated with him at his birth. This is because he changes over time, and whatever properties he may have when very young may be lacking when he is older. But if Ḍittha, at all these stages, has a universal of Ḍitthahood, then we can correctly apply the term. For Buddhists such as Kamalaśīla, though, what it means for there to be such a universal is very different than what it means for a Mīmāṃsaka. In this context, a universal is mere conceptualization of whatever every momentary stage of Ḍittha has in common, since on the Buddhist view, persons lack selves which form an essence or a perduring core of their identity.To what extent, if any, Mukula is drawing on this discussion is not clear, since he does not identify his interlocutor, but as we will see elsewhere, he is not averse to drawing on Buddhist philosophy.

14 Again, if this were taken to be Bhartṛhari's view, we could say that each of these utterances manifest the "burst" which is distinct from any phonemic features belonging to a speaker's accent, etc.

15 For recent discussion of this term in brahminical and Buddhist philosophy of language, see Tzohar (2018). More relevant to Mukula's context, Ānandavardhana uses the term *upacāra* for one of two subvarieties of secondary meaning (*guṇa-vṛtti*), where the other subvariety is *lakṣaṇā*. He uses *lakṣaṇā* to refer to a particular kind of secondary meaning which is based in relationships like association or proximity—anything other than similarity, which is for him the basis of *upacāra*. Mukula alters this terminology, using *lakṣaṇā* as the broadest category and *upacāra* as a subdivision.

16 The Sanskrit *gaṅgāyām*, meaning Ganges, is in the locative case, where *ghoṣaḥ*, meaning a village, is in the nominative and is the subject of the sentence (with an implied predicative "is"). Pāṇini 1.4.45 describes the function of the locative as *ādhāro 'dhikaraṇam* or "'locative' means locus." Vasu (1897: 185). The term "locus" (*adhikaraṇa*) used to gloss "locative" (*ādhāra*) is defined as having three meanings, according to Patañjali: close contact or proximity (*aupaśleṣika*), pervasion or being within (*abhivyāpaka*), and content or topic (*vaiṣayika*). Those theorists who say that *gaṅgāyāṃ ghoṣhaḥ* is an example of indication do so because the locative case ending cannot be understood literally. According to them, strictly speaking, the locative should be taken as one of these, but in this context it cannot be:The village is on (proximity/*aupaśleṣika*) the Ganges. The village is in (pervasion/*abhivyāpaka*) the Ganges.The village is about (topic/*vaiṣayika*) the Ganges.

17 Adapted from Seto (1999:104).

18 Example adapted from Camp (2017), which discusses the way in which metaphors are especially apt for insults. The original example, from Moran (1989), is: "George is a tailwagging lapdog of privilege." This complicates the example, since "tailwagging" (and perhaps "privilege"?) might be taken in a secondary manner as well.

19 For discussion of this figure, see Gerow (1971:124-125).

20 Postulation is accepted as its own kind of epistemic instrument by Mīmāṃsā and Vedānta thinkers, but not Nyaiyāyikas, who argue that it is reducible to inference.

21 Sections of what follow are taken, with minor revisions, from Keating (2017).

22 Bhāṭṭa Mīmāṃsakas following Kumārila think that, in some cases, a linguistic content is understood (in what they call "verbal postulation")

whereas Prābhākara Mīmāṃsakas following Prabhākara think that there is only a single kind of postulation, in which a fact or state of affairs is understood. Although Mukula avoids this debate, in his emphasis on incongruity, or what would otherwise be incongruous (*anyathânupapatti*), his position is more in line with Bhāṭṭa thinkers.

23 I thank Parimal Patil for discussion of the details of this example and emphasizing the point about the exclusive nature of the interpretive choices involved.

24 For more on this, see McCrea (2008:273-274).

25 Elsewhere, in Keating (2013a), I have argued in more detail that Mukula, along with Bhāṭṭa Mīmāṃsakas, understands a close connection between all varieties of indication and postulation. In light of Guha (2016), I should emphasize a few things. First, this claim is nowhere made explicit in the text, although in what follows I will give evidence that it is indeed assumed by the author. Further, Guha is right to emphasize that indicated meanings need not always be understood via postulation—we will see discussion of frozen, conventional indication later, for instance, which is understood like a primary meaning. However, Mukula seems to argue that this is the default manner in which they are understood, and that they are understood by an epistemic instrument is important for his arguments against Ānandavardhana. As well, although in print I have defended the view that postulation may be a kind of inference to the best explanation (IBE) or variety of abduction, I have come to believe that this may not be the case, even though much work remains to be done investigating how postulation is understood by a range of thinkers. Although contemporary philosophers of language would tend to view Gricean implicatures (which have much structurally in common with indication via postulation) as understood by IBE, the necessity of postulation seems to be a crucial aspect of its status of an epistemic instrument, even for poetic language. Finally, Mukula's understanding of postulation fits well with other Mīmāṃsā philosophers. They also claim that postulation is the means by which incomplete utterances like "the door, the door" are completed, showing its importance for completing incomplete testimony of various kinds. See Keating (2017b).

26 This is not to say that there are no similarities which could be possible. Later, Mukula refers to the possibility that some small similarity could be pointed out for any two objects. The point is just that the speaker is not aiming to express similarity but some other relationship.

27 Some of this discussion is also found in the ancient commentary known as the *Vṛtti* which may or may not have been written by Bhartṛhari. For our purposes, we will treat them as at least holding consistent views, being agnostic about authorship.

28 See Iyer (1977:124-125) and Sanskrit in Iyer (1983:116), although the relevant verses start at 285 in the English and 286 in the Sanskrit. Iyer identifies the proponent of this view as being some Mīmāṃsakas, citing Śabara. For more details, see discussion in Iyer (1968).

29 Although they might accept transfer of meaning in the sense of the nature of the sound /ox/ as a word type. This is not discussed, either way, by Bhartṛhari in his arguments against the view.

30 The Pañcāla people lived in the north of India in the late Vedic period, around 1200 BCE and forward, and were, for a time, a very powerful political entity. Their name is derived from *pañca*, meaning "five" and probably referred to a collection of five tribes—Mukula does not mention this aspect of the meaning of the name, although it would be relevant to his discussion of etymological meanings later.

31 For details, see Joshi (1993) and Cardona (2007).

32 "For the word '*rājan*,' is the basis *kṣatriya*-hood or is the basis functioning like a *rājan*?" *kiṃ kṣatriyatva-nimmitto rāja-śabda uta rājya-karaṇa-nimmitta iti*. Sastri (1932: 150).

33 See Bharṭhari's *Treatise on Sentences and Words* at 3.3.40-41, as well as the commentary, discussed in Houben (1995:257-262) and translated in Iyer (1971:99-101). That Mukula has this in mind is, of course, uncertain, but if he does, it again points to his repurposing of earlier concepts for his own theory.

34 Ingalls (1990:562) "But from secondary usage also, suggestiveness differs from both nature and in object"; *kintu tato 'pi vyañjakatvaṃ svarūpato viṣayataśca bhidyate,* Śāstri (1940:422).

35 Set theory is a way to represent precisely how collections or groups of things, known as "sets," are related to one another. For instance, we could consider a list of employees on a payroll as one set and a list of government identification numbers as another set. The relationship between these two sets is known as a "function" when each member of the set of employees is paired with only one corresponding member of the set of identification numbers. Functions can also be used to represent cognitive processes, where an input (in the first set) results in an output (in the second set). For a basic introduction to set theory, see Steinhart (2009). I thank Brendan Gillon and Anand Vaidya for helpful discussion of this section.

36 While the footnotes in Ingalls's English translation explaining Ānanadavardhana's use of the sentence might lead the reader to think otherwise, nowhere does Ānandavardhana use "The village is on the Ganges" as an example of suggestion. This discussion is only found in Abhinavagupta's *Eye*, at 1.4, Ingalls (1990:87) and Śāstri (1940:60). Its presence suggests, though is not conclusive evidence, that Abhinavagupta is responding to Mukula, although the former's list of suggested properties

is not identical to Mukula's list. It may be the case that Mukula was the first to use this stock example as an illustration of putatively suggested meaning, albeit in an attempt to show that meaning is attained through indication. See McCrea (2008:194, fn 45) for more discussion.

37 A codomain is a set of possible objects which can be mapped, whereas a range is the set of objects which have been mapped.

38 "The denoted meaning is something directly connected with the word. The other meaning, being implied by the capability of the denoted meaning, is something connected with that with which the word is connected," Ingalls (1990:554) at 3.33e; *vācyo hy arthaḥ sākṣāc chabdasya sambandhī tad itaras tv abhidheya-sāmarthyâkṣiptaḥ sambandhi-sambandhī,* (Śāstri 1940: 417).

39 I am intentionally setting aside more technical questions regarding function composition. Modern set theory works here mostly as a heuristic to understand Ānandavardhana's distinctions between these functions.

40 However, we should observe that while he addresses the argument in terms of verbal functions, Ānandavardhana makes a further claim in this section which Mukula does not address, which is that suggestion functions even in cases of music, and so it should not be understood as a verbal function at all! Ānandavardhana argues that the *rasa*s such as love, heroism, and so on, are suggested by great musical performances. This claim fits with his argument that *rasa*s are suggested even by the phonemes in poetry, such as harsh or soft sounding letters (See *Light* 3.3-4). Clearly, Mukula's account will not be able to explain these cases, since he is focusing on words and sentences—linguistic communication. But there is a reply available. Immediately after his observation about music being suggestive, Ānandavardhana goes on to reiterate that there are three verbal functions, the primary, secondary, and suggestive. So while suggestion may be a phenomenon that goes beyond language, it is still linguistic, in some cases. Thus Mukula might be ignoring phonemes and music simply because they are not relevant to Ānandavardhana's claims about verbal functions. Abhinavagupta takes this as a possible reply to the identification of suggestion with secondary meaning in his discussion of this section, arguing that it would then make more sense to equate suggestion with the primary function rather than the secondary. Still, the idea that suggested *rasa* is a result of music seems to pose a difficulty for Ānandavardhana's theory, if only because this complicates the question of where *rasa* and suggested meaning should be found. He only takes this question up in a few places, always identifying the locus as within the text. However, to say that the *rasa* of musical performances is found in the composition seems wrong—instead, what is suggested seems to be an emotion or aesthetic experience in the hearer, which is not how Ānandavardhana characterizes it. This difficult question is left for later thinkers, for which see Pollock (2016).

41 Now, strictly speaking, this is more a case of what is called "punning" in English, and in Sanskrit literary theory, *śleṣa*. Yigal Bronner (2010) has coined "bitextuality" to refer to it, as it involves multiple registers of meaning. This is because it isn't really the nature of a ham sandwich which is semantically shading the indicated meaning (the customer) but the double meaning associated with "ham." However, the focus of Mukula's discussion is represented in this case, where there isn't merely a referential use of indication, but that there is also a semantic influence of the primary meaning.

42 A fuller treatment of the way in which Mukula's theory is commensurable with structured lexical entries can be found in Keating (2013a).

43 I indicate the effects of the emphatic particle *eva* (*gaur eva ayaṃ*) by the exclamation mark at the end.

44 The principle of *Fixity* applies to the other categories of words, including pronouns (called *sarva-nāma*, or "names for everything," in Sanskrit). Despite pronouns having variable referents, depending on context, they also have a nature which is fixed, which can be understood through the same observational principles as the other word categories. For discussion of Sanskrit philosophers on pronomial reference and meaning, see "*Sarvanāma*: Indexicality and Pronominal Anaphora" in Ganeri (2011).

45 See discussion in Rajendran (1984).

46 Translation adapted from Ingalls (1990:704). Sanskrit: Śāstri (1940:568).

47 In light of Ānandavardhana's allusions to Buddhist philosophy, this term might also be identified with *ākara* (nature) which is part of the frequent triad, *deśa-kālâkāra-nimitta* (the basis which is place, time, and nature) found in such texts as Dharmakīrti's *Drop of Reasoning* (*Nyāya-bindu*). (This was suggested to me by Lawrence McCrea.)

48 See *Light* 3.16.

49 Mukula here uses another term (*vailakṣaṇya*) but uses the same Sanskrit word *svā-lakṣaṇya* in his other mention of the factor at the end of the section, suggesting he sees no important difference between these words.

50 While this is possibly a reference to the notion of *sva-lakṣaṇa* in Buddhist philosophers such as Dharmakīrti (whom Ānanadavardhana refers to elsewhere), its use in Mukula at least does not seem to require the metaphysical commitment to momentarily existing, irreducibly unique particulars. Individuality can be understood simply as the various natures of ordinary objects.

51 *kathaṃ paratra vartate paraśabda iti. guṇavādas tu. guṇād eṣa vādaḥ. katham aguṇa-vacano guṇaṃ brūyāt. svârthâbhidhānana iti brūmaḥ*, Sastri (1932:315). As Mukula does not want to explain every figurative statement in terms of property transfer, as we have seen, he omits the intervening mention of "a statement due to properties." In this passage, such

statements are distinguished from statements which depend on indication or *lakṣaṇā*, the term Mukula prefers for both varieties.

52 *lakṣaṇā 'pi hi laukikī nanu uktam asaṃvādo vade na hy ūrgudumbara iti.* Sastri (1932:9).

53 Śabara is here concerned with a section from the *Yajur Veda* which describes the very important and complex horse sacrifice. At one point, the passage says, "Let the . . . Udumbura fig tree [aid you] with strength," and the question is whether to take this expression as an injunction or motivating speech. Śabara's interlocutor tries to find an interpretation which has the least incongruity with reality—this is the resolution which ought to be postulated. Specifically, here, the Udumbura fig tree isn't a source of food, and the interlocutor argues that a false utterance is suspect and would not promote the purposes of encouraging an action. Śabara, however, points to the immediate context of the phrase, in which the sacrificial post is made out of Udumbura wood. This supports an interpretation in which the word "Udumbara" refers to the sacrificial post through figurative meaning. However, Śabara argues that this happens through a statement referring to properties and not indication—and it is in this context that he remarks that indication is merely ordinary or customary speech. So, again, in the original context, there is a distinction between indication and figurative language involving properties that Mukula would not accept. While Mukula does not quote Kumārila's commentary on Śabara here, given Mukula's earlier discussion of postulation, it is worth observing that the terms "postulation" (*arthāpatti*) and variations of "posit" (*kḷp)* occur here. In his lengthy discussion of the correct interpretation, Kumārila argues against the opponent on their view that "moreover, the praise, which is being implied through the rest of the sentence, would not be posited from the injunction's implications through postulation." (*prarocanā 'pi ca vākya-śeṣād upapadyamānā na arthāpattyā vidhy-uddeśād eva kalpitā bhaviṣyati,* Sastri (1932:39). This suggests that the correct interpretation is attained through postulation.

54 Without explicitly saying so, Mukula gives room for this distinction, insofar as he defines *loka* in terms of certain ordinary epistemic instruments (*pramāṇa*). These are the ones such as perception which can be validated by people's everyday experiences. Earlier, he has highlighted the importance of these everyday experiences in the opening sentences, where human action requires knowledge of the things at which we aim. The epistemic instrument of postulation has appeared in his discussion of the Fat Devadatta case, and we will see him use vocabulary specific to that knowledge source throughout the rest of the text.

55 For instance, Kumārila illustrates the primary denotation with the important term red (*aruṇa*), a term which has a chapter devoted

entirely to its explication in an important Vedic injunction. See McCrea (2008:74ff) for discussion on this single sentence and its relationship to Sanskrit poetics in Ānandavardhana.

56 This, and all poetic examples which follow, are stanzas, made up of two verses, subdivided each into two quarters. Typically, each English line in translation corresponds to a quarter-verse. Some examples are excerpted from larger works, while some may have been composed as a "stray verse" (*muktaka*), meaning a single stanza appreciated as a coherent work without a larger context. Some examples are unknown, and it is unclear to which category they belong. For a general discussion of Sanskrit poetic meter and related conventions, see Ingalls (1965), and for a scholarly history, see Lienhard (1984).

57 Sanskrit: *arthântara-saṅkramita-vācya dhvani*. This category is discussed in more detail below.

58 Ingalls (1990: 204) and Śāstri (1940:169). For discussion of this verse, which may be from a lost play and its treatment in Indian poetic theory, see Warder (1983:386-387).

59 See the section, "Rains," in Ingalls (1965) for examples.

60 Māgha's work is frequently quoted by treatises on poetry, and he is well-known not only for his skill in meter, but his punning word play. See Winternitz (1985: 722ff) and Bronner and McCrea (2012). There are now two English translations of *The Killing of Śiśupāla*, Dundas (2017) and Rajendran (2017).

61 For discussion of these legends, see Doniger (2014).

62 Though see Peterson (1989) and McCrea (2010) for discussion of this focus on single stanzas, and the relationship of literary theory to literary praxis.

63 The term *subhāṣita* or "beautifully spoken," is a word for single stanza compositions, thus "sparkling single stanza" in the context of a treasury of jewels (*ratna-kośa*).

64 Ingalls (1990:83). Collected in *The Seven Hundred* (*Sattasaī*) 2.75.

65 However, it is difficult to understand precisely how this helps the woman whose affair is in danger of being interrupted by the monk. This took multiple commentaries to determine, for which see Pollock (2001).

66 See "The Wanton" in Ingalls (1965) for discussion (in which this stanza also appears).

67 Thanks to my students in Classical Indian Philosophy of Language, 2016, for coming up with these ideas.

68 For more discussion of Ānandvardhana's analysis of the meaning, see Ingalls (1990: 330-31) and McCrea (2008: 107-108).

69 In this section, Mukula may also be drawing on Vāmana (c. 750 CE). Vāmana distinguishes between imagining and hyperbole in terms of the

intensity of the superimposition involved. Likewise, Mukula explains hyperbole as involving transfer (*upacāra*) and also superimposition (*adhyavasāna*), making it, as Bronner (2016:117) puts it, "more layered imaginative act." More understanding of the relationship between Mukula and Vāmana, who also understands indication (*lakṣaṇā*) as involving similarity, is a desideratum.

70 Bronner (2016:94).

71 The Sanskrit term, *utprekṣā,* like many others in poetic theory, has no standard English translation. Bronner (2016) prefers "seeing as," Gerow (1971) calls it "ascription," Ingalls (1990), "poetic fancy." I follow McCrea and Patil's suggestion of "imagining," understood here as a technical term and not as encompassing all imaginative acts.

72 Abhinavagupta, in his commentary, again seems to have Mukula in mind when he characterizes this as, in addition to metaphor, a case of imagining combined with a figure known as "doubt" (*sasandeha*). Likewise, he argues that the figure is not understood because of any impossibility (*anupapatti*), which seems to be a response to Mukula's discussion as well. He argues that there are other possible explanations of the ocean's doubts, which shows that this case cannot be one of implying but must be suggestion. Ingalls (1990:331–332), Sanskrit in Śāstri (1940:231–233).

73 There is no clear origin for these verses, nor are they found in Ānandavardhana.

74 Translation Ingalls (1990:311).

75 See Raja (1990:176–187) for an overview and Ingalls (1990:579n1) for discussion of its use in Ānandavardhana.

76 Likely the "five fires" are referring to self-mortifying practices in which one is surrounded by four ritual fires, with the fifth being the sun. Pārvatī is said to have performed this practice to win the heart of Śiva, which may be a further allusion here (in which case perhaps the heavy breasts are not being observed by a male speaker but are being endured by a female speaker?).

77 The later Mahima Bhaṭṭa, who is a critic of suggestion like Mukula, seems to do the same sort of thing, though in more detail. See McCrea (2004).

78 For a detailed look at the rules involved in the derivation of these compounds, see Scharf (2011).

79 The *aṆ*-affix is an *Ṇit pratyaya* (see 1.3.9).

80 Translation adapted from Vasu (1897, Vol 1:849).

81 Vasu (1897, Vol 1:849).

82 Thanks to Jo Brill and R. K. Sharma for discussing this passage and Pāṇinian grammar more generally during the summer of 2013 at Ananda Ashram. Of course, any errors here are my own.

83 The example which seems out of place is the example of "Fat Devadatta does not eat during the day," as one might think that the sentence "Devadatta eats at night" is indicated by the entire preceding sentence. However, Mukula argues that it is the word "fat" which carries the indicated meaning, in a manner analogous to "cow" in "The cow is to be sacrificially bound."

84 In fact, there is much more in how Mīmāṃsā understands imperatives, but it is not directly relevant to this text. Suffice it to say that Mīmāṃsā was well aware of the need to distinguish between moods, and to account for how it is that the imperative mood has a compelling force, in contrast to assertions.

85 The phrase here is *viśeṣaṇa-viśiṣṭa*, often called "qualifier-qualified." Any syntactic relationship between two word meanings falls under this, so it includes verbs taking indirect objects, adjectives qualifying nouns, and so on.

86 Probably this is alluding to Maṇḍana Miśra's *Brahma-siddhi,* circa 700 CE (I thank Parimal Patil and Larry McCrea for pointing me to this discussion). Maṇḍana's larger purpose in using the example "O priest, your son is born" is different than Mukula's, as it is part of a larger argument to show that knowledge of Brahman is possible through testimony. However, his point is that injunctions are not the only purpose for language. Sometimes we simply inform people, and a further meaning (like joyfulness for someone who lacks a son) comes on the basis of that assertion. See summary in Thrasher (1970: 359–62) and corresponding text in Śastri (1937:25).

87 For discussion of this idea, see Siderits (1991).

88 See Siderits (1991) for more on this idea, that Prābhākara thinkers have a theory of sense, not just reference.

89 That he calls this view *samuccaya*, which is a Mīmāṃsā technical term for apparently exclusive options in a ritual context which are in fact together obligatory, may also suggest that he sees this debate as misguided. See Kane (1962:1327-1328) on Jaimini's *Aphorisms on Exegesis* (*Mīmāṃsā-sūtra*) 10.4.6.

90 The theory of *apoha* is a way of explaining word meaning without appealing to ontologically troublesome things like individuals, properties, and universals, which Buddhists like Dignāga and Dharmakīrti take to conflict with radical particularity, momentariness, and other metaphysical commitments. Thus "cow" does not refer to an individual or a universal, but it excludes non-cows. See Siderits, Tillemans and Chakrabarti (2011) for an introduction to the topic.

91 Thakur (1997:299).

92 Prasad (1994:335) makes a point on something like this when he says that Naiyāyikas have a theory of "compositional-cum-contextual significance," though he identifies the two views as representing the combination from syllables to words, then words to sentences, which is not Mukula's point here. Further, he does not identify which Nyāya philosopher might hold such a view, and since Naiyāyikas differ among themselves on sentence meaning, I hesitate to say Mukula's description fits all Nyāya treatments of the topic.

93 Vātsyāyana, in Dasti and Phillips (2017:147).

94 Translation adapted from Iyer (1977:168). Sanskrit: *sahasthitau virodhitvaṃ syād viśiṣṭāviśiṣṭayoḥ | vyabhicārī tu saṃbandhas tyāge 'rthasya prasajyate* (Iyer 1983:149), numbered as 2.393.

95 For a sense of this debate, see Cardona (1999).

96 *Treatise on Sentences and Words* 3.6.26: *paramârthe tayor eṣa bhedo 'tyantaṃ na vidyate* (Iyer 1963:228).

97 In fact, the meaning and the sound are also a whole, and the relationship between subject and object as well. Brahman is the ultimate reality, and he is identified with language. However much these ideas are in the background for Mukula—and they clearly are as we see in the conclusion to his work—he is scant on details.

98 While Ānandavardhana does not take up the problem of how suggestion relates to theories of sentence meaning, Abhinavagupta discusses the theories which Mukula takes up here in his comments on 1.4b, for which see Ingalls (1990:83-98). Again, this suggests that perhaps he has Mukula's objections in mind in his commentary. Notably, though, he does not take up the combined view, only the other three, and it is the combined view which is Mukula's strongest argument against suggestion.

99 We do not have his works except through citations in other texts in which he takes up an opposing position to Śabara. Abhinavagupta quotes the same passage from Bhartṛmitra in the *Eye*, using two different versions of the quote, although neither is identical with Mukula's quotation. See Ingalls (1990:67, fn 4) for discussion.

100 For discussion of some issues with the text at this point, see the transliteration.

101 See discussion at Houben (1995:340, fn 564).

102 Although since some residents along the Mississippi might argue with this claim, insert any other river which is unholy and not beautiful.

103 *The Seven Hundred* (*Sattasaī*) 618, Khoroche (2009:185). A trumpetflower is an orange-colored flower whose honeysuckle-shaped petals look like trumpets.

104 See Appendix C in Rajendran (2003) for discussion of these points. Thanks also to C. Rajendran for discussing this with me in connection with Mukula.

105 MS 1.4.23 *liṅga-samavāyāt para-śabdaḥ paratra vartate. yathā chatriṇo gacchanti ity ekena cchatriṇā sarve lakṣyante* . . . Sastri (1932: 316). In his discussion of this example, Kumārila observes that this case is like "The staffs enter," where the staffs are associated with brahmins.

106 For instance, Coward and Raja (1990: 326).

107 Thanks to Michael Yoshitaka Erlewine for suggesting this in conversation.

108 See Daniel (2013). Kiparsky (2010) discusses the associative in the context of Vedic Sanskrit and compounds.

109 Surnames and personal pronouns are exceptions in English. So "we" can refer to a group of people speaking or to the speaker and her associates. Likewise, "the Smiths" can refer to "Mr. Smith and his wife" or "Mr. Smith and his family" (Michael Daniel 2013).

110 There is some difficulty with this term, for which see Keith (1970:69), where he notes that the term is used in its literal sense for royal people, which is not how Bharata describes its use. So the history of its use is unclear.

111 Sanskrit: *svāmi iti yuva-rājas tu kumāro bhartṛ-dārakaḥ | śaumya bhadra-mukha ity evaṃ he pūrvaṃ ca adhamaṃ vadet ||* Ghosh (1967:100).

112 See Bronner (2010) for discussion.

113 See *Light on Suggestion* 2.21 and Bronner (2010).

114 Translation adapted from Ingalls (1990:173), at 1.13m. Sanskrit, Śāstri (1940:136).

115 A terminological note: Mukula uses the same Sanskrit term for the category of unintended expression as Ānandavardhana (*avivakṣita-vācya*). However, he does use different Sanskrit terms for "intended to be expressed" (*vivakṣita-vācya*, not *vivakṣitânya-para-vācya*) and what he calls "expressed meaning that is entirely displaced" (*atitiraskṛta-vācya*, not *atyanta-tiraskṛta-vācya*). His decision to use a different term for the first category is important since, for him, intentionally expressed indication is not always subordinate to another meaning (*anya-para-vācya*).

116 Venugopalan (1977:262, fn 92).

117 McCrea (2008:204, fn 79).

118 Ānandavardhana's statement: *anena hi* ***vyaṅgya-dharmântara-pariṇataḥ*** *sañjñī pratyāyyate na saṃjñimātram* (Śāstri 1940:169). Mukula's statement: *atra hi rāma-śabda-vācyaṃ dāśa-rathi-rūpaṃ* ***vyaṅgya-dharmântara-pariṇatatvāt*** *sva-paratvena anupāttam tasmād*

avivakṣitam na tv atyaṇtaṃ tiraskṛtam vyaṅgya-dharma-dvāreṇa vākyârthe kathaṃcid anvitatvāt.

119 Ingalls (1990:571, fn 6). Ingalls argues that this sense is implied in 1.17, where Ānandavardhana says that secondary meaning or *guṇa-vṛtti* "reveals" (*darśana*) an object. Though Ānandavardhana is happy to admit that secondary meaning can make a new meaning manifest, unless that meaning is especially beautiful, it doesn't constitute *vyaṅgya* in the narrow, technical sense he's offering—the sense which requires a special linguistic function. There is also a second use of the term in a related sense, where he says that all sentences are *vyaṅgya* in that they "make manifest" a speaker's intention. Here, though, what is *vyaṅgya* is rather the primary meaning. Since sentential aim (*tāt-parya*) is involved in Ānandavardhana's explanation of the case of Rāma, where he uses the phrase involving *vyaṅgya*, this might support Mukula's interpretation of the term in this "wide" sense. For more discussion of this second wide/narrow reading, see Ingalls (1990: 583, fn 1).

120 Some of this discussion has been published as Keating (2013a) although in that discussion I did not take into account the additive/associative plural distinction.

121 McCrea (2008: 307).

122 For discussion, see Gerow (1971:223-225).

123 Thanks to Tyler Richard for the example. The stress on the first syllable in English may sometimes disambiguate between compounded and uncompounded word combinations, see Plag, et al. (2008).

124 Translation adapted from Ingalls (1990: 207). Sanskrit in Śāstri (1940:270): *tadā jāyante guṇā yadā te sahṛdayair gṛhyante* | *ravikiraṇânugṛhītāni bhavanti kamalāni kamalāni* || although the verse is originally Prakrit, probably from a play of Ānandavardhana's own writing.

125 For a more detailed discussion of this point and other aspects of Ānandvardhana on *śleṣa*, see McCrea (2008:141-147) and Bronner (2011:211-212).

126 Ingalls 345. Sanskrit Śāstri (1940: 272) *ramyā iti prāptavatīḥ patākāḥ rāgaṃ viviktā iti vardhayantīḥ* | *yasya amasevanta namadvalīkāḥ samaṃ vadhūbhir valabhīr yuvānaḥ* || From *The Killing of Śiśupāla* 3.53.

127 In yet another tantalizing possible connection between Abhinavagupta and Mukula, the former argues in his commentary on this stanza that it cannot be understood by verbal postulation, like the sentence "Fat Caitra does not eat by day." As elsewhere, he does not mention Mukula by name as a proponent of this alternative view, but his goal here is to argue that since nothing is incomplete in the primary meaning, this is a "non-primary" (*anmukhya*) capacity, and is suggestion. Ingalls (1990:356-47), Śāstri (1940: 274-75).

128 Venugopalan (1977: 263, fn 99).

129 Deshpande (2009:43).

130 For discussion of Bhartṛhari's views on the language principle (*śabda-tattva*), see Aklujkar (2001) and Desnitskaya (2006) as well as Houben (1995: 300- 311) and further citations in footnote 490 of that text. He identifies Brahman with the language principle, but what that identification amounts to is a matter of significant debate, debate which does not bear directly on Mukula's point here, although he is surely alluding to Bhartṛhari with his choice of language.

131 Translation adapted from Houben (1995:309).

132 Translation adapted from Houben (1995: 301).

133 Venugopalan notes in connection with these remarks, the *Treatise* 3.57-58, in which Bhartṛhari discusses the relationship between the world and our cognition of it, a cognition which is in some crucial ways, interrelated with language. Again, this topic is beyond the scope of commenting on Mukula's immediate aims, but Bhartṛhari's views were adopted by Kashmiri thinkers. Among them is Bhaṭṭa Kāllaṭa, who Mukula says is his father in the closing verse of the text. It is tempting to read this broader context into Mukula's closing remarks, and see him as drawing connections between Kashmiri Śaivite appropriation of Bhartṛhari and his rejection of Ānandavardhana's theory. However, to postulate such a second meaning would require (as Mukula has shown us) clear evidence of a motive as well as a relationship between the primary and secondary meaning. Lacking these, we can only speculate about Mukula's other commitments and their relationship to this text.

134 "A poem's ability to communicate [to the reader] any *rasa,* an ability which is found operative in all *rasa*s and styles, is called clarity (*prasāda*)," Ingalls (1990:259). *samarpakatvaṃ kāvyasya yat-tu sarva-rasān prati* | *sa prasādo guṇo jñeyaḥ sarva-sādhāraṇa-kriyaḥ* || 2.10. Śāstri (1940: 212)".

135 Discussion of this formulation and its origins is found at http://indianphilosophyblog.org/2015/06/19/pada-vakya-pramaṇa-since-when, where Elisa Freschi cites Veṅkaṭanātha: "The knowers of the śāstra divide the śāstra into three, according to the division into words, sentences and means of knowledge" (*pada-vākya-pramāṇa-bhedena hi tredhā vibhajanti śāstraṃ śāstra-vidaḥ*) and Andrew Ollett cites Anaṅgaharṣa Mātrarāja's *Tāpasavatsarāja* as saying *pada-vākya-pramāṇeṣu sarva-bhāṣā-viniścaye* | *aṅga-vidyāsu sarvāsu paraṃ prāvīṇyam āgatā.* And at http://elisafreschi.com/2015/06/18/pada-vakya-pramaṇa-since-when/, Bāṇa's *Kādambarī* is mentioned as a possible earlier source.

136 These are the *puruṣârtha*: right living (*dharma*), wealth (*artha*), pleasure (*kāma*), and liberation (*mokṣa*).

137 Given the resonance of both terms "speech" (*vāc*) and "lord" (*īśvara*) in Kashmir Śaivism, reading the compound as a play on words may be possible: through mastery of the appropriate disciplines, a language-user becomes one with primordial Speech, the absolute Lord, Śiva. But this speculation goes beyond the plain words of the text unwarrantedly unless we have more evidence about Mukula's relationship to Kashmiri Śaivism.

Part IV

Introduction

1 According to the *Codicum Manuscriptorum Bibliothecae Bodleianae*, the title of this work is given as *abhidhāvṛttimātṛkā* in one manuscript as well as *abhidhāvṛttamātṛkā*. See Winternitz (1905:143). However, the catalog notes that the latter is most likely the title. In any case, whether *vṛtti* or *vṛtta* is the correct reading does not change the title nor our understanding of the text much, as the first is a *varia lecto* for the second.

2 D, F, V: *prāmāṇyam*. A, M: *prādhāṇyam*. The latter would mean "supremacy" or "primacy" rather than "authority" or "knowledge-conductivity." As Venugopalan (1977:245, n. 1) notes, in Mammaṭa's *SVV*, which quotes Mukula's *AVM*, the reading is *prāmāṇyam*, further supporting the emendation. See Dvivedi (1974) edition of *SVV*.

3 A, D, M: *vyavahārōparohanibandhanam*

Verses 1–15

1 A, M: *śākhādiyāntena*

2 D inserts *gaur anubandhya iti.*

3 To construe the adjective *nityā* with the masculine nominative plural *paramāṇutvâdayaḥ* and *gunāḥ*, I have emended it to read *nityāḥ*.

4 F: *na tu*

5 D: *saṃjñi*; F: *atra abhidhīyate. guṇe kriyāṃ śabdasaṃjñi vyaktīnām;* M: *saṃjña.* As *śabda-saṃnjñā* is the more common term ("proper name"), this emendation, as Venugopalan (1970:250, n. 22) notes, makes sense of the compound as a *dvandva* containing four items: particulars, proper names, actions, and properties.

6 A, M, D: *vicitrā iva syād iti*; F: *vicitryeṇa syuriti* or possibly *vicitryeṇa spuriti;* V: *vaicitryeṇa sphurati*, probably on the basis of F. The reading

vicitryeṇa is ungrammatical. The reading *syur iti* is possible as the optative third singular of *as*, whereas *spuriti* is ungrammatical.

7 A,S,D: *bhāvā llakṣaṇā*; F, V: *bhāvalakṣaṇā*

8 V: inserts *pura* on the strength of Śabara's *MS* 2.3.3: *nanu yo yo janapadapurapariakṣaṇam karoti* . . . (252, n. 36). But the phrase *paripāla* is attested in several places in Kumārila's *TV* ad *MS* 2.3.3, for instance: *tacca rājyaṃ janapadaparipālanaṃ nāma sarvalokaprasiddham*, in *Mīmāṃsā-darśanam* (1932:172).

9 All printed texts except for V: *viddhâviddhârthâvagāhitvena.* Venugopalan remarks, "The printed text reads *viddhāviddhārthāvagāhitvam.* This means nothing. One of the manuscripts consulted reads *tathāvidhārthāvagāhitvena* which means the implication of such (i.e. previously described) Secondary Sense. Hence the emendation" (255:n. 55). In contrast, A and S gloss *viddhâviddha* as, respectively, *sampṛkta* and *asampṛkta*, and *saṃbaddha* and *asaṃbaddha*, roughly the same meaning.

10 D: *tvasatyoktaḥ* though it is marked with a question mark; V: *satyo 'rthaḥ*; F: *atra satyorthaḥ*

11 All printed editions save V read *vācyātmabhiḥ* but Udbhaṭa's text reads *vācyevādyātmabhiḥ.*

12 F: omits *vākyāpekṣayā ca*

13 D, S: [*vācyatvāt*]

14 All printed editions read *evam abhihitânvayâdi-pakṣa-catuṣṭaye* in place of *idānīm etasyā*, except for V, who notes in footnote 80 that this does not fit. It seems to be a dittography. V inserts *idānīm etasyā* on the evidence of an unnamed manuscript. This reading is found in F at folio 22.

15 D: *prati āsannatvamāt*

16 All other printed texts: *tena*; V: omits *tena* on the basis of intelligibility and the authority of an unnamed manuscript. F: *kena* at the start of Folio 23.

17 All other printed texts: *tad-vyatirikta-vastv-antara-gatasya* but F has *tad-vyatiriktam* which construes with *yat prayojanam uktam.*

18 All other printed texts: *saṃvijñāna-padasya* but footnote 84 in V remarks that the term must be *asaṃvijñāna-pada* on the basis of its use in *VP* 1.119. The reading *asaṃvijñāna-padasya* is found in F, folio 23.

19 All other printed texts: *sambodhanânyathânupapattyā*, but F inserts *ādi.* V notes this reading as preferable in footnote 87. Given *lectio difficilior potior*, and the stanza itself being discussed, *ādi* is better, as it probably refers to the incongruities such as bees being able to speak and think, not just their being addressed.

20 F: *tad evaṃ nibandhana-traya-samudbhavatā lakṣaṇā vṛttasya uktā*. M: *tad evaṃ nibandhana-tritaya-samudbhavatā lakṣaṇa-trayasya uktā*. All other printed texts: *tad evaṃ nibandhana-tritaya-samudbhavatā lakṣaṇā-trayasya uktā.*
21 F: *vā*; All other printed editions: *ca.*
22 F: *na tv atyantaṃ*; V: *vivakṣitâvivakṣitatve na tasya atyantaṃ (na tv atyantam) tiraskāraḥ.*
23 A: *tathā*; D: inserts [sambandhe] in brackets after *tatra.*
24 V: omits *upādane* on grounds of redundancy (290:fn90).
25 F: *vivakṣitânapara-vācyatā*
26 A: *tasya arthântara-saṃkramitatvāt;* V: *avivakṣitatatārthāntar asaṅkramitatvāt*; D: omits *lakṣaṇe tu,* sentence reads *vācyasya arthāntarasaṃkramitatvāt.* See McCrea (2008:303, fn77) for discussion of this emendation.
27 V, F: *krama*. All other printed texts: *artha.*
28 A, D: *vivarttamāne*
29 F: *svarūpaṃ*
30 F: *prati vivaṃśa*
31 F: *yasya sāhitye*; V: inserts [*sāhitye sarga-bandhâdau*] after *sāhityâdau*
32 F: inserts *saṃ-* before *saṃcārayati.*
33 D: *vṛtti*, though he notes alternate reading of *vṛtta* discussed above under title.
34 F, V: *vṛtti.*

Part V

Mukula Bhaṭṭa on Sentence Meaning and the Semantics-Pragmatics Distinction

1 Contingently named things are essentially objects of proper names, since the name-bearer is thought to be referred to in virtue of the speaker's desire to use a particular expression as a name, not in virtue of any property in the name-bearer. See commentarial chapter on Verse 2.
2 Though see commentarial chapter on Verses 7b-9a for some speculation about possible historical inspiration.
3 Parts of this chapter are adapted from Keating (2013b). I no longer think, as I argued in that essay, that Mukula was unaware of the distinction between so-called "semantic indication" and "pragmatic indication." Rather, I think that he was aware, which is clear from his discussion of sentence meaning, a discussion which has received less attention than the rest of his treatise.

Mukula Bhaṭṭa on Primary and Secondary Meaning

1 Page numbers for Mukula's text refer to this volume.

2 The treatment of imperatives (and other grammatical forms with imperatival force) is a significant topic, however, especially in Mīmāṃsā philosophy, concerned with Vedic injunctions. See Ollett (2013) for an overview.

3 Here we set aside, as does Mukula, the ontology of universals (*jāti*, *sāmānya*) in Indian philosophy, and their precise relationship to particulars.

4 The relationship between *rasa* and linguistic meaning comes to be the subject of complex discussion after Mukula, but at this point, a *rasa* is taken to have the same status as other meanings understood through language. It is not an emotion the hearer experiences. Rather, we might think of what is understood as the fact that there is love-in-separation on the part of the narrator or poet.

5 This is the only point where Mukula uses the term *tātparya* which comes to be taken by some thinkers as its own linguistic capacity alongside of the primary and indicatory function. For discussion of early use of the term in this sense, in Abhinavagupta and Jayanta Bhaṭṭa, both of whom are close to Mukula's time, see Graheli (2016).

6 This view is the *sphoṭa* or "burst" theory of the grammarian Bhartṛhari, who argues for it in his *Treatise on Sentences and Words*. An introductory discussion of the view can be found in Raja (1969).

7 These theories are discussed in more detail in Chakrabarti (1989), Graheli (2016), Matilal and Sen (1988) Siderits (1991), and Taber (1989).

8 The term *apekṣayā* is derived from a verb root *īkṣ* and a prefix *apa*, which in combination mean "have in view, pay regard to, mind," MacDonell (2001:47), so essentially just meaning "with respect to." The term is ordinary, but what it means for Mukula's attempt at synthesis is not so clear.

9 This point is not explicitly made in Mukula, though perhaps he alludes to it when he says, on this view, that words convey the relationships (along with the entities) "because words have natural expressive capacities which are incorporated into a universal of some kind" (88). That a universal is involved at some point in sentence meaning seems clear in Śālikanātha (Paṇdurangi 2004), who argues in his *Exposition in Five Chapters* (*Prakaraṇa-pañcikā*) that particulars and universals are apprehended together in cognition (72-73), and Pandurangi (2006:437) also argues that it is the universal that one is reminded of by a word, before its referential capacity.

A Contemporary Approach to What is Said: François Recanati

1 Recanati (2004) and Recanati (2010) are his two book-length treatments of this topic, although he has published many articles as well.

2 For Recanati, minimalist philosophers include Kent Bach, Emma Borg, and John Perry. This discussion is found in Recanati (2004:5-21). In the fourteen years since that text, quite a lot has been written on this topic, and it is not possible to survey the debate in any detail here. A relatively recent handbook is Börjesson (2014) and a representative collection of essays is found in Preyer and Peter (2007).

3 On Bach's version of minimalism, it is even possible for what is said to be semantically incomplete, that is, not expressing a complete propositional content. This would be the case for a sentence like "Peter's bat is grey," since the genitive construction is ambiguous. This might be the bat Peter owns, one he has picked out, one he is holding, etc. Thus, according to Bach, what is said by this sentence is a propositional radical, something schematic, but not yet truth-evaluable. See also Bach (1994) and Bach (2006).

4 Minimalists disagree on whether this semantic content should be characterized as truth-conditional or propositional (and what the relationship is between these two options). For discussion, see Carston (2002), Cappelen and Lepore (2005), and Soames (2002).

5 Recanati (2004:16).

6 This is a point where he has come in for criticism, however, since he seems to be characterizing Gricean implicature as a theory of comprehension, not a rational reconstruction of what is necessary for a certain implicature to be present. My concern here, though, is Recanati's account, whether or not it is entirely accurate to the views he is treating (just as my concern has been Mukula's account, whether or not it is entirely accurate to the Sanskrit thinkers he is drawing on).

7 Recanati (2004:53).

8 He begins with the level of sentence meaning, but does say on page 55 that what the sentence says is determined "by semantic interpretation."

What is Said, What is Expressed

1 Here I have in mind something like what Siderits (2017) has called "fusion" or "confluence" philosophy, glossed by Chakrabharti and Weber (2016) as "borderlerless."

2 For an example of this debate, which typically, but not always centers on Chomsky's universal grammar, see Devitt (2006), along with responses such as Smith (2006) in the same issue of the *Croation Journal of Philosophy*.

3 They did, however, make connections between syntax and semantics, as in the controversy over what the optative suffix (known as *liṄ* in Pāṇini's system) conveys—the impulse to do something or the thing which is to be done. Thinkers such as Jayanta Bhaṭṭa argued for their position on the basis of observing what meanings are understood in different contexts (with and without the optative), illustrating the relationship between syntactical and semantic theory and phenomenological reflection. See Bhattacharyya (1978:728) and corresponding Sanskrit in Sastri (1983:72).

4 "A relationship between word and meaning is understood, since what the speaker and hearer understood would be incongruous without it" (76).

5 This example appears in Recanati (2004:135-136), along with citations where it is discussed.

6 Freschi (2011) discusses this point explicitly in relationship to speech act theory.

7 For some discussion about this in relation to Mukula's text, see Keating (2013) and the reply in Guha (2016).

8 Recanati characterizes this as a Gricean approach, but as Bach (2007) points out, Grice's theory is a rational reconstruction, and not a theory of how language users actually process inferences to what is implicated.

9 In fact a later thinker, Mammaṭa, criticizes Mukula for not explaining how hearers understand speaker motive. See Agrawal (2008) and McCrea (2008) for discussion.

Lessons and Future Inquiry

1 García-Carpintero (2006:58) calls this the "phenomenological fallacy."

Bibliography

Primary sources

Ānandavardhana. *The Dhvanyaloka of Anandavardhana with the Locana of Abhinavagupta*, edited by Daniel H. H. Ingalls, Sr. and translated by Daniel H. H. Ingalls, Sr., Jeffrey Moussaieff, and Patwardhan M. V. Masson. Harvard Oriental Series 49. Cambridge: Harvard University Press, 1990.

Ānandavardhana. *The Dhvanyāloka with the Locana of Abhinavagupta and Bālapriyā of Rāmaśāraka*, edited by Paṭṭābhirāma Śāstri. Kashi Sanskrit Series 135. Varanasi: Chaukhambha Sanskrit Santhan, 1940.

Bharata. *The Nāṭyaśāstra: ascribed to Bharata-Muni*, translated by Manomohan Ghosh. Calcutta: Granthalaya Private Limited, 1967.

Bhartṛhari. *The Vākyapadīya of Bhartṛhari: Chapter II: English Translation with Exegetical Notes*, translated by K. A. Subramania Iyer. New Delhi: Motilal Banardsidass Publishers, 1977.

Bhartṛhari. *The Vakyapadiya of Bhartṛhari: Chapter III Part I: English Translation*, translated by K. A. Subramania Iyer. Poona: Deccan College, 1971.

Bhartṛhari. *Vākyapadīya Kāṇḍa 3*, edited by K. A. Subramania Iyer. Poona: Deccan College, 1963.

Bhartṛhari. *Vākyapadīya Kāṇḍa II with Ṭīkā of Puṇyarāja and the Ancient Vṛtti*, edited by K. A. Subramania Iyer. New Delhi: Motilal Banarsidass Publishers, 1983.

Gautama. *The Nyāya-sūtra: Selections with Early Commentaries*, translated by Matthew Dasti and Stephen Phillips. Indianapolis: Hackett, 2017.

Jaimini. *Śrīmajjaiminipraṇīte Mīmāṃsādarśane*, edited by V. Sastri. Samskrita Granthavali 97. Punya: Anandashram, 1932.

Jayanta Bhaṭṭa. *Nyāya-mañjarī*, edited by Janaki Vallabha Bhattacharyya. Vol. 1. Delhi: Motilal Banarsidass, 1978.

Jayanta Bhaṭṭa. *Nyāyamañjarī of Jayanta Bhaṭṭa Part Two with the Commentary Granthibhaṅga*, edited by Gaurinath Sastri. Vol. 5. Varanasi: M.M. Śivakumāraśāstrigranthamālā, 1983.

Kumārila Bhaṭṭa. *Ślokavārttika*, translated by Gaṅganātha Jha. Delhi: Sat Satguru Publications, 1983.

Kumārila Bhaṭṭa. *Ślokavārttika of Śrī Kumārila Bhaṭṭa with the Commentary Nyāyarathākara of Śrī Pārthasārathi Miśra*, edited by Ganganatha Jha. Varanasi: Tara Publications, 1978.

Māgha. *Śiśupālavadha of Mahākavi Māgha*, translated by C. Rajendran. New Delhi: Sahitya Akademi, 2017.

Māgha. *The Killing of Shishupala*, translated by Paul Dundas. Murty Classical Library of India 11. Cambridge: Harvard University Press, 2017.

Mammaṭa. *Śabdavyāparavicāraḥ*, edited by Resa Prasad Dvivedi. Vidyamāna Saṃskrta Granthamāla 166. Varanasi: Caukambā Vidyamāna, 1974.

Mammaṭabhaṭṭa. *Kāvyaprakāśa of Mammata Bhaṭṭa with the Critically Edited Commentary* Rasaprakāśa *of Śrī Śrīkṛṣṇa Śarman*, translated by S. N. Ghoṣāl Śāstri. The Jaikrishnadas Kirshnadas Prachyavidya Granthamala 7. Varanasi: Chowhamba Sanskrit Series Office, 1973.

Maṇḍana Miśra. *Brahmasiddhi*. Madras Government Oriental Series 4. Madras: Madras Government Oriental Mansuscripts Library, 1937.

Mukulabhaṭṭa. "Abhidhāvṛttimātṛkā." In *Abhidhāvṛttimātṛkā of Mukula Bhaṭṭa and Shabdavyāpāra-vichāra of Rājānaka Mammatāchārya*, edited by Mangesh Rāmakrishna Telang. Bombay: Nīrnāya Sagar Press, 1916.

Mukulabhaṭṭa. *Abhidhāvṛttimātṛkā*, edited by Ramprasad Dvivedi. Varanasi: Vidyābhavana Saṃskṛta Granthamālā 165, 1973.

Mukulabhaṭṭa. *Abhidhāvṛttamātṛkā*, edited by Brahmitra Avasthi and Indu Avasthi. Delhi: Indu Prakashan, 1977.

Mukulabhaṭṭa. "Abhidhāvṛttimātṛkā," translated and edited by K. Venugopalan. *Journal of Indian Philosophy* 4: 203–64, 1977.

Mukulabhaṭṭa. *Abhidhāvṛttimātrkā with Subodhini First Sanskrit Commentary and Sangamani Hindi commentary*, edited by Sugyan Kumar Mahanty and translated by Sugyan Kumar Mahanty. Varanasi: Caukhmba Samskrta Akadami, 2008.

Pāṇini. *The Ashtādhyāyī*, translated into English by Srisa Chandra Vasu. 2 Vols. Benares: Sindhu Charan Bose, 1897.

Pāṇini. *The Aṣṭâdhyāyī of Pāṇini with Translation and Explanatory Notes*, edited by J. A. F. Roodbergen and S. D. Joshi. New Delhi: Sahitya Akademi, 1993.

Patañjali. *The Vyākaraṇa – Mahābhāṣya of Patañjali*, edited by F. Keilhorn and K. V. Abhyankar. Pune: Bhandarkar Institute Press, 2005.

Śabara. *Śābara-bhāṣya*, edited and translated by Ganganatha Jha. Gaekwad's Oriental Series 66. 3 Vols. Baroda: Oriental Institute, 1933.

Śālikanātha. 2004. *Prakaraṇapañcikā of Śālikanātha with an Exposition in English*, edited by K. T. Pandurangi. New Delhi: D.K. Printworld.

Uddyotakara. Nyāyabhāṣyavārttika *of Bhāradvāja Uddyotakara*, edited by Anantal Thakur. New Delhi: Indian Council of Philosophical Research, 1977.

Secondary sources

Agrawal, M. M. "Mukulabhaṭṭa and *vyañjanā*." In *Linguistic Traditions of Kashmir: Essays in Memory of Paṇḍit Dinanath Yaksha*, edited by Mrinal Kaul and Ashok Aklujkar, 28–40. New Delhi: D.K. Printworld, 2008.

Aklujkar, Ashok. "The Word is the World: Nondualism in Indian Philosophy of Language." *Philosophy East & West* 51(4): 452–73, 2001.

Bach, Kent. "Review, François Recanati, Literal Meaning." *Philosophy and Phenomenological Research* 75(2): 487–92, 2007.

Bach, Kent. Speaking Loosely: Sentence Nonliterality. In *Midwest Studies in Philosophy, Vol. 25. Figurative Language*, edited by Peter French and Howard Wettstein, 249–63. Oxford: Blackwell Publishers, 2001.

Bezuidenhout, Anne. "Metaphor and What Is Said: A Defense of a Direct Expression View of Metaphor." *Midwest Studies In Philosophy* 25(1): 156–86, 2001.

Borg, Emma. *Pursuing Meaning*. Oxford: Oxford University Press, 2012.

Bronkhorst, Johannes. "Études sur Bhartṛhari, 1: L'auteur et la date de la Vṛtti." *Bulletin d'Études Indiennes* 1: 105–43, 1998.

Bronkhorst, Johannes. "The Peacock's Egg: Bhartṛhari on Language and Reality." *Philosophy East & West* 51(4): 474–91, 2001.

Bronner, Yigal. *Extreme Poetry: The South Asian Movement of Simultaneous Narration South Asia Across the Disciplines*. New York: Columbia University Press, 2010.

Bronner, Yigal. "Undertanding Udbhaṭa: The Invention of Kashmiri Poetics in the Jayāpīḍa Moment." In *Around Abhinavagupta: Aspects of the Intellectual History of Kashmir from the Ninth to the Eleventh Century*, edited by Eli Franco and Isabelle Ratié, 81–147. Berlin: LIT Verlag, 2016.

Bronner, Yigal. "What is New and What is Navya: Sanskrit Poetics on the Eve of Colonialism." *Journal of Indian Philosophy* 30: 441–62, 2002.

Bronner, Yigal and Lawrence McCrea. "To Be or Not To Be Śiśupāla: Which Version of the Key Speech in Māgha's Poem Did He Really Write?" *Journal of the American Oriental Society* 132(3): 427–55, 2012.

Cahill, Timothy. *An Annotated Bibliography of the Alaṅkāraśāstra*. Leiden: Brill, 2001.

Camp, Elisabeth. "Why Metaphors make Good Insults: Perspectives, Presupposition, and Pragmatics." *Philosophical Studies* 174(1): 47–64, 2017.

Cardona, George. "Approaching the Vakyapadiya." *Journal of the American Oriental Society* 119(1): 88–125, Jan-Mar 1999.

Cardona, George. "On the Structure of Pāṇini's System." In *Sanskrit Computational Linguistics*, edited by Amba Kulkarni, Peter Scharf, and

Gérard Huet. ISCLS 2007, ISCLS Lecture Notes in Computer Science, 5402. Berlin, Heidelberg: Springer, 2008.
Carston, Robyn and Deirdre Wilson. "Metaphor, Relevance and the 'Emergent Property' Issue." *Mind & Language* 21(3): 404–33, 2006.
Chakrabarti, Arindam. "Sentence-holism, Context-principle and Connected-designation Anvitabhidhāna: Three Doctrines or One?" *Journal of Indian Philosophy* 17(1): 37–41, 1989.
Charkabarti, Arindam, editor. *The Bloomsbury Research Handbook of Indian Aesthetics and the Philosophy of Art*. New York: Bloomsbury, 2016.
Chakrabarti, Arindam and Ralph Weber. "Introduction." In *Comparative Philosophy Without Borders*, by Arindam Chakrabarti and Ralph Weber, 1–34. New York: Bloomsbury, 2016.
Coward, Harold G. *The Sphoṭa Theory of Language: A Philosophical Analysis*. Delhi: Motilal Banarsidass, 1980.
Coward, Harold G., and K. K. Raja. *Encyclopedia of Indian Philosophies, Vol V: The Philosophy of the Grammarians*. Delhi: Motilal Banarsidass, 1990.
Daniel, Michael, and Edith Moravcsik. "The Associative Plural." In *The World Atlas of Language Structures Online*, edited by Matthew S. Dryer and Martin Haspelmath. Leipzig, 2013. Accessed April 26, 2018. http://wals.info/chapter/36.
Davidson, Donald. "What Metaphors Mean." *Critical Inquiry* 5(1): 31–47, 1978.
Depraetere, Ilse, and Raphael Salkie. *Semantics and Pragmatics: Drawing a Line*. Cham: Springer, 2017.
Deshpande, Ganesh T. *Indian Poetics*. Translated by Jayant Paranjpe. Mumbai: Popular Prakashan, 2009.
Deshpande, Madhav. "Language and Testimony in Classical Indian Philosophy." *The Stanford Encyclopedia of Philosophy* (Fall 2016 Edition), edited by Edward N. Zalta, 2016. URL = <https://plato.stanford.edu/archives/fall2016/entries/language-india/>.
Deshpande, Madhav. *The Meaning of Nouns: Semantic Theory in Classical and Medieval India:* Nāmārtha-nirṇaya *of Kauṇḍabhaṭṭa*. Studies of Classical India 13. Dordrecht: Springer, 1992.
Desnitskaya, Evgeniya. "Antinomy of One and Many in Bhartṛhari's Vākyapadīya." *Acta Orientalia Vilensia* 7(1–2): 209–21, 2006.
Devitt, Michael. *Ignorance of Language*. Oxford: Clarendon Press, 2006.
Dirven, Rene and Ralf Pörings. *Metaphor and Metonymy in Comparison and Contrast*. Berlin: Mouton de Gruyter, 2000.
Doniger, Wendy. "The Submarine Mare in the Mythology of Shiva." In *On Hinduism*. Oxford: Oxford University Press, 2014.
Dravid, Raja Ram. *The Problem of Universals in Indian Philosophy*, edited by Kanshi Ram. Delhi: Motilal Banarsidass Publishers, 2001.

Ezcurdia, Maite, and Robert J. Stainton. *The Semantics-Pragmatics Boundary in Philosophy.* New York: Broadview Press, 2013.

Franco, Eli. "On the Periodization and Historiography of Indian Philosophy." In *Periodization and Historiography of Indian Philosophy*, edited by Eli Franco, 1–25. Vienna: Publications of the De Nobili Research Library, 2013.

Frauwallner, Erich. *History of Indian Philosophy*, translated by V. M. Bedekar. 2 Vols. New York: Humanities, 1974.

Freschi, Elisa. *Duty, Language and Exegesis in Prābhākara Mīmāṃsā*. Leiden: Brill, 2012.

Freschi, Elisa. "The Study of Indian Linguistics. Prescriptive Function of Language in the Nyāyamañjarī and in the Speech Act Theory." In *Open Pages in South Asian Studies*, edited by William Vanderbolt and Dominik Wujastyk. Moscow: Centre for South Asian Studies, Russian State University for the Humanities, 2011.

Ganeri, Jonardon. *Artha: Meaning*. Oxford: Oxford University Press, 2006.

Ganeri, Jonardon. *Semantic Powers: Meaning and the Means of Knowing in Classical Indian Philosophy*. Oxford: Clarendon, 1999.

Ganeri, Jonardon. *The Lost Age of Reason*. Oxford: Oxford University Press, 2011.

Gerow, Edwin. *A Glossary of Indian Figures of Speech*. The Hague: Haris-Mouton, 1971.

Gerow, Edwin. *Indian Poetics*. Wiesbaden, Germany: Harrassowitz, 1977.

Gillon, Brendan. "Panini's *Aṣṭâdhyāyī* and Linguistic Theory." *Journal of Indian Philosophy* 35(5–6): 445–68, 2007.

Gnoli, Raniero. *The Aesthetic Experience According to Abhinavagupta*. Roma: Instituto per il Medio ed Estremo Oriente, 1956.

Goldman, Robert P. and Sally J. Sutherland Goldman. *Devavāṇīpravaśikā*. Berkeley: University of California, 2004.

Gonda, Jan, editor. *History of Indian Literature*. 10 Vols. Leiden: Brill, 1974–86.

Graheli, Alessandro. "The Force of *Tātparya*: Bhaṭṭa Jayanta and Abhinavagupta." In *Around Abhinavagupta: Aspects of the Intellectual History of Kashmir from the Ninth to the Eleventh Century*, edited by Eli Franco and Isabelle Ratié. Berlin: LIT Verlag, 2016.

Grice, Herbert Paul. "Logic and Conversation, Lecture 2." In *Studies in the Way of Words*, 22–40. Cambridge: Harvard University Press, 1989.

Guha, Nirmalya. "On Arthāpatti." *Journal of Indian Philosophy* 44(4): 757–76, 2016.

Halbfass, Wilhelm. *On Being and What There Is: Classical Vaiśeṣika and the History of Indian Ontology*. Albany: SUNY Press, 1992.

Houben, Jan. *The Saṃbandha-samuddeśa (Chapter on Relation) and Bhartṛhari's Philosophy of Language*. The Netherlands: Egbert Forsten, 1995.

Ingalls, Daniel H. H. *Sanskrit Poetry from Vidyākara's "Treasury."* Cambridge: Harvard University Press, 1965.

Iyer, K. A. Subramania. "Bhartṛhari on the Primary and Secondary Meanings of Words." *Indian Linguistics* (Linguistic Society of India) 29: 97–112, 1968.

Jaszczolt, K. M. *Semantics and Pragmatics: Meaning in Language and Discourse.* London: Longman, 2002.

Keating, Malcolm. "(Close) the Door; the King (is Going): The Development of Elliptical Resolution in Bhāṭṭa Mīmāṃsā." *Journal of Indian Philosophy* 45(5): 911–38, 2017a.

Keating, Malcolm. "Metonymy and Metaphor as Verbal Postulation: The Epistemic Status of Non-Literal Speech in Indian Philosophy." *Journal of World Philosophies* 2(1): 67–80, 2017b.

Keating, Malcolm. "Mukulabhaṭṭa's Defense of *Lakṣaṇā*: How We Use Words to Mean Something Else, But Not Everything Else." *Journal of Indian Philosophy* 41(4): 439–61, 2013.

Keating, Malcolm. "Speaking Indirectly: Theories of Non-Literal Speech in Indian Philosophy." PhD diss, University of Texas at Austin, Austin, 2015.

Keating, Malcolm. "'The Cow is to be Tied Up': Sort-Shifting in Classical Indian Philosophy." *History of Philosophy Quarterly* 30(4): 311–32, 2013.

Keating, Malcolm. "The Literal-Nonliteral Distinction in Classical Indian Philosophy." The *Stanford Encyclopedia of Philosophy* (Winter 2016 Edition), edited by Edward N. Zalta, 2016. URL = <https://plato.stanford.edu/archives/win2016/entries/literal-nonliteral-india/>.

Keith, Arthur B. *The Sanskrit Drama in its Origin, Development, Theory and Practice*. Oxford: Oxford University Press, 1970.

Khoroche, Peter and Herman Tieken. *Poems on Life and Love in Ancient India: Hāla's* Sattasaī. Albany: SUNY Press, 2009.

Kiparsky, Paul. "*Dvandvas*, Blocking, and the Associative: The Bumpy Ride from Phrase to Word." *Language* 86(2): 302–31, 2010.

Lepore, Ernest and Matthew Stone. "Against Metaphorical Meaning." *Topoi* 29(2): 165–80, 2010.

Lienhard, Siegfried. *A History of Classical Poetry: Sanskrit, Pali, Prakrit*, edited by Jan Gonda. Vols. A History of Indian Literature, Volume 3. Wiesbaden: Otto Harassowitz, 1984.

Macdonell, Arthur. *A Sanskrit Grammar for Students*. First Indian Edition. Delhi: Motilal Banarsidass, 1974.

Matilal, Bimal K. *Epistemology, Logic, and Grammar and Indian Philosophical Analysis*, edited by Jonardon Ganeri. Oxford: Oxford University Press, 2005.

Matilal, Bimal K. *The Word and the World: India's Contribution to the Study of Language*. Oxford: Oxford University Press, 2001.

Matilal, B. K. and P. K. Sen. "The Context Principle and Some Indian Controversies over Meaning." *Mind* 97(385): 73–97, 1988.

McCrea, Lawrence. "Mahimabhatta's Theory of Poetic Flaws." *Journal of the American Oriental Society* 124(1): 88–93, 2004.

McCrea, Lawrence. "Poetry in Chains: Commentary and Control in the Sanskrit Commentarial Tradition." In *Language, Myth, and Poetry in Ancient India and Iran*, 239–56. Israel: Israeli Academy of Sciences and Humanities, 2010.

McCrea, Lawrence. "'Resonance' and its Reverberations: Two Cultures in Indian Epistemology of Meaning." In *The Bloomsbury Research Handbook of Indian Aesthetics and the Philosophy of Art*, edited by Arindam Chakrabarti, 25–41. London: Bloomsbury, 2017.

McCrea, Lawrence. *The Teleology of Poetics in Medieval Kashmir*. Cambridge: Harvard University Press, 2008.

Moran, Richard. "Seeing and Believing: Metaphor, Image and Force." *Critical Inquiry* 16(1): 87–112, 1989.

Ollett, Andrew. "What is *Bhāvanā*?" *Journal of Indian Philosophy* 41: 221–62, 2013.

Perrett, Roy. *An Introduction to Indian Philosophy*. Cambridge: Cambridge University Press, 2016.

Peterson, Indira Viswanathan. Playing with Universes: Figures of Speech in Kāvya Epic Descriptions. In *Shastric Traditions in Indian Arts*. Vol. 1, by Anna Libera Dallapiccola. Stuttgart: Steiner Verlag Wiesbaden GMBH, 1989.

Plag, Ingo, Gero Kunter, Sabine Lappe, and Maria Braun. "The Role of Semantics, Argument Structure, and Lexicalization in Compound Stress Assignment in English." *Language* 84(4): 760–94, 2008.

Pollock, Sheldon. *A Rasa Reader: Classical Indian Aesthetics*. New York: Columbia University Press, 2016.

Pollock, Sheldon. *The Language of the Gods in the World of Men: Sanskrit, Culture, and Power in Premodern India*. Berkeley: University of California Press, 2006.

Pollock, Sheldon. "The Social Aesthetic and Sanskrit Literary Theory." *Journal of Indian Philosophy* 29: 197–229, 2001.

Pollock, Sheldon. "The Theory of Practice and the Practice of Theory in Indian Intellectual History." *Journal of the American Oriental Society* 105(3): 499–519, 1985

Prasad, Hari Ram. "The Context Principle of Meaning in Prabhākara Mīmāṃsā." *Philosophy East & West* 44(2): 317–46, 1994.

Preyer, Gerhard, and Georg Peter. 2007. *Context-Sensitivity and Semantic Minimalism: New Essays on Semantics and Pragmatics*. Oxford: Oxford University Press.

Raja, K. Kunjunni. *Indian Theories of Meaning*. Adyar: Adyar Library and Research Centre, 1969.

Rajendran, C. "References to Buddhistic Philosophy in *Dhvanāloka*." *Vishveshvaranand Indological Journal* 22: 208–13, 1984.

Rajendran, C. *Vyaktiviveka: A Critical Study*. Delhi: New Bharatiya Book Corporation, 2003.

Recanati, François. *Literal Meaning*. Cambridge: Cambridge University Press, 2004.

Ruppel, A. M. *The Cambridge Introduction to Sanskrit Website*. March 1, 2017. Accessed April 10, 2018. http://cambridge-sanskrit.org/.

Scharf, Peter M. "On the Semantic Foundation of Pāṇinian Derivational Procedure: The Derivation of *kumbhakāra*." *Journal of the American Oriental Society* 131(1): 39–72, 2011.

Scharf, Peter M. The Denotation of Generic Terms in Ancient Indian Philosophy: Grammar, Nyāya, and Mīmāṃsā. *Transactions of the American Philosophical Society, American Philosophical Society, NS* 86(3), 1996.

Scharfe, Hartmut. *Grammatical Literature: Vol. 5, A History of Indian Literature*. Edited by Jan Gonda. Wiesbaden, Germany: Otto Harrassowitz, 1977.

Searle, John. "Metaphor." In *Expression and Meaning*, 76–116. New York: Cambridge University Press, 1979.

Seto, Ken-ichi. "Distinguishing Metonymy from Synechdoche." In *Metonymy in Language and Thought*, edited by Klause-Uwe Panther and Günter Radden. Philadelphia: John Benjamins, 1999.

Siderits, Mark. "Comparison or Confluence In Philosophy." In *The Oxford Handbook of Indian Philosophy*, edited by Jonardon Ganeri, 75–92. Oxford: Oxford University Press, 2017.

Siderits, Mark. *Indian Philosophy of Language: Studies in Selected Issues*. Dordrecht: Kluwer Academic Publishers, 1991.

Siderits, Mark. "The Sense-Reference Distinction in Indian Philosophy of Language." *Synthese* 69(1): 81–106, 1986.

Siderits, Mark. "The Sense–Reference Distinction in Indian Philosophy of Language." In *Studies in Buddhist Philosophy*, by Mark Siderits and Jan Westerhoff, 160–81. Oxford: Oxford University Press, 2016.

Siderits, Mark, Tom J. F. Tillemans, and Arindam Chakrabarti. *Apoha: Buddhist Nominalism and Human Cognition*. New York: Columbia University Press, 2011.

Smith, Barry. "Why We Still Need Knowledge of Language." *Croatian Journal of Philosophy* 6(18): 431–57, 2006.

Soames, Scott. *Beyond Rigidity: The Unfinished Semantic Agenda of "Naming and Necessity."* Oxford: Oxford University Press, 2002.

Soames, Scott. "Linguistics and Psychology." *Linguistics and Philosophy* 7(2): 155–79, 1984.

Staal, J. F. *A Reader on the Sanskrit Grammarians*. Cambridge, MA: MIT Press, 1972.

Stainton, Robert. *Words and Thoughts: Subsentences, Ellipsis, and the Philosophy of Language*. Oxford: Oxford University Press, 2006.

Steinhart, Eric. *More Precisely: The Math You Need to Do Philosophy*. Peterborough: Broadview Press, 2009.

Taber, John. "A Road Not Taken in Indian Epistemology." In *Indian Epistemology and Metaphysics*, by Joerg Tuske, 243–69. New York: Bloomsbury, 2017.

Taber, John. "The Theory of the Sentence in Pūrva Mīmāṃsā and Western Philosophy." *Journal of Indian Philosophy* 17: 407–30, 1989.

Thrasher, Allen W. "Maṇḍana Miśra, *Brahmasiddhi*." In *The Encyclopedia Of Indian Philosophies: Advaita Vedanta Up To Samkara And His Pupils*, edited by Karl Potter, 347–419. Delhi: Motilal Banarsidass, 1970.

Tubb, Gary. "*Vastutas tu*: Methodology and the New School of Sanskrit Poetics." *Journal of Indian Philosophy* 36(5–6): 619–32, October 2008.

Tubb, Gary and Emery Robert Boose. *Scholastic Sanskrit: A Handbook for Students*. New York: American Institute of Buddhist Studies, 2007.

Tzohar, Roy. *A Yogācāra Buddhist Theory of Metaphor*. Oxford: Oxford University Press, 2018.

Warder, A. K. *Indian Kavya Literature: The Ways of Originality (Bāṇa to Dāmodaragupta)*. Vol. 4. Delhil: Motilal Banarsidass, 1983.

Winternitz, Moriz. *Catalog of Sanscrit Manuscripts in the Bodleian Library: Begun by Moriz Winternitz, Continued and Completed by Arthur Berriedale Keith*. Vol. 2. Aufrecht: Clarendon Press, 1905.

Winternitz, Moriz. *History of Indian Literature*. Vol. 3. Delhi: Motilal Banarsidass, 1985.

Index of Names, Works, and Terms

Note: The index uses English alphabetical order, so while diacritics are present in the Sanskrit terms, they do not influence word order. (E.g., a word beginning with *ś* is treated as beginning with *s*.) Bolded page numbers refer to glossary entries, italicized numbers to the translation.

abductive inference. *See* inference, to the best explanation

abhidhā 88, 90, **247**. *See also* primary meaning

Abhinavagupta

- commentator on *Dhvanâloka* 22, 37, 40–41, 193
- relationship to Mukula 134, 269 n.36, 270 n.40, 274 n.72, 276 n.98, 278 n.127

absorption (*adhyavasāna*) *53–6*, 110–17, 124–5, **247, 252**

action (*kriyā*)

- double meanings connected with *67–72*, 164–6, 172–4, 183–4
- habitual *63*, 146–8
- meaning of verbs 12, 22–3, 29, 31, *49–50*, 94–6, 99, 127, 151–3, 224, **247**
- ordinary linguistic behavior (*vyavahāra*) *73–4*, 101, 131, 242, **250**

adhyavasāna. *See* absorption

aesthetics 7, 21–2, 34. *See also alaṅkāra-śāstra*

ākāṅkṣā (syntactic expectancy) 31, 151, 240, **248**

alaṅkāra-śāstra 21, 34–8, 243

ambiguity. *See* homonyms

Ānandavardhana

- arguments for suggestion 5–9, 33–4, 118–20
- dependence on earlier theorists 35
- later responses to 36–8, 40–1
- Mukula's replies to 10–16, 90, 91, 103–4, 116–24, 129–49, 160, 163, 165, 174–93

Anumāna. *See under* inference

apoha (exclusion) 158, 275 n.20

artha. *See* meaning

arthāpatti. *See* postulation

asaṃvijñāna-pada 165. *See also* novel uses of language

āsatti. *See saṃnidhi*

assertion 33–4, 127

Aṣṭâdhyāyī (*Eight Chapters,* Pāṇini) 20, 92, 145–8

Atiśakyôkti. *See* hyperbole

atyanta-tiraskṛta-vācya. *See* meaning, entirely displaced

Bach, Kent 232–4, 239–40, 242, 284 n.3

Bhartṛhari

- language principle (*śabda-tattva*) 188–91

Mukula's engagement with 20–1, 112–13, 118, 165
sentence meaning 161–3
sphoṭa ("burst" theory) 23, 25, 30–2, 40, 98–9, 127
Bhartṛmitra 28, *67*, 164–5, 173
Bhāṭṭa *See* Mīmāṃsā
bitextuality
śleṣa (pun) 68–9, 172–4, 178, 183–6, 190
term's origin 271 n.41
yamaka (twinning) 35, 183–4
Borg, Emma 232
Bronner, Yigal 35, 41, 262 n.13, 271 n.41
Buddhism 23, 40, 129, 158, 192, 243, 266–7 n.13. *See also* Dharmakīrti

cognition
determinate (*niścaya*) 15, 45, 88–9, 131
knowledge 23, *73*, 104, 107, 189, **247**
of primary and secondary meanings 27, *47*, *55*, 109, 119, 125, 223
referential 23–5, 50, 55, 99
of sentences 31, 127, 151, 226, 236–7
comparison
indication as 8, 12, *53–4*, *70*, *72*, 110, 137, 185–6
object *53–4*, *72*, 110, **250**
philosophical 242
subject *53–4*, *72*, 110, **251**
compatibility. *See* semantic fit
connotation 97, 137
content
known in linguistic practice *60*, *66*
minimal and maximal 231–3
motive *67*
primary and secondary meaning *47*, *48*, *64*, 96, 105, 118–19
context
free enrichment 233, 240
Frege's principle 236
indexicals 232, 241
language learning 23–4, 151, 155
meaning varying with 5–6, 16, 22, 25–6, *61*, 92–4, 113, 115, 118–20, 126–8, 182
poetic 134, 137, 176, 179
saturation 234
sentence meaning 30, 155–7, 158–60, 227, 239
truth conditions 238
contextualism 231, 235, 236, 242
convention
fixes meaning *54–6*, *66*, *73*, 114, 117, 124–6, 129–38
motive for speaking *67*, 164–5
as ordinary linguistic practice (*vyavahāra*) *58*, *64*
and poetic tropes 15, *59*, 139, 168

Davidson, Donald 260 n.1
deception *60–1*, 139–40
denotation. *See also* reference
primary 23, *58*
sentence 29, *63–6*, 149–63
word *51*, *58*, **248**
desire, speaker's *48*, *56*, 97, 125, 152, 240, **251**. *See also* motive
dharma 132
Dharmakīrti 37, 169, 243, 247
Dhvanyâloka (*Light on Suggestion*). *See Ānandavardhana*
distinguishing features (*upādhi*) *48–50*, 95–101, 116, **266**
dhvani. *See* suggestion
double meaning. *See* bitextuality

ellipsis 19, 29
epistemic instrument. *See also* inference, postulation
certainty of 15, 239

for knowing *dharma* 132
importance for Mukula's argument 20
in Indian thought 19, 22–3, **248**
relationship to communicative function 16, *46, 52, 66, 73–4,* 89, 106–10, 189, 191–3
etymology 92, 116, 173, 183–6
expressions. *See* language

Frege, Gottlob 232
figurative meaning. *See under* meaning
function (*vyāpara, vṛtta, vṛtti*)
communicative (*śabda-vyāpara, abhidhā-vṛtta*) 5, 223, 237
domain and codomains of 119–21, 123
indicatory (*lākṣaṇika-vyāpara*) 10, *46, 47, 51, 56, 57,* 90, 103, 123, **249**
primary (*mukhya-vyāpara*) *46,* 223, **250**

genre 12, 139, 149, 159
grammar
associative plural 26, 170, 182
flaws in 145–8
Sanskrit 99
Sanskrit textual discipline (*vyākaraṇa*) 20, 22, 24, 33, 36, 39, *74,* 88, 160–3, 191–2, 243
syntax and meaning 237, 239
grammarians *49,* 97–8
Grice, H.P. 18, 232–3, 260 n.1
Guha, Nirmalya 260 n.6, 268 n.25
guṇa. See properties
guṇa-vṛtti (secondary meaning) 267 n.15, 278 n.119

homonyms 115, **248**. *See also śleṣa*
hyperbole (*atiśayokti*) *61–2,* 142–3, **249**

imagining (*utprekṣā*) *61–2,* 142–3, **249**
implicature 18, 232, 233, 235, 260 n.1 262 n.14, 268 n.25
indexical 232, 234, 241, 272 n.44
indication. *See* secondary meaning
inference
anumāna 20, 37, 192, 243
based on positive and negative correlations *57, 64,* 128, 151, **249**
inference to the best explanation (*see also arthāpatti*) 239, 260, 268
Ingalls, Daniel H.H. 40, 181
insults 125, 172
intention, speaker. *See* motive
irony 11, 35, 166, 171–2, 179–80

Jaimini. *See under* Mīmāṃsā
jāti. See universal

Kashmir 2, 33, 41, 193, 279 n.133
kāraka. See grammar
kāvya 21, 35, 173, 191
Kāvya-prakāśa (*Illumination of Poetry*, Mammaṭa) 37
Keating, Malcolm 268 n.25, 271 n.42, 282 n.3
Knowledge. *See* epistemic instrument
Kumārila Bhaṭṭa. *See under* Mīmāṃsā

language
changing meanings of *53–6,* 110–17, 124–5
conventional. *See* convention
and knowledge. *See* epistemic instrument
learning 23–4, 28, 89, 128, 151, 155, 227–8, 237–8
lakṣaṇā. See secondary meaning, indication
lies. *See* deception
literal meaning. *See under* meaning
Locana (*The Eye*, Abhinavaupta) 22
logic 15. *See also* inference, postulation

Māgha. *See Śiśupālavadha*
Mahā-bhāṣya (*Great Commentary*, Patañjali) 20, *48*, 88
Mammaṭa 2, 22, 36–8, 99, 187
McCrea, Lawrence 22, 36–7, 41, 131, 173, 181
meaning (*artha*)
 basis of (*nimitta*) *46, 49, 70,* 100–1, 115, 152 (*see also* distinguishing features)
 expressed (*vācya*) 1–12, *57, 59–66, 69–73*, 128–30, 135, 138, 143–4, 149–51
 expressed meaning that is discarded *72*, 178, 184–6
 expressed meaning that is entirely displaced (*atyanta-tiraskṛta-vācya*) *70*, 174, 175, 177, 179
 expressed meaning that is shifted (*arthântara-saṅkramita-vācya*) 175
 figurative 21, 27, 35, *54*, 111, 114, 132, 144 (*see also* secondary meaning)
 indicated. *See* secondary meaning
 intended to be expressed (*vivakṣita-vācya*) 33, 174–5, 176–7, **249**
 intended to be expressed and subordinate (*vivakṣitânya-para-vācya*) 175
 literal. *See* primary meaning
 not entirely discarded (*na atyantaṃ tiraskāraḥ*) *70, 71, 72*, 174, 177, 180–3
metaphor. *See also* secondary meaning
 failure of semantic fit as trigger 31–2, 152
 frozen 111
 relation to Indian linguistic categories 7–9, 28, 40, 105, 112
 meaning as indicated 11–12
 meaning as primary 127
metaphysics 92–5, 102, 163, 188, 199, 226
metonymy 7, 26, 32, 105, 128
Mīmāṃsā
 Bhāṭṭa thinkers 24, 27, 29, 32, 126, 151–4, 161, 226
 Jaimini 132
 Kumārila Bhaṭṭa 22, 24, 28, *58*, 92, 133
 Prābhākara thinkers 24, 32, 126, 154–7
 Prabhākara Miśra 24, 30
 Śabara Miśra 22, *58*, 132
 Śālikanatha Miśra 155–6, 283 n.9
Mīmāṃsā-sūtra (*Aphorisms on Exegesis*) 132
morphology 22, 99, 146–7
motive (*prayojana*)
 absence of *60*
 author's 12, 137
 to convey hidden meanings *60*
 necessary condition for indication 6, 10, 15, *66–7*, 164
 novel and conventional *67–9*, 164–74, 180
 speaker's 13, 241
mukhya. See primary meaning

names. *See* proper names
nimitta. See meaning, basis of
niścaya (determinate cognition). *See under* cognition
novel uses of language 15, 25, *67–8*, 165, 168
Nyāya 24, 27, *74*, 158–60, 192, 243–4
Nyāya-sūtra (*Aphorisms on Logic*, Gautama) 158

Ontology. *See* metaphysics

Pāṇini 22, *63*, 145–8, 191
paraphrase 233
Patañjali 20, 24, *48*, 88–9, 93, 96, 102–3

phonemes *48*, *73*, 97–8, 134, 188–9, 270 n.40
poetry. *See also alaṅkāra-śāstra, kāvya*
conventions of 15, 140, 167
examples in Mukula 11–12, *58–62*, 68–9
rasa 7, *62*, 133–4, 138, 143–4
suggested meanings 7–9, *70*, 133, 135
postulation (*arthāpatti*)
in Abhinavagupta 278 n.127
importance for argument against suggestion 177, 186, 193
and indication 13–15, 19–20, *52*, 106–10, 141, 149, 154, 169, **250**
in Jayanta Bhaṭṭa 261 n.7
logical structure of 13–15, 239
in Mahima Bhaṭṭa 37
in Mīmāṃsā 132, 267, 267 n.22, 268 n.25, 272 n.53
Prābhākara. *See* Mīmāṃsā
pragmatics 27, 221–3. *See also* indication, secondary meaning
prayojana. See motive
pramāṇa. See epistemic instrument
pravṛtti. See use
pratibhā 25
primary meaning (*mukhya*)
actions (*kriyā*) 29, *48*, 98–9, **247**
blocked *51*, *58*, *59*, *66*, *67*, *68*, **247**
division into four kinds *48*, 95, 221
properties (*guṇa*) *48*, *49*, 99–101
semantically imbued *48*, 96, **251**
something contingent (*yad-ṛcchā*) *48*, *50*, 97–8, **251**
universals (*jāti, sāmānya*) *47*, *48*, *49*, *50*, *52*, 99–101, **252**
proper names *48*, *50*, 96–7, 101, 266 n.13
properties
manifested. *See vyaṅgya*
semantic 15, 35, *47*
similar 27–8, *51*, *53–5*, *56*, *59*, *61–2*, *68*, 136, 142, 168
as referent of adjectives *48–50*
without a specific term (*asaṃvijñāna-pada*, *see* novel uses of language)
propositions 232, 234–5, 240–1
puns *See* bitextuality

qualities *See* properties

Raja, K. Kunjunni 37
rasa
Ānandavardhana's view of 7–9, 33, 133–4, 138–9, 175–6, 186, 191, 270 n.40
dramaturgy 34
Mukula's view of 10, 12, *62–3*, 133, 143–5, 225, **250**
Reader. *See* sensitive critic
Recanati, François 231–5, 238–41, 242
Reference. *See* primary meaning

Śabara. *See under* Mīmāṃsā
Śabda. See language principle, phonemes, word
Śabda-vyāpāra-vicāra (*An Investigation into the Function of Speech*, Mammaṭa) 37
śabda-tattva (language principle) *73*, 188–9, 191–2
sahṛdaya. See sensitive critic
saṃnidhi (contiguity) 31–2, *64–5*, *67*, 151–3, **248**
scripture. *See* Veda
secondary meaning
inclusion 14, *51–3*, *55*, *62–3*, *69*, *70*, 106–9, 117–18, 140–1, 174–80, 186, **249**
indication, varieties of *73*, 94, 111, 116, 118, 130, 177–8, 190 (*see also* language)

indirect expression *51, 52–3, 54, 55, 69, 70,* 106, 109–10, 121–2, 174, **249**
intermediated indirect expression *54,* 114
facts (*vastu*) as content of 139
figures of speech (*alaṅkāra*) as content of *61–2,* 138, 140–3
properties, involving *53–6,* 111, 114–16, 122, 125–6, 141–3
semantic distance from primary *55–7,* 116, 125–6
semantically imbued (*uparakta*) *55, 56,* 116, 118, 112, **251**
of sentences. *See* sentence
superimposition (*āropa*) *53–6, 61–2,* 110–11, 141–3, 144, **251**
transfer, involving (*upacāra-miśra*) *51, 53,* 103, 105–6, 110–12, 121, 125, **249**
transfer, lacking (*śuddôpacāra*) *51,* 106–10, **249**
rasa as content of *62,* 143–5, 149
semantics 27, 170, 224, 232, 237, 239, 242–3. *See also* reference
semantic fit (*yogyatā*) 31, *64,* 151, 224, **252**
semantic power (*śakti*) *58,* 223. *See also* function
sense-reference distinction 25, 186
sensitive critic (*sahṛdaya*) 36, *63, 69, 72,* 145, 180, 184–6, **251**
sentence
abhihitânvaya (denotation-through-the-connected) theory of *64–5,* 154–7
anvayâbhidāna (connection-of-the-denoted) theory of *64, 65,* 151–4
definition of *57,* **251**
indication based on *61–2,* 140–3
samuccaya (combined) theory of *64, 65, 66,* 157–60, 162, 228–9, 239–40
science of (Mīmāṃsā) 16, 19, *74,* 191
sphoṭa (burst, undivided) theory of 25, 30, *64, 65, 66,* 98, 160–3
Siderits, Mark 237
simile (*upamā*) 35, 168, 184–5
Śiśupālavadha (*The Killing of Śiśupāla,* Māgha) *59,* 136–7
śleṣa. See under bitextuality
Soames, Scott 237
Sound. *See* phonemes
speaker
definition of *57*
indicated meaning due to relationship with *60–1,* 138–40
intention. *See* motive
stipulating meaning *48–9,* 97–8
speech. *See* language principle, phonemes
sphoṭa. See under sentence
synonym. *See* homonym
syntax. *See also ākāṅkṣā,* Pāṇini
plurals 26, 170, 182
Sanskrit (*see under* grammar)
suggestion (*dhvani*)
arguments for 5–7, 118–20, 175–6
arguments against 14–15, *72,* 109, 120–4, 129–36, 137–45, 148–9, 160, 176–88
influence of 36–8
varieties of 7–9
superimposition. *See under* secondary meaning

Tantra-vārttika (*Exposition on Ritual Practice,* Kumārila Bhaṭṭa) *58,* 92
tātparya (sentential aim) 36, *62,* 225, 241, 243, 283 n.5
testimony 23, 27, 107, 126, 156
truth
communicating in a hidden way *60, 68,* 171
deception 11, *61,* 140

relativity in semantic theories 161–2
and semantic content 232, 238, 240, 260 n.7
twinning. *See under* bitextuality
transfer. *See* metaphor, secondary meaning
type-token distinction 22, 25, 27, 98, 113, 115, 183, **252**

Udbhaṭa 35–6, *62*, 142–3
Understanding. *See* cognition
universal (*jāti*)
general metaphysics of *49*, **252**
referent of words 24, 27–30, *47–50*, *57*, 82, 93–6, 99–103, 108–9, 224
in theories of sentence meaning *64–5*, 113, 151, 156–8, 160–1
upacāra (transfer)
indication involving (*upacāra-miśra*) *51, 53–5,* 103, 110–17, **249**
indication lacking (*śuddhôpacāra*) *52–3,* 103–10, **249**
in Nyāya 160
upādhi. See distinguishing features
upamā. See simile
use (*pravṛtti*) *46, 48, 50, 54, 55, 56, 57,* 96, 100. *See also* function, meaning
utterance
actions paired with 88–9, 131
comprehension stages 226–7
meaning paired with *46*, 91, 98, 109
motives for *60*, 94, 135, 225
sounds of 33, 162
types (having a universal of) *50,* 102, 115
utprekṣā. See imagining

vācya. See meaning, expressed
vākya. See sentence
Vākya-padīya (*Treatise on Sentences and Words,* Bhartṛhari) 20, *49*
Vāmana 22, 273 n.69
Veda 20, 22, 93, 189
verbs *See* action
vivakṣita. See meaning, intended to be expressed
vivakṣitânya-para-vācya. See meaning, intended to be expressed and subordinate
vṛtti. See use
vyākaraṇa. See grammar
Vyakti-viveka (*Analysis of Suggestion*, Mahima Bhaṭṭa) 37, 243
vyaṅgya (manifested) *71*, 180–1, 278 n.119
vyāpāra. See function
vyavahāra. See under action

word. *See also* primary meaning, reference
as hypothetical construct *65, 66* (*see also* Bhartṛhari, *sphoṭa*)
compositionality 126–7 (*see also* sentence)
learning (*see* actions, ordinary linguistic behavior)
primary meanings of 22–9, 40, *46*, *64*, 88–9, 99–103, 126–8
secondary meanings of (*see* secondary meaning)
types and tokens 115

yamaka (twinning). See under bitextuality
yogyatā. See semantic fit

www.ingramcontent.com/pod-product-compliance
Ingram Content Group UK Ltd.
Pitfield, Milton Keynes, MK11 3LW, UK
UKHW021904220326
469204UK00008B/183